The Public Policy Process

PEARSON
Education

We work with leading authors to develop the
strongest educational materials in politics, bringing
cutting-edge thinking and best learning practice to a
global market.

Under a range of well-known imprints, including
Longman, we craft high quality print and electronic
publications which help readers to understand and
apply their content, whether studying or at work.

To find out more about the complete range of our
publishing, please visit us on the World Wide Web at:
www.pearsoned.co.uk

The Public Policy Process

MICHAEL HILL

Fourth edition

PEARSON
Longman

Harlow, England • London • New York • Boston • San Francisco • Toronto • Sydney • Singapore • Hong Kong
Tokyo • Seoul • Taipei • New Delhi • Cape Town • Madrid • Mexico City • Amsterdam • Munich • Paris • Milan

Pearson Education Limited
Edinburgh Gate
Harlow
Essex CM20 2JE
England

and Associated Companies throughout the world

Visit us on the World Wide Web at:
www.pearsoned.co.uk

Fourth edition published 2005

© Prentice Hall UK 1997
© Pearson Education Limited 2005

ISBN 0 5828 9402 6

British Library Cataloguing-in-Publication Data
A catalogue record for this book is available from the British Library

Library of Congress Cataloguing-in-Publication Data
Hill, Michael J. (Michael James), 1937–
    The publc policy process / by Michael Hill. – 4th ed.
        p. cm.
    Rev. ed. of: The policy process in the modern state. 3rd ed. 1997.
    Includes bibliographical references and index.
    ISBN 0–582–89402–6 (pbk.)
        1. Policy sciences. 2. Bureaucracy. I. Hill, MIchael J. (Michael James), 1937– Policy process in the modern state. II. Title.

H97.H35 2005
320.6–dc22

2004053544

10 9 8 7 6 5 4 3 2 1
08 07 06 05

Typeset in Stone Serif by 3
Printed and bound by Bell & Bain Limited, Glasgow

The publisher's policy is to use paper manufactured from sustainable forests.

Contents

Part 3 Analysis of the policy process

Preface

The roots of this book lie in a book I published with Chris Ham in 1984, *The Policy Process in the Modern Capitalist State*. That underwent a substantial revision when I produced *The Policy Process in the Modern State* on my own in 1997. This is a fundamental revision of the later book, not only updating it to introduce more recent theory and research, but also reshaping the text. The latter involves increasing the emphasis upon the complexity of the whole system and paying more attention to variations in policy content and institutional context.

This is a book about the process by which public policy is made. Efforts to influence the policy process, the concern of much policy analysis writing, need to be grounded in an understanding of it. Making policy embraces the emergence of policies on the agenda, policy formulation and policy implementation. It is a continuous process, with many feedback loops, carried out by diverse actors. This is something that was recognised in the earlier books but is made much more explicit here.

The book starts with an introductory chapter (Part 1) which sets the study of the policy process in the context of the wider policy studies literature and examines some of the key underlying concepts and methodological issues. It is then followed by five chapters (Part 2) which set out the various theoretical approaches to policy process analysis. Part 3 comprises seven chapters which explore the application of those approaches. These start with an examination of the implications of policy diversity for any analysis. This is followed by separate explorations of policy formulation and policy implementation. Two chapters then look explicitly at issues about the roles of organisations in the policy process (making a distinction between inter- and intra-organisational issues). After that one chapter pays special attention to issues about the roles of 'street-level' workers in the policy process. The book ends by exploring the impact of concerns about accountability for the operation of the policy process.

Despite all the changes, the book obviously still owes a great deal to the original collaboration with Chris Ham, and I am very grateful to him for his original contribution and for then letting the book evolve in my way. We developed *The Policy Process in the Modern Capitalist State* when we worked together on a teaching programme on the policy process for the master's course in public policy studies at the School for Advanced Urban Studies at Bristol University.

Over the years that I have been engaged on writing about the policy pro-cesses my debts to colleagues and students, both in the institutions in which I have worked and in many other places at home and abroad, have cumu-lated to the extent that I cannot acknowledge them all. I will confine myself to some of those who have been particularly helpful in the recent past. After I left Bristol I used the book for undergraduate teaching at the University of Newcastle. During that period I revised the original book twice. Wendy Ranade, Bob Hudson and John Vail were very helpful at that stage.

During that period I developed collaborative work with Pieter Degeling and with Peter Hupe. Subsequently I wrote *Implementing Public Policy* with Peter Hupe. That collaboration has had a big impact upon my thinking about how to analyse the policy process. I have learnt a great deal from Peter, who brings an analytical eye to the subject and a Dutch scepticism about some of the things the British take for granted. This book draws heavily on recent work with him. Recent teaching at Goldsmiths College and at the University of Brighton has enabled me to develop my ideas further, as have a variety of guest lecturing opportunities in Britain and abroad.

I am grateful to Caroline Hollingworth for the help she has given me in preparing this manuscript. I would like to thank Morten Fuglevand and Emma Travis of Pearson for their support for the preparation of this edition, my copy-editor, Katy Coutts, and the five anonymous referees who fed in some very helpful comments.

Finally, I must thank my wife for her tolerance of the extent to which inroads have been made into my half-retirement as I have become increas-ingly preoccupied with the book over the past few months.

Acknowledgements

We are grateful to the following for permission to reproduce copyright material:

Box 1.3 adapted from *Government and Public Policy in the UK*, Oxford University Press (Richards, D. and Smith, M., 2002, Table 2.2); Figure 7.1 adapted from 'Synthesising the implementation literature' in *Journal of Public Administration Research and Theory*, Oxford University Press (Matland, R.E., 1995); Figure 11.2 from 'From a national system locally administered to a national system nationally administered: The new Leviathan in education and training in England' in *Journal of Social Policy*, Cambridge University Press (Ainley, P., 2001); Box 11.5 adapted from 'Joined-up government in the Western world in comparative perspective' in *Journal of Public Administration Research and Theory*, Oxford University Press (6, P., 2004); Table 13.2 adapted from *Implementing Public Policy*, Sage Publications Ltd (Hill, M. and Hupe, P., 2002, Table 8.5).

Part

1

Introduction

1 Studying the policy process

SYNOPSIS

After this introductory chapter the book is divided into two further parts. Part 2 (Chapters 2–6) explores a range of theories that have been developed to explain all of, or key aspects of, the policy process. After Chapter 6 there is an 'intermezzo' which summarises and draws some overall conclusions from the discussion of theory. Then Part 3 (Chapters 7–13) looks at various aspects of the policy process, essentially developing and applying some of the main ideas from the first part. Connections between the theories in the first part and the discussions of the issues in the second part will be made in various ways, including summarising observations at the ends of chapters.

This introductory chapter looks at some important overall considerations about the study of the policy process. It starts with an exploration of the relationship between the 'descriptive' aim of this book and the 'prescriptive' objectives that motivate much policy analysis. This is followed by an examination of what may be meant by 'policy', and what is distinctive about the study of public policy. The examination of the latter topic ends with a recognition of the extent to which there are problems with identifying a distinctive public sector, a topic which is emphasised in modern stresses upon the extent to which 'government' needs to be seen as 'governance'.

There is then a general exploration of what is involved in studying the policy process, both in terms of its relationship to political science and other social science disciplines, and in terms of the methodological challenges facing those academic disciplines. This leads to an examination of the most fundamental of those challenges – that offered by postmodernist theory. Here a stance is taken that rejects the most extreme forms of relativism embodied in that theory, but recognises that the study of the policy process must be very alive to the extent to which there are competing discourses in which interests and values are embedded. The chapter ends by exploring one such discourse, dominant in the early history of the study of the policy process, but which has now been shown to contain problematical assumptions: the notion of the process as involving a system of stages or cycles.

Introduction

We are all critical of public policies from time to time. Most of us have ideas about how they could be better. When we engage in ordinary conversations about the defects of policies we put forward, or hear advanced, various propositions about why they are defective. Those propositions tend to involve views about policy makers as ignorant or misled or perhaps malign. They often embody views that policies would be better if only different people had more influence on policy, including, of course, perhaps ourselves.

This book is based on the belief that before you can really start to suggest alternative policies to the ones we have, or to suggest alternative ways of making policy, it is essential to try to understand how policy is made. Many of the popular prescriptions for improving policy rest upon essential misunderstandings of the nature of the policy process. For example:

- Views about the need for policy makers to be more aware of 'the facts' often disregard the way the facts are actually matters of dispute between different 'interests'.

- Suggestions for taking 'politics' out of policy making disregard the fact that politics is much more than simply the interplay of politicians.

- Statements about the roles of politicians (including many they themselves make) suggest that they have much more influence over the policy process than in fact they do.

The view taken in this book is that the policy process is essentially a complex and multi-layered one. It is essentially a political process, but in the widest sense of that term. The policy process is a complex political process in which there are many actors: politicians, pressure groups, civil servants, publicly employed professionals, and even sometimes those who see themselves as the passive recipients of policy.

Description and prescription in policy analysis

Some policy analysts are interested in furthering understanding of policy (analysis *of* policy); some are interested in improving the quality of policy (analysis *for* policy); and some are interested in both activities (see Parsons, 1995, for an overview of the many approaches). Further, cutting across the distinction between 'analysis of' and 'analysis for' policy are concerns with *ends* and concerns with *means*, together with writers who are concerned about both and are not happy about separating them in this way. Indeed, we will explore later the arguments that these two cannot be separated (see pp. 15–19).

The typology set out in Box 1.1 identifies a range of different kinds of policy analysis.

Box 1.1	Different kinds of policy analysis

Analysis *of* policy

- *Studies of policy content*, in which analysts seek to describe and explain the genesis and development of particular policies. The analyst interested in policy content usually investigates one or more cases in order to trace how a policy emerged, how it was implemented and what the results were. A great deal of academic work concentrates on single policies or single policy areas (social policy, environment policy, foreign policy, etc.).

- *Studies of policy outputs*, with much in common with studies of policy content but which typically seek to explain why levels of expenditure or service provision vary (over time or between countries or local governments).

- *Studies of the policy process*, in which attention is focused upon how policy decisions are made and how policies are shaped in action.

Analysis *for* policy

- *Evaluation* marks the borderline between analysis *of* policy and analysis *for* policy. Evaluation studies are also sometimes referred to as impact studies as they are concerned with analysing the impact policies have on the population. Evaluation studies may be either descriptive or prescriptive.

- *Information for policy making*, in which data are marshalled in order to assist policy makers to reach decisions. An important vein of contemporary studies of this kind manifests a pragmatic concern with 'what works', trying to ensure that policy and practice are 'evidence based' (Davies, Nutley and Smith (eds), 2000).

- *Process advocacy*, in which analysts seek to improve the nature of the policy-making systems through the reallocation of functions and tasks, and through efforts to enhance the basis for policy choice through the development of planning systems and new approaches to option appraisal. Much of the academic work in the sub-field of 'public administration' has this concern.

- *Policy advocacy*, which involves the analyst in pressing specific options and ideas in the policy process, either individually or in association with others, perhaps through a pressure group.

Typology based upon ones offered by Gordon, Lewis and Young (1977) and by Hogwood and Gunn (1981, 1984).

This book's concern is primarily with the third of the varieties of policy analysis identified in Box 1.1. However, many studies of policy outputs contribute to our understanding of the policy process. Similarly, evaluation studies give much attention not merely to what the policy outputs or outcomes were but also to questions about how the policy process shaped them. Much the same can be said of studies that seek to offer information for policy making, since 'what works' may be determined by the way the policy process works. Overall, to reiterate the point already made, it is often not easy to draw a clear line between 'analysis of' and 'analysis for' policy.

The desire to examine how the policy process works was in many respects a minor concern in the period between 1950 and 1980 when policy studies in their own right mushroomed dramatically. If the right policies could be found, and their design difficulties solved, then progress would be made towards the solution of society's problems. Only a minority – radical analysts on the 'Left' who doubted that modern governments really had the will to solve problems, and radical analysts on the 'Right' who were sceptical about their capacity to do so – raised doubts and suggested that more attention should be paid to the determinants of policy decisions. While many of the leading figures in the development of policy analysis certainly moved between prescription and description, endeavouring to ground solutions in political and organisational realism, prescription was dominant in policy studies.

This book's original predecessor (Ham and Hill, 1984) was, when it was first published, comparatively unusual in asserting that it was appropriate to concentrate on description, to explore the nature of the policy process, to help to ensure that proposals about policy content or about how to change policy should be grounded in the understanding of the real world in which policy is made. Nowadays that is a much less exceptional stance to take towards the study of policy. Rather, the problem may instead be that scepticism is so widespread that it is hard to make a case for the development of more sophisticated approaches to the policy process. That contributes to a widening gulf between the practical people – politicians, civil servants, pressure group leaders, etc. – whose business is achieving policy change and the academic analysts of the policy process. This book's stance, then, is to assert that we must continue to try to understand the policy process – however irrational or uncontrollable it may seem to be – as a crucial first step towards trying to secure effective policy making.

The meaning of 'policy'

A textbook on the policy process obviously cannot evade a definitional problem concerning the meaning of the term 'policy'. Chambers's dictionary defines policy as 'a course of action, especially one based on some declared and respected principle'. That definition clearly sees policy as something more than simply a decision: it embodies the idea of action – indeed, rational action – inasmuch as some 'principle' is involved. In everyday speech we sometimes say things like 'my policy is always to . . .'. This book is, of course, about *public* policy. Interestingly, the *Oxford English Dictionary* describes the following as 'the chief living sense' of the word 'policy': 'A course of action adopted and pursued by a government, party, ruler, statesman . . .'. We come back to this issue below.

These definitions do not get us very far towards identifying a policy. Perhaps we can do no more than adopt the very British pragmatism of Cunningham, a former top British civil servant, who argued that 'Policy is rather like the elephant – you recognise it when you see it but cannot easily define it' (1963, p. 229). A rather similarly vague approach is adopted by Friend and his colleagues, who say: 'policy is essentially a *stance* which, once articulated, contributes to the context within which a succession of future decisions will be made' (Friend, Power and Yewlett, 1974, p. 40). However, others have sought to do better than that. Box 1.2 sets out some examples.

Box 1.2   **Definitions of policy**

- Heclo's definition of policy, like the Chambers's dictionary one set out in the text, emphasises action: 'A policy may usefully be considered as a course of action or inaction rather than specific decisions or actions' (1972, p. 85).

- Easton offers a variant of this, noting that 'a policy . . . consists of a web of decisions and actions that allocate . . . values' (1953, p. 130).

- Jenkins sees policy as 'a set of interrelated decisions . . . concerning the selection of goals and the means of achieving them within a specified situation . . .' (1978, p. 15).

- Smith suggests that 'the concept of policy denotes . . . deliberate choice of action or inaction, rather than the effects of interrelating forces': he emphasises 'inaction' as well as action and reminds us that 'attention should not focus exclusively on decisions which produce change, but must also be sensitive to those which resist change and are difficult to observe because they are not represented in the policy-making process by legislative enactment' (1976, p. 13).

The definitional problems posed by the concept of policy suggest that it is difficult to treat it as a very specific and concrete phenomenon. Policy may sometimes be identifiable in terms of a decision, but very often it involves either groups of decisions or what may be seen as little more than an orientation. The attempts at definition also imply that it is hard to identify particular occasions when policy is made.

Let us look a little more at the implications of the fact (emphasised in Easton's and Jenkins's definitions in Box 1.2) that policy involves a course of action or a web of decisions rather than just one decision. There are several aspects to this. First, a decision network, often of considerable complexity, may be involved in producing action. A web of decisions, taking place over a long period of time and extending far beyond the initial policy-making process, may form part of the network.

A second aspect is that policy is not usually expressed in a single decision. It tends to be defined in terms of a series of decisions which, taken together, comprise a more or less common understanding of what policy is.

Third, policies invariably change over time. Yesterday's statements of intent may not be the same as today's, either because of incremental adjustments to earlier decisions, or because of major changes of direction. Also, experience of implementing a decision may feed back into the decision-making process. This is not to say that policies are always changing, but simply that the policy process is dynamic rather than static and that we need to be aware of shifting definitions of issues.

Fourth, it is therefore important not to fall into the trap of seeing the policy process as if it exists on a desert island. Most of the policies that are likely to be studied in the modern world are changes to existing policies. Even when they seem to address a new issue or problem they will nevertheless be entering a crowded policy space, impacting upon and being influenced by other policies. Hence, as Wildavsky puts it, 'any major move sets off a series of changes, many of which ... inevitably transform any problem they were originally supposed to solve' (1979, p. 71).

Fifth, a development of this point is that much policy decision making is concerned, as Hogwood and Gunn (1984) have stressed, with attempting the difficult task of 'policy termination' or determining 'policy succession' (see also Hogwood and Peters, 1983).

Sixth, the corollary of the last three points is the need to recognise that the study of policy has as one of its main concerns the examination of non-decisions. This is what Heclo and Smith are pointing to (see Box 1.2) in their references to inaction. It has been argued that much political activity is concerned with maintaining the status quo and resisting challenges to the existing allocation of values. Analysis of this activity is a necessary part of the examination of the dynamics of the policy process.

Finally, the definitions cited raise the question of whether policy can be seen as action without decisions. It can be said that a pattern of actions over a period of time constitutes a policy, even if these actions have not been formally sanctioned by a decision. Dery takes this point even further to argue that often we can write of 'policy by the way ... the by-product of policies that are made and implemented to pursue objectives other than those of the policy in question' (1999, pp. 165–6). In this sense policy may be seen as an outcome, which actors may or may not want to claim as a consequence of purposive activity.

Writers on policy have increasingly turned their attention to the action of lower-level actors, sometimes called 'street-level bureaucrats' (Lipsky, 1980), in order to gain a better understanding of the policy process. It has been suggested that in some circumstances it is at this level in the system that policy is actually made. It would seem to be important to balance a decisional, top-down perspective on policy with an action-oriented, bottom-up perspective. Actions as well as decisions may therefore be said to be the proper focus of policy analysis.

Later we will explore some of the issues surrounding the evolution of policy, noting writers who see the policy process as involving distinctive stages or a cycle and a literature (including earlier versions of this text) which draws a stronger distinction between policy making and implementation (see pp. 19–21). Such an approach rests very much upon a taken-for-granted version of the Chambers's definition set out above. It may be contrasted with a view that in many respects policy needs to be seen as what happens, rather than as what politicians say will happen.

The view that policies may simply be outcomes of political and bureaucratic processes as opposed to courses 'of action adopted and pursued' leads to two important themes for the study of the policy process: (1) the relationship between policy and politics, and (2) the dominance in much that is said and written about policy of the view that political action is (or should be) purposive.

A deeper exploration of the *Oxford English Dictionary* reveals that the word 'policy' has an interesting history in English. Amongst usages of the word that are now obsolete are the notions of policy as a 'prudent, expedient or advantageous procedure' and as a 'device, expedient, contrivance . . . stratagem, trick'. Parsons points out that Shakespeare used 'policy' in various ways:

> Policy encompassed the arts of political illusion and duplicity. Show, outward appearance and illusions were the stuff of which power was made. Shakespeare employed the terms of Machiavellian philosophy . . . Power cannot be sustained purely with force. It needs, in a Machiavellian sense, *policy*: and 'policy sits above conscience', as the bard tells us in *Timon of Athens*. (Parsons, 1995, p. 14)

Furthermore some languages, including French and Italian, do not draw a clear distinction between 'policy' and 'politics'.

The purpose of this very brief excursion into linguistic history is to emphasise not merely that policy has been seen as a simple and expedient, even duplicitous, ingredient in political strategy but also that this may still be an appropriate way to think of it. We need to ask: what is being said when someone stresses that they have a policy? May they not simply be trying to convince us that they are acting effectively and purposefully? Edelman (1971, 1977, 1988) has devoted considerable attention to the 'symbolic' uses of the concept of policy. Further, even if people can convince us, we still need to ask: what are the implications of their policy? Phenomena like proclaimed 'equal opportunities policies' particularly need unpacking in this way. The notion here that policies are 'claims' takes us back to the simplest of the dictionary definitions, that is, that when we (and by the same token politicians) say we have a 'policy' we are in a sense making a claim to have a 'property'.

It is a particular feature of the modern discourse about policy that it is seen as desirable that politicians should have policies – so that electorates may make choices – and that governments should enact those policies in a systematic way. It was suggested above that the very rise of the study of policy was dominated by that perspective, and that many contributions to policy analysis are motivated by a desire to assist a rational policy-making process. Yet politicians do not necessarily see their roles in this way – power may be more important to them than policy, and power may be used for personal ends rather than to try to solve problems in the way presumed in discussions of policy analysis.

What, then, needs to be understood as we examine the policy process is that although the concept of policy is vague and elusive, it is nevertheless widely used to suggest a rational process. Readers need to be sceptical about writing which takes it for granted that a policy-making process is organised and has specific goals. It may be desirable that it should be like this, but whether it actually is or not must be an issue for research.

Public policy

The *Oxford English Dictionary* definition of policy quoted above refers to action 'by a government, party, ruler, statesman, etc'. But it goes on to note the more private usage of 'any course of action adopted as advantageous or expedient'. It was noted that individuals sometimes talk of adopting 'policies'. Organisations of all kinds regularly do so. This book is about 'public policy'. Is there anything intrinsically different about the definition arising from the fact that it is the state or state organisations that are seen as the makers of the policy? The answer to that is surely 'no' as far as the simple characteristics of policy are concerned, but 'yes' inasmuch as special claims are made about the legitimacy of state policy and its primacy over other policies. This takes us into two difficulties – one about the nature of the state, the other about the special justifications used for the role of the state as a provider of policies.

The basic definition of the state is as a set of institutions with superordinate power over a specific territory. It can be defined in terms of both the institutions that make it up and the functions these institutions perform. State institutions comprise legislative bodies, including parliamentary assemblies and subordinate law-making institutions; executive bodies, including governmental bureaux and departments of state; and judicial bodies – principally courts of law – with responsibility for enforcing and, through their decisions, developing the law. State institutions are located at various levels – national, regional and local.

But there are also supra-state institutions which act, to some degree, as superordinate states. These include both international organisations – the United Nations, the World Trade Organisation, etc., which may seek to impose policies on nation states – and organisations like the European Union which operate quite specifically as supra-national law makers. The very fact that this superordinate power is controversial and is to some degree challenged by nation states offers a reminder of the fact that many states have gone through a process of struggling to achieve a legitimate superordinate role. Institutions vary considerably in the degree of freedom they enjoy from central agencies.

The identification of a complex of institutions as making up the state introduces another complication. This is that the state may operate through institutions which have many features that are regarded as private rather than public. In the past, particularly in the early years of state formation, states hired mercenary armies, subcontracted tax collection and delegated law enforcement to local, quasi-autonomous barons. In many of the early nation states the whole apparatus of government was initially no more than an extension of the royal household. In other societies the establishment of a centralised governmental system was very much a partnership between the sovereign and a religious body.

The modern manifestation of the phenomena discussed in the last paragraph has been a deliberate shift to the delegation of what had become accepted as governmental functions. What this implies is a contract between government and a 'private' body to operate all or part of a public service. This is often presented as simply a mechanism for policy 'implementation' with policy making remaining in government hands, but it will be shown later in this book that this policy making/implementation distinction is not easily drawn. The delegation of a major activity, particularly a monopoly activity, tends to involve some shift of control over policy. A related phenomenon is a public/private partnership where resources are drawn from both publicly collected revenues and private sources; policy control is obviously particularly likely to be shared in these circumstances. Finally, in introducing this subject the word 'private' was deliberately put in inverted commas. Like the concept 'public', this is hard to define when there is a complex partnership between different elements, including state ones. Furthermore, 'private' does not necessarily imply a private profit-making organisation – in this respect institutions bringing voluntary organisations into association with the state may be seen as ways of further integrating state and society and increasing democratic participation.

These complications, arising both from the increasing importance of supra-state bodies and from changes within the nation state (sometimes described as the 'hollowing out' of the state – see Milward, Provan and Else, 1993) have led many contemporary writers to speak of a movement from 'government' to 'governance'. Richards and Smith thus say:

> 'Governance' is a descriptive label that is used to highlight the changing nature of the policy process in recent decades. In particular, it sensitizes us to the ever-increasing variety of terrains and actors involved in the making of public policy. Thus, it demands that we consider all the actors and locations beyond the 'core executive' involved in the policy making process. (Richards and Smith, 2002, p. 2)

That definition perhaps gives insufficient emphasis to the supra-state issues, that is, that the key actors may be outside as well as inside the nation state.

There is a debate about the extent to which globalisation and the development of international governing institutions are important for contemporary governance (see Pierre, 2000).

Pierre and Peters explore the use of the term 'governance', suggesting that it is confusing since it is used both to describe empirical phenomena and to explore how those phenomena operate (2000, p. 12). Some writers emphasise a need for a shift from government to governance because of new realities, while others use this terminology to analyse how processes are actually changing.

Richards and Smith (2002) also portray the way these developments make the policy process more complicated as a shift to a 'postmodern state' (see Box 1.3). This usage has been adopted by others (see, for example, Bogason, 2000). However, readers need to be careful about the expression 'postmodern', which is used in various ways. Whilst in this context it simply refers to new sources of complexity for the analysis of the policy process, another usage of postmodern offers a methodological challenge which is in no way implicit to this formulation. This is explored later.

Box 1.3	The Weberian state vs. the postmodern state

Weberian bureaucratic state	A postmodern state
Government	Governance
Hierarchy (Weberian)	Heterarchy (networks, etc.)
Power (1): zero-sum game	Power (1): positive-sum game
Power (2): concentrated	Power (2): diffuse
Elitist	Pluralist
Unitary, centralised, monolithic state	Decentralised, fragmented, hollowed state
Strong, central executive	Segmented executive
Clear lines of accountability	Blurred/fuzzy lines of accountability
State central control	State central steering
Single homogeneous public service ethos	Heterogeneous service cultures

Note: the notions implicit in the idea of the Weberian state are explained on pp. 199–202.
Source: Richards and Smith, 2002, p. 36, Table 2.2. By permission of Oxford University Press.

Studying the policy process

As an issue for academic study, the exploration of the policy process is most evidently a part of political studies or political science. We are concerned here with the explanation of the outputs of politics – the 'how' aspect of

Lasswell's terse definition of the study of politics as being about 'who gets what, when, how' (1936). At the same time, much of the study of politics is about how power is acquired and used, without reference to outputs, inasmuch as it is concerned with elections, legislative processes and so on.

Any discussion of the public policy process needs to be grounded in an extensive consideration of the nature of power in the state. Any consideration of how the process works will tend to involve propositions about who dominates. Omission of this, in statements about the policy process, will tend to have the implication that there are no dominant elements in the state. That is in itself a stance on this much debated subject, congruent with the pluralist perspective that power is evenly spread and openly contested. This has been widely opposed by views which draw upon Marxist theory or elite theory, which see power as very distinctively structured or which suggest that dominance is very much embedded in the nature of the machinery of the state itself.

An important element in the controversy about control over the state concerns the nature of power itself. This will be explored further in the next chapter. Controversy about the state and about power is closely related to the debate about democracy. Broadly, there is a conflict about the extent to which it is possible to identify, in the society that is under scrutiny – in much of the English language literature it is of course the United States or Britain – a system of power over the state which can be regarded as reasonably according with some of the criteria for a democracy. Whilst modern political scientists recognise problems about the realisation of any ideal model of democracy, there are differing views about the scope any specific system offers for public participation. Sometimes these differences seem like little more than debates about whether the bottle is half full or half empty. However, there has been a strong division between a pluralist camp, taking an optimistic view of democracy, particularly American democracy, and a neo-Marxist or elitist camp emphasising, for example, the dominance of the 'military–industrial complex' (Mills, 1956).

Having identified the study of the policy process as so closely related to the study of politics, it is pertinent to note, without going too deeply into the argument, the problems about adopting too restrictive a view of the 'political'. Hay, in exploring what is meant by 'political analysis', makes the following point:

> the political should be defined in such a way as to encompass the entire sphere of the social. The implication of this is that events, processes and practices should not be labelled 'non-political' or 'extra-political' simply by virtue of the specific setting or context in which they occur. All events, processes and practices which occur within the social sphere have the potential to be political and, hence, to be amenable to political analysis. The realm of government is no more innately political, by this definition, than that of culture, law or the domestic sphere. (Hay, 2002, p. 3)

Hay goes on from that to argue for the need for political analysis to include 'extra-political variables', to be concerned with economic and cultural processes, for example. He thus argues: 'Political analysts cannot simply afford to leave the analysis of economics to the economists, history to historians and so forth' (ibid., p. 4). But there is also a need to turn that argument the other way about and acknowledge that economists, historians, etc. can make a contribution to the understanding of the policy process.

In some parts of this book attention will be paid to arguments about the nature of the policy process that derive from economics: arguments about the extent to which it can help us to understand the policy process if we identify some or all of those engaged in it as 'rational actors' following their interests, and engaged in forms of gaming, that have much in common with the way economists analyse human behaviour in the 'marketplace'. We will also have to examine a very different kind of economics which sees decision making as determined by powerful economic forces.

Another discipline which contributes to the understanding of the policy process is sociology. It may be argued that analysis of political behaviour is political sociology. But quite apart from that, the sociology of organisations makes an important contribution to the study of the policy process, inasmuch as most policy making occurs within institutions. The sociology of organisations is particularly important for the interpretation of the translation of policy into action, exploring issues about the behaviour of workers within complex organisations (amongst which state bureaucracies loom large).

It is important to stress that there is no reason to suggest that the study of policy processes is any different from any other social science research enterprise. However, a little more needs to be said about the way in which the characteristics of the policy process pose certain problems for research.

The object of study is normally a unique sequence of events. This means that there will be little scope for testing earlier research by looking for a situation in which a process is replicated. Policy experiments are rare, and when they occur they are not necessarily set up in ways which make research evaluation easy (Bulmer (ed.), 1987; Booth, 1988). The political environments in which they are conducted mean that they are very unlikely to run their course without ongoing adjustments. When they do occur, the very fact that they are atypical limits the lessons that can be drawn from them. Furthermore, the impact of the presence of researchers on the behaviour of the researched will also distort the impressions they give of processes.

Policy process studies are very often case studies, using qualitative methods. Where quantitative methods are used they are likely to deal with impact, from which deductions can be made back to process. Perhaps the ideal here is some combination of qualitative observation of process with quantitative work on impact.

One area of policy studies where quantitative methods are used to some effect in the examination of processes is in comparative studies. Many such studies have sought to explain similar activities in different countries (or different local governments) by reference to contextual variables – demographic data, economic data, information on levels of support for particular political positions, etc. There will be some discussion of these in

Chapter 6. They have played an important role in the evaluation of some of the broad hypotheses about power systems but they leave much unexplained.

There are many relevant activities that are very hard to observe. This brings us back to the issue of power. The fact that many power processes are covert – indeed, their very success may depend upon them being so – is acknowledged in many colloquial expressions ('the power behind the throne', the 'kitchen cabinet', the '*éminence grise*'). Official secrecy is openly used as a justification for restricting access to situations or data necessary to evaluate policy processes. Very much more is just kept secret without any attempt to offer a justification for doing so.

Analysts of policy processes are thus thrown back on methods which must involve inference from the data they can secure. They also find themselves in situations in which – like journalists – they cannot validate their findings by revealing their sources. All social scientists are open to accusations that their theories and ideologies predispose them to particular interpretations of their data. Those who study the policy process are particularly vulnerable to this charge.

One interesting way of trying to deal with this problem is to openly acknowledge the validity of competing frames of reference and then to explore a case study using each as an alternative lens (likely to amplify some parts of the subject and obscure others). Allison's (1971) use of this approach is examined in Chapter 7 (see p. 116). A number of other writers have followed Allison's lead, using different models. A particular concern has been to try to evaluate the evidence for the interpretations of policy processes to be discussed in the next chapter, as fairly open and competitive ones or as ones that are strongly structured or biased in favour of particular actors or interests (Ham, 1992; Blowers, 1984; Hill, Aaronovitch and Baldock, 1989).

In the social and political sciences we recognise how complexity, change and the consciousness of the actors we are studying limit our scope for the establishment of generalisations. We also recognise how, particularly in a field like the study of policy, we cannot use experimental methods and we must often use qualitative techniques to study phenomena. Hence, whilst the study of the policy process is claimed to be an academic discipline (Lasswell, 1951, 1968, 1970) upon which the more active contributions to policy analysis need to be based, there is a need not to overwork that distinction. People describe because they want to prescribe. Conversely, people who dedicate themselves directly to prescription will always want to root what they have to say in a realistic appreciation of what 'is', whether derived from academic studies or from their own practical experience. However, a number of books have taken this observation further to pose a challenge to efforts to generalise about the policy process. This challenge is examined in the next section.

The postmodernist challenge to the study of the policy process

Some theorists (who are here labelled 'postmodernist') argue that it is impossible to draw a distinction between 'analysis of' and 'analysis for' policy. The starting point for their argument is a view that few realistic social scientists will contest, namely that when we attempt to study a topic on which we have strong views on what 'ought' to happen that may distort our interpretation of what does happen. That distortion is then even more likely if we have difficulties in developing a methodology for our work which enables the establishment of undisputable facts. What we face here, of course, are the issues about the extent to which social or political studies can be called 'scientific'. In debates in English about the claim that social sciences are scientific, the core of the argument is about the extent to which 'positivist' methods can be used, involving the formulation and testing of hypotheses. The difficulties about doing this are partly practical problems about the extent to which it is possible to set up experimental situations and control some of the variables so that the impact of others may be tested. These problems are tackled by those who subscribe to positivist approaches by seeking situations in which there are variations between research sites in the extent of the presence of key variables. Sophisticated statistical methods are used to sort out the impact of a complex mix of variables. But there are other problems. When we try to develop explanations of what people do we need to be aware that they have their own explanations of their behaviour; and their behaviour is influenced by the way they think and speak about what they are doing. Then we must also not forget that researchers themselves are people developing hypotheses about other people. Hence, not only do they bring biases to their studies but they are also likely to be in situations in which their views and what they are doing will be communicated to those whose activities they are researching and thus will be influencing future behaviour. While even in the physical sciences there are some problems about the relationship between researchers and the 'matter' they study, in the social sciences these problems are fundamental. The objects of studies can understand what is being hypothesised and can react to that.

The notion of positivist 'policy science' has, not surprisingly, therefore come under attack. Postmodernist theorists argue that when reporting 'facts' the observer is an active shaper both of the message sent and of the message received. Farmer argues that:

> the view that social science is a matter of cumulative accretion of knowledge through the work of the human subject neutrally observing the action and interaction of the objects – letting the facts speak for themselves – is untenable. (Farmer, 1995, p. 18)

Another important contributor to this literature, Fischer, while preferring to refer to his work as postempiricist rather than postmodernist, describes his approach as 'An epistemological orientation that seeks to move beyond an "objectivist" conception of reality' (2003, p. 12). What this signifies is the 'adamant' rejection of

> the idea that a unified understanding of science methodology can be applied to all research questions. Underlying this argument is the rejection of the possibility of a neutral observational vocabulary that can be used to test and conclusively prove or falsify explanatory variables. (Fischer, 2003, p. 13)

For postmodernists, the language with which evidence is reported is important. The social construction of reality involves discourses and the presentation of 'texts' in which issues about language usage are at the core of the postmodern argument. For Farmer:

> Hermeneutics (the study of relationship between reason, language and knowledge) concerns texts; it is concerned with interpreting, with specific significance, with achieving intelligibility. Texts, in this case, can be written texts or texts in the form of social practices, institutions, or other arrangements, or activities. (Farmer, 1995, 21)

What is involved then, it is argued, is reflexive interpretation. Hence, as Yanow expresses it:

> a key difference between interpretation and positivism is the former's focus on meaning. In application to policy and implementation analysis, it calls on us to ask: What does a policy mean? To whom, aside from its drafters and implementers, does it have meaning? and How do various interpretations of meaning affect policy implementation? These are the sorts of questions that need to be answered with respect to specific policies. There is also a set of questions about the more general processes, common to many situations, by which policies acquire and convey their meanings. Asking 'how' a policy means is asking how a policy accrues meaning; where meanings reside; how they are transmitted to and among various policy stakeholders; how they come to be shared or not shared; how they may be destroyed. (Yanow, 1993, p. 41; see also Yanow, 1996, for a development of this perspective)

Fox and Miller (1995, Chapter 5) offer a particularly forthright attack on the way in which these 'discourses' in the analysis of public policy are used in defence of interests. They support the claims of 'feminists and others' that the Enlightenment discourse was simply 'the special pleadings of white, propertied, patriarchal, Eurocentric privileged classes'.

At its strongest, then, the postmodernist perspective challenges all attempts to generalise about the policy process. Some observations on the implications of this, recognising connections between this specific literature and other related literatures, are set out in Box 1.4. It is often not clear in

this 'postmodernist' writing whether it is only being argued that more attention needs to be paid to discourse, and the need to deconstruct dominant
discourses, or whether an entirely relativist stance is being taken. In much
postmodernist writing there is an emphasis on the need for the 'democratis-
ation of discourse' (Drysek, 1990; Fox and Miller, 1995; Fischer, 2003). This
is particularly important for the issues about evidence in political analysis.
Clearly, the acceptance of truth claims is influenced by dominant discourses;
the question is then whether it is appropriate to use that argument against
all positivist science (as Fischer does, 2003, p. 125). The alternative to
empiricist social science offered from this perspective replaces truth claims
by consensus derived from competing perspectives (ibid., p. 131). If the
latter is the case then any of the discourses of the oppressed are as potentially dismissible as the discourses of the dominant. It is strange that the
avowedly radical concern of Fischer seems to involve not replacing dominant discourses by ones which draw rather better on evidence of, for
example, poverty or discrimination but rather adding them to the 'tower of
babel'. This involves not simply an unworldly expectation of achieving a
democratic discourse, but also a relativistic approach to evidence. Fischer
counters the latter argument by attacking the dogmatism of those
who claim to have found the truth. But that is rather a debating chamber
answer. Surely there is not simply an either/or choice between dogmatism
and relativism.

Box 1.4	The postmodernist challenge in its most extreme forms

At a university the author visits from time to time a range of sound bites
about education are displayed in a passageway to one of the entrances. One
of these is a quotation from Nietzsche, one of the rather ancient founding
fathers of postmodernism: 'There are no facts, only interpretations'. The
author is tempted to add a graffiti comment: 'if you believe this, do not
bother to continue into the university', since in its absolute form it renders
irrelevant any attempt to make sense of the world. Dawkins (2003) offers a
challenge to this point of view from a scientist's perspective. But in relation
to the concerns of this book the debate amongst historians is more relevant.
It is an issue that has been of particular concern with reference to the understanding of some of the more horrific events of modern history. What
follows from the absolute denial of factual evidence can include the denial
of the evidence for the Holocaust (see Evans, 2001, for a discussion of the
challenge to historiography posed by this work).

The position taken in this book is to support the positivist 'project' inasmuch as it involves the systematic search for truth, in a context in which
there are great difficulties about either accumulating good evidence or
avoiding biases. But there must be a concern to recognise the significance of
discourse (see further discussion in Chapter 5, pp. 84–6) and to allow for the
possibility of alternative interpretations of evidence. This position has been

described as 'critical modernist', explained by Pollitt and Bouckaert as still holding to 'the importance of the empirical testing of theories and hypotheses, although accepting that this is only one kind of test, and that arguments concerning whether the appropriate conditions for falsification will be met will never cease' (2000, p. 23). They go on to emphasise that 'reality is socially constructed, but not all constructions have equal claim to our credulity', and that there is a need to 'discriminate between more – and less – adequate descriptions and explanations' (ibid.).

Nevertheless, one of the particular benefits to our subject that flows to a large extent from the 'postmodernist' work has been a challenge to conventional frameworks for the study of public policy which particularly flow from 'top-down' views of the policy process. Some of the issues around this are explored in the next section.

The traditional approach to seeing the policy process as a system, and some of the problems with that

The theory of representative democracy sees expressions of the popular will as an 'input' into the political system leading through various processing stages to a policy outcome as an 'output'. An influential nineteenth-century essay stressed a need for a clear distinction, during that process, between politics and administration (Wilson, 1887). Accordingly, what may be described as a 'stagist model', or policy cycles model, was developed.

Models of policy stages or policy cycles have been developed to assist comprehension of the complexities of the process of decision making. The systems approach outlined by David Easton (1953, 1965a, 1965b) has gained considerable prominence. Easton argues that political activity can be analysed in terms of a system containing a number of processes which must remain in balance if the activity is to survive. The paradigm that he employs is the biological system, whose life processes interact with each other and with the environment to produce a changing but none the less stable bodily state. Political systems are like biological systems, argues Easton, and exist in an environment which contains a variety of other systems, including social systems and ecological systems.

In Easton's model, one of the key processes of political systems is inputs, which take the form of demands and supports. Demands involve actions by individuals and groups seeking authoritative allocations of values from the authorities. Supports comprise actions such as voting, obedience to the law, and the payment of taxes. These feed into the black box of decision making, also known as the conversion process, to produce outputs, the decisions and policies of the authorities. Outputs may be distinguished from outcomes, which are the effects policies have on citizens. Easton's analysis does not end here, for within the systems framework there is allowance for feedback, through which the outputs of the political system influence future inputs into the system.

The main merit of systems theory is that it provides a way of conceptualising what are often complex political phenomena. In emphasising processes as opposed to institutions or structures, the approach is also useful in disaggregating the policy process into a number of different stages, each of which becomes amenable to more detailed analysis. For all of these reasons the systems model is of value, and this no doubt helps to account for its prominence in the literature. Other writers who do not necessarily share Easton's systems framework have also used the idea of stages in the policy process for the purposes of analysis (see Box 1.5).

Box 1.5	Variations on Easton's systems model

Jenkins (1978, p. 17) elaborates the Easton model considerably, recognising complex feedback flows and identifying the following stages:

- initiation
- information
- consideration
- decision
- inplementation
- evaluation
- termination

Hogwood and Gunn (1984, p. 4) offer a more complex model in which they identify the following:

- deciding to decide
- deciding how to decide
- issue definition
- forecasting
- setting objectives and priorities
- options analysis
- policy implementation, monitoring and control
- evaluation and review
- policy maintenance, succession and termination.

The advantage of a stages model is that it offers a way of chopping up, if only for the purposes of analysis, a complex and elaborate process. It is useful as a heuristic device but potentially misleading about what actually happens (Parsons, 1995, pp. 79–81). It is important to recognise the extent to which both the systems model and the stages 'discourse' rest upon a model of the representative democratic policy process in which politicians make decisions, senior civil servants help to translate them into specific legislation, and junior civil servants implement them. This is a widely held view of what 'should' happen. From the standpoint of this book the most important problem with this perspective is that the use of the stages model imposes upon the analysis of what actually happens a potentially distorting framework if what really happens is radically different from this.

From an empirical perspective, policy processes are in many respects continuous processes of evolution in which a realistic starting point may be far back in history. It was noted in considering the definitions of the term 'policy' that it is inappropriate to get into a model of the way policy processes occur which might only apply to a newly annexed desert island where nothing had been done before. Inasmuch, therefore, as it is possible to identify policy 'initiation', it may start anywhere in the system. Whilst there are grounds for seeing the stages as involving the progressive concretisation of policy (or involving a nesting of decisions in which some are logically prior to others), this offers no basis for prediction about how much will occur at any stage (in other words, whilst some policies may be formulated in very explicit terms early in the process, others may gradually manifest themselves as they are implemented).

Stages are not insulated from each other and there may be a succession of feedback loops between them – often the same actors are involved at different stages and the policy games they play will be carried on through different parts of the process (this remark is particularly applicable to the policy making/implementation distinction). Friedrich summed up this alternative perspective long ago when he argued: 'Public policy is being formed as it is being executed and it is likewise executed as it is being formed' (1940, p. 6).

The stages model has been discussed here because it is still widely used. This discussion has suggested, however, that its use can mislead. The problem – as John, one of the model's severest critics, has recognised – is that there is a pragmatic case for the model as it 'imposes some order on the research process' (1998, p. 36). What had to be recognised in shaping this book was that if every process is continuously seen as interacting with every other process, there is no way to divide up discussion into separate chapters or sections. Hence, limited use is made of the stages model by recognising rather that there are somewhat different things to say about agenda setting, policy formulation and implementation respectively. At the same time, interactions are regularly stressed.

CONCLUSIONS

This chapter has stressed that this book deals with the description of the policy process. It will proceed from a discussion of the relevance of competing theories of power to the examination of various aspects of the policy process.

In doing this it will not attempt to offer prescriptions for policy making and implementation. However, it has been noted that it is impossible to maintain a rigid distinction between description and prescription because so many of those who have written about the policy process have combined the two. Descriptions have been offered in order to justify or criticise the way policies are made and implemented. Some of the most important controversies in policy analysis have been between analysts who differ on what they observe and what they want to observe.

A particularly important aspect of the way in which description and prescription are mixed is that concerns about accountability, managerial or democratic, have been of overriding importance in policy analysis. This is a theme to which the last chapter will return.

One widely quoted proposition from Karl Marx is: 'The philosophers have only *interpreted* the world in various ways; the point, however, is to *change* it' (1845, in Marx, 1958, vol. 2, p. 405). Marx was clear that he needed to offer a realistic description of the world in order to establish his political programme. The study of policy processes has been dominated by people concerned to show how power is concentrated or how politicians may be called to account or how administrators distort the intentions of their political chiefs and so on. Whilst this account attempts to achieve a measure of neutrality in that respect, it would be foolish of its writer to pretend that his prescriptive biases will not show through from time to time. And in the last resort Marx is right – the justification for trying to understand is a desire to do things better.

Part

2

Policy theories

2 Theories of power and the policy process

SYNOPSIS

This chapter, as the first of five exploring theoretical approaches to the analysis of the policy process, deals with some of the most fundamental issues about power in society, which are of importance for explaining the policy process. It shows how a pluralist perspective on representative government was developed, one which saw power as fragmented yet relatively equally distributed. That view of power challenged, and was in turn challenged by, perspectives that stressed a view that power is concentrated in unrepresentative hands. It shows that a debate about what power is and how it may be studied is very important for the analysis of these respective positions.

The chapter goes on to examine theories that stress power inequalities. The first one to be examined is elite theory, which is shown to be rather diffuse in nature. By contrast, the next approach examined, Marxist theory, has a very explicit approach to explaining power inequalities in terms of economic inequalities. The chapter then shows that much Marxist theory involves a perspective on the state embodying a form of structural determinism: seeing state action as determined by the economic order (capitalism, in the modern world).

That leads on to a general consideration of forms of structural determinism, the most important of which – amongst theories in current vogue – is globalist theory. The exploration of globalist theory suggests that some of its forms are closely related to Marxist theory and that most aspects of it raise important questions about the complex nature of the relationship between social structure and political action. Reasons are then suggested for recognising structural constraints, moving beyond narrow economic determinism to embrace considerations about inequalities introduced by analysts of gender and ethnic inequalities, but avoiding a narrowly determinist approach to them.

Introduction

The study of the policy process is essentially the study of the exercise of power in the making of policy, and cannot therefore disregard underlying questions about the sources and nature of that power. These questions have been the subject of widespread controversy. In that controversy there are two particularly important themes: about the extent to which systems have power distributed in a relatively egalitarian way and about the extent to which power is concentrated or fragmented. Figure 2.1 expresses these as two dimensions. All four positions represent generalised versions of different theoretical positions which will be discussed further here and in the following chapters. The two top positions (1 and 2) show what are often presented as alternative models of democracy, but the concern here is with alternative types of power systems, not with the arguments about what constitutes a democratic system of government. The diagram has been deliberately drawn to involve four quadrants rather than axes, but of course in reality different theories take different positions about the extent of the fragmentation of power or about the extent to which its distribution is egalitarian. In the process of arguments between theorists, new modified positions are adopted. This means that contemporary exponents of any of these perspectives are likely to take positions closer to the axes than their predecessors. For example, a classical Marxist position would be way out on the margins of quadrant 3 if a continuum was used, and a classical pluralist one would be at an alternative extreme position in quadrant 2, but many modern theorists will be much closer to the axis. A great deal of the literature on power and theories of the state does indeed focus upon the arguments between theorists who are broadly in quadrants 2 and 3. The perspective represented by quadrant 1 has come under considerable attack from all sides, while in quadrant 4 will be found some recent writers (including some of the postmodernists discussed on pp. 16–19) who see the political process as exceptionally incoherent.

Figure 2.1   Basic models of the policy process

	Power concentrated	Power fragmented
Power distributed relatively equally	1. Representative government in which a unified executive is responsive to popular will	2. Pluralist government in which popular will prevails through competition between groups
Power distributed unequally	3. Government by an unrepresentative elite, or in the grip of external influences	4. Unpredictable and chaotic government, buffeted by multiple pressures

Origins of pluralist theory: rescuing the theory of representative democracy

Reference was made in Chapter 1 to the way in which descriptions of the nature of the policy process are often very much linked with prescription of how it should work. That mixture lies right at the centre of the debate about pluralism. Defenders of democratic ideals have had to come to terms with the large and complex institutional structures of states. An Athenian ideal of democracy – that is, one involving direct participation – has been seen to offer an unworkable model. The alternative has been to see democracy as a representative system. A limited number of people participate in the day-to-day business of government but they may be the representatives of the people as a whole. The early model for this representation was still seen to involve a relatively personal relationship between the elected politician and the comparatively small electorate that elected him (it was always 'him' at that stage of the development of political institutions). With the enlargement of the electorate and the increasing need to organise within the legislature, another institution developed to make the connection between elector and elected more indirect – the political party. Schumpeter (1947) defines democracy as 'that institutional arrangement for arriving at political decisions in which individuals acquire the power to decide by means of a competitive struggle for the people's vote' (p. 269).

However, in addition, the processes of government increasingly began to involve other groups, organisations of public interests who might try to influence voting decisions at elections or the legislative programmes of political parties. Once established, moreover, these 'pressure groups' were likely to try to influence the policy process at any stage – negotiating the details of legislation, establishing links to influence the implementation process, monitoring policy outcomes and so on. Thus, it is argued that the pressure groups that have grown up alongside the formal institutions of government have come to play an important direct part in representing the views of specific interests. Talking about the United Kingdom, Beer (1965) notes the development of a collectivist theory of representation legitimising a much greater role for groups than earlier conceptions of representative government. Beer argues that as governments sought to manage the economy they were led to bargain with organised groups of producers, in particular with worker and employer associations. Governments of both political parties sought the consent and cooperation of these associations, and needed their advice, acquiescence and approval. Similarly, the evolution of the welfare state stimulated action by organised groups of consumers, such as tenants, parents and patients. The desire by governments to retain office led them to consult and bargain with these consumer groups in attempts to win support and votes. Beer's thesis has been developed in the work of Richardson and Jordan (1979; see also Jordan and Richardson, 1987), who have argued that the United Kingdom is a 'post-parliamentary democracy' in which policies are developed in negotiation between government agencies and pressure groups organised into policy communities. According to Richardson and Jordan, pressure groups influence public policy from the point at which issues emerge onto the agenda to the stage of implementation.

What has been described here, then, is a replacement of the view of government portrayed in quadrant 1 of Figure 2.1, 'representative democracy', in which an executive responsible to a legislature was seen as making policy on behalf of the people, by a more complex pluralist model (as in quadrant 2). As far as some countries are concerned, particularly the United Kingdom, this perspective on the system is still contested – if not by political scientists then at least by some politicians – inasmuch as claims are made that the government 'in parliament' is still paramount, with a mandate to legislate. The empirical question to which we will need to return, therefore (particularly in Chapter 8), is the extent to which policies emerge directly and untainted by the influence of pressure groups from political manifestos and promises in some societies.

The pluralist school of thought in political science described and charted the developments described above, exploring how political parties really worked and the roles played by pressure groups. But many in this school also argued that this was how a modern democracy should work. Theorists like Truman (1958) and Bentley (1967) gloried in the institutional complexity of their society, contrasting it favourably with less open societies where they perceived much group activity to be limited or even suppressed. Hence pluralism should be seen, in Schwarzmantel's words, 'both as a normative theory and as a way of explaining and analysing the power structure of the liberal-democratic system' (Schwartzmantel, 1994, p. 48). Schwarzmantel amplifies this as follows:

> Because pluralism takes its starting point to be a modern society in which there are different interests, popular power is realised through group activity, the working of political parties and pressure groups or interest groups, each of which represents one of the many interests into which a developed society is split. Pluralist perspectives salute and emphasise this diversity of interest, and like liberal theorists they see this variety as a necessary and positive dimension of social life. (Schwarzmantel, 1994, p. 50)

Clearly, then, opposition to the pluralist perspective can take two forms. One of these is to argue that this is not a satisfactory model for democracy (it is too indirect or it is impossible to realise the 'general will' through such diversity). This is not the concern of this discussion. The other is to argue that pluralism provides a misleadingly optimistic picture of the way power is organised in those societies described as pluralist. This may, of course, then lead back to a critique of the ideal, or, as in the case of the work of the socialist pluralist Herbert Laski (1925), to a set of proposals for strengthening pluralism by countering the biases in the system (see also Cohen and Rogers, 1995, for a modern version of this approach).

Perhaps the most influential exponent of pluralist theory, and certainly a very important one for the study of policy processes, has been Robert Dahl. Dahl (1958) argues that power in many Western industrialised societies is widely distributed among different groups. No group is without power to influence decision making, and equally, no group is dominant. Any group can ensure that its political preferences and wishes are adopted if it is sufficiently determined. Dahl's main empirical contribution to the study of power is described in Box 2.1.

Box 2.1   Dahl's study of power

Dahl analysed power in the town of New Haven, and reported the study in his book *Who Governs?* (Dahl, 1961). In asking 'Who governs?' in New Haven, Dahl examined a number of more specific questions, including whether inequalities in resources of power were cumulative or non-cumulative, how important decisions were made, and if the pattern of leadership was oligarchic or pluralistic. He concluded that in the period from the 1780s to the 1950s, the town had gradually changed from oligarchy to pluralism. No one person or group was dominant.

What Dahl did in New Haven was to select a number of key political issues and examine who won on those issues. One of the criteria used in identifying key issues was that there should be disagreement among two or more actors about what should be done. An issue was key, in other words, if there was open conflict. Analysis of the handling of three key political issues in the 1950s – urban redevelopment, public education and political nominations – revealed a situation in which power was not concentrated in a single group. Rather, because the resources that contributed to power were widely dispersed in the population, power itself was fragmented between different actors. Different interests were active on different issues, and there was no consistent pattern of success or failure. Indeed, one of the points Dahl notes is that interests opposed on one issue might join together on another. The only actor consistently involved was the mayor, but he was by no means dominant. Only a few people had direct influence over key decisions, but most people had indirect influence through the power of the vote.

Dahl and colleagues such as Nelson Polsby (1963) argued that their position is not that power is equally distributed. Rather, pluralist theory argues that the sources of power are unequally though widely distributed among individuals and groups within society. Although all groups and interests do not have the same degree of influence, even the least powerful are able to make their voices heard at some stage in the decision-making process. No individual or group is completely powerless, and the pluralist explanation of this is that the sources of power – like money, information, expertise and so on – are distributed non-cumulatively and no one source is dominant. Essentially, then, in a pluralist political system power is fragmented and diffused, and the basic picture presented by the pluralists is of a political marketplace where what a group achieves depends on its resources and its 'decibel rating'.

There is an issue here, to which we will return in the next three chapters, about the way that pluralist theory deals with the role of government agencies. In much pluralist work the state, as such, is little investigated. While some writers argue that government is neutral and acts essentially as a referee in the struggle between groups (Latham, 1952), the dominant theme in the work of Dahl is that government agencies are one set of pressure groups among many others. According to the latter interpretation, government both pursues its own preferences and responds to demands coming from outside interests.

The critique of pluralism

In the discussion in the previous section, the case for the pluralist perspective was made without acknowledging that much of the theoretical work, and particularly Dahl's contribution, was an attack on earlier work which stressed power concentrations. In an article published in 1958 Dahl argues that 'the evidence for a ruling elite, either in the United States or in any specific community, has not yet been properly examined so far as I know' (p. 469). Dahl's article and the criticisms it contains were aimed explicitly at two studies which had claimed to find a ruling elite in the United States. In Dahl's view, there is a need for researchers interested in the power structure to examine neither power reputation nor organisational position, but rather to focus on actual decisions and to explore whether the preferences of the hypothetical ruling elite are adopted over those of other groups. Only in this way is it possible to test the assertion that a ruling elite exists. As the studies summarised in Box 2.2 had not adopted this test, Dahl maintains that the ruling elite model has not been examined properly.

Underpinning Dahl's critique is a straightforward definition of power which states: 'A has power over B to the extent that he can get B to do something that B would not otherwise do' (Dahl, 1957, p. 203). This draws attention to the fact that power involves a relationship between political actors. These actors may be individuals, groups or other human aggregates, and Dahl emphasises that power must be studied in cases where there are differences of preferences between actors. Actors whose preferences prevail in conflicts over key political issues are those who exercise power in a political system. It follows that the student of power needs to analyse concrete decisions involving actors pursuing different preferences. Careful study of these decisions is required before the distribution of power can be described adequately.

| Box 2.2 | Studies stressing power concentrations criticised by Dahl |

The first study, by Floyd Hunter (1953), examined the distribution of power in Atlanta, Georgia. By analysing the reputation for power of local leaders, Hunter concluded that control rested with a small group of key individuals. The second study, by C. Wright Mills (1956), focused on the United States as a whole, and argued that a power elite drawn from the military, from business corporations and from state agencies governed American society. Dahl contends that the research methods used by Hunter and Mills were not sufficiently rigorous to justify their conclusions. In particular, Hunter's approach of examining the 'reputation' for power of local leaders, and Mills's strategy of identifying those in key positions in large-scale organisations, did not meet the test Dahl proposes should be required of those claiming to find a ruling elite.

The problem with this is that it treats the exercise of power as something that is likely to be very visible. Critics of Dahl have pointed out that much power is exercised more covertly and through the subtle cultural processes which influence how people determine their activities and interests. Attempts have been made to deal with this issue by using other words – 'authority', 'influence' and 'domination', for example. Changing the words does not really solve the problem, but it does draw attention to the variety of ways in which power is exercised. Knoke offers a useful approach, using 'influence' to describe what 'occurs when one actor intentionally transmits information to another that alters the latter's actions' (Knoke, 1990, p. 3) and 'domination' where 'one actor controls the behaviour of another actor by offering or withholding some benefit or harm' (ibid., p. 4). This helps to get away from a simple model of the way power is exercised, but it does not deal with the problem of deeply structured power.

Dahl came under attack from Bachrach and Baratz, who, in an article published in 1962, argue that power does not simply involve examining key decisions and actual behaviour. Bachrach and Baratz assert that 'power is also exercised when A devotes his energies to creating or reinforcing social and political values and institutional practices that limit the scope of the political process to public consideration of only those issues which are comparatively innocuous to A' (1962, p. 948). Borrowing a term from Schattschneider, Bachrach and Baratz describe this as 'the mobilisation of bias' (Schattschneider, 1960, p. 71), a process which confines decision making to safe issues. What this suggests is the existence of two faces of power: one operating, as Dahl indicates, at the level of overt conflicts over key issues; the other operating, through a process which Bachrach and Baratz term 'nondecision-making', to suppress conflicts and to prevent them from entering the political process. The implication of Bachrach and Baratz's analysis is that the methodology adopted by researchers such as Dahl is inadequate, or at least partial. A more complete analysis needs to examine what does not happen as well as what does happen, and to unravel the means by which the mobilisation of bias operates to limit the scope of debate.

But what does nondecision-making actually involve? In a second article, published in 1963, Bachrach and Baratz define nondecision-making as 'the practice of limiting the scope of actual decision-making to "safe" issues by manipulating the dominant community values, myths, and political institutions and procedures' (p. 632). Bachrach and Baratz argue that a nondecision-making situation can be said to exist 'when the dominant values, the accepted rules of the game, the existing power relations among groups, and the instruments of force, singly or in combination, effectively prevent certain grievances from developing into full-fledged issues which call for decisions' (ibid., p. 642). In this respect Bachrach and Baratz distinguish nondecision-making from negative aspects of decision making such as deciding not to act and deciding not to decide. In their view, nondecision-making differs from these other phenomena in that when nondecision-making occurs, issues do not even become matters for decision. That is, issues remain latent and fail to enter the decision-making process because of the impact of the mobilisation of bias.

Bachrach and Baratz emphasise the means by which vested interests are protected by nondecision-making. In their model of the political process, Bachrach and Baratz argue that demand regulation is not a neutral activity, but rather operates to the disadvantage of persons and groups seeking a reallocation of values. These may be expected to be those who are disadvantaged by the status quo.

The pluralists responded to Bachrach and Baratz's critique by claiming that nondecision-making was unresearchable (Merelman, 1968; Wolfinger, 1971). How, they asked, could nondecisions be studied? On what basis could social scientists investigate issues that did not arise and conflicts that did not emerge? Bachrach and Baratz replied by amplifying and to some extent modifying their position. In their book, *Power and Poverty* published in 1970, they maintain that the second face of power operates to keep grievances covert. A nondecision – defined as 'a decision that results in suppression or thwarting of a latent or manifest challenge to the values or interests of the decision-maker' (p. 44) – can be investigated through the identification of covert grievances and the existence of conflicts that do not enter the political arena. If no grievances or conflicts can be discovered, then a consensus exists and nondecision-making has not occurred (see Box 2.3).

Bachrach and Baratz also argue that power may be exercised by anticipated reactions. That is, an actor, A, may be deterred from pursuing his or her preferences because he or she anticipates an unfavourable reaction by another actor, B. Anticipated reactions may operate when a community group fails to mobilise because it anticipates an unfavourable response by decision makers, or when decision makers themselves do not act because they expect opposition from key political actors. Although these examples involve an exercise of power, Bachrach and Baratz note that this 'is not nondecision-making in the strict sense' (1970, p. 46). This last point is explored in a study of air pollution policies in the United States, described in Box 2.4.

Box 2.3	**Bachrach and Baratz's examples of the different forms that nondecision-making can take**

- The use of force to prevent demands from entering the political process. For example, the terrorisation of civil rights workers in the southern United States.

- The use of power to deter the emergence of issues. The co-optation of groups into decision-making procedures is an illustration.

- Rules or procedures used to deflect unwelcome challenges. Referring issues to committees or commissions for detailed study is one example; labelling demands as unpatriotic or immoral is another.

- Reshaping rules and procedures to block challenges.

Box 2.4	**Different approaches to air pollution policy in the United States**

Matthew Crenson (1971) compared two cities with respect to action taken to control dirty air. The cities, Gary and East Chicago in Indiana, are adjacent steel towns. While East Chicago passed a law controlling air pollution in 1949, Gary did not act until 1962. Crenson explains the differences between the two cities in terms of the existence in East Chicago of many different steel companies and the domination of Gary by a single corporation, US Steel. The delay in legislating in Gary resulted, Crenson suggests, from the power reputation of US Steel. Although the company was not politically active, the economic power of US Steel, which was exercised through anticipated reactions, was decisive. Thus, indirect influence was important, with political leaders anticipating that US Steel might move from Gary and adversely affect its prosperity if restrictive legislation were passed. In contrast, in East Chicago the fragmentation of the steel industry meant that it was easier for those seeking to control pollution to secure favourable action.

Crenson observes: 'if indirect influence can work for ordinary community residents, then there is no reason why it cannot work for US Steel or General Motors or bank presidents or members of families in the Social Register' (1971, p. 108). Crenson maintains that observable action provides an incomplete guide to the distribution of political power. The comparative method as used in Crenson's study, described in Box 2.4, and the operation of indirect influence through anticipated reactions, illustrates the way in which the nondecision-making thesis can be tested.

The debate about power was taken a stage further by Lukes (1974), who argues that power must be studied in three dimensions. First, there is the exercise of power that occurs in observable, overt conflicts between actors over key issues: the pluralists' approach. Second, there is the exercise of power that occurs in covert conflicts between actors over issues or potential issues: Bachrach and Baratz's method. Third, there is the dimension of power that Lukes adds, which involves the exercise of power to shape people's preferences so that neither overt nor covert conflicts exist. In other words, when the third dimension of power operates, there is latent conflict.

Lukes states that latent conflict exists when there would be a conflict of wants or preferences between those exercising power and those subject to it were the latter to become aware of their interests. In this context, the definition of power employed by Lukes is that 'A exercises power over B when A affects B in a manner contrary to B's interests' (1974, p. 27). In Lukes's view the existence of a consensus does not indicate that power is not being exercised, for as he argues:

> is it not the supreme and most insidious exercise of power to prevent people, to whatever degree, from having grievances by shaping their perceptions, cognitions and preferences in such a way that they accept their role in the existing order of things, either because they can see or imagine no alternative to it, or because they see it as natural and unchangeable, or because they value it as divinely ordained and beneficial? To assume that the absence of grievance equals genuine consensus is simply to rule out the possibility of false or manipulated consensus by definitional fiat. (Lukes, 1974, p. 24).

The difficulty with Lukes's formulation is that it suggests that 'true interests' can readily be identified, and that in this sense the researcher can identify something that the objects of his or her study cannot. While there is something to be said for this when what is at stake are policies (like pollution) that may actually poison us and shorten our lives, there is otherwise a problem about this approach. Hay suggests that one way out of this problem is not to follow Lukes in identifying a third dimension of power but to suggest that there are two uses of power which he describes as 'conduct shaping' and 'context shaping'. He argues about the latter that:

> To define power as context-shaping is to emphasise power relations in which structures, institutions and organisations are shaped by human action in such a way as to alter the parameters of subsequent action. (Hay, 2002, pp. 185–6)

Hay's formulation fits with the way in which Lukes's third dimension of power suggests for Gaventa and others a 'deep structure' conditioning policy options. It also draws attention to identifiable actors in the policy process whose indirect influence is difficult to chart, in particular the mass media.

The shaping of power can be studied, for example through the examination of 'social myths, language, and symbols and how they are manipulated in power processes' (Gaventa, 1980, p. 15). In his elaboration of Lukes's work, Gaventa explores the way in which power is exercised in all three dimensions and stresses the need to see how successful operation on one 'dimension' affects another:

the total impact of a power relationship is more than the sum of its parts. Power serves to create power. Powerlessness serves to reinforce powerlessness. Power relationships, once established, are self sustaining. (Gaventa, 1980, p. 256)

Identifying a 'shaping' activity in respect of power can, however, also suggest scope for activities that do not take existing power structures for granted. From the point of view of Marilyn Taylor, exploring the possibilities for the empowerment of disadvantaged communities, it carries a 'more positive message that power is not fixed and immutable and that it is possible to seize opportunities to redefine assumptions and divert the flow of power into new directions' (2003, p. 102).

These issues have been given considerable attention by theorists who have explored issues about the role of discourses in the power structure. Habermas (1987) has emphasised the importance of communication in securing the acceptance of the unequal distribution of power, and of the policy consequences that flow from it. Foucault (1980) goes further, to see power relations as flowing from taken-for-granted discourses. A perspective on political discourse that is particularly relevant here is Edelman's analyses of political language (1971, 1977, 2001). The postmodernist concern with discourse was discussed in Chapter 1 (pp. 16–19) and is further discussed in Chapter 5 (pp. 84–6).

The pluralists rethink?

It is important to note again that all of the more sophisticated exponents of the pluralist position, and in particular Dahl, do not claim that power is likely to be equally distributed. Their theory has two crucial components: one is that the political stage is accessible to all, the other is that the elites who mount that stage do so largely as the representatives of larger groups of people.

Such statements need to be located in times and places: they cannot be taken to be generalisations about everywhere. They might only be applicable to the places that were studied. Indeed, it is not without relevance that Floyd Hunter's study which Dahl set out to refute was carried out in a city in the south of the United States in the 1950s, whilst Dahl's was carried out in a northern city, host to a major university. Bachrach and Baratz's study was conducted in Baltimore, a 'border' city between North and South where the black population has become very much more politically assertive in the years since that research was carried out. However, much of the debate was carried out in terms which applied it to the whole of the United States, and often beyond.

That is not to belittle the important methodological and conceptual issues that figured in this debate, but it is to stress that the degree of concentration of power and the extent of suppression of interests ought to be regarded as empirical questions not simply resolvable by taking sides in the debate. The contributions from Bachrach and Baratz and from Lukes have raised issues about how power should be studied that cannot be disregarded.

It is interesting to note, therefore, a significant shift in position adopted by some of the key protagonists in the debate on the pluralist side. Dahl and Lindblom's 1953 collaboration *Politics, Economics and Welfare* was revised in 1976 and prefaced with a strong statement on political inequality. Parsons describes it as reflecting on

> many of the failures of policy-making which were becoming evident in the 1970s ... After Vietnam, Watergate, the 'imperial presidency', the growth of urban decay, and social and economic inequality, Dahl and Lindblom confessed to changing their minds on the question of who governs. (Parsons, 1995, p. 253)

Lindblom's *Politics and Markets* (1977) also offered powerful evidence on the limitations imposed upon pluralist democracy by the working of business and markets.

In terms of the quadrants in Figure 2.1, these qualifications to pluralist theory can be seen as bringing it closer to the perspective embodied in the third quadrant, emphasising inequalities and recognising, as Schattschneider so memorably put it, that 'The flaw in the pluralist heaven is that the heavenly choir sings with a strong upper-class accent' (Schattschneider, 1960, pp. 34–5).

However, there are two rather different ways of conceptualising a revised pluralist position, both of which represent compromises between the pluralist perspective and other perspectives, though they are rather different in character. One is to reconceptualise pluralism as 'democratic elitism' (Bachrach, 1969), which involves a sort of reconciliation between Dahl and the writers like Hunter and Wright Mills whom he originally set out to attack. The other is to take the arguments about the limitations upon pluralism in a much more structuralist direction. The next section addresses the first of these options, leading discussion on towards the stronger statements about power concentration that are associated with Marxism. The latter leads on to the discussion of structuralist perspectives.

The elitist perspective

The classical elitist position was set out at the end of the nineteenth century by an Italian, Gaetano Mosca:

> Among the constant facts and tendencies that are to be found in all political organisms, one is so obvious that it is apparent to the most casual

eye. In all societies – from societies that are very meagrely developed and have barely attained the dawnings of civilisation, down to the most advanced and powerful societies – two classes of people appear – a class that rules and a class that is ruled. The first class, always the less numerous, performs all political functions, monopolises power and enjoys the advantages that power brings, whereas the second, the more numerous class, is directed and controlled by the first, in a manner that is now more or less legal, now more or less arbitrary and violent. (Mosca, 1939, p. 50; original publication in Italian, 1896)

The classical elitist thesis maintains that political elites achieve their position in a number of ways: through revolutionary overthrow, military conquest, the control of water power (a key resource in oriental societies: see Wittfogel, 1963), or the command of economic resources. In the modern state, the position of elites is related to the development of large-scale organisations in many areas of life, with the result that there are different kinds of elites, not just those holding formal political power. Bottomore makes a distinction between the political *elite*, which is made up of 'those individuals who actually exercise power in a society at any given time' and which 'will include members of the government and of the high administration, military leaders, and, in some cases, politically influential families of an aristocracy or royal house and leaders of powerful economic enterprises', and the political *class*, comprising the political elite but also leaders of political parties in opposition, trade union leaders, businessmen and politically active intellectuals (1966, pp. 14–15). Defined in this way, the political elite is composed of bureaucratic, military, aristocratic and business elites, while the political class is composed of the political elite together with elites from other areas of social life. What this suggests is that elite power may be based on a variety of sources: the occupation of formal office, wealth, technical expertise, knowledge and so on. To a certain extent, these resources may be cumulative, but power is not solely dependent on any one resource.

In the twentieth century, the growth of large firms, the establishment of trade unions, and the development of political parties – all institutions in which effective power is likely to rest with an oligarchic leadership – underline the significance of organisational control and institutional position as key political resources. Of particular importance in this context was the creation of bureaucratic systems of administration to carry out the increasing responsibilities taken on by the state from the nineteenth century onwards. As Weber (1947) notes, bureaucracies have both positive and negative aspects: positive, in that they offer an efficient way of organising administration; negative, because they open up the possibility of power being vested in officials who are accountable neither to the public nor to politicians. The growth of bureaucracies may, in Weber's view, lead to control of the economy by bureaucrats. In this line of argument, elite theory draws attention to the need to look at the state itself. This theme has been echoed by various writers who have seen the modern state as a technocracy (Ellul, 1964; Meynaud, 1965). We will also see other variants on this theme in the rational choice theory explored in the next chapter, and in theories stressing the importance of policy communities in Chapter 5 and institutions in Chapter 6.

C. Wright Mills (1956) draws attention to institutional position as a source of power, and suggests that the American political system is dominated by a power elite occupying key positions in government, business corporations and the military. The overlap and connection between the leaders of these institutions helps to create a relatively coherent power elite. Reference has already been made to Mills's book and to the work of Hunter on local power. But can a realistic distinction be drawn between the sort of modified pluralist perspective set out in the last section and the elitist one? The elitist case is not helped by the fact that many alternative sources of elite power have been suggested. That tends to reinforce the pluralist case, and may be seen as the basis of the theory of 'democratic elitism' mentioned above. That theory argues that regular elections based on competition between the leaders of political parties, together with participation by pressure group elites in between elections, and interaction between these elites and the bureaucratic elites, are the ways in which democracy operates in the modern state. The fact that different elites operate in different issue areas is a protection against domination by one group.

There is a problem with sustaining a simple elite theory position inasmuch as there are difficulties in specifying the mechanisms by which power is seized and the techniques used to hold on to it. One now very unfashionable elite theorist, Paretto, who worked in Italy around the same time as Mosca, offered an answer to that question inasmuch as he saw elite domination as based upon the special qualities possessed by the elite (Paretto, 1966). But even he posited a kind of pluralist process by which the 'circulation of elites' occurs as old elites weaken and new ones arise.

There are, however, two ways in which the debate about how power is exercised needs to be taken further. One, as indicated above, is to bypass the question about how power is acquired but to argue that once that has happened then the institutions of the state offer the means for an elite to perpetuate its power. The detailed examination of this will have to await Chapter 5. The other approach to this question is to emphasise the importance of economic power. Where it does this, elite theory begins to merge with another very important approach to the study of power, Marxist theory, to the extent that some of the key exponents of the position set out above (for example, Wright Mills) are only distinguishable from Marxists by their comparative reluctance to quote Marx in their support. The next section therefore picks up on those aspects of Marxist theory that concentrate on the role of individual actors in the pursuit of power.

Elite theory, in both classical and modern guises, represents an important alternative to pluralism. Yet, while some writers have attempted to reconcile elitism and pluralist democracy, others have used the findings of elitist studies to argue that the power elite is but a ruling class by another name. That is, it is suggested that institutions may well be run by minority groups, but that these groups come from similar social backgrounds and are therefore exercising power in the interests of a dominant group.

It must be noted that the bridging concept between elitism and Marxism is the idea of a 'ruling class'. However, until recently this class analysis has led to a disregard of the extent to which other forms of social stratification, particularly stratification in terms of gender and ethnicity, may be significant for the distribution of power. Now, both within feminist literature and in the analysis of racism, a lively debate has developed about the extent to which these other forms of stratification may operate independently of, or in association with, class divisions, to structure and bias the policy process. We will return to this later.

Marxism

In his book *The State in Capitalist Society* (1969), Miliband takes as his starting point not the political process itself but the form of economic organisation or the mode of production. In advanced Western industrialised societies the capitalist mode of production dominates, giving rise to two major social classes – the bourgeoisie and the proletariat. Miliband's analysis of the distribution of income and wealth, and changes in this distribution over time, demonstrates the continued concentration of wealth in a small section of the population. The question Miliband then asks is whether this economically dominant class exercises decisive political power. In other words, he explores the relationship between economic power and political power.

Taking their cue from Karl Marx, writers like Miliband argue that the state is not a neutral agent, but rather is an instrument for class domination. Marx expressed this view in the *Communist Manifesto*, where he wrote that 'The executive of the modern state is but a committee for managing the common affairs of the whole bourgeoisie' (quoted in McLellan, 1971, p. 192). Miliband suggests three reasons why the state is an instrument of bourgeois domination in capitalist society. First, there is the similarity in social background between the bourgeoisie and members of the state elite – that is, those who occupy senior positions in government, the civil service, the military, the judiciary and other state institutions. Second, there is the power that the bourgeoisie is able to exercise as a pressure group through personal contacts and networks and through the associations representing business and industry. Third, there is the constraint placed on the state by the objective power of capital. In these ways, Miliband contends, the state acts as an instrument which serves the long-term interests of the whole bourgeoisie.

Marxism is today seen, above all, as the ideology that sustained the Soviet empire until its collapse and is argued to continue to hold sway in China. But it must be remembered that Marx's original purpose was to analyse the system of economic power dominant within capitalist societies and to show how that system contained within it the seeds of its own downfall. The fact that it has not fallen in the way Marx predicted does not necessarily invalidate the whole of his analysis, particularly those parts relating to the significance of ownership or control of the means of production for power within the state.

The original theory set out by Karl Marx, though complicated and stated in rather different ways at different times in his life, postulated a theory of history in which the means of production is a dominant and determining force. The 'executive of the modern state' was a committee to manage the 'affairs of the whole bourgeoisie' not because the latter was able to control it, but because it could be nothing else so long as society remained capitalist. In other words, mainstream Marxist theory takes the issues about the determination of policy in a very different direction to the concerns of this chapter so far, to suggest that a power *structure* determined by the means of production is of dominant importance.

Structuralist aspects of the Marxist perspective

This section will deal fairly briefly with Marxist structuralism since direct use of this form of analysis has declined significantly in recent years. Yet it is worth a little attention as an alternative approach to the explanation of unequal power in the policy process, seeing what may be called 'economic imperatives' as a crucial influence, a view that we will then see echoed by some theorists who would not see themselves as Marxists.

According to classical Marxist theory, the social structure of a capitalist society is essentially a 'class structure'. The two classes that confront each other in a capitalist society (at least in the last resort) are the bourgeoisie (the owners of the means of production) and the proletariat (who work for the bourgeoisie). Some of Marx's work deals with other classes, but his logic indicates that they will eventually be sucked into the fundamental class struggle. That struggle will then intensify, as the nature of competitive production forces the bourgeoisie to systematically reduce the rewards going to the proletariat. This process of 'immiseration' will eventually lead the increasingly unified proletariat to rise up to overthrow the bourgeoisie. That revolution will lead to the replacement of capitalism by socialism, just as earlier the logic of industrial change led capitalism to replace feudalism. In other words, at the core of classical Marxist theory there is an essentially determinist argument. Our position in relation to the means of production determines our long-run political interests. Our fate is set by the working out of that dialectic. Notwithstanding that position, Marx urged the proletariat to organise politically, to work towards the ultimate revolution. In that sense there is a contradiction at the core of classical Marxism, which has left it open for some to reinterpret the theory in a very much less deterministic way.

Our concern here is with the role of the state in the determinist model. The idea, set out above, of the state as 'the executive committee of the bourgeoisie' is, in this interpretation, the only thing it can be. Its role is a supportive and subsidiary one in relation to capitalism. In his determinist 'mood' Marx was not very interested in the role of the state. The problem is that in his more activist 'mood' he urged the organisations of the proletariat to mobilise to try to take over the state. This engendered an argument within Marxism about the purpose of such activity. Was it just to prepare for, or practise for, or advance, the revolution, since the state could neither be transformed nor transform capitalism? Or was there a peaceful road to revolution by way of securing control over the state? It was this alternative that engendered a social democratic form of Marxism which the revolutionary followers of Marx repudiated.

Hence, whilst generating an elaborate controversy about the state within Marxist ranks (which became increasingly complicated as the role of the state changed in the twentieth century in ways that did not seem to accord with Marxist predictions), the classical Marxist position is to suggest that the capitalist state's main function is to assist the process of capital accumulation. This means creating conditions in which capitalists are able to promote the production of profit. The state is seen as acting to maintain order and control within society.

Twentieth-century Marxist theory has elaborated this in a variety of ways, partly to explain phenomena that Marx had not expected to occur. In specific terms, assisting accumulation means providing physical resources such as roads and industrial sites, while maintaining order is carried out both through repressive mechanisms like the police and through agencies such as schools, which perform an important legitimation function. The accumulation process is further assisted through state intervention in the provision of services such as housing and health to groups in the working population. One of the functions of these services is to reduce the cost of labour power to capital and to keep the workforce healthy.

O'Connor (1973) classifies these different forms of state expenditure as social investment, social consumption and social expenses. Social investment increases labour productivity through the provision, for example, of infrastructure and aid to industry; social consumption lowers the cost of reproducing labour power as, for example, in the provision of social insurance; and social expenses serve to maintain social harmony. In practice, nearly all interventions by the state perform more than one of these functions.

O'Connor's analysis suggests that state expenditure serves the interest of monopoly capital, and that the state is run by a class-conscious political directorate acting on behalf of monopoly capitalist class interests. In a similar vein, Gough (1979) makes use of O'Connor's typology to show how the modern welfare state serves the long-term interests of the capitalist class.

The key point overall is that Marxist theory tends to take a stance which treats state action as to a considerable extent constrained and *determined* by economic institutions. It will be suggested below that this simple proposition is echoed today by many who would certainly not wish to be portrayed as Marxists.

Other structuralist perspectives

Thompson puts the underlying theoretical issue about the relationship between explanations of social action that emphasise actions and those that emphasise structure as follows:

> The problem of the relation between the individual and society, or between action and social structure, lies at the heart of social theory and the philosophy of social science. In the writings of most major theorists ... this problem is raised and allegedly resolved in one way or another. Such resolutions generally amount to the accentuation of one term at the expense of the other ... the problem is not so much resolved as dissolved. (Thompson, 1989, p. 56)

Structuralist theories that see political action as determined by powerful forces outside human control have a long history in the social sciences. Writers have postulated distinct patterns of human evolution or a determinist approach to history which have challenged the view that individuals have the capacity to determine their own social and political institutions. Theories of this kind have taken forms that suggest a need to accept the status quo, to regard political choices as predetermined by demographic, social and economic factors. They have also come in 'critical' forms – concerned to analyse what are seen as powerful constraints upon human action which have to be attacked in order to achieve fundamental change. That contrast draws attention to the problem within much of this theory: that in dealing with the factors that determine social stability in changing societies it has to try to specify conditions under which change can occur. Its proponents have, particularly in its critical forms, to try to answer questions about the conditions under which actions to effect social change may be appropriate.

Structuralist theory has, in short, to take a stance on the relationship between structure and action. The former determines the latter yet the latter feeds back to alter the former. All but the most simplistic forms of structural theory – with which we need not bother ourselves because they are so unrealistic – acknowledge some measure of scope for action to secure change. Further distinctions can be made between different kinds of structural theory about the extent to which they are totally determinist. These differences particularly concern the extent to which there are strong evolutionary forces in societies.

Related to this issue of variations in the extent to which theories are determinist is the issue of what is seen as the source of that determinism – demography, technological evolution and economic forces being perhaps the most widely identified sources. A sort of determinism which lies at the very weakest end of structural theory sees the institutional and ideological configurations that have been established as imposing strong constraints upon future actions.

Hence, structuralist Marxism sits alongside other structuralist perspectives. In sociology 'structure functionalist theory' has been influential but is now seen as fairly dated. Yet it is worth a brief mention (a) because of the way in which it poses questions about structural influences that – at least when postulated in a very weak form – still need attention, and (b) because as a theoretical perspective it occupies an important place in relation to Marxism as a set of propositions which partly support and partly offer a contradiction of that perspective.

Structural functionalism involves a fusion in sociological theory between propositions from early anthropological studies – which suggested that social institutions reinforce each other in ways which support the status quo in allegedly 'static' societies – and propositions from social Darwinism, which traced processes of social evolution. Sociologists in this tradition in the United States or western Europe saw their own societies as 'progressing', with their institutions adapting in response to evolving social needs. Where Marxists saw an evolutionary process leading towards social crisis, these theorists saw a progressive adaptation occurring.

What this perspective implied for political choices – and thus for the policy process – was a series of imperatives to which the political system would respond. The evolutionary element in this perspective led some scholars to proclaim that their own societies had reached 'the end of ideology' (Bell, 1960) – in which political battles would be muted by a common acceptance of the benefits of the status quo – and less 'developed' societies would follow to evolve along the same progressive path. Economic development is seen as the generator of a wide range of social changes (Kerr, 1973). In addition to its contribution to the growth of the standard of living it is a source of urban development. These changes are then held to have influenced patterns of social behaviour, including choices about marriage and family size.

Comparative studies have thus aimed to explain the emergence of public policies – particularly social policy – by correlating their incidence with the phenomena of economic growth, industrialisation, urbanisation and demographic change linked together in a package of ingredients of 'modernisation' (Hofferbert, 1974; Wilensky, 1975).

Some versions of the modernisation thesis go beyond these issues to try to identify a postmodernist or a post-industrial order with its own distinctive policies. We will find some traces of this approach later in the book when we examine organisational arrangements and find that there are suggestions that we are now in a postmodernist, or more specifically post-Fordist, era in which old bureaucratic and hierarchical models for the organisation of industrial and administrative life are giving way to new forms. Clearly, technological changes – the development of computers and other electronic control devices – facilitate the development of these new forms of organisation. Readers should be suspicious of arguments about these phenomena which come in deterministic forms, however. It is one thing to say that people are trying new approaches to the organisation of complex activities, aided by new technology, but quite another to dress this up in a technologically determinist form which seems to deny any role for human choice.

The question is: have we here a set of determinist theories suggesting that public policy developments can be read off from these economic and social developments? Or are these theories merely making the point that there is

(a) a general association between economic growth and state growth across the broad band of prosperous nations in the past, together with (perhaps)

(b) a certain critical threshold that nations have to pass before significant levels of public services, imposing high costs on the nation, become feasible in developing societies, and

(c) further – picking up on the last part of this section – that there is a later generation of technological developments which are further transforming some of the record keeping and surveillance options open to governments?

To go further would be to pay too little attention to the choices made by actors or to variations in response from place to place (Ashford, 1986).

Economic determinism without Marxism

Perspectives can be identified on economic determinism which either diverge so far from classical Marxism that it is inappropriate to call them Marxist, or which involve propositions about the dominance of economic considerations in the policy process of a kind that have no foundations in Marxist theory. The most important of these propositions are those that stress the significance of 'global' economic forces. These will be discussed separately following this comparatively brief look at other theories that embody forms of economic determinism.

There is a perspective which suggests that there is built into the politics of any but the poorest societies a set of concerns about the need for advances in the standard of living that any politicians will disregard at their peril. Related to this – particularly since the collapse of communism – is the view that only capitalist economic institutions can provide those advances. This perspective is obviously advanced in philosophical works which celebrate capitalist economic institutions (Hayek, 1944, 1960), and is more generally taken for granted in much contemporary political analysis. The pronouncement by the Chinese leader Deng Xiaoping – to justify his flirtations with capitalism – that it does not matter what colour the cat is so long as it can catch mice (Shambaugh, 1995, p. 88), perhaps sums up this post-Marxist consensus.

It is interesting to note how implicit economic determinism crops up in the ranks of thinkers from all parts of the ideological spectrum. Arguably, there is a thread of thinking from the 'Right' which is very like Marxist structuralism, but without any theory of change or revolution. This is the view that there has been a process of evolution to the ideal economic order (capitalism) and the ideal political order (representative democracy) and that the kind of 'directional history' embodied in the theories of Hegel and Marx has come to an end (Fukuyama, 1992). Such a perspective suggests that:

> All countries undergoing economic modernisation must increasingly resemble one another: they must unify nationally on the basis of a centralized state, urbanize, replace traditional forms of social organisation like tribe, sect and family with economically rational ones based on function and efficiency, and provide for the universal education of their citizens ... the logic of modern natural science would seem to dictate a universal evolution in the direction of capitalism. (Fukuyama, 1992, pp. xiv–xv)

Fukuyama explores this theme with a caution not evident in the quotation, but he does in many respects advance a 1990s version of Bell's earlier 'end of ideology' thesis (see p. 43).

More pragmatic versions of this perspective involve taken-for-granted assumptions about the need to limit public expenditure or taxation – with the implicit consequences of this for other policies – in the interests of the maintenance of the capitalist economy. Clearly there is here a kind of structuralist perspective, specifying a distinct limit to the extent to which politicians can disregard economic forces.

Globalism

A closely related kind of determinist theory, deserving of a section of its own because of the wide attention it is given, is globalism. This sees a sequence of worldwide economic developments as of determining importance for contemporary policy making. Globalist theory has developed on a massive scale, and in the process branched in many directions. It embodies various themes – the development of global financial markets, the cross-national diffusion of technology, the emergence of transnational or global corporations (and the increasing economic pressure upon large corporations to 'think globally') and the emergence of global cultural flows. All these trends offer challenges to state autonomy and stimulate new political formations beyond the nation state. More cautious statements on this topic stress the extent to which this is in some respects a gradual change, acknowledge that complex supranational economic developments have a long history and recognise that the speed of modern communications heightens awareness of the phenomenon.

There are variants of globalism that are close to classical Marxism, in that they see the processes described by Marx as now taking place on a world scale (Wallerstein, 1979; Cox, 1987). This is a view that George and Wilding describe as 'Marxissant', with 'the fundamental premise that the driving logic of capitalism for constantly increased profitability has been the major force behind globalisation' (2002, p. 7). This is a view that is not particularly new: it was set out originally by Lenin in 1917. It suggests that there is a complicated working through of the postulated conflict between capitalists and proletariat across the world, postponing the eventual crisis and raising difficult tactical problems for international Marxists who have to face difficulties in getting the proletariat to think globally rather than to accept national interpretations of exploitation.

Within Marxist thinking there are distinctions to be found between those who see capitalism as an increasingly international phenomenon and those who argue that companies are rather more supra-national than global (that is, they spread out from a national base) and that their power is not necessarily an external imposition upon nation states but something established within them (see Panitch, 1994). As Panitch puts it in a rhetorical question:

> Is it really to international finance that governments in London or Ottawa are accountable when they prepare their budgets? Or are they accountable to the City of London or to Bay Street? (Panitch, 1994, p. 74)

Alternatively, globalist theory may accept that capitalist economic relationships are increasingly organised on a world scale but not set out that view in Marxist terms. The question that emerges for this discussion is then to what extent a globalist position is really a determinist one. Is globalist theory saying that here is a series of structural developments about which politicians can do little? Or is it merely saying that the issues about the power of economic interests – which even pluralist writers like Lindblom have come to accept as critical for the policy process – need to be analysed in supra-national terms? In other words, this is not so much a determinist point of view as one which emphasises *either* that national policy makers must increasingly be able to deal with interests organised outside their country *or* that effective policy processes need to be supra-national too (Hirst and Thompson, 1992). The latter position may lead to a pessimistic stance on the feasibility of achieving solutions to political problems in the face of institutional complexity, but it is not ultimately a determinist stance. This is certainly the position reached by analysts of issues about pollution policy (see, for example, Hurrell and Kingsbury, 1992), energy policy (see Yergin, 1991) and monetary policy (Walter, 1993).

Hay offers a useful alternative slant on the determinist element in the globalist perspective arguing that:

> Whether the globalist thesis is 'true' or not may matter far less than whether it is *deemed* to be true – or, quite possibly, just useful – by those employing it. (Hay, 2002, p. 258)

Hence, Hay argues that decision makers may believe either that there is no alternative but to respond to perceived global economic forces, or that globalisation 'may provide a most convenient alibi, allowing politicians to escape the responsibility they would otherwise bear for reforms which might otherwise be rather difficult to legitimate' (ibid., p. 259). That puts a very interesting slant on the structure/action relationship, seeing decision makers as active 'agents' within structures. But those structures are not all determining, and how those structures are perceived or 'used' may be crucial.

That observation on globalism leads to two others. First, it is obviously not a determinist approach in itself to pay attention to the extent to which pressures upon policy decisions come from sources outside the nation state. In that sense it is quite feasible to adopt a pluralist analysis (whether modified or not by concerns about power concentrations), taking into account the extent to which interest groups organised outside the nation state or across several nation states have an impact upon policy in any specific state. Second, if governments are more aware of international developments then this may affect how they respond to economic interests within their own country. Hence, as Pierre and Peters put it:

> The need to develop closer links ... with private industry is driven by a strategy to maintain or increase the international competitiveness of the domestic industry. (Pierre and Peters, 2000, p. 60)

Other variants of structuralism

Some of the structuralist arguments originating from feminism link very closely with Marxist theory. For some writers, gender divisions in society are seen as further ways in which the proletariat are divided and controlled. The growth of a female workforce which is poorly paid and insecure is seen as a particularly insidious development in the 'reserve army of labour' that keeps the proletariat cheap and weak (Barrett, 1980).

Other feminist theory focuses rather more upon male domination of economic and political institutions *per se*, not seeing it in the Marxist context of class divisions (Millet, 1970; Delphy, 1984). Inasmuch as this perspective is structuralist in nature, it opens up a very important issue with ramifications beyond the relations between the genders. What is involved is an argument that there is a range of institutions – the family, the church, the economy, the state – that are linked together in a structure that has a powerfully determining impact upon what gets on the agenda. We are back here with Lukes's third face of power. This structure influences culture, discourse and behaviour, defining the political agenda. As such it *defines out* many female concerns. Schwarzmantel makes a direct parallel with Marxism using the concept of 'deep structure':

> Both feminism and Marxism take a common stance, in that both are concerned to reveal ... a 'deep structure' or power dimension which exists in

the liberal-democratic state and the society that surrounds it, and in other forms of state and society as well. The power dimension is in both cases seen as a 'fault line' or basic division which is to some extent hidden from view. (Schwarzmantel, 1994, p. 115)

Rhetorics of equality are seen as masking real inequalities of power. An ideology of male domination is seen as embodied in a division between the 'public' sphere and the 'private' sphere. The public sphere for long excluded women, whilst, in the private sphere, behaviour within the household was regarded as outside the realm of political interference. This has had the effect of keeping issues about domineering behaviour by men within the household off the agenda.

Schwarzmantel perhaps takes the parallels between feminist theory and Marxist theory too far. What the general feminist position brings into the discussion is a good example of how policy processes have been structured with the effect that they support the status quo and suppress certain issues in the way described by Lukes. They take us into a very much looser and more general approach to the way in which policy processes are structured.

Before we look at that it is important to recognise that the arguments deployed here also apply to ethnic divisions. The equivalent of radical feminism's development of Marxist theory is a body of work that stresses the way ethnic divisions function to keep the proletariat divided (Solomos et al., 1982). The term 'ethnicity' needs to be interpreted widely here – going far beyond recognised biological differences (which are in any case ambiguous and contestable) to comprise national, linguistic, cultural and religious divisions which create or are used to create divisions of an 'ethnic' kind. In this case there is a connection back, too, to the issues about globalism. There are economic differences associated with divisions between countries, where the 'national interest' is invoked to both attack and defend inequalities. The world 'division of labour' has ethnic dimensions. Migration has then further complicated this by contributing to the reproduction of these divisions within countries (Cohen, 1987).

Just as there is a conflict within feminist theory between those who link gender and class issues and those who focus primarily on gender, so in the analysis of ethnic divisions there are those whose analyses are embedded in Marxist theory and those who see that perspective as too limiting for a satisfactory analysis of the exploitation of ethnic groups (Rex, 1986). In the analysis of ethnic divisions, as in the exploration of gender divisions, there is a need to analyse structural constraints upon political action in historical terms, examining both the establishment of institutions which privileged some and disadvantaged others, and the development of ideologies which set out to justify inequalities. In the case of ethnicity, the establishment of cohesive nation states involved the deployment of rules to define who did and who did not belong, and ideologies to justify those rules.

In this section, as in the last, it is open to question whether the phenomena being explored should be described as 'structural'. What is being described is divisions within societies, which are maintained and reinforced in various ways. It is implicit in feminist theory and in attacks upon ethnic divisions that there is a politics of challenge to these divisions. Where the structuralism comes in is in regarding challenging such divisions as a difficult political task. It is a task, moreover, where policy processes have to involve not just changing distributive or regulatory rules but also challenging the ideologies that have underpinned those rules. Here we are back to the point made by Hay in relation to globalism, that we have here ideas about society and its culture – discourses, if you like (and here the postmodernist approach discussed on pp. 16–19 is very relevant) – that sustain patterns of power.

This discussion of structural determinants of policy processes has moved from theories which seem to be strongly determinist – structural functionalism and classical Marxism – to perspectives that many would not call structuralist at all since they merely spell out factors which are likely to have a strong influence on political choices. Parsons (1995, pp. 608–9) argues that some of these may simply be incorporated into accepted constraints:

> The distinction between politics and economy and society . . . needs to be revised to take account of the argument that the world of 'facts' and social and economic forces is not simply 'out there'.

He goes on:

> it may well be that external environments are better understood as mirrors or projections of the values, beliefs and assumptions which frame the internal policy-making process.

That is, however, perhaps to make too little of some powerful forces at work. The case for a discussion of structuralist theory lies not primarily in a need to outline what are in many respects rather over-deterministic theories, but in a need to stress that there is running through any policy process a series of strong biases or influences on action. This may be described as an influential 'deep structure' (Schwarzmantel, 1994) or in terms of Lukes's 'third face of power' or Hay's 'context-shaping power' (see p. 34). Social change – in which the policy process plays an important part – involves a dynamic in which structure influences action and is at the same time altered by that action.

It has been shown that structural perspectives do not necessarily put 'class interests' and 'economic forces' as the only kinds of determining agents. Implicit in the concept of structure is a system which gives dominance to a range of powerful groups (see Degeling and Colebatch, 1984). Such groups will include professional and bureaucratic elites, males, specific ethnic, religious, linguistic groups, and so on. This dominance is given structural form by customary practices and modes of organisation. It may well be built into language, and manifested symbolically in a variety of ways.

Structures are not fixed and immutable. In giving attention here to formalised political institutions, it must not be forgotten that they vary considerably in strength and in the extent to which they are formalised. A distinction may perhaps be drawn between structures and institutions, where the latter are seen as 'regularized practices *structured* by rules and resources deeply layered in time and space' (Thompson, 1989, p. 61). They are changed by action, and some actions may be specifically directed at trying to change structures. The prevailing order is continually being renegotiated. This is clearly not an easy process, but in addressing the determinants of decision making, it is one which must not be entirely disregarded (this sort of approach to the relationship between structure and action is explored in the sociological writings of Giddens, 1976, 1984).

CONCLUSIONS

This long chapter started by outlining a simple way to classify discussions of power in terms of four quadrants illustrating arguments about the extent to which it is fragmented and the extent to which it is distributed equally. It rather quickly dismissed the 'representative government' model (Figure 2.1, quadrant 1) which sees power as neither fragmented nor unequally distributed.

Figure 2.1 was used to help to give shape to the discussion. Since it was described as a way to distinguish positions in an argument, readers may reasonably ask where the author puts himself. The answer is – if the quadrant is seen instead as two dimensions – very close to the axis, accepting that a characteristic of most democratic societies is a very unbalanced pluralism.

The discussion showed that the main arguments seem to have been between pluralists who see power as fragmented but relatively evenly distributed, and a variety of theorists who identify ways in which it is concentrated in the hands of small groups, often described as elites. Identifying Marxism as, at least historically, the most important version of the latter theory, it went on to explore the way in which Marxists have been split between those who identify capitalists as actors in their own interests and those who adopt a more structuralist explanation of the (for them temporary) dominance of capitalism.

Interestingly, then, it is this structuralist version of Marxism that tends to continue to exert influence, detached from its origins in an evolutionary theory, in the variety of ways in which economics is seen as exerting a deterministic influence upon the policy process. The most important modern form of this determinism is globalist theory.

The chapter ended by looking at challenges to determinism, seeing the extent to which it involves discourses used to support the existing distribution of power or to enhance the power of specific interests. In the end it needs to be conceded that actions occur within structures, and are influenced by those structures, but that what this implies in practice is very complex. The next three chapters pick up this theme in different ways, since much of the theoretical work considered is concerned with the relationship between structure and action.

3 Rational choice theory

SYNOPSIS

Rational choice theory involves the application of notions from economics (and to some extent from mathematics) to the analysis of the way in which self-interested behaviour by individuals may influence the policy process. It is seen as an extension of pluralist theory. It suggests that predictive propositions can be derived from generalisations which equate self-interest and rational behaviour and assume that they will be dominant. It assists the analysis of the policy process by reminding us of the importance of self-interest and of the extent to which public policy problems emerge from the incapacity of market mechanisms to solve many collective action problems.

The basic notion of the political marketplace is introduced. This is followed by a discussion of the way in which collective action problems have been analysed from an economic perspective, principally to assist with the development of prescriptive approaches, but in ways which also help with the analysis of the development of public policies. Game theory, with its roots in mathematics rather than economics, is then briefly examined as a further extension of that approach.

Finally, the economic theory of bureaucracy is examined. It is seen as a theoretical approach which contributes to insights about the behaviour of public sector bureaucrats, particularly when it is modified in ways which retain its concern to stress self-interested behaviour but show that it may lead to varied predictions of the way in which actual behavioural choices will be structured. A final note warns against the underlying determinism of theory that puts self-interest into so strong a predictive role.

Introduction

There are a number of approaches to the analysis of the policy process which draw upon economic theory. These are given various names, but essentially they are variants of what is called rational choice theory or public choice theory. Assumptions about choices made in competitive market situations are applied to political processes. A key characteristic of this sort of theory is the way its assumptions are derived from the notion that individuals act in their own best interests. It is in this sense that the word 'rational' is used. While there are good grounds for arguing that economists have here appropriated the word 'rational' for a rather particular restricted use, since it seems now to be the term most commonly used to describe this kind of theory, it will be used here.

The emphasis upon interests clearly contains echoes of the similar concern to analyse interests in classical pluralist theory, and the notion that it should be possible to predict what those interests will be seems to suggest that with this addition pluralism will have more predictive power. We will look here, therefore, at a linked group of theories about choices in political processes, about the relationship between individual interests and collective interests and about how actors inside the policy system (particularly bureaucrats) may also have predictable interests. This kind of theoretical work offers a corrective to an idealistic view of the policy process as involving impartial problem solving, but it will be shown that it, too, suffers from problematic simplifying assumptions.

The development of the idea of the political marketplace

The idea of politics as a marketplace in which leaders compete for votes is developed in the work of Downs (1957), who uses economic theory to analyse political behaviour. This perspective develops pluralist theory by adding an element of economistic reasoning which sees self-interest as the dominant motive force in political behaviour. In the political marketplace, parties compete to win power by responding to the demands of pressure groups (see Auster and Silver, 1979; Tullock, 1976; Brittan, 1977). There is a very strong pressure upon governments to yield to those demands, and thus to enhance the role of the state as a giver of benefits (using that word in its general sense, to embrace jobs, contracts, services and tax concessions as well as direct cash benefits). This is not very effectively restrained by the fact that these benefits have to be paid for, because of the extent to which these costs can be hidden in the short run (by deficit financing) or spread in ways which lead benefits to be more readily perceived than the mechanisms to pay for them. For example, in 1991 in Britain a dramatic cut in an unpopular direct local tax (the 'poll tax') was funded by a percentage increase in an indirect sales tax rate (which had a slight and gradual impact upon prices paid by consumers). Interest groups seek specific benefits for themselves (business subsidies, welfare services, etc.) whose costs are diffused amongst taxpayers as a whole (Moe, 1980). The whole process involves what is often described as 'rent-seeking behaviour' in which interests secure larger gains for themselves than they would if they were competing in a free and open market.

Public choice theorists argue (Tullock, 1976; Brittan, 1977) that as a result of political responses to plural demands the state grows in power and importance in ways which may be damaging to the working of the capitalist economy. They also suggest that these pluralist (or demand-side) pressures for government growth may be reinforced by monopolistic interests on the part of state suppliers, bureaucrats and professions in enhancing their 'empires'. At this point rational choice theory diverges from classical pluralist theory in giving a significant role to the state as an autonomous actor. This is a theme to which we will return below.

Another theme emerging from this school of thought has been the notion that there is a 'government business cycle' in which government expenditure, to satisfy demands and curb unemployment, is pushed up before general elections (Nordhaus, 1975; MacRae, 1977). The consequences of this are problems of inflation and adverse trade balances that will need to be dealt with in the post-election period. Hence, it is argued that political behaviour may contribute to the cyclical problems of the modern capitalist state. While it is comparatively easy to find specific examples of behaviour to support this thesis, it is less plausible as a general hypothesis. The empirical data is not conclusive (see Mosley, 1984), the feasibility of this kind of behaviour depends upon electoral systems, fitting political activities to economic trends is a difficult activity, and there have been alternative attempts to make economic rectitude a political asset (see Dearlove and Saunders, 1991, pp. 66–7).

Rational choice and collective action

Rational choice theory has particularly been developed by those who think it preferable to use market mechanisms to settle collective choice problems. It aims to show that public policy choices are made in ways that are no different from market choices, and that in some respects, therefore, commercial marketplaces deal with choice problems better than political marketplaces. It is argued that policy initiatives ostensibly developed to deal with the deficiencies of markets (market failure) need to take into account corresponding deficiencies of the state (state failure). In this respect, rational choice theory is more concerned with advocacy about the way public policy *should* be made than with analysis of *how* it is made. Hence, there is a close connection between rational choice theory and an economics literature which attempts to define the circumstances in which state (or at least collective) intervention may be justified, for those who believe that market systems are the right ones to settle most social distribution questions.

It may seem to be something of a digression to look at this literature inasmuch as it does not so much explain how public policy is made as examine justifications for public interventions. However, it is worth examining briefly for the way it leads on to analyses of decision-making situations in which actors will be likely to conclude that following self-interest is problematical, and thus seek other ways of solving collective action problems.

Three key concepts are used in the discussion of this topic:

- externalities
- market inefficiencies
- monopoly.

Box 3.1	The tragedy of the commons

Where there is common land on which peasants are entitled to graze livestock, if there is no regulation of numbers, each individual will see it as not in their interest to restrict use. They will reason that a few more animals will not make any difference. Yet when all behave in this way the consequence is the destruction of the common pasture.

Externalities arise when market activities have consequences, either *positive* or *negative*, for people who are not party to those activities. Failure to deal with negative externalities has been described as 'the tragedy of the commons' (Hardin, 1968), referring to the collective consequences of self-interested individual decisions (see Box 3.1). Failure to give attention to externalities means that all suffer in the long run. One of the most obvious examples of this arises in relation to pollution. In the course of producing something, a manufacturer expels waste products up a chimney or into a water course. Neighbours etc. suffer the consequences of this action. Here, then, is a case for state intervention: to prevent a nuisance which its producer has no incentive to prevent, given that any individual sufferer from it is likely to lack the resources to take action alone.

Positive externalities are not, in themselves, a source of problems. However, the difficulty in this case is that the creator of a positive externality is likely to resent the 'free riders' who will benefit from something they do not pay for. If someone builds a sea wall to protect their property from flooding, their neighbours are likely to share that benefit. There may, of course, in this case also be negative consequences somewhere else down the coast, in which case the combination of positive and negative effects further reinforces the case for collective action.

Faced with a high-cost item, and the likelihood of 'free riders', an individual is likely to try to secure agreement to collective action (the sharing of the cost amongst the potential beneficiaries). As far at least as the community surrounding the builder of the hypothetical sea wall are concerned, the wall constitutes what is sometimes called a 'public good'. No one can be prevented from benefiting from it. There are other examples where the benefiting community may be very much larger. Perhaps the largest example is a national – or even international – defence system. If it is true that a nuclear deterrent preserves peace then everyone benefits. The case for a state monopoly of defence (assuming acceptance of that state's legitimacy by its population) is overwhelming. There are similar issues here with regard to policing within a country.

Furthermore, whilst there have been efforts by states to delegate these tasks, states often then have to deal with severe control problems. Power has been given – in a very strong sense because weapons are involved – to a body of people who owe no ultimate allegiance to the state. Mercenaries merely have a contract to receive payment and/or spoils in return for their 'work'. It is not surprising that mercenary armies have sometimes switched allegiance, particularly when the capacity of the state to deliver on its part of the bargain has been in doubt (as it would be if the very action for which the mercenaries had been hired seemed to be failing). Some rather more modern issues also arise around the nature of the 'contract' between the state and the implementing actors, in the situations in which the latter seem to have no wider basis for 'allegiance'.

Returning, however, to the notion of externalities: how wide are the implications of positive and negative effects? Do they extend well beyond the examples given so far of environmental protection, law and order and defence? There are some other cases where the free rider problem can be brought under control: roads, bridges and parks may be provided privately, their use paid for through tolls. Then the argument for public provision lies in questions about the inefficient or inequitable use of resources.

But then the externalities argument can be widened further. For example, to what extent does everyone benefit if their fellow citizens are kept healthy? The 'external' impact of infectious diseases is clear enough, but there are other wider senses in which everyone benefits from living in a healthy community. What about education? – do not benefits similarly arise from living in an educated nation? Finally, what about 'externalities' relating to income distribution? If the elimination of extreme inequalities makes people with resources safer – from burglary, assault, revolution even – there are surely externalities which derive from income maintenance policies.

Most economic theorists would probably answer 'no' to my response to that last question, and say that this is stretching the concept too far. If they accepted the case they would probably want to discuss 'trade offs' with other indirect consequences of state interventions. However, as stressed above, the concern here is not with the philosophical argument but rather with the fact that there has been a recognition within capitalist economies of a range of justifications for state intervention, often stretching far beyond the obvious examples of 'public goods'. Some economists have added another related concept to the list of special cases – merit goods (Musgrave, 1959), where the collectivity (state) regards it as desirable that people should have something whether they want it or not (in economists' terms this means they are prepared to and can afford to buy it). Education and health services are sometimes put into this category.

However, there may be reinforcing reasons for state action. One such reason, which lies very close to economic analysis, involves the extent to which state systems make it easier for employers to socialise costs. Public education and training systems reduce costs for employers, and reduce the disadvantage they encounter when other employers poach those upon whom they have spent training money. Help for the old and sick makes it easier for employers to discard inefficient workers. Unemployment benefits similarly may make the laying off of labour at a time of work shortage a less controversial matter, and may help those out of work to deal with their relocation problems in a more economically efficient way.

Pure economic theory is based upon assumptions of full awareness by all parties of all their options as buyers and sellers. Real-world economics concedes that there are many imperfections in the market arising from incomplete knowledge. That suggests that there may be a role for the state in helping to reduce knowledge imperfections. The case for labour market interventions, introducing buyers of labour to sellers of labour, certainly seems to have been based primarily upon this concern. That example is, however, one designed to deal with an essentially short-run problem. There are also long-term problems inasmuch as citizens may find it very difficult to act in the way the economic model presupposes (this is particularly the case when individuals are unwell or disabled). There was some recognition, even by the tough-minded theorists who designed poor law systems, that there might be individuals who could not be expected to behave like 'economic men'.

Another issue is that of monopoly, concerning principally the difficulties that competing suppliers might have in entering a market. Ironically, extreme market liberals accept a role for the state in preventing the abuse of monopoly power – the 'night-watchman state' has a duty to restrain those who try to act in restraint of the market. But another issue concerns the variety of situations in which the nature of the activity is such that it is in practice very hard to sustain competition. The crucial situation here is one in which there is a monopoly or near monopoly supplier and a competing supplier would find the costs of market entry prohibitively high. Examples of this are found in the supply of water, electricity and gas. To a lesser extent they also exist in transport systems (particularly where – like railways – they use fixed plant) and in large institutions like hospitals and schools. There is then an argument for state ownership or regulation to prevent any existing institution from exploiting its position, or perhaps (more controversially) for state intervention or subsidy to help create a second supplier.

Economic theory about externalities, incomplete knowledge and monopoly thus provides a series of justifications for public policies, both regulatory and redistributive, of a kind likely to be taken seriously by states in capitalist societies. But there are logical problems about how far to take these arguments. If it is believed that externalities are all-pervasive, incomplete knowledge is the norm and not the exception and monopoly tendencies are endemic, then the logical position reached is a state socialist one. But then, as pragmatic socialists have had to come to recognise, there are arguments to weigh on each side – setting the evidence on 'market failure' against what is sometimes called 'state failure', the incapacity of public institutions to function efficiently or equitably (see Self, 1993 for a good discussion of this issue).

It will be evident that much of the analysis in this section relates to arguments about what the state *should* do rather than about what it actually *does*. The implications of this for analysis of the policy process are (1) that justifications for intervention and for non-intervention are embodied in this literature, and (2) that, in the hands of those analysts who are convinced of the general superiority of markets, it offers rather deterministic explanations of policy problems (state failure) which arise when insufficient attention has been paid to the underlying logic.

Game theory

Another body of theory closely linked to rational choice theory is game theory, which also contributes to the exploration of the issue of why public policy solutions to collective action problems are adopted. This theory arises not so much from economics as from a branch of mathematics which has explored the logic of various situations in which there are conflicts of individual interests. Game theory develops a variety of models in which issues are explored about the extent to which individuals do best if they cooperate and those in which they do best if they, in the jargon of the theory, 'defect' – that is, refuse to act cooperatively. It is possible to construct scenarios in which there can only be one winner (zero sum) and games in which collaboration logically brings the best result (positive sum), but much of the relevant work of game theory focuses on games where it is not so easy to point to an obvious choice for the individual players. These games are described as 'mixed-motive games' by Scharpf, who goes on to say that in them:

> the preferences of players are partly harmonious and partly in conflict. Of these, four 'archetypal' constellations have achieved the most notoriety, even among social scientists who otherwise profess to game-theoretic illiteracy. They are known by the nicknames of 'Assurance', 'Battle of the Sexes', 'Prisoners' Dilemma' and 'Chicken'.
>
> In discussing the implications of these mixed-motive constellations, the strategies available to both players are conventionally labelled 'cooperate' (C) and 'defect' (D) depending on whether the strategy is intended to realize the common interest of ego and alter or to maximize the advantage of ego at the expense of alter. (Scharpf, 1997, p. 73)

The best known of these games, 'The Prisoners' Dilemma', is set out in Box 3.2 overleaf. While it uses what may seem a very artificial situation, it can be argued that its equivalent arises in the policy process in many situations in which conflicting actors (particularly actors that may not communicate particularly well with each other, such as nation states) are clear enough about what they have to do in their own interest and do not trust each other.

| Box 3.2 | **The Prisoners' Dilemma** |

Two prisoners who conspired to commit a crime are caught. They are put in separate cells and each told that if they confess they will receive a mild punishment. If they remain silent it is possible that both will secure moderate punishments. The dilemma for each is the fear that if the other confesses and they do not, this will result in a severe punishment for themselves. There are therefore four potential outcomes, as shown in the table. The optimum for both is strategy 4, but can they trust each other to stay silent in the face of the temptation to avoid a severe punishment?

	Prisoner A confesses	Prisoner A does not confess
Prisoner B confesses	1. Mild punishments for both	2. Severe punishment for A, light one for B
Prisoner B does not confess	3. Severe punishment for B, light one for A	4. Possible avoidance of punishment for both

---

The game theory approach is thus used to explore to what extent in the real world situations emerge in which actors will be likely to move from conflicting to collaborative strategies. Particularly pertinent here will be the fact that games are rarely 'one shot' events. There are likely to be repeated interactions between actors so that experience from one game influences the next, and so on. What this leads to is a consideration of the extent to which games occur within structures, a topic to which we will return.

The economic theory of bureaucracy

The economic theory of bureaucracy applies assumptions about self-interest to the behaviour of public officials. The rational choice theory discussed above sees competition to win political support as an activity that can be analysed like economic 'market' behaviour. This is a 'demand-side' theory about state behaviour. The economic theory of bureaucracy reinforces it by a 'supply-side' argument which is concerned with the consequences of the fact that public bureaucracies tend to be monopoly providers of goods and services. This perspective then draws upon economic theory on monopoly, which stresses the absence of constraints upon costs when these can be passed on to consumers and the extent to which in the absence of market limitations a monopolist will tend to oversupply commodities. It is thus particularly central for the notion of 'state failure'. It is argued that bureaucrats will tend, like monopolists, to enlarge their enterprises and to use resources extravagantly (Niskanen, 1971; Tullock, 1967; Buchanan and Tullock, 1962). Thus Tullock argues:

> As a general rule, a bureaucrat will find that his possibilities for promotion increase, his power, influence and public respect improve, and even the physical conditions of his office improve, if the bureaucracy in which he works expands. (Tullock, 1976, p. 29)

This theory has an intuitive plausibility, but comparatively little empirical evidence has been produced to support it. Self argues that 'these descriptions of the political process can be seen to be ... overdrawn and exaggerated' (1993, p. 58). Earlier in the same book he describes the work of the key theorist on this topic, Niskanen, as 'logically and mathematically elegant ... [but] empirically wrong in almost all its facts' (ibid., pp. 33–4). Self goes on to make the following five critical points:

1. The salary of a bureau chief is *not* closely related to the size of his bureau ...
2. Bureaus are not necessarily monopolistic ...
3. Political controllers are not as starved of information as Niskanen claims ...
4. In any case bureau chiefs are ... subject to the control of super bureaucrats ...
5. It is impossible to say that bureaus produce an excessive output if there is no objective way of valuing the output. (Self, 1993, p. 34)

It is not necessarily the case that bureaucratic success is measured by bureau enlargement. Brian Smith (1988, p. 167) points out how some of the most powerful and highly paid roles in civil services – in central finance departments, for example – are in small organisations. Self has observed that 'Bureaucratic self-interest takes many different forms, depending on the different career patterns and normative constraints found in different public services' (Smith, 1988, paraphrasing Self, 1985). Indeed, the political attack on big government has led to situations in which civil servants have been rewarded for their skills at cutting budgets, privatising public services and so on.

The use of such an economic model to theorise about public bureaucracy does, however, help us to analyse such organisations. This theory is closely related to what is described as principal/agent theory, which focuses on situations in which the 'agent' – that is, the person or persons delegated authority – has motives for disregarding the instruction of 'principals' (Wood and Waterman, 1994; Horn, 1995). This goes beyond the simple proposition about bureau enlargement to explore, from a rational choice perspective, the top-down concern about control over implementation (see Chapter 9). It has led to a diligent search for situations in which 'perverse incentives' may be built into the day-to-day work of public organisations (see, for example, an influential examination of this issue in relation to the British National Health Service in Enthoven, 1985).

The model has also produced an interesting development which has rather more complex implications. Where market considerations apply, organisations are likely to try to externalise costs. Without the constraints imposed by markets, bureaucracies may also, Dunleavy has suggested (Dunleavy, 1985, 1986, 1991), internalise costs. Where theorists like Niskanen stress the negative aspects of this – it creates opportunities for the exploitation of public office – there may also be positive ones. Examples of this include: exemplary employment practices (in relation to wages, equal opportunities, employee welfare, etc.), responsiveness to clients' needs and interests (appeals procedures, opportunities for participation on policy issues, etc.) and, indeed, general openness to political intervention. Demands that bureaucracies operate as if they were private firms therefore directly challenge a variety of 'benefits' (that is, the costs that have been internalised) that have often been taken for granted as characteristics of the public service. Privatisation of such organisations, Dunleavy argues (1986), may both undermine the provision of these benefits and create situations in which there are incentives to externalise costs (pollution, income mainten-ance needs arising out of low wage policies, health consequences of employment practices, etc.).

Dunleavy accepts that bureaucrats will tend to engage in self-interested activities that are directed towards maximising their own welfare; but he shows that whether or not this will involve maximising the size of their organisations will depend upon the task of the organisation, the external (including political) pressures upon it and their own roles within the organ-isation. He describes their strategies as 'bureau shaping'. He sums up his position as follows:

> Rational bureaucrats therefore concentrate on developing bureau-shaping strategies designed to bring their agency into line with an ideal configu-ration conferring high status and agreeable work tasks, within a budgetary constraint contingent on the existing and potential shape of the agency's activities. (Dunleavy, 1991, p. 209)

Hence rational choice theory has both provided a set of arguments to support an attack on public bureaucracy *and* stimulated thinking about how we analyse organisational outputs. The attack on the public sector has taken the form of both outright privatisation and efforts to create competition between or within bureaucracies (see Olson, 1965, 1982 for the development of a rationale for this). Nevertheless, in both this theory and Dunleavy's alternative to it, it must be noted that the emphasis, as in classical economic theory, is upon what can be expected from an individual acting upon 'rational' self-interest. There remains a need to test whether actual behav-iour is determined in this way.

The limitations of rational choice approaches

This chapter has portrayed public or rational choice theories as building upon pluralist theories. The discussion of pluralist theories in the previous chapter ended not only by challenging the failure of many of the early variations of pluralism for their disregard of inequalities of power but also by setting the individualistic assumptions of pluralism against arguments that identify the importance of structures. Both of these considerations also apply to rational choice theories. While rational choice theories direct us perhaps even more strongly than classical pluralist theory to attach overwhelming importance to self-interest in the explanation of public policy decision making, they do not really deal with the issues about power inequalities within the interest structures they analyse. Clearly they could do this rather more, and in this sense Dunleavy's reformulation of the economic theory of bureaucracy indicates a move in that direction (by recognising the way in which top bureaucrats may have both rather different interests and rather more power than others). But in general the use of an individual interest model pays little attention to the issues about the manipulation of interests that so concerns theorists like Lukes.

On the other hand, a curious feature of rational choice theory is the way in which, while it can be counterpoised to theories that emphasise the determination of interests, it contains a form of determinism of its own. This has been highlighted by Hay, who argues that the 'rationalism' of rational choice theory

> deals with the problem of the contingency otherwise injected into social systems by agency ... by denying that agents exercise any meaningful choice at the moment of strategic deliberation. They have, if you like, a nominal choice between rationality and irrationality but, as rational actors, always opt for the former. ... It relies ... on a convenient assumption that we know to be false: that individuals in a given context will always choose the same (rational) option. In so doing it translates what would otherwise be a moment of contingency and indeterminism (at least from the political analyst's point of view) into one of complete and absolute determinism. (Hay, 2002, p. 53)

That formulation is only seeking to deal with the logic of the economic rationality assumption. Behind that, as Hay is of course fully aware, lie problems about the notion that self-interested behaviour and rational behaviour can be equated. Other theorists, although starting out from an economistic mode of reasoning, recognise that other behavioural modes may determine action. Le Grand, for example, makes a distinction in the analysis of public officials between 'knaves', motivated by self-interest, and the more public-spirited altruists, whom he calls 'knights' (1997, 2003). Jones and Cullis similarly seek to apply evidence from psychology to economic analyses of motivation (2003). Yet even with these modifications, surely Hay's strictures about determinism apply. What is merely being pointed out is that what is determined may vary.

It is Le Grand's approach to the problem that brings us closest to seeing policy determination as arising out of the influence of structures, paying attention to variations in the extent to which 'knavish' or 'knightly' behaviour is rewarded. In that sense he follows a position taken by institutionalist theorists (to be discussed in Chapter 5). For example, Thelen and Steinmo argue:

> people don't stop at every choice they make in their lives and think to themselves, 'Now what will maximise my self-interest?' Instead, most of us, most of the time, follow societally defined rules, even when so doing may not be directly in our self-interest. (Thelen and Steinmo, 1992, p. 8)

CONCLUSIONS

The irony is that inasmuch as rational choice theory has been taken seriously it has had a certain self-fulfilling effect. Strategies to control bureaucrats and professionals which assume that self-interest is the crucial motivating force in their lives tend to reinforce that phenomenon (through incentive structures) and to undermine altruistic behaviour by controls which send the message that the official is not regarded as trustworthy. Self puts a related point, with particular reference to the use of insecurity as a device to control bureaucrats:

> The problem of moral hazard, according to the theory, is that the bureaucrat will always tend to substitute his own personal wishes . . . However a short-term contractual relationship may well increase this danger . . . An official on limited contract will have less commitment to the public service and may be more disposed to use his position to establish useful contacts and opportunities in the public sector. (Self, 1993, p. 166)

But we must beware of simply replacing one form of determinism by another. If behaviour in the policy process cannot just be read off from a simple model of self-interest, it should equally not be read off from some more complex form of determinism which sees behaviour as the product of predetermined circumstances. In this sense we return to the conclusion of the last chapter, that individuals make choices in situations that may have a strong impact upon their freedom, or perceptions of freedom, to make those choices. But it would be foolish to deny the power of self-interest in this context.

4. From pluralism to networks

SYNOPSIS

Chapter 2 showed how classical pluralist theory came under attack both from those who emphasised power inequalities and from those who saw the system of power as in various respects structured. In this chapter, particular attention will be given to approaches to the modification of pluralism which accepted the force of these criticisms without at the same time accepting either the very unitary vision of much Marxist work or going very deeply into the sources of structuration. A crucial concern here will be with the extent to which interest groups are aggregated to provide more coordinated systems of power. The central concern will be to look at network theory, but the chapter will start with a consideration of a body of theory which can be seen as in many respects a precursor of network theory, the theory of corporatism. While it will be argued that the latter theory has now been largely discredited, it is important to look at it, not merely because of the place it occupies in the evolution of theory but also because corporatist tendencies can still be identified in the policy-making systems of some countries.

Corporatist theory, or corporatism

Schmitter describes corporatism as a system of interest representation. He defines the ideal type of corporatism as:

> a system of interest representation in which the constituent units are organised into a limited number of singular, compulsory, non-competitive, hierarchically ordered and functionally differentiated categories, recognised or licensed (if not created) by the state and granted a deliberate representational monopoly within their respective categories in exchange for observing certain controls on their selection of leaders and articulation of demands and supports. (Schmitter, 1974, pp. 93–4)

In Schmitter's analysis there are two forms of corporatism: state and societal. State corporatism is authoritarian and anti-liberal. The label is applied to the political systems of Fascist Italy and Nazi Germany. In contrast, societal corporatism originated in the decay of pluralism in western European and North American political systems. Schmitter hypothesises that in the latter systems changes in the institutions of capitalism, including concentration of ownership and competition between national economies, triggered the development of corporatism. The need to secure the conditions for capital accumulation forced the state to intervene more directly and to bargain with political associations. The emerging societal corporatism came to replace pluralism as the predominant form of interest representation.

Much of the English language literature on corporatism has explored that concept's applicability to the United States and Britain. Its use to encapsulate the policy process in some of the continental European countries – particularly Scandinavia, Austria and the Netherlands – has been rather more taken for granted. For example, writing about the last-named country, Kickert and van Vucht say:

> The threat of labour revolt and rising socialism was countered at the end of the 19th century by the creation of 'corporatism': the institutionalisation of socio-economic cooperation between ... organised capital, organised labour and government. Based on this ... the Netherlands developed into an extreme example of the modern non-statist concept of *neo-corporatism*. This concept emphasises the interest representation by a number of internally coherent and well-organised interest groups which are recognised by the state and have privileged or even monopolised access to it. (Kickert and van Vucht, 1995, p. 13)

This emphasis upon an organised and legally recognised system certainly highlights a difference from the rather uncertain evolution of the 'Anglo-Saxon' systems in this direction. Speaking primarily of these, Winkler (1976) argues that the state in capitalist society has come to adopt a more directive and interventionist stance as a result of a slowing down of the process of capital accumulation. Winkler points to industrial concentration, international competition and declining profitability in the British economy as examples of significant changes in the economic system which prompted the shift towards corporatism.

In his writings Winkler stresses the economic aspects of corporatism, seeing it as a system of private ownership of the means of production combined with public control. According to Winkler, examples of corporate involvement by the state in the United Kingdom are provided by the development of policies on prices and incomes and the attempt during the 1970s to develop planning agreements with industry. These policies were worked out by the state in collaboration with business and trade union elites. However, Winkler does not specify precisely the role of the state in a corporate economy, nor does he discuss in detail the sources of state power. What seems clear, though, is that, according to this view, the state is not controlled by any particular economic class or group, but plays an independent and dominant role in its relationship with labour and capital.

The political history of corporatism in Britain has been outlined most fully by Middlemas (1979, 1986). Middlemas argues that a process of corporate bias originated in British politics in the period 1916–26, when trade unions and employer associations were brought into a close relationship with the state for the first time. As a consequence, these groups came to share the state's power, and changed from mere interest groups to become part of the extended state. Effectively, argues Middlemas, unions and employers' groups became 'governing institutions' (1979, p. 372), so closely were they incorporated into the governmental system. By incorporation, Middlemas means the inclusion of major interest groups into the governing process and not their subordination. The effect of incorporation is to maintain harmony and avoid conflict by allowing these groups to share power.

The impact of Margaret Thatcher's policies led some British writers to dismiss British applications of corporatist theory as merely a description of a passing phase (see, for example, Gamble, 1994). During the 1980s the trade unions were dismissed from the 'triangular' relationship, and at times even the role of business seemed to be downgraded. But this evidence surely only discredits those who proclaimed, borrowing Marxist historicism, that we entered, in the 1970s, the 'age of corporatism'. Corporatism remained in other countries, and could return in Britain, as a way in which the state may 'manage' its relations with key economic actors.

In the United States the relevance of the corporatist thesis has been questioned by observers such as Salisbury (1979), who have argued that Schmitter's model of societal corporatism does not fit the American experience. A different stance is taken by Milward and Francisco (1983), who note important trends *towards* corporatism in the United States (see Box 4.1).

Box 4.1	Milward and Francisco's (1983) theory of 'corporatist interest intermediation'

This perspective, applied to the United States, stresses the development of corporatist institutions in some policy sectors and particularly those based on government programmes. In these sectors, state agencies support and rely on pressure groups in the process of policy formulation. The result is not a fully developed corporate state but rather 'corporatism in a disaggregated form'. In Milward and Francisco's view, neither federalism nor the separation of powers has precluded the development of corporatist policies because corporatism is based on policy sectors which cut across both territorial boundaries and different parts of government.

It is apparent that corporatism is viewed in different ways by different writers. Theorists such as Winkler define corporatism mainly as an economic system, to be compared with syndicalism, socialism and capitalism. In contrast, Schmitter, Middlemas, and Milward and Francisco discuss corporatism as a political system or sub-system. Reviewing different approaches to the use of the concept of corporatism, Panitch (1980) argues for a limited definition. In his view, corporatism is not a total economic system, as Winkler argues, but rather a specific and partial political phenomenon. More concretely, corporatism is a political structure within advanced capitalism which 'integrates organised socio-economic producer groups through a system of representation and cooperative mutual interaction at the leadership level and mobilisation and social control at the mass level' (ibid., p. 173).

Those who see corporatism as a total system take up a position that is perhaps closer to Marxism than pluralism, particularly if they see it not as a tripartite division of power between capital, labour and the state but as an accommodation between capital and the state. It has been shown in Chapter 2 that a key element in neo-Marxist theory is a recognition of the role of the state as helping to deal with the crises of late capitalism (see in particular O'Connor, 1973, and Gough, 1979). Wolfe (1977) sees corporatism developing as one response to this crisis. Noting the tension between the demands of the accumulation of capital and the need for legitimation within capitalism, Wolfe argues that political alternatives have been exhausted and that one response to government overload is a corporatist organisation of the state. In Wolfe's analysis this can involve, among other things, the economy being under the domination of monopolies making private investment decisions; the state planning apparatus working closely with these monopolies to further their investment decisions; representatives from trade unions acting as consultants to planning agencies; and the institution of price and wage controls.

The corporatist thesis has been criticised by Marxists for failing to develop an adequate theory of the state. Thus, Westergaard argues that in Winkler's analysis the state 'figures in a curiously disembodied form' and 'its ability to put the powers which it has acquired to uses of its own is only asserted, not demonstrated' (1977, p. 177). Westergaard goes on to maintain that the principles that guide corporatism are merely those of capitalism, and that corporatism is not a distinctive economic system. For his part, Winkler does not argue that corporatism favours redistribution or equality, nor does he quarrel with the view that the state acts to restore private profitability and to enhance capital accumulation. Where Winkler and other writers in the corporatist tradition take issue with the Marxists is in their analysis of the role of the state and its autonomy. The corporatist thesis is that the state has moved from a position of supporting the process of capital accumulation to directing that process. In making this shift, new patterns of relationships have developed between the state and the major economic interest groups, and the state, although constrained by these interests, has autonomy deriving from its command of legal, organisational and other resources. It is this autonomy that enables the state to act in the interests of capital, labour and other interests as appropriate.

For some writers, corporatism is seen as the best way of managing the conflict between the needs of the economy and the demands of consumers, highlighted as a problem for democracy by rational choice theory (see Mishra, 1984). This brings us back to the more cautious formulations of corporatist theory discussed above. They talk about a variety of looser links between interest groups and the state. These formulations have generated a rather different way of conceptualising relationships between interest groups and the state. Grant has summed up the fate of corporatist theory in Britain under the impact of political change and academic elaboration:

> By the time they had developed a conceptual apparatus to analyze the phenomenon, and had managed to organize large-scale research projects, the object of study was already dwindling in importance. The corporatist debate did, however, help to stimulate a new wave of theoretical and empirical work on pressure groups promoting a re-examination of pluralist theory, and thereby encouraging the development of new forms of pluralist analysis such as the idea of policy communities. (Grant, 1989, p. 36)

It seems on balance as if 'corporatism' is more a descriptive label than a theory. Whilst some corporatist theorists have adopted the Marxist-like argument that there are inevitable tendencies operating in this direction, few have accepted that view, and events in places like the United Kingdom have suggested that corporatist tendencies may come and go as matters of political choice rather than be inevitable developments. In any case, corporatist theory has paid little attention to interests outside the key productive processes. Corporatist theory, however, highlights the way in which interests may be aggregated, and the extent to which the state may play a role in bringing capital and labour together in ways which may (and this is very much a hypothesis) limit the power of the former. This theoretical work thus draws our attention to the possibility that collaboration within networks may be a feature of the policy process. This brings us to the next section.

Policy networks and policy communities

Corporatist theory indicates that there is a need to pay attention to the ways in which powerful interest or pressure groups outside the state and groups within the state relate to each other. But it tends, in a rather generalised way, to develop a single model which gathers the 'parties' to this relationship into three overarching groups: capital, labour and the state. Much other pluralist theory, however, sees neither capital nor labour as single interests, easily brought together in all-embracing institutions. The same point may be made about the state. Analysts of government have recognised that it is very difficult to get departments to act corporately. Many policy issues are fiercely contested between departments, even within relatively unitary systems of government, between central and local governments and between the many different elements in complex systems like that of the United States.

It has been suggested, therefore, that there may be, rather than corporatist systems, a variety of separate linking systems between interests within government and those outside. One such formulation postulates the existence of a variety of 'iron triangles' embracing the state and both sides of industry and operating in specific industrial sectors and not necessarily across the economy as a whole (Jordan, 1986; Thurber, 1991; Salisbury, 1979).

A related alternative formulation, using the concept of corporatism, comes from Dunleavy (1981), who argues that it is possible to identify systems of 'ideological corporatism' (p. 7) in operation in policy communities. These systems derive from 'the acceptance or dominance of an effectively unified view of the world across different sectors and institutions' (ibid.). In many cases the unified view of the world emanates from a profession – the medical model is a good example – and provides 'ideological cohesion' (ibid.). Dunleavy goes further, suggesting that:

> underlying apparent instances of policy shaped by professional influences it is possible on occasion to show that structural parameters and dynamics shaped by production relations and movements of private capital play a key role in shifts of welfare state policy. But I doubt if fairly specific policy changes can ever be reduced to explanation in such terms alone. (Dunleavy, 1981, p. 15)

These formulations suggest relatively strong links between actors: *iron* triangles or policy *communities*. Others have borrowed from transaction theory and from the sociological study of inter-organisational relationships to suggest that where powerful institutions need to relate to each other over a period they develop a variety of ways of doing business which assume a measure of stability (see Knoke, 1990). Furthermore, it should not be assumed that these relationships are simply one-way. Pluralist theory can be seen as stressing the amount of competition between groups to try to influence the state. Marxist theory goes to the other extreme of regarding the state as the 'creature' of capitalism. An alternative view is that both sides need each other – the pressure groups need to influence policy, the institutions of the state need support from powerful groups outside it. The exchanges may even be more explicit than that – when the two sides need to trade knowledge, expertise and influence over other actors. Hence, another contribution to the understanding of these relationships comes from the application of exchange theory (see Rhodes, 1981). State institutions and non-state institutions can be seen as linked by both reciprocal connections and more complex network relationships. Smith thus argues that:

> The notion of policy networks is a way of coming to terms with the traditionally stark state/civil society dichotomy ... State actors are also

actors in civil society, they live in society and have constant contact with groups which represent societal interests. Therefore the interests of state actors develop along with the interests of the group actors and the degree of autonomy that exists depends on the nature of policy networks. (Smith, 1993, p. 67)

Smith explores the relationship between the two concepts outlined above: 'policy networks' (the expression 'issue networks' is also used in this literature) and 'policy communities'. These are closely related ideas, between which there is *no need* to make a choice whilst formulating a policy theory drawing upon them. Communities are stronger versions of networks. Clearly, therefore, networks may cohere into communities and communities may disintegrate into networks. There may be some issues where communities are more likely than networks and vice versa. There may also be some institutional situations, and even societies, where one pattern is more likely than the other and so on.

Smith's analysis was developed from the work of Jordan and Richardson (1987), which tends to use the expression 'policy communities' for a range of relationships of varying stability, and that of Rhodes (1988) and Marsh and Rhodes (1992), which identifies networks of varying cohesiveness. The main features of *policy communities* are set out in Box 4.2. By contrast, *issue networks* have rather different characteristics, as set out in Box 4.3.

Box 4.2	Features of policy communities

- Comparatively limited memberships often with economic or professional interests, sometimes consciously excluding others
- Shared values and frequent interaction
- Exchange of resources, with group leaders able to regulate this
- A relative balance of power amongst members.

Box 4.3	Characteristics of issue networks

- Large and diverse
- Fluctuating levels of contacts and lower levels of agreement than policy communities
- Varying resources and an inability to regulate their use on a collective basis
- Unequal power.

What is particularly important about this work – distinguishing networks and communities from simple pluralist clusters of organisations – is the emphasis upon the state interest in fostering them. Smith (1993), drawing on Jordan and Richardson (1987), identifies, for the British case, four reasons for this:

■ Networks and communities facilitate a consultative style of government.

■ They reduce policy conflict and make it possible to depoliticise issues.

■ They make policy making predictable.

■ They relate well to the departmental organisation of government. An example of this is the grouping associated with the development of British agricultural policy after the Second World War, which is set out in Box 4.4.

Box 4.4	The British agricultural policy 'network' or 'community'

It has been argued that this has involved close consultation between the government department responsible, the associations representing farmers' and landowners' interests and the major suppliers of fertilisers and pesticides. This grouping has been seen as working in a concerted way, resisting influences from consumer interests and anti-pollution lobbies, presenting itself as the manager of the countryside in opposition to other government departments as well as to outside pressure groups (Lowe, 1986). Between the 1940s and the 1970s this could be described as a typical policy community; more recently it has weakened and has had to consult more widely and is perhaps now more appropriately described as a policy network.

Both concepts – particularly that of policy communities – postulate a stable pattern of interest organisation, so there are some important issues that need to be addressed about how such systems change over time. Smith suggests (1993, pp. 91–8) that change may be engendered by external relationships, general economic and social change, new technology, internal divisions within networks, and challenges between networks and within communities. In the case of agriculture (outlined in Box 4.4), that change has come about partly because of Britain's membership of the European Community, partly because of the growth of a rural population with no commitment to agriculture (people working in or retired from the towns) and partly because of other events that have put consumerist and environmental issues on the political agenda.

In later work with Marsh, Smith has come back to the issues about change (Marsh and Smith, 2000). An important feature of this work has been a concern to take on board issues about networks as 'structures' and actors as 'agents' (see the discussion of the structure/agency issue in Chapter 2, pp. 49–50). This involves recognising the way in which actors change networks. Marsh and Smith then develop an examination of the impact of exogenous factors, as outlined in the last paragraph, to stress the dialectic relationship between a network, agents and the wider environment.

Other refinements of this theory have sought to be more specific about the way in which networks and communities may relate to each other. Wilks and Wright (1987) suggest the idea of a continuum from communities to networks, with the former term reserved for situations in which there is a common policy focus. Others have argued that more specific communities will often be 'nested' within larger networks (Dudley and Richardson, 1999; Chadwick, 2000).

There is a need for situations in which it is possible to test the extent to which (a) communities really are unified, as there is general agreement that communities vary in this respect, and (b) unified communities get their own way. Box 4.5 offers an exploration of this through an empirical study.

Box 4.5	Toke and Marsh's (2003) study of policy networks and the genetically modified (GM) crops issue

Toke and Marsh describe their study as deploying 'a dialectical model of policy networks' designed to analyse 'the interaction between agents and structure, network and context and network and outcomes to understand and explain how policy change has occurred' (p. 229).

This study explores how a policy on which there appeared to be a cohesive 'policy community' in favour of GM came under challenge. In the process of that challenge they see the policy community being transformed into a more open network in which some environmentalist groups have been incorporated and have been able to change policy towards a much more cautious approach to GM crops. It has been significant that key actors here have emerged from relatively 'establishment' pressure groups, notably the widely supported Royal Society for the Protection of Birds and from a government-supported agency English Nature. Also important has been wider public recognition of a potential 'problem' with GM crops.

In general, Marsh and Toke's study provides an example of agenda change emerging out of interest group politics. However, it does also indicate the way in which a government minister, sympathetic to the environment protection lobby, may have played a key role. What is interesting about this, however, is that he was in a comparatively junior position, with a viewpoint not supported by the Prime Minister. Here, then, we have an example of low-key policy change coming about not through a direct political initiative but through policy network transformation, yet involving a politician, and a not insignificant movement in public opinion.

There is also a danger here of getting into self-fulfilling statements, like explaining why ideas are on (or off) the policy agenda by arguing that this is because communities want them on or off. The fact that educationalists dominated the United Kingdom education system between 1945 and 1979 can just as plausibly be attributed to the fact that other powerful actors were quite content to let this happen as to the fact that the education policy community had the power to keep it that way. Notwithstanding this, we can at least end up with a simpler proposition: that the policy agenda will be more organised and more predictable when unified policy communities are allowed to dominate. There may then be some interesting comparative questions about differences between societies in this respect (corporatist theory propositions are relevant here). But explaining this may be very difficult, particularly when (as seems to have happened in the United Kingdom in the last quarter of the twentieth century) quite dramatic shifts have occurred in the toleration of this policy community dominance. Of course, the ideological attack upon insider control over policy systems (particularly embodied in public choice theory – see Chapter 3) can be demonstrated. But the question remains why that ideology should have become so influential, and found echoes (for example in the pro-participation Left) way outside the ranks of the leaders of the attack from the political Right. We are back here to some interesting issues about political choice, undermining social scientists' generalisations about the policy process!

The core executive

Rhodes, one of the theorists most involved in the development of network theory, has, in his work with Dunleavy, added another element to the analysis of the involvement of networks in government. Rhodes describes the term 'core executive' as referring 'to all those organisations and procedures which co-ordinate central government policies, and act as final arbiters of conflict between different parts of the government machine' (1995, p. 12). John (1998) discusses the efforts of Dunleavy and Rhodes to define the core executive in Britain as a contribution to institutional theory (see the discussion of this approach in the next chapter). However, according to Rhodes, 'The core executive is the set of networks which police the functional policy networks' (1997, p. 14). As such it needs to be seen as a refinement of network theory.

It is important to recognise how these different emphases upon networks range across a variety of policy issues and concern themselves with different aspects of the policy process. Inasmuch as network theory is an advance upon the pluralist theory of power, it concerns itself with domination (or its absence) across the policy process as a whole. But network ideas can also be found very much in evidence in relation to questions about policy implementation: in concerns about the sharing and modification of policy goals and about the determination of effective action in complex inter-organisational contexts. They have been very important for critiques of the top-down approach to the examination of implementation (see Chapter 9). Clearly, therefore, it is possible that network or community explanations for policy outcomes may be used for parts of policy processes where other explanations (stressing concentrations of power, or even determinist theories, or the institutional theories examined in the next chapter) are offered as prior structuring influences.

The advocacy coalition approach

Paul Sabatier has developed an approach to the analysis of the policy process that has much in common with the work of scholars who emphasise the importance of networks and policy communities. His particular contribution has been to try to refine the way the implementation process is analysed. In work with Jenkins-Smith he has developed what he calls an 'advocacy coalition' approach (see particularly Sabatier and Jenkins-Smith, 1993). This complex theory sees the policy process – from policy inception through to implementation – as involving an 'advocacy coalition' comprising actors from all parts of the policy system. Advocacy coalitions consist of 'actors from a variety of institutions who share a set of policy beliefs' (Sabatier, 1999, p. 9). Sabatier and Jenkins-Smith's approach involves the acceptance of ultimately coordinated action between actors both in favour of and against specific policy goals, and of change over time in response to events inside and outside each 'policy subsystem'. This approach can be seen to be sharing with the

Box 4.6	The advocacy coalition framework's key features

Sabatier and Jenkins-Smith summarise their approach as follows:

1. Reliance upon the policy subsystem as the principal aggregate unit of analysis.

2. A model of the individual based upon (a) the possibility of complex goal structures and (b) information-processing capabilities that are limited and, most important, involve perceptual filters.

3. Concern with policy-oriented learning as an important source of policy change.

4. The concept of advocacy coalitions as a means of aggregating large numbers of actors from different institutions at multiple levels of government into a manageable number of units.

5. Conceptualizing both belief systems and public policies as sets of goals, perceptions of problems and their causes, and policy preferences that are organized in multiple tiers.

6. Coalitions that seek to manipulate governmental and other institutions to alter people's behavior and problem conditions in an effort to realize the coalitions' belief systems.

(Sabatier and Jenkins-Smith, 1999, p. 154)

other approaches here the notion of a network and of the existence of a degree of consensus (coalition), but going beyond it to embody concerns about the wider political and institutional context. Sabatier, Loomis and McCarthy (1995) use this approach to some effect to explore planning decisions in the forest service in the United States. The key features of the advocacy coalition approach are set out in Box 4.6. The particular concern with 'policy learning' in this version of network theory is clearly important for the issues about inter-organisational collaboration that will be discussed in Chapter 11.

Problems with the use of network theory

It has been noted that network theory offers a way to analyse the clustering of interests in the policy process, which has advantages over both simple pluralism and corporatist theory. Rhodes sees policy networks as 'a long-standing feature of British government' (Rhodes in Hayward and Menon, 2003, p. 65). Yet he goes on in the same essay to argue:

> To talk of the governance of Britain is to say the Westminster model is no longer acceptable and we have to tell a different story of the shift from government (the strong executive) to governance through networks. (Hayward and Menon, 2003, p. 67).

Here, then, is a potential for confusion. If one of the key justifications for the use of the term 'governance' is the importance of networks, is Rhodes saying 'we, political scientists, now see this to be the case', or is he saying that the system has changed? Probably he would reply, 'a bit of both', and of course we must remember that the categories we use influence what we see (see Chapter 1, p. 15). However, there are grounds for concern that some of those who write about the contemporary importance of networks seem to take a stance on the evolution of the policy process very like that taken by earlier theorists who saw the emergence of the 'age of corporatism'. A very different stance will be taken in this book. Issues about networks as one amongst several 'modes of governance' will feature in many places in the book. But the author very much agrees with Lowndes and Skelcher that:

> A crude periodization of modes of governance can also carry with it the myth of progress – bureaucracy as all-bad, markets as a necessary evil and networks as the 'new Jerusalem'. (Lowndes and Skelcher, 1998, p. 331)

There is, furthermore, a problem with policy community and policy network theory rather similar to that with the weaker versions of corporatist theory, that it offers a description of how policy decision processes are organised but not any explanation of why they are organised in that way. This body of theory perhaps only refers to a tendency – one of the ways relationships between the state and interest groups may be regulated. Drawing upon empirical studies it is particularly suggestive of the way in which relationships between the state and interest groups are likely to be regulated in a comparatively stable political system. Smith's (1993) book explores parallels between Britain and the United States, suggesting characteristics of the system of government in the latter that make networks more likely than communities, but he argues that a great deal still depends upon the policy sector. Studies in other societies suggest the existence of similar phenomena (see, for example, Kickert and van Vucht, 1995, on the Netherlands). But it is interesting to observe how difficult it is, despite a strong state tradition and extensive and lively interest groups, to encapsulate within any single theory the characteristics of relationships between the state and groups in France (see Box 4.7). Network theory comes out best, but it explains little. In a case like this, as elsewhere, as Howlett and Ramesh (2003, p. 155, drawing on Coleman and Perl, 1999) argue, it may be important to identify whether or not the state is a dominant actor.

Box 4.7	Policy networks in France

Knapp and Wright's examination of 'the state and the pressure groups in France' (2001, Chapter 11) contrasts four models:

- 'the domination-crisis model', which interprets French culture in terms of ambivalence towards authority, with the consequence that there is an endemic tendency for confrontations to arise between an often authoritarian state and intransigent interest groups;

- 'the endemic and open conflict model', which shares the characteristics of the first model but sees the conflict to be rooted in a lack of accommodating institutions;

- 'the corporatist and concerted politics model', which highlights the many ways in which interest groups and the state work together;

- 'the pluralist model', which stresses the diversity, and the importance, of interest groups.

Knapp and Wright see France as:

a State capable, at times, of considerable autonomy, even high-handedness, in its actions; interest groups often both fragmented within each sector and internally divided; the frequent resort of groups to extra-institutional action, leading, in extreme cases, to crises . . . But if these features offer a distinctive view of State–group relations in France, it is far from an exhaustive one. The other two models, developed for other political systems, are important reminders of other characteristics, more banal but no less present: the free competition of pluralism, the quiet collusion of corporatism. Typical traits of all four models may be discerned in France, but in different proportions in different sectors at different times. (p. 335)

In the light of this, Knapp and Wright nevertheless suggest that policy network theory offers a 'mixed model' making a 'minimum of sense out of the apparent chaos' (p. 326), a remark which highlights both the strength and the weakness of such theory.

John argues that the crucial problem with network theory is that

> the all-encompassing nature of networks creates a problem. They are both everything and nothing, and they occur in all aspects of policy-making. But the concept is hard to use as the foundation for an explanation unless the investigator incorporates other factors, such as the interests, ideas and institutions which determine how networks function. The result is an endless circle of argument whereby the network idea is extended to breaking-point to try to explain something it only describes. (John, 1998, pp. 85–6)

Network theory is not alone in this respect: indeed, a problem running through the study of the policy process is that much theory describes rather than explains. However, it can perhaps be said that network theory in particular describes rather little except that most activities involve networks. This is the sense in which Dowding (1995) attacks network theory as offering no more than a 'metaphor' for the policy process. A slightly less negative way in which this point may be put is to suggest that it provides a 'framework' rather than a theory. This is a point that Sabatier and Jenkins-Smith consider about their approach, agreeing that it 'started as a framework' (1999, p. 154), but they still argue that as they have worked with it they have begun to develop testable hypotheses.

CONCLUSIONS

The emphasis upon networks and communities offers an important corrective to accounts of the political system and the operation of the state which treat them as homogenous and unified entities. It also offers a way of challenging the 'stagist' approach to the policy process (see pp. 19–21) inasmuch as it emphasises that networks and communities function in a relatively integrated way throughout the policy process.

But network theory lacks explanatory power. Drawing our attention to the importance of networks and policy communities tells us little about how they actually influence the policy process. Moreover, it tends to provide too stable a picture of the world of policy makers. While their protagonists recognise the fluidity of networks (indeed, the work analysing the relationships between networks and policy communities is very concerned with this issue), and that there may be overlapping networks and networks within networks, there is a difficulty in giving any sense of dynamism to the resultant processes. Recognition of the need to explore issues about networks in terms of interactions between actors, and to site them in a wider environment, helps to deal with this. But there remains a problem, one that is shared with the institutional theory that will be discussed in the next chapter.

Institutional theory

SYNOPSIS

This chapter explores the contribution made by institutional theory to understanding the public policy process. While some writers have argued that it is a relatively recently discovered approach, the first part of the chapter will suggest that it has deep roots in the sociological analysis of policy processes, and that it has also been influenced by institutional economics. Then will follow an exposition of the theory today, showing how the concept of 'institution' has been used very widely to embrace cultural and ideological phenomena. The next part of the chapter explores the way in which theorists have sought to address the problem that an emphasis on institutions tends to imply a stress on stability and the absence of policy change. The two main solutions to this are either simply to stress, as March and Olsen (1984) have, that actually the theory does little more than assert that the organisation of political life makes a difference, or to develop a way of analysing critical points at which opportunities emerge for system change. A number of approaches to the latter solution are explored. This leads to a short discussion of a related policy theory: on policy transfer.

The chapter concludes that institutional theory faces some of the same problems as network theory, inasmuch as its explanatory uses are limited, but indicates that this in many ways simply emphasises the extent to which the analysis of the policy process is an intuitive art.

Introduction

It has been suggested that during the time in the 1950s and 1970s when academic political science developed rapidly in the United States and Britain, there was a tendency to neglect the study of state institutions (Nordlinger, 1981; March and Olsen, 1984). The claim that there was a need for work 'bringing the state back in' (Evans, Rueschemeyer and Skocpol, 1985) rather exaggerated the earlier neglect. State functionaries, including the military, figured as key concerns in elite theory, yet it was true that classical Marxist theory tended to see the state simply as a supporting player for the capitalist system and that early pluralist theory largely treated it as a neutral institution which groups in society would compete to control.

Various alternative conceptions of the state are set out in Box 5.1. While it rather exaggerates their positions, it can be said that both early pluralist theory and classical Marxist theory largely embody the first of the models set out in the box. Some elite theory, corporatist theory and the simpler versions of the public choice model criticised by Dunleavy (see p. 60), by contrast, tend to give the state an active but unitary character (Model 2). Network theory comes close to Model 3 inasmuch as it sees the state as containing members of more than one network or community, but it pays little attention to conflict between these. The theories discussed in this chapter particularly emphasise Model 4, but in doing so they contain elements of Models 2 and 3.

Box 5.1	Ways the state may be conceptualised

Model 1   As a passive entity to be influenced/captured
Model 2   As an active entity with interests of its own
Model 3   As containing actors with potentially conflicting interests
Model 4   As a structured system influencing and perhaps constraining action

March and Olsen contrast institutional theory with pluralist theory as follows:

> There are two conventional stories of democratic politics. The first story sees politics as a market for trades in which individual and group interests are pursued by rational actors. It emphasises the negotiation of coalition and 'voluntary' exchanges. The second story is an institutional one. It characterizes politics in a more integrative fashion, emphasizing the creation of identities and institutions as well as their structuring effects on political life. (March and Olsen, 1996, p. 248)

Their model, at least as expounded in their 1996 essay, sees the need for a fusing of the two approaches: the latter framing the former but being open to change under various circumstances.

The roots of institutional analysis of the policy process

Some writers draw distinctions between different kinds of institutional theory. Hence, John portrays institutional analysis as having a 'central place in political science, particularly during the origins of the discipline', since 'the founding scholars of political science treated institutions, such as legislatures and courts, as a key part of public life and worthy of study in their own right' (1998, p. 38). He then goes on to chart the various ways in which scholars dealt with institutions until about the 1980s, and at the same time notes how behaviourist studies paid little attention to issues about the impact of institutions. After a critique of older institutional studies John then charts the rise of 'new institutionalism' in the 1980s, which placed the 'state at the centre of analysis' with institutions as 'manifestations of the state' crucial for the explanation of outcomes' (ibid., p. 57).

The present author, while recognising (as indicated above) the importance of the revival of interest in institutions, does not consider that so clear a distinction can be made between earlier and later work. Perhaps that is because his own roots are in political sociology, and he published a book called *The Sociology of Public Administration* back in 1972. Certainly, one sociologist whose work will be discussed below, Selznick, has been a seminal figure, saying things still pertinent for modern analyses of institutions. Selznick has reasonably been critical of the clear line modern institutionalists have tried to draw between their work and his (1996), but then academics have to try to claim originality!

In some respects institutional analysis is fundamental for the discipline of sociology, raising questions about the extent to which human actions are structurally determined. It is then given an emphasis that is particularly important for organisational activities. The importation of ideas from organisational sociology to the study of the policy process has its roots at least as far back as Selznick's classic study of the Tennessee Valley Authority, which was published in 1949. Even earlier, Barnard (1938) stressed the need to see policy decision making in its organisational context. This theme was picked up by Simon in his *Administrative Behaviour* (1957).

A distinction is made in much of the sociological work between 'organisations' and 'institutions'. Here Selznick is a key influence, arguing:

> The term 'organization' thus suggests a certain bareness, a lean no-nonsense system of consciously coordinated activities. It refers to an expendable tool, a rational instrument engineered to do a job. An 'institution' on the other hand, is more nearly a natural product of social needs and pressures – a responsive adaptive organism. (Selznick, 1957, p. 5)

This distinction emphasises the social world within which organisations are created, drawing attention both to the impact of the external environment and to the way people bring their own needs and affiliations into organisations which then shape the social systems that develop there. Selznick describes this phenomenon very clearly in the following observations:

> All formal organizations are moulded by forces tangential to their rationally ordered structures and stated goals. Every formal organization – trade

union, political party, army, corporation etcetera – attempts to mobilize human and technical resources as means for the achievement of its ends. However, the individuals within the system tend to resist being treated as means. They interact as wholes, bringing to bear their own special problems and purposes; moreover the organization is embedded in an institutional matrix and is therefore subject to pressure upon it from its environment, to which some general adjustment must be made. As a result, the organization may be significantly viewed as an adaptive social structure, facing problems which arise simply because it exists as an organization in an institutional environment, independently of the special (economic, military, political) goals which called it into being. (Selznick, 1949, p. 251)

Selznick's approach has been criticised as too deterministic, but the general thrust of his argument remains pertinent. Later work has emphasised the need to see institutions as 'cultural rules' (Meyer and Rowan, 1977) and to identify the way in which a process of 'structural isomorphism' occurs, which means that organisations working in similar 'fields' tend to develop similar characteristics (DiMaggio and Powell, 1983). An important modern writer on the sociology of organisations, Scott, writes about three 'pillars' of institutions:

- regulative, resting upon 'expedience' inasmuch as people recognise the coercive power of rule systems;
- normative, resting upon social obligations;
- cognitive, depending upon taken for granted cultural assumptions. (Scott, 1995, p. 35)

This sociological work tackles the issues about the policy process from a rather different direction to that of the political scientists. It is not concerned with questions about how public policy develops but with how organisations work. But then policy processes are generally also organisational processes. Chapters 10 and 11 will pick up some themes from the sociology of organisations.

Another feature of the development of institutional analysis has been the recognition of the need to employ historical analysis, to trace the evolution of policy over a long period of time. Some of the key theorists have described themselves as 'historical institutionalists'. They see themselves as drawing inspiration from 'a long line of theorists in political science, economics and sociology including Polanyi, Veblen and Weber' (Thelen and Steinmo, 1992, p. 3).

It is pertinent too to note some relevant work on the impact of institutional arrangements on decision making emerging from economics. Some of the rational choice work, discussed already in Chapter 3, particularly that on the interests of bureaucrats, is concerned with the influence of institutions on behaviour. We will come back later in this chapter to some modern work that is explicitly concerned with the structuring of 'rational choice' by institutional arrangements (see p. 87). Also relevant is the development within economics of an institutional perspective that challenged the relatively context-free way in which classical economics analysed market relationships, pointing out the importance of seeing these exchanges within structures with their own rules and expected practices (Coase, 1937; Williamson, 1975). This has found interesting echoes in modern discussions about appropriate organisational arrangements for policy delivery.

Institutional theory today

March and Olsen explain their view of the importance of the institutional approach as follows:

> Political democracy depends not only on economic and social conditions but also on the design of political institutions. The bureaucratic agency, the legislative committee, and the appellate court are arenas for contending social forces, but they are also collections of standard operating procedures and structures that define and defend interests. They are political actors in their own right. (March and Olsen, 1984, p. 738)

Hall makes a rather similar point in stressing the ways policy actors' behaviour is shaped:

> Institutional factors play two fundamental roles in this model. On the one hand, the organisation of policy-making affects the degree of power that any one set of actors has over the policy outcomes ... On the other hand, organisational position also influences an actor's definition of his own interests, by establishing his institutional responsibilities and relationships to other actors. In this way, organizational factors affect both the degree of pressure an actor can bring to bear on policy and the likely direction of that pressure. (Hall, 1986, p. 19)

Hall's approach involves stressing institutional influences outside the formal institutions of government. He asserts that he 'ranges more widely to consider the role of institutions located within society and the economy' (ibid., p. 20). His study of economic policy making in Britain and France pays considerable attention to the ways in which economic interests are formally represented in the political process. His perspective is very close, therefore, to that of the writers on policy communities discussed in the last chapter.

The quotations above tend to project a static view of the institutional approach. They suggest that an examination of the policy process needs to be seen as occurring in organised contexts where there are established norms, values, relationships, power structures and 'standard operating procedures'. But much of the work in this tradition is also concerned with looking at how those structures were formed, and to elucidate the extent to which they impose explicit constraints and the circumstances in which they are subject to change. As March and Olsen say, 'while institutions structure politics, they ordinarily do not determine political behaviour precisely' (1996, p. 252).

Box 5.2	The use of institutional analysis in the exploration of social policy in the United States by Skocpol and her associates

In the United States in the nineteenth century, democratic political institutions (only for white males, of course) predated the elaboration of public administration. This created a situation in which patronage practices were the main form of response to political demands as opposed to distributive policies using a state bureaucracy. For example, pension provisions for Civil War veterans were extended as political favours way beyond their original intentions. Political institutions were functioning to deliver benefits to some, but to limit the scope for more fundamental state-driven reform.

In the context of a federal constitution requiring complex alliances to secure social reform, policy change was difficult to achieve. Many promising movements for reform failed to put together winning coalitions. This remained the situation until an economic crisis in the 1930s enabled the leaders of the 'New Deal' to put together a coalition of the Northern urban working class with the whites of the rural and racist South which could initiate new policies and offer a brief challenge to the older interpretation of the constitution. But the changes achieved were limited because the President still had to carry a resistant legislature.

The legacy of the policy changes in the 1930s continued into the postwar period, and into the period when emergent black groups had some success in challenging the status quo and the constitution. But such social policy legislation as had been achieved in the 1930s had added the Northern white working class, who had gained through the development of social insurance pensions, to the coalition against more radical reform. This was then a source of resistance to more radical change, particularly change favouring black people.

Skocpol (1994) and her associates (Weir, Orloff and Skocpol, 1988) have used the institutional approach to good effect to explain the long-term evolution of social policy in the United States (see Box 5.2). They show how policy change at one point in time created institutions which served as a barrier to change at a later point. As March and Olsen say:

Programs adopted as a simple political compromise by a legislature become endowed with separate meaning and force by having an agency established to deal with them. (March and Olsen, 1984, p. 739 – drawing here upon Skocpol and Finegold, 1982)

Analysis like that set out in Box 5.2 is taking a general point, which is quite often made, about the barriers to political change imposed by the United States constitution, and expanding it into an analysis of both barriers to and opportunities for policy change in a context in which one set of changes then sets the structure for future events (and thus perhaps for nondecision-making).

Immergut (1993) has carried out a somewhat similar analysis on a comparative basis, exploring the evolution of health policy in Switzerland, France and Sweden. She writes of a policy game being played within a set of rules. In her study, other events, over a turbulent period in European history, had an influence on the 'rules'. These events had an impact in different ways in each country upon 'veto' points (where those opposed to change, principally the medical profession, could successfully challenge it) and 'access' points (where agents for change could succeed). Box 5.3 features another study which used Immergut's approach.

Box 5.3	Hwang's use of Immergut's approach to institutional analysis

In a study of health reform in Taiwan, Hwang (1995) shows how a generalised commitment to state health policy originating in the republican constitution developed on the mainland of China in the 1920s and a series of limited ad hoc social insurance developments in the period between 1950 and 1980 to help engender social support for the authoritarian regime set a framework, including access points, for rapid moves towards a national health insurance scheme as Taiwan democratised in the late 1980s and early 1990s.

If it is to work satisfactorily, the institutional approach must handle the relationship between structure and action. It is not enough just to emphasise institutional constraints. It is only too easy, as suggested above, to treat, for example, the United States' constitution as a straitjacket which effectively makes it impossible to get some issues on the agenda. An examination of the history of efforts to secure a universal health insurance scheme in that country encourages that view (see Skocpol, 1994, Chapter 9). Yet the US constitution has been amended many times, and, perhaps even more importantly for the policy process, it has been subject to reinterpretation in ways that in the 1930s widened the scope for federal action and in the 1960s opened the door for the civil rights movement. Political activity is not just a game played within rules, it also often involves efforts to renegotiate those rules. The revision or reinterpretation of those rules ('meta policy making') is important. From a study of the development of Swedish labour market policy which examines the way trade union interests were built into the policy process, Rothstein suggests that:

> In some, albeit probably rare, historical cases, people actually create the very institutional circumstances under which their own as well as others' future behavior will take place. (Rothstein, 1992, p. 52)

The other point, which Skocpol's work particularly emphasises, is the way successful action generates new constraints (rules or structures). But constraints may be ideas as well as structures and rules. The next section explores this further.

Institutional theory, ideas and discourses

March and Olsen draw attention to the work of Bachrach and Baratz discussed in Chapter 2, and by implication also to Lukes's and Hay's ideas, in arguing that so-called 'rules' embody implicit assumptions of exclusion:

> Constitutions, laws, contracts, and customary rules of politics make many potential actions or considerations illegitimate or unnoticed; some alternatives are excluded from the agenda before politics begins ... but these constraints are not imposed full blown by an external social system; they develop within the context of political institutions. (March and Olsen, 1984, p. 740)

A related point is made by Thelen and Steinmo, who argue that the use of class differences in explaining political behaviour needs to be supplemented by exploring 'the extent to which it is reinforced through state and societal institutions – party competition, union structures, and the like' (1992, p. 11).

Clearly, the institutional approach to the study of the policy process involves interpretation. It does not suggest that outcomes can be easily 'read off' from constitutional or institutional contexts. Immergut sets out her games analogy as follows:

> Institutions do not allow one to predict policy outcomes. But by establishing the rules of the game, they enable one to predict the ways in which policy conflicts will be played out. (Immergut, 1992, p. 63)

In this way, modern institutional theory embodies 'cognitive and normative frames' which 'construct "mental maps"' and 'determine practices and behaviours' (Surel, 2000, p. 498).

Hall argues that

> politicians, officials, the spokesmen for social interests, and policy experts all operate within the terms of political discourse that are current in the nation at a given time, and the terms of political discourse generally have a specific configuration that lends representative legitimacy to some social interests more than others, delineates the accepted boundaries of state action, associates contemporary political developments with particular interpretations of national history and defines the context in which many issues will be understood. (Hall, 1993, p. 289)

But then the interesting feature of Hall's work is that it is concerned with policy change. He explores the rise and fall of Keynesian economic dominance in government, seeing constraints not so much in structures as in dominant ideologies and charting how these change over time (Hall, 1986). Hall presents Keynesian economic theory and then monetarist theory as successive dominant paradigms. Hence he sets out to explain a 'paradigm shift' in which the emergence of new policy options required an ideological shift, facilitated in the British case by the victory of a government disposed to encourage that.

In using notions of dominant ideas or paradigms, institutional theorists face questions about the extent to which these shifts can be explained independently of other events. It seems necessary, as Surel argues, to see exogenous influences as important for this. For him, 'transformations of economic conditions, and/or a serious crisis' are crucial (Surel, 2000, p. 503). Hence there may be differences between nations, and differences between policy subsystems, in the extent to which such changes occur.

This form of institutional analysis may need to lay so strong an emphasis upon specific configurations of institutional situations and actors that all it can offer is an account of past events, from which little generalisation is possible. In other words, the example from Hall's work quoted above may involve no more than quoting, with the benefit of hindsight, all the things that reinforced the Keynesian orthodoxy at one point in time and then undermined it later. This is the direction in which some of the things March and Olsen had to say about the institutional approach seem to be heading:

> the new institutionalism is probably better viewed as a search for alternative ideas that simplify the subtleties of empirical wisdom in a theoretically useful way.
>
> The institutionalism we have considered is neither a theory nor a coherent critique of one. It is simply an argument that the organisation of political life makes a difference. (March and Olsen, 1984, p. 747)

There are two parts to this problem. One is that institutional theory brackets together a very wide range of potential constraints, from constitutions and laws, through institutional self-interest and standard operating procedures to ideologies. To some extent this mixing of the formal and the informal is justifiable. Sociologists have rightly warned us against treating constraints built into rule books as if they are necessarily firmer than custom and practice, particularly when the latter have penetrated into our language. But in analysing policy constraints we do need to make some distinctions in order to explore what a breach of those constraints may involve.

The way in which some of the institutional theorists go far beyond emphasis on the structuring provided by formal governmental arrangements to include accepted rules, norms and even ideologies has been described as 'the big tent theory of institutions', which implies that 'today we are all institutionalists' (Frederickson and Smith, 2003, p. 69). While such a development is compatible with the usages by sociologists (see, for example, the discussion of the work of theorists like Giddens, on p. 50) it has been criticised, in much the same way as network theory has been (see pp. 49–50), for encompassing so much that it explains little or nothing. John argues:

> The main problem with the new institutionalist approach is its definition of what counts as institutional. By incorporating values and norms as part of institutions, they include too many aspects of political life under one category. The resulting amalgam of processes appears to explain change under the rubric of institutions, but in reality it disguises the variety of interactions and causal mechanisms that occur between the contrasting elements of the political system. (John, 1998, p. 64)

If the object is to try to achieve theoretical parsimony, this extension of institutional influences to include ideas and ideologies may be a weakness. However, its strength is that it recognises the soft and pliable nature of institutional systems. Fischer (2003), who welcomes modern institutional theory for the attention it gives to discourses, highlights the need to see institutions in the following way:

> A political system ... is a linguistic concept discursively invented and employed to describe a set of relationships that we can only partly experience – one goes to the voting booth, appears as a witness in a court case, visits parliament, speaks with a political representative, and so on. But no one ever sees an entire political system. While we can directly encounter parts of a political system or discover its effects, the system itself remains a set of formal and informal relationships that can be constructed and discussed only through language. (Fischer, 2003, p. 45)

Problems with the use of institutional theory

It will be evident from what has been said above that a critical issue for institutional theory concerns the identification of the conditions under which change occurs. Immergut conceptualises these in terms of 'access points' (Immergut, 1992). But there is clearly a methodological difficulty here: these conditions may be readily identified with the benefit of hindsight, but can they be recognised in advance? Another approach to this issue explores differences in the extent to which institutional arrangements are 'embedded', that is, reinforced by ideological paradigms (Hall, 1993).

To put the issue more generally, what we are concerned with here is a problem that confronts all theories that emphasise structure: they are better at explaining stability than change. If we go back to classical Marxist theory we see this difficulty being tackled with a sort of evolutionary theory which argues that contradictions within systems accumulate to the point where they force change – in that case, of course, revolutionary change. We find a variety of efforts to deal with this problem in a not dissimilar way within the more mundane everyday world of policy processes. There have been attempts to do this using concepts like 'critical junctions' (Collier and Collier, 1991) or 'performance crises' (March and Olsen, 1989). A more fully argued through exploration of this issue uses the concept of 'punctuated equilibrium' (Krasner, 1984; Baumgartner and Jones, 1993). Baumgartner and Jones explore the way in which feedback from policy decisions builds up critical problems over time, hence accelerating the process of movement from stability to crisis.

A different take on these issues is contained in the work of Kiser and Ostrom, whose concern is to combine an emphasis upon rational choice (as explored in Chapter 3) with the fact that this occurs in an institutional framework. Kiser and Ostrom (1982, p. 184) specify three related but distinct levels of analysis. They thus separate decisions taken at the *constitutional level*, which structure the design of the context within which choices are made, from the *collective choice level*, at which key decisions about the management of policy are made, and the *operational level*, which explains the world of action. In Chapter 1 it was suggested that there are problems with the use of the traditional 'stages' framework for the analysis of the policy process. However, clearly some decisions set contexts for subsequent ones, particularly if institutions are created. There is a 'nesting' process in which some kinds of decisions have a particularly strong impact upon the context for later ones, hence the idea of *constitutional level* and *collective choice level* decisions. The present author and Peter Hupe used this idea in their discussion of the implementation process (Hill and Hupe, 2003, Chapter 8).

Another approach to the issue of the relationship between structuration and change involves the use of biological analogies. This occurs in the work of both Kingdon and John. Kingdon (whose very careful analysis of agenda setting in the policy process will be explored further in Chapter 8) sees the flowing together of forces for policy innovation into an equivalent of 'primeval soup' in which they combine together to produce change.

Warning that evolutionary theory seems to carry with it a Darwinian notion of progress and the survival of the fittest, John points out that contemporary analyses of evolution (as in the work of Dawkins, 1976) do not contain these elements. Hence he sees it as feasible to see policy change as a process in which

> the elements to policy systems continually interact over time. Combinations of ideas and interests constantly seek to dominate decision-making and to interact with institutions, patterns of interest groups and socio-economic processes which are also slowly changing and evolving over time. The notion is that some ideas are successful in this context, but that change defines the nature of modern public policy. (John, 1998, p. 195)

Theorists like Baumgartner and Jones, Kiser and Ostrom, Kingdon and John are all engaged in trying to integrate the emphasis on stability that comes from a consideration of the impact of institutions with sources of change. None of them is dogmatic about the influence of structure. Kingdon, for example, is at great pains to emphasise the extent to which 'processes are dynamic, fluid and loosely jointed' (1995, p. 230). In many respects these theorists bring us back to the notion of structured choice already emphasised in earlier chapters (see pp. 49–50 and 61–2).

Policy transfer

It is appropriate to interpose here a brief exploration of another theory, which is not explicitly institutional theory but which addresses similar issues about (a) the importance of ideas and (b) their role in policy change. This is known as policy transfer. Some scholars have suggested a case for 'policy transfer theory' as a distinct and separate contribution to the study of the policy process.

One aspect of globalist theory that is fairly self-evident is that in the modern world a great deal of effort is put into policy transfer. Not only do national policy makers look around at what is occurring elsewhere when they design their own policy, but it is also the case that there are a number of international organisations that are explicitly in the business of offering policy prescriptions – notably the various United Nations agencies, the World Bank and the Organisation for Economic Co-operation and Development. The question here is not whether policy transfer occurs – that is indisputable – but rather whether there is a case for developing a distinctive theory of policy transfer as a contribution to policy process theory.

Box 5.4	James and Lodge's critique of theories of lesson drawing and policy transfer (2003, p. 179)

First, can they be defined as distinctive forms of policy making separate from other, more conventional forms? 'Lesson drawing' is very similar to conventional accounts of 'rational' policy making, and it is very difficult to define 'policy transfer' distinctly from many other forms of policy making. Second, why do 'lesson drawing' and 'policy transfer' occur rather than some other form of policy making? The proponents of 'policy transfer' put a set of diverse and conflicting theories under a common framework, obscuring differences between them. Third, what are the effects of 'lesson drawing' and 'policy transfer' on policy making and how do they compare to other processes?

'Policy transfer' is seen as a new approach to or 'framework of' policy analysis (see Dolowitz and Marsh, 1996, 2000; Dolowitz et al., 2000). It builds on Rose's work on 'policy learning' (1991, 1993). Yet since attempts to transfer policies are so widespread, a theory of 'policy transfer' either has a slightly banal quality or tends to invest too much importance in the migration of ideas as a driver of policy change. It leaves questions unanswered about how decisions are made to accept or reject ideas from elsewhere (see Box 5.4 for some of the key critical points).

There are obviously some important issues to raise about the conditions under which policy transfer occurs. There are clearly problems that arise from uncritical policy transfer. But the notion that a 'theory of policy transfer' can be developed must be viewed with some scepticism. On the other hand, policy transfer theory can be seen, both in terms of the general notion that new ideas and new discourses develop and are spread around the world, and in terms of its concern with circumstances in which policy transfer is or is not facilitated by existing institutional arrangements, as another contribution to institutional theory in its more wide-ranging forms.

From institutional theory to garbage cans

The discussion has suggested some difficulties with the use of institutional theory which have been met by responses that tend to deal with these objections by widening its scope. The overall problem with institutional theory is well put by Thelen and Steinmo, who say it is 'that institutions explain everything until they explain nothing' (1992, p. 15). They go on to argue that their concept of 'institutional dynamism' addresses the problem by identifying situations 'in which we can observe variability in the impact of institutions over time but within countries' (ibid., p. 16). The problem remains, however, that work from this school involves the interpretation of case studies where the reader is invited to share the writer's understanding of events.

Going even further down this problematical path, March and Olsen have given us, from their work with Cohen, a memorable expression to typify an extreme version of the institutional approach: 'the garbage can model'. They say, almost as if distancing themselves from their own idea:

> In the form most commonly discussed in the literature, the garbage-can model assumes that problems, solutions, decision makers, and choice opportunities are independent, exogenous streams flowing through a system. (Cohen, March and Olsen, 1972)

> They come together in a manner determined by their arrival times. Thus, solutions are linked to problems primarily by their simultaneity, relatively few problems are solved, and choices are made for the most part either before any problems are connected to them (oversight) or after the problems have abandoned one choice to associate themselves with another (flight). (March and Olsen, 1984, p. 746; see also March and Olsen, 1989)

There is a problem that once any attempt to generalise is left behind in this way, the student of the policy process is being required to take a position like that of a purist atheoretical historian, determined to let the facts speak for themselves without any principles to help organise attention or lessons to draw from the study. Or is he or she being urged to look to psychology to offer some organising principles? Certainly there has been a whole range of policy analysis literature which suggests the need to draw upon psychology. There is obviously no objection to this. However, except in some forms of social psychology which are very closely linked to organisational sociology in endeavouring to explain how structures influence attitudes and thus actions, the problem is that much of this literature does no more than tell us that individual attitudes, emotions, etc. will influence decisions. Parsons makes this point well about Young's (1977) essay on the 'assumptive worlds' of policy actors:

> The problem is ... how can we students of public policy actually study this 'assumptive world?' ... Surface, observable forms of politics are somewhat straightforward as compared with 'values', 'beliefs', 'assumptions', and the 'subconscious aspects of policy-making'. (Parsons, 1995, p. 379)

There is obviously a need to be sensitive to unique juxtapositions of events and the unique responses of individual actors, but if we are sitting in the 'garbage can' watching the latter deal with the former, we can do little but describe what happens on each unique occasion.

CONCLUSIONS

Clearly, the extreme positions described in the last few paragraphs are not typical of the institutional school, but they do remind us how much institutional analysis of the policy process is an intuitive art. Institutionalist writers offer a critique of other approaches to policy analysis. For example, Immergut portrays her work as 'a break with "correlational" thinking' (1992, p. 57), arguing that it goes beyond the static perspectives of interest group theory (p. 66) and asserting that 'the view that institutions are somehow congealed social structure is not especially helpful' (p. 85). But do they actually replace or supplement other theoretical approaches?

However, perhaps the remark above about 'intuitive art' is applicable to all policy process studies. The discussion of postmodernist theories in Chapter 1 (pp. 16–19) highlighted the way in which this perspective merges into one which sees attempts to offer generalisations and a systematic account of the policy process as impossible. The author's reluctance to go all the way down that road was explored there.

The institutionalist approach is very often operationalised through comparisons between countries, since good opportunities for looking at similar policy processes in different institutional contexts are obviously provided by national institutional differences. Equally, it can be said that comparative work leads naturally to attention to questions about the ways in which institutions matter. Thus the next chapter, which explores some relevant comparative work, can be seen in many respects as an extension of this rather short chapter.

6 Comparative perspectives on the analysis of the policy process

SYNOPSIS

In this chapter there will be an exploration of some relevant comparative perspectives. This is not offered as another theoretical approach; rather, all the approaches examined so far need – at least in theory – to be tested out in comparative ways to explore their claims either to universality or to situational specificity. Hence, this chapter should be seen as supplementary to the other chapters and particularly as offering more understanding of the problems implicit in very determinist theories and of the insights offered by institutional approaches.

Particular attention will be given to two specific groups of comparative studies:

- studies of policy differences – where efforts to explain those differences raise issues about policy process differences;
- studies of institutional differences – where these throw light upon how policies are made.

The chapter is followed by an 'Intermezzo' which sums up the first part of the book. The propositions set out in Figure 2.1 at the beginning of Chapter 2 are restated in modified ways and examined. Whilst acknowledging that in many respects choices between theories and perspectives have to be made by readers themselves, given the absence of hard evidence and the ideologically loaded nature of some of the ideas the author suggests ways in which he considers it feasible to integrate aspects of the different perspectives.

Introduction

Given the very limited scope for experimental methods in political science, it is very important to test theories by making comparisons between them. The use of comparison generally gives a wide range of possible ways of looking at more than one situation separated by time, space, or even policy issue. Obviously much of this can be done within one country. Nevertheless, it is comparison between countries that offers a particular challenge to theories. That is what this chapter will look at.

Comparative work is vital for the development of policy theory if we do not want its propositions to be seen as merely observations about specific occurrences in a particular place and even at a particular point in time. This is the sense in which, long ago, Dahl asserted that claims of a 'science of public administration' needed a set of generalisable principles independent of their national setting (1947). A more modern formulation of this proposition is to be found in a leading textbook on comparative politics:

> Comparison is the methodological core of the scientific study of politics. Comparative analysis helps us develop explanations and test theories of the way in which political processes work. (Almond et al., 2004, p. 31)

Comparative work can be seen as testing the universality of theories about the policy process. In the case of two of the groups of theoretical approaches, the need for comparative work to test theories flows directly from the nature of the theories. Any theory that embodies deterministic propositions about influences on the policy process suggests that countries with similar characteristics will tend to have similar policies. Many forms of Marxist theory suggest that policy similarities will arise at similar stages in the development of capitalism, more general theories of socio-economic development embody comparable propositions, whilst many forms of globalist theory suggest widespread uniformities in responses to issues, particularly those with economic implications across nations.

The other group of theories where the case for comparison is implicit is institutional theories, in which the central proposition is often almost the direct opposite of that embodied in much determinist theory: that countries will differ because of their different institutional configurations. Whilst it is easier to show that systems diverge rather than converge, there is, nevertheless, a sense in which institutional theory, at the very least, needs comparison to demonstrate how divergence occurs. Moreover, some propositions from institutional theory do embody suggestions of a determinist form (though they are usually more cautiously specified than in the main forms of economic determinism). They may claim that there may be specific combinations of institutional influences that can be identified in particular situations, particularly, that is, situations inhibiting or assisting policy change. If such propositions have any general validity they may be expected to be applicable in more than one country.

That last point about institutional theory is one that may be applied to all the theoretical approaches. Questions about the universal applicability of theories require the examination of the extent to which they translate into other contexts. Relevant questions are, for example:

- To what extent does classical pluralist theory embody generalisations that are much more likely to apply to the highly differentiated institutional situation that exists in the United States than elsewhere?
- Are corporatist arrangements simply characteristic of some European accommodations between the state and organised economic interests in a particular era?

This leads us to a further issue: if some generalisations about the policy process are more valid in some societies than others, it may then be the case that some kind of typology of societies can be developed. Perhaps there can be generalisations of this kind that fall somewhere between strong determinism and the assertion of institutional uniqueness.

Studies of policy differences

Studies of policy differences use differences in the *characteristics* of policy (particularly those that can be quantified, such as expenditure on specific objectives and policy outputs) as *dependent variables* which may be seen as subject to influence by *independent variables*. Inevitably, the hypotheses used to determine which independent variables to examine have been influenced by the theories discussed in the earlier chapters – in particular, the extent to which outputs are determined by factors external to the national policy system (the wider social and economic environment and the impact of global forces), pressure groups and political parties, and national institutional arrangements.

Whilst the comparative study of policy outputs is developing in relation to all substantive policy areas, it is in the study of social policy that a particularly sophisticated literature has grown up. This is partly because variations in levels of social policy expenditure and the way in which social policy institutions have developed are particularly salient across the more economically developed nations, with questions about whether 'welfare states' are boons or banes being particularly prominent in ideological debates. But it must also be partly attributable to the fact that social policy expenditure is a large item in the budgets of many states, and that its ingredients and implications are widely measured and reported in a variety of international databases which facilitate relatively accurate comparisons between countries. Moreover, aspects of social policy can be more easily measured for comparative purposes than, say, differences in ways of managing the economy, or conducting relations with other nations, or regulating activities and behaviour. Hence, the following discussion will outline the way in which the comparative study of social policy has developed, with particular reference to the extent to which findings have contributed to our understanding of the policy process.

The earliest systematic comparative studies of welfare states followed a largely determinist line (for example, Wilensky and Lebaux, 1965), contributing a view that social policy development was a largely unidimensional growth in which rising gross domestic product (GDP) would inevitably bring with it growing state expenditure on social policy. Later, this approach was challenged by scholars who felt dissatisfied with the high level of generality in these studies, which emphasised broad trends and paid little attention to variation in policy content (Higgins, 1981; Jones, 1985). A particular concern developed to explore the extent to which 'politics matters', looking at political inputs including ideologies (Rimlinger, 1971; Castles, 1985). Since an interest in welfare seemed to distinguish parties of the Left from those of the Right, it was obviously relevant to ask whether political orientation had any real effect.

The most influential comparative study on this theme is Esping-Andersen's *Three Worlds of Welfare Capitalism* (1990). Esping-Andersen analyses aspects of the characteristics of social policy systems in terms of their contributions to social solidarity. This leads him to identify three regime types (see Box 6.1).

Box 6.1	Esping-Andersen's regime types

1. The '"liberal" welfare state, in which means-tested assistance, modest universal transfers, or modest social-insurance plans predominate' (Esping-Andersen, 1990, p. 26). This indicates low levels of 'decommodification' (see discussion below). Esping-Andersen puts Australia, the United States, New Zealand, Canada, Ireland and the United Kingdom in this category.

2. Nations where 'the historical corporatist–statist legacy was upgraded to the new "post-industrial" class structure'. In such nations 'the preservation of status differentials' is more important than either 'the liberal obsession with market efficiency' or 'the granting of social rights' (ibid., p. 27). This second category includes Italy, Japan, France, Germany, Finland, Switzerland, Austria, Belgium and the Netherlands.

3. Countries 'in which the principles of universalism and decommodification of social rights was extended also to the middle classes'; in these places 'the social democrats pursued a welfare state that would promote an equality of the highest standards' (ibid.). Denmark, Norway and Sweden are the nations in this category.

The approach to comparative analysis adopted by Esping-Andersen is rooted in the notion that some social policy systems may reflect and contribute to social solidarity. The concept of 'decommodification' is used by Esping-Andersen to suggest that some policy systems achieve a universalism which treats all sections of society alike. The decommodified systems of Scandinavia are contrasted with corporatist and liberal systems which more clearly reflect labour market divisions and market ideologies. These are attempts to classify national systems as a whole; the inclusiveness of the Scandinavian systems is seen relative to other systems.

Esping-Andersen's notion of regime types brings together three key issues relevant to policy process theory:

- His starting point is a view that 'politics matters', using an essentially neo-pluralist perspective emphasising variations in the representation of class interests within politics.

- However, the notion that there may be rather different systems with different institutional and/or cultural characteristics introduces an element of the institutional perspective. Particularly interesting here is the distinction between the second and third of the regimes outlined in Box 6.1, where differences in political representation do not seem to have sufficient explanatory power on their own.

- The use of the notion of 'regime types' involves a typology which highlights institutional issues but suggests a distinct clustering of institutional approaches.

Esping-Andersen's work has been widely criticised, particularly by scholars who have suggested that his early, seminal work gave insufficient attention to comparative issues in respect of the gender dimension in social policy (Lewis, 1992, 1993, 1997; Sainsbury, 1994; Daly, 2000). However, his emphasis upon broad social policy 'regimes' is not challenged by such work. Rather, it simply widens the debate about ideologies and sources of power. Familist ideologies are shown as influencing the politics of social security and determining the expectations embedded within it (a point Esping-Andersen acknowledges in his later work (1999)). Attention has been drawn, in this respect, to the extent to which there is a Roman Catholic and/or southern European (see Ferrara, 1996) approach to the design of social policy.

It is perhaps pertinent to interpose here what is perhaps the most fundamental problem with Esping-Andersen's approach, since it bedevils all comparative research on policy, and suggests that it gets progressively more difficult as it penetrates into the more complex aspects of the policy process. Esping-Andersen's work depends very much upon what can be measured. Clearly, social security expenditure and related issues about its redistributive effects can be put into a comparative model very much more easily than can differences in services, where gross expenditure comparisons tell us very little about how systems actually work. Box 6.2 cites an example of a study that emphasises this point. Clearly, the same point could be made very forcibly about other areas of public policy: about comparing efforts to regulate economic activity, or control pollution, or develop transport policies and so on.

In the mainstream work on comparative social policy, many studies since Esping-Andersen's have been concerned to chart the more specific pressures in play. The work of Pierson (1994, 2001) is particularly important in this respect since it uses institutional theory much more explicitly, with two key features. One is that it equates regimes with institutional configurations that will channel new policy initiatives. The other is that it suggests that the relative success of interest groups will depend upon institutional arrangements. Reference was made in Chapter 5 to Immergut's comparative analysis of

Box 6.2	An example of difficulty with comparative generalisation in a complex policy area

Anttonen, Baldock and Sipila argue, in their recent book *The Young, the Old and the State: Social Care Systems in Five Industrial Nations* (2003), that they found it impossible to develop a systematic theoretical approach to comparison using a modified version of regime theory. They see a need to situate interpretations of current policy in their historical contexts. Hence, they offer carefully documented accounts of very partial developments in the five nations they studied. These were complicated in the case of childcare by the way the female labour market is evolving in each country and by ideological expectations about female roles, whereas in the case of the care of elderly people what was particularly relevant was developments in health and income maintenance policy and varying expectations of family roles. Hence, they assert that it is the welfare mix of state, family, community and market that makes the comparative task so difficult, together with the fact that social care policy interacts in complex ways with social security, employment, health and education policies.

health policy in terms of the presence or absence of 'access points' and 'veto points' in different societies. Box 6.3 illustrates some applications of this theme, with particular reference to policy cutbacks. In general, a variety of scholars suggest that particular institutional approaches set up 'pathways' which influence future developments. Path-dependencies seem to be particularly important in income maintenance systems, where pension schemes imply long-run expectations (a theme to be explored further in Chapters 7 and 8) and often embody social insurance arrangements, which themselves build very strong, long-run political expectations and therefore obligations.

Box 6.3	Interest groups, institutional configurations and policy change

Pierson (1994) explores the way in which pressure from interest groups inhibited the cutback aspirations of Ronald Reagan in the United States and Margaret Thatcher in the United Kingdom. Béland (2001) has addressed the same theme rather differently in a study of pension reform in France and the United States, showing that the extent to which group interests are institutionalised will have an impact. His contrast is between the influence of labour unions in the two countries, and he argues that while union membership is actually proportionately lower in France than in the United States and the control over the pensions systems is in both cases firmly in the hands of the state, nevertheless French unions have benefited from the fact that their right to be consulted about pension issues is formally embedded in the institutional arrangements. Taylor-Gooby (2001, 2002) similarly explores the impact of institutional arrangements upon social policy cuts in Europe.

The attempt to explain differences in the extent of welfare cuts is, not surprisingly, an important theme in contemporary social policy analyses. As well as looking at arguments about the power of interests and the rigidity of institutional arrangements for research into welfare cuts, this literature makes a contribution to the debate about the power of global forces. In this case, however, the important point is not the conflicting explanations for differences in resistance to cuts but the fact that these differences occur, posing a challenge to any simple determinist version of the impact of globalism.

Box 6.4	Comparative social policy theory and the East Asian nations

The early determinists' comparative theory suggests that all the East Asian nations will have developed, or will be developing, social policy institutions and that those that have reached Western levels of wealth will have reached Western levels of expenditure. Clearly they have not, but there seems to be a tendency in that direction – perhaps we merely have to allow for a time-lag effect. Alternatively, can the highly industrialised Eastern economies (Japan, South Korea, Taiwan, Singapore, Hong Kong) be fitted into Esping-Andersen's typology at least as later 'arrivals'? There does seem to be a case for seeing the first three (the other two have perhaps been too influenced by British colonial policies) as joining Esping-Andersen's 'corporatist–statist' group (Ramesh, 2004). An alternative is to see them as having features that are more specifically Eastern, which explain areas of limited development. The main argument along these lines has been the suggestion that Confucian family ideologies lead to a greater delegation of welfare responsibilities to the family and extended family (Jones, 1985). The problems with this argument are that (a) in any under-developed income maintenance system the family will, *faute de mieux*, have to take on greater responsibilities, and (b) the use of Confucian ideologies as a justification for inaction by the political elite is not evidence that political demands can and will be damped down in this way in the absence of evidence of the acceptance of that reasoning by the people.

A book on South Korea by Dong-Myoen Shin (2003) expresses doubt about the applicability of Esping-Andersen's regime model to Korea, on the grounds that it gives too little attention to political institutions. It is important that Korea has a government that, according to Shin, has no doubt about its role as a supervisor and regulator of economic policy, the first requirement for being an effective innovator in social policy. This has set up significant 'pathways' in that society.

Similar challenges are offered by the study of social policy systems in countries that are comparatively late developers of social policy, in particular the industrialised nations of East Asia and the ex-communist countries of eastern Europe. Box 6.4 explores some of the debate about the former group. A consideration of the increasingly lively debate about social policy change in East Asia seems to bring us back to a key point made earlier, alongside theories that emphasise pressures, influences and constraints, about the continuing importance of policy choice. It is important in comparative studies not to lose sight of the extent to which policy learning takes place over time and between nations. The newly industrialised Asian economies have the opportunity to observe the strengths and weaknesses of the policies adopted previously and to learn from them selectively. They have also inevitably been drawn into the new global debate about the economic costs of generous welfare benefit systems (see Esping-Andersen, 1996) and have wanted to draw their own conclusions.

This section has explored the way that approaches to the explanation of policy differences in the study of social policy have evolved from an initial concern to test determinist propositions, through a literature that introduced a rather more pluralist view of policy determination, to contemporary perspectives that have a strong institutionalist character (particularly inasmuch as many institutionalist perspectives embrace issues about culture and ideology). The arguments about globalism have forced a measure of return to the exploration of economic determinism, but the evidence suggests that responses to global economic influences have been diverse. Here, however, it is important not to lose sight of Hay's argument, explored on pp. 46–7, about the extent to which globalism has an impact inasmuch as decision makers believe the propositions about globalist theory to be true in a world in which policy transfer is widespread and is encouraged by international organisations.

We turn now to approaches to comparison which start quite explicitly from efforts to compare institutions.

Studies of institutional differences

Not surprisingly, the comparative question that has excited political scientists a great deal has been whether nations can be compared in terms of the extent to which they are democratic. This has naturally led on to an exploration of the different institutional forms that allegedly democratic government may assume. It is not appropriate to go deeply into this literature here, but it clearly has some relevance for questions about the way policy processes vary from country to country.

Perhaps the most relevant comparative work on democratic systems is that of Lijphart, who argues that definitions of democracy raise the fundamental question of

> who will do the governing and to whose interests should the government be responsive when the people are in disagreement and have divergent preferences? (Lijphart, 1999, p. 1)

He goes on to contrast two answers to that question: 'the majority of the people' (the 'Westminster model') and 'as many people as possible' (the 'consensus model'). He goes on to deploy evidence that suggests that consensual democracies (often operating through corporatist policy-making processes) are more effective and implicitly more responsive. But his comparative analysis does not only contrast countries in respect of the extent to which their systems correspond to either the Westminster model or the consensus model. He also examines variations along another dimension: that between strong federalism at one extreme and high degrees of unification at the other. Lijphart displays his comparative data in terms of these dimensions. Table 6.1 simply sets out his schema in terms of quadrants (with just a few examples), to illustrate the idea without getting tangled up in some of the finer (and more contestable) distinctions along the dimensions. Hence, we see countries like the United Kingdom (before devolution) and New Zealand as having systems that are majoritarian and unitary, and the United States and Canada as having majoritarian but federal systems. Switzerland and Germany are good examples of consensus but federal systems (particularly the former), whilst the Scandinavian countries are consensus but unitary systems.

Table 6.1   Lijphart's types of democracies

	Majoritarian	Consensus
Unitary	UK, New Zealand	Sweden, Denmark
Federal	United States, Canada	Switzerland, Germany

Lijphart is clearly engaged in a very bold attempt to produce what Lane and Ersson call 'grand social theory' (2000, p. 224). They prefer to break down their approach to the same topic into somewhat more modest attempts to produce 'middle range' generalisation. But what is particularly pertinent to this discussion is the way in which this work suggests that even if all the so-called democratic systems included in Lijphart's study are in some sense 'pluralist', there are some very different versions of pluralism operating, integrating interests into the decision process in very different ways. We will return to this theme in Chapter 8 when we look at agenda setting.

However, looking at the way interests may be aggregated in the parliamentary process in the way Lijphart does still treats the state as a very passive entity, with a fixed set of institutions to which interests can relate. A rather different comparative concern has been with the distinction between 'weak' and 'strong' states. This offers, as we shall see, a very different perspective which cuts across Lijphart's dimensions.

Dyson's analysis (1980) of the differences between the way the state is conceptualised involves describing Britain and America as 'stateless'. This involves a rather deliberate exaggeration, and to describe societies in which the state is large and costly in this way violates common sense. His object is to emphasise both an absence of ideologies which ascribe a special role for the state in society and to show that a fragmented view of the state is dominant in the way institutions work. In this book the formulation 'strong' and 'weak' states (Katzenstein, 1977) is preferred to 'states' and 'stateless societies'.

Dyson argues that the concept of state, inasmuch as it means more than an actor in international relations, involves:

- 'a legal conception which attributes a distinct personality to a particular institution or complex of institutions';

- 'a political conception which establishes the unique character of ... the exercise of public power'; and

- 'a sociological conception which refers both to an institution endowed with a remarkable coercive power and to a special type of communal bond capable of generating sentiments of affection and disaffection'. (Dyson, 1980, p. 206)

These characteristics are more evident in some societies than others. Dyson describes strong states as resting upon a tradition which involves

> a widespread sense of the legitimacy of public action ... and ... a willingness to define 'public power' as distinctive and to exercise it authoritatively. (Ibid., p. 256)

Such states do not necessarily have bigger governments: Dyson's proposition is about how power is exercised. Weak states, by contrast,

> are characterised by the strength of pluralism, representation and the debating tradition in the political culture; an instrumental view of government and a pragmatic conception of politics ...; a pervasive informality in politics ...; a preference for 'social' models of the constitution or economic analyses of politics which emphasize the role of elites rather than institutions. (Ibid., p. 52)

The 'strong state' idea occurs in a different form in relation to analyses of the role of the state in development and nation building. In this respect Pusey (1991) provides an interesting examination of the Australian state, a country which otherwise might be expected to be very much in the Anglo-American 'camp' (see Box 6.5). The examination of the case of Australia draws attention to other societies where a very positive role for the state has been adopted – Japan, South Korea and Taiwan, for example. Whilst the Japanese case may have parallels with the shift from absolutism traced by Dyson in Europe (see, for example, Harrop (ed.) 1992), South Korea and Taiwan are examples of societies where states have accepted a crucial modernising role from the outset (inasmuch as these states only assumed their modern forms in the 1940s). The East Asian model of state-led development has of course attracted widespread attention (Lau, 1986; Sandhu and Wheatley, 1990). It is interesting that Japan, South Korea and Taiwan were all in a sense American 'protectorates' in the post-war period. Whilst there were distinctive efforts to implant 'pluralist' political ideas in these societies, the initial defensive need for the 'strong state' was evident. Confucian doctrines about the state and the roles of its servants seem also to have had some influence on the subsequent translation of these into strong economic roles.

Box 6.5	The Australian state

Pusey (1991) sees Australia as a 'nation building state', or alternatively as 'born modern', in that from an early stage in its existence the state took upon itself the role of steering economic development and protecting the interests of its working people. Crucial to this view of Australia is the importance of the establishment of protective trade barriers and a minimum wage policy (and also, of course, and less to its credit, the 'white Australia' policy) at the beginning of the twentieth century (Macintyre, 1985).

The Australian case is the subject of controversy in the comparative analysis of social policy, too. While it is seen by Esping-Andersen (1990) as a typical 'liberal' state, it has been alternatively argued that its distinctive stance of egalitarian economic management makes it rather different from Britain and America (Castles, 1985; Castles and Mitchell, 1992).

There are dangers in using the concepts of 'strong' and 'weak' states. Atkinson and Coleman (1989) have pointed out that their application needs to be modified both by taking into account the extent to which there is centralisation and, even when there is not, by recognising the variations there may be between policy sectors. Their analysis of state strength also goes on to remind us that if the concept is used there needs to be some consideration of the strength of the elements in society that the state is striving to influence and regulate. Strength is a relative concept – a so-called 'strong state' may not look so strong when it is dealing with a unified and well-organised group of economic actors. Howlett and Ramesh, citing the work of Haggard and Moon on South Korea (1990), go on from that point to argue that 'there is no reason to believe that strong states will necessarily make policies that serve the interests of society as a whole, rather than those of self-serving groups' (Howlett and Ramesh, 2003, p. 61). In other words, do not allow usage of the concept of the 'strong state' to lead to a begging of questions about the respective power of the state and other groups involved in the policy process.

Putting Lijphart's theory and Dyson's theory together, one could clearly have a rather different version of Table 6.1, one that maintains the majoritarian/consensus distinction but contrasts it with another distinction between strong and weak state traditions as in Table 6.2 (you could, if you like, try to envisage a three-dimensional table which also keeps the unitary/federal distinction – but this will not be attempted here).

The United Kingdom has been deliberately left out of Table 6.2, as a rather ambiguous case. A Canadian, applying state theory to a comparison

Table 6.2   Types of states

	Majoritarian	Consensus
Strong state tradition	Australia, New Zealand, Taiwan	Sweden, Denmark, Germany
Weak state tradition	United States	Switzerland

between her country and the United States, suggests that 'political structures that adhere to a parliamentary system of government, have a propensity for party discipline and executive dominance, a tradition of a permanent, low profile, independent and experienced civil service, and a long history of interventionist social policy, produce a potentially strong and autonomous state in relation to social institutions' (Boase, 1996, p. 290). That description seems to fit Britain well. Since the arrival on the scene of the Labour Party, and the related shift away from 'economic liberalism' by the Liberals, at the beginning of the twentieth century, the British policy-making scene has been dominated by strong programmatic stances by the political parties. The electoral and parliamentary institutions have tended to polarise political debate into distinctive 'Left' and 'Right' positions. Furthermore, one side in that polarity – the Left – has tended to need to strengthen the state in order to realise its goals. Hence, there is a need to be cautious about the typification of Britain as a 'weak state', a point that is further exemplified by the paradox around the way in which the Thatcher government used the state to weaken the state (see Box 6.6).

Box 6.6   Britain – a strong or a weak state in the era of Thatcherism?

The title of Gamble's analysis of 'the politics of Thatcherism', *The Free Economy and the Strong State* (1994), encapsulates the crucial point here. As Gamble suggests, 'The idea . . . involves a paradox. The state is to be simultaneously rolled back and rolled forward' (ibid. p. 36). It can perhaps be said that state strength was used to weaken the state, at least in relation to the industrial sector. Hall makes the same kind of point in a rather different way, emphasising ideology, in his exploration of Thatcherite economic policy. He argues that 'A coherent and technically plausible set of ideas, commanding the support of some body of experts, can confer a degree of independence on the state' (Hall, 1986, p. 128). There was in the period of political leadership by Margaret Thatcher, in effect, the weakening of the state by the state – a paradoxical development only possible because of the weakness of countervailing interest groups such as the public sector trade unions.

The further general point that needs to be made here is that the importance of party politics in the British system makes the role of the state an area of controversy in a way that it is not in the United States (this is discussed further in Chapter 8). The peculiar impact of the dominance of a single party in Britain throughout much of the recent past has been highlighted in

Dunleavy's analysis of 'policy disasters'. It is suggested that 'five main factors seem to be involved in generating policy disasters: scale aggregation, overly speedy legislation and policy making, political hyperactivism, the arrogance of Whitehall, and ineffective core executive checks and balances' (Dunleavy, 1995, p. 59). The first two and the last are essentially institutional factors – unitary government, a simple law-making process ('the fastest law in the west', Dunleavy says, taking this expression from a comment on the government of a smaller, similar case, New Zealand) and very centralised power. 'Political hyperactivism' can be seen as a characteristic of the contemporary ideological climate, whilst Dunleavy's fourth point emphasises the way in which 'political responsiveness and policy activism' (ibid., p. 62) is at a premium in the top civil service.

The capacity for 'action' in the United Kingdom has been seen as making for very positive government, not weak government. The appellation 'weak' therefore draws attention to wider cultural and ideological considerations that inhibit positive government and/or undermine the legitimacy of government. On the other hand there is a very important distinction to be made between the UK and the USA which amounts not just to different positions on the unitary/federalism scale but also to the fact that the United States has a very divided system even at the centre (between President, two Houses of Congress and the Supreme Court). In the UK modern prime ministers have been described as presidential (Kavanagh and Seldon, 2001), but what is misleading about that appellation is that prime ministers have a level of control over Parliament beyond a US president's wildest dreams. In the words of Gamble, observing how the 'royal prerogatives' are now the Prime Minster's: 'the Prime Minister has no need to become a President because he is already a Monarch, a position of considerably greater scope' (2003, p. 11).

It has been shown that the strong state/weak state dichotomy is of limited use. An alternative is the policy styles literature, which involves a much more complex exploration of institutional differences. Jeremy Richardson and his associates have developed an analysis of 'policy styles' (1982) (see Box 6.7 overleaf). Styles are seen as varied, not merely on account of national differences, but also because of differences in the policy issues at stake. This is an approach linked to ideas about 'policy communities' (see p. 69) – hence the suggestion is that different policy styles may be manifested in different policy communities even within the same country, let alone between countries. Smith (1993) picks this idea up in his discussion of the distinction between 'policy networks' and 'policy communities', suggesting that features of the United States make the former more likely than the latter in that country. This is another way of saying that bargaining processes are more likely to be evident in that large country with its complex constitutional structure.

At the end of his edited book, in which this model is explored through case studies, Richardson is cautious about labelling countries in terms of policy styles. Nevertheless, Bovens, 't Hart and Peters, in introducing a study of *Success and Failure in Public Governance* (2001, pp. 18–19), offer expected 'styles' for the six countries they studied. However, they qualify their prediction by offering an alternative prediction that they may see 'roughly similar

Box 6.7	Richardson's (1982) analysis of policy styles

This involves two dimensions:

- an anticipatory style as opposed to a reactive one;
- a consensus-seeking style as opposed to one which tends to impose decisions on society.

This model is then used to identify four quadrants:

1. Anticipatory and consensus-seeking
2. Anticipatory and imposing decisions
3. Reactive and consensus-seeking
4. Reactive and imposing decisions.

governance in each of the sectors [to be studied], and major differences between sectors even between cases set in the same country' (ibid., p. 18). Hence, we see suggestions that different national policy styles affect how policy is formulated, but then this is interestingly qualified by Bovens and his colleagues with suggestions that this may very much depend upon policy area. Differences in the characteristics of policy areas are explored further in Chapter 7. While a brief quotation cannot do justice to a lengthy and complex analysis, the conclusions set out in Box 6.8 are worth attention.

Box 6.8	Bovens, 't Hart and Peters' conclusion on policy styles after examining four contrasting policy areas in Britain, Germany, France, the Netherlands, Sweden and Spain

Bovens, 't Hart and Peters argue as follows:

> The empirical evidence here seems to allow us to argue that the policy styles of some countries are more stable and clearly defined than are those of others. In particular, the Netherlands and Sweden emerged as consensual in almost all the cases, as would be expected from the conventional discussions of politics in these two countries. Germany also emerges as relatively consensual, as does Spain. The latter case is the more interesting: given its political history and its majoritarian governments it might be expected to rely more on imposition. In general, the governing style of all these countries emerged as more consensual than might have been expected from the literature, reflecting perhaps continuing changes in the style of politics in all industrialized democracies.
>
> If we examine the other dimension of policy style, reactive versus anticipatory, there was considerable variation among the policy areas in the way the actors involved attempted to deal with the future course of policies. For most of the policies the Netherlands, Spain and the UK tended

to be relatively anticipatory, while the other states tended to be reactive. The findings for financial regulation were somewhat the reverse, with Spain and France being more anticipatory systems. (Bovens, 't Hart and Peters, 2001, p. 646)

CONCLUSIONS

The most obvious and simple comparative question about the policy process is whether systems tend to converge (as most determinist theory and particularly globalist theory suggest) or diverge (as institutional theory suggests, at least in its most general forms). The evidence from contemporary comparative studies is rather more in support of the second proposition. At this stage in the book, in which there has been much discussion of the difficulties that face efforts to generalise about the policy process, this conclusion will not come as much of a surprise. More interesting questions arise about quite explicit attempts to encourage convergence on the one hand and about the ways these are resisted on the other.

However, there is a need to go beyond the dichotomy explored in the last paragraph to a range of interesting comparative questions about the extent to which distinct approaches to policy making are shared by groups of countries. The regime theory that has become so dominant in the comparative analysis of social policy and the interest in types of states both suggest that there is a case for analyses that identify distinct clusters of states. Such work, moreover, may help the exploration of some of the questions about rather different degrees of pluralism in different societies and about the extent to which networks converge into corporatist arrangements in some places.

Yet much of this work takes the shape of a rather academic game in which individuals contest typologies. The curious thing about some of this typologising is that it may at one and the same time help us to gain insights into the characteristics of systems yet fall to pieces when pursued to its logical limits. In this chapter the distinction between 'strong' and 'weak' states has been seen in these terms, raising interesting thoughts about how policies are made in different societies but ending up leaving us puzzled as to why the United Kingdom or Australia can be called strong states by some and weak states by others. The policy styles literature goes down a similar road but avoids getting too much into typifying states by recognising the importance of differences between policies.

The main functions of this chapter have, then, been to explore further the way in which comparative studies illuminate the theoretical arguments and to introduce some of the arguments about the ways in which policy process differences are apparent in different societies. Comparative material of a more specific kind will be used further in many places in the rest of the book. Meanwhile, before we go any further, we need to sum up where the theoretical analysis has taken us thus far.

Intermezzo: Drawing conclusions from the review of theories

Chapters 2–6 have reviewed a wide range of theoretical approaches to the public policy process, pointing out the strengths and weaknesses of each. Where does that leave readers? Should they just make their own choices bearing in mind these points but guided by their own ideological predispositions? Well, the answer is 'yes, up to a point'. However, it is important to recognise that what has been described is a succession of ideas developed over a long period of time, in the course of which some degree of consensus has developed about which are most helpful for our understanding of the policy process and which are less so. In the rest of the book connections will be made back to these theories, highlighting their usefulness where applicable. This book does not reject altogether the social-scientific search for truth, at least in the form of the view that some explanations are better than others. So it is reasonable to expect the author to 'get off the fence' and indicate his view of the validity of various perspectives.

In Chapter 2, a simple figure (Figure 2.1) was presented to sum up the key dimensions along which accounts of the policy process differ. This is reproduced below, followed by another chart along the same lines (Figure IM1). In the second chart the headings are omitted, but four propositions about the policy process are set out, each of which has something in common with the four in the first chart.

Statements 2–3 in the second figure are identifiable as modified versions of the pluralist position and the elitist (or neo-Marxist) position explored in Chapter 2. It was recognised there that they have converged into formulations that reasonably comfortably combine both. Then Chapters 3 and 4 explored ways in which the pluralist position has been made more sophisti-

Figure 2.1 (repeated)   Basic models of the policy process

	Power concentrated	Power fragmented
Power distributed relatively equally	1. Representative government in which a unified executive is responsive to popular will	2. Pluralist government in which popular will prevails through competition between groups
Power distributed unequally	3. Government by an unrepresentative elite, or in the grip of external influences	4. Unpredictable and chaotic government, buffeted by multiple pressures

Figure IM1   Models of the policy process restated

1. The institutions of government are important, but must be regarded with scepticism. The discourses and ideologies that surround them may be more important than their formal characteristics.	2. There is extensive competition between groups to influence government and this is likely to be organised in networks in which the interests of those inside government will be involved as well as those outside.
3. Power is distributed unequally both inside and outside government, having an impact as much upon what is on the agenda and the context in which decisions are taken as on the decision process itself.	4. There is a great deal of confusion and incoherence in the policy process, but nevertheless we can identify choices made by actors, who may be able to learn from earlier events and choices.

cated through the recognition of (a) strategies used in the pursuit of interests, (b) the salience of interests inside government, and (c) the ways in which interests are organised in networks and policy communities. People naturally continue to differ about how unequal and how concentrated the distribution of power is, but the divergence is not as striking as it once was. This author's position is still to regard power inequalities as very salient but to be sceptical about the extent to which power is concentrated. In both cases, however, there is wide variation, both between countries and between policy areas. The latter topic will be looked at further in the next chapter.

Statement 4 in Figure IM1 is in many respects simply a restatement of the original statement in Figure 2.1. The important addition is the emphasis on policy choice, something that has been stressed at various points in previous chapters. Recognition of the importance of policy choice is also relevant for the rejection of the more structurally determinist positions embedded in some theoretical propositions (particularly those represented by statement 3). A view that there is both a measure of chaos and a measure of choice in the policy system does not contradict the account of power provided in the last paragraph. The chaos benefits some interests more than others (particularly the defenders of the status quo), and some actors have more opportunities to choose or to influence choice than others.

Statement 1 in Figure IM1 is of course very different from the original statement 1 in Figure 2.1. Instead of a complacent statement about representative democracy there is here simply an acknowledgement that institutional configurations matter (and, of course, the institutions of representative democracy are important in most of the policy process systems that are discussed in this book). Also important for the new statement 1 is an emphasis upon what people (again, particularly the powerful) consider those institutional configurations to be. Moreover, it is through the deployment of discourses about institutions that power may be exercised. There is no necessary conflict between statement 1 and statements 2 and 3. But statement 4 does seem to be rather in conflict with statement 1. It is interesting how the institutional theory discussed in Chapter 5 includes positions that emphasise both of these statements. We find kindred (in many respects) theorists emphasising on the one hand structured pathways and on the other 'primeval soup' and the institutional 'garbage can'.

However, this potential contradiction between those who emphasise the factors that contribute to stability in the system and those who emphasise the uncertainties and points at which choice is fundamental is no more than a version of the difficulties involved in reconciling the evidence of stability and the evidence of change that lie at the heart of social science discourse. Under the influence of the sociologist Giddens, perhaps the most popular contemporary exploration of this uses the terms 'structure' and 'agency' (see pp. 49–50).

These propositions have, finally, to be recognised as offering an emphasis upon influences from within the nation state. There is a need not to forget the complexity of modern *governance*. This means that 'institutions of government' (statement 1) may be international, that groups (statement 2) may be organised outside and across individual states, that issues about inequalities of power (statement 3) need to be analysed globally, and that choices are made by actors (statement 4) who are increasingly conscious that they are playing on an international stage.

With the qualifications in that last paragraph added in, what is set out in Figure IM1 are propositions about the policy process, all of which will be kept in mind during the discussion in Part 3 of the book. While there are conflicts between them, it is possible to take the view that all are important. Then, of course, there are various shades of difference of emphasis between writers on our subject, corresponding with differences in the interpretation of the relevance of the four propositions. It will also be the case that there are differences between countries, or between different points in time in the same country, or even between different policy areas, in the extent to which each of the points is relevant. Power may be more unequal, or institutional constraints may be greater, or networks may be more important, or decision processes may be more coherent, in some places or situations than in others. In this sense readers may find it helpful to explore issues by contrasting the strengths and weaknesses of different perspectives along the lines mentioned in Chapter 1 (see p. 15), where reference was made to Allison's use of contrasting perspectives.

A final point about these propositions is that they may in various respects provide the theoretical foundations for hypotheses about the policy process. In this respect it is appropriate to interpose a methodological point. Some discussions of policy analysis theory (notably Hay, 2002 and Howlett and Ramesh, 2003) stress the need to distinguish inductive and deductive approaches (see Box IM1). Since each approach involves, in principle, the generation and testing of hypotheses, there is no reason, for the purposes of this discussion, to suggest that one approach should be preferred to the other. However, Howlett and Ramesh do appropriately warn us that 'many deductive-oriented researchers often seem to forget the contingent nature of their hypotheses and the need to constantly test and refine their assumptions against empirical evidence' (2003, pp. 46–7). Hay explicitly criticises the use of so-called 'rational' assumptions about self-interest in rational choice theory (see Chapter 3) in these terms. But a similar warning needs to be sounded about the more deterministic theories. There is a temptation to take on board these approaches as offering a more exciting approach to generalisation about the policy process than those (which in some respects do not merit description as theories) that do no more than urge us to focus our attention on the behaviour of interest groups, the relevance of networks and communities and the salience of institutions. The stance taken in this book, accepting the undesirability of imposing an assumed model of the physical sciences on the study of public policy and acknowledging the very tentative nature of most generalisations on offer, means that a very pragmatic perspective will be a key influence on the discussion that follows in the rest of the book.

Box IM1	Inductive and deductive theories

- Inductive approaches start from empirical observations, try to generalise from them and thus develop theory which may then generate further testable hypotheses.
- Deductive approaches start from theory and generate hypotheses, which may then be tested and fed back to improve the theory.

Part 3 Analysis of the policy process

7 Looking at policy: types, stages and instruments?

SYNOPSIS

While it is obvious that studying the policy process means studying the making of policy, we noted in Chapter 1 that policy is by no means a simple phenomenon. Furthermore, since different policies have different substantive contents it must be expected that policy will be made manifest in many different ways. Two approaches to handling this problem seem to be on offer from past literature: one of these is to divide analysis into stages, the other is to use policy typologies. Comments have already been made in Chapter 1 about the limitations of the former of these two approaches.

It was decided that the best way to go into the issues about policy differences in the rest of this book would be to look first at some examples of very different policy areas, accepting the likelihood that there will be extensive differences but making no assumptions about how these might be categorised. These areas will be labelled in terms of their substantive content and explored to illustrate the diversity of public policy and highlight the very different analytical issues that emerge in each case. The policy areas that will be considered are:

- making war
- trying to control the economy
- providing income maintenance (or social security)
- providing education
- trying to prevent pollution
- reorganising local government.

This will be followed by a section comparing and contrasting these areas of policy in terms of the extent to which the stages model is applicable to their analysis. The chapter ends with a discussion of policy typologies and policy instruments, again using these policy examples to illustrate the problems with these approaches to policy analysis.

Introduction

At the start of the part of the book where we move away from overarching theory to the examination of parts of the policy process, we need to consider how this large subject can be divided up. In Chapter 1 reference was made to writers who have seen the policy process as involving discrete stages or cycles. Some problems with this approach were identified, particularly that the policy process takes many forms, with many feedback loops, and that it is undesirable to impose upon its analysis a model that has been strongly influenced by a view of the way the process *should* proceed rather than by analysis of the way it actually does occur. Nevertheless, a pragmatic argument for the stages approach is that it offers a way to divide up a large subject.

Another way to divide the subject up is to focus upon different *kinds* of policy. There are obviously divisions in the literature in respect of policy content, often with distinct areas of scholarship in respect of foreign policy, economic policy, social policy and so on. These areas are often further subdivided: hence, for example, within social policy we find specialists on health policy, education policy, housing policy, income maintenance policy and so on. Prima facie, there are good grounds for arguing that what we have here are very different policy 'contents' and that these will have an influence on the characteristics of the policy process. We will explore this point rather more precisely below.

It is pertinent to comment before we go any further that some discussions of politics and the policy process make a distinction between the 'high politics' of managing external relations and the economy and the 'low politics' of delivering services and regulating everyday life. The first two policy areas to be explored here – making war and trying to control the economy – belong in the 'high politics' category, therefore, and the rest (generally speaking) belong in the 'low politics' category. The choice of the first two was dictated by a desire to highlight some of the characteristics of two policy areas that get little attention from the general run of discussions of policy processes and have vast, rather separate literatures of their own. The low/high distinction has been used to emphasise rather different configurations of interests. Jordan, for example, uses it in relation to those who see the European Union largely in terms of inter-governmental relations, who he says tend to emphasise the high politics, and those who stress the development of multi-level governance, who are particularly concerned with low politics issues (2001, p. 204). John (2001) mentions the way in which it has been used to indicate the policies that are particularly likely to be delegated to local government. These points are relevant to any consideration of the extent to which the policy processes in relation to making war or controlling the economy are rather different, but the point should not be exaggerated as each policy area has some distinctive characteristics of its own.

Making war

The study of policy decisions about the making of war are peculiarly absent from the mainstream policy process literature. Indeed, in political science the examination of this issue comes within the remit of international relations, a topic that is often rather hived off from the rest of the discipline. For example, the only discussion of war in Almond et al.'s *Comparative Politics Today* (2004), which is subtitled *A World View*, is a brief comparison of different national experiences of military violence (p. 146). It is thus rather risky for the present author, whose academic work has been confined to issues about domestic politics, to make comments on the study of this issue. Nevertheless, it does seem inappropriate to try to generalise about the policy process without any mention of this very important aspect.

Given the fundamental impact of war upon society, it can reasonably be argued from a prescriptive point of view that the making of war should be (a) under democratic control and (b) involve a most careful (rational? – see the discussion in Chapter 8, on pp. 150–2) exploration of the case for action before it occurs. Yet probably these two phenomena are unlikely to occur. The journalistic treatment of the negotiations between nations, fundamental for decisions about making war, tends to personalise the policy process. It is thus treated as being primarily about the aims and aspirations of political leaders and about the bargaining between them. In many respects this is treated as a kind of chess game of moves, gambits and bluffs. The international relations literature seems to adopt a similar approach, except that much of the personalisation of the journalists is replaced by the reification of nation states (America argues this, France did that, etc.). Hay's analysis of the various approaches to the study of international relations suggests that many of them use rational models (the chess game approach) but with varying assumptions about the idealism of the underlying goals (2002, Chapter 1).

One study about issues of war and peace (in this case the avoidance of war) that has had a great influence on the study of policy processes is Allison's (1971) study of the Cuban missile crisis. In 1962 the Russians began to install missiles in Cuba. The Americans, seeing this as a direct threat to themselves, challenged this action. After threats and fraught negotiations the Russians pulled back. This crisis, probably the most dangerous event in the history of the Cold War, since the Americans certainly contemplated using nuclear weapons, has been extensively analysed. Even a very compelling film has been made of the event. Allison's analysis of the account involves comparing three alternative models of the policy process. The details of this are set out in Box 7.1 overleaf.

What is significant about the story from our point of view is that domestic political pressures (other than from within the core executive) within the United States seem to be entirely absent from the account. The early stages of the negotiations were kept very quiet and at no stage was

Box 7.1	Allison's (1971) analysis of the Cuban missile crisis, using three models

First, Allison considers the 'rational actor model', which sees actions as being formed by purposeful agents with certain goals and objectives. These agents have to choose between alternative courses of action in order to achieve their goals. Alternatives are assumed to have a set of consequences attached, and rational choice consists of selecting the best alternative in these terms. This version of the story highlights the roles of the two national leaders, Kennedy and Khrushchev, as decision makers, as do most popular accounts of the crisis.

Second, Allison considers the organisational process model which sees action not as rational choice but as the output of organisational behaviour. This behaviour is largely the enactment of established routines in which sequential attention is given to goals and standard operating procedures are adopted. The concern here is with how the decision systems worked in the two countries, a topic on which there is of course much better evidence from the United States than from Russia.

Allison's third model is the bureaucratic politics model, which sees action as neither choice nor output but as the result of bargaining between groups and individuals in the political system. Here questions are raised about the interests of the key actors in the crisis. Crucial here is the issue of the power of the military. Accounts of events in the United States suggest that Kennedy came under enormous pressure from the 'hawks' within the military, who wanted to bomb Cuba, but resisted with the support of the more cautious State Department (see also Dallek, 2003, Chapter 16).

Critics of Allison's work (Bendor and Hammond, 1992) suggest that there are not three models here but two, and that the contrast is between the 'rational actor' model and models that stress the roles of institutions.

there the kind of political debate that would have opened the decision making to any direct democratic influence. President Kennedy, ever a calculating politician, would certainly have given consideration to the impact of his decisions upon his electoral chances, but that simply implies a worry about the trade-off between having been seen to be weak on the one hand and the damage entailed in war on the other.

In that last sense we can see the politics of peace and war throughout the second half of the twentieth century as still influenced by the events that preceded the Second World War, when Hitler expanded his power rapidly whilst the allies sought to 'appease' him (Gilbert and Gott, 2000). Probably (though poll data from that period is not very good), appeasement was the popular (democratic) option. Such thinking seems to have continued to influence decisions about military action to this day. The 2003 war against Iraq was pursued (certainly on the part of the United Kingdom; the evidence on the United States is more ambiguous) in the face of widespread opposition both amongst the general public and in the ranks of the ruling United Kingdom Labour Party. The arguments of the Labour leader, Tony Blair, about the need for war certainly included a view about the need to cease to appease a dictator. At the time of writing, at a distance of no more than a few months from the Iraq war, it is foolish to try to reach a definitive explanation of that event, but it is worthwhile mentioning here a few of the explanations on offer, each of which is suggestive of the peculiar nature of the policy process when it comes to war (see Kampfner, 2003 and Shawcross, 2003 for contrasting accounts). These explanations are summarised in Box 7.2. Clearly, whatever explanation is used seems to testify to the relatively narrow circle of actors who played key roles in decisions about war and peace. In Chapter 8, when we explore issues about policy agenda setting, we will examine the role of political manifestos in that process. One thing we will not find is statements of intention to go to war. On the other hand, we *will* find generalised comments on intentions to prevent war, and, to be fair, the 'do not appease' rationale implies a willingness to risk war, or conduct small wars, to avoid worse. But the interesting thing about this is the way that evolution into war then involves an incremental process (see pp. 147–50 for a further discussion of this) in which, rather than there being an overall analysis of the options, there tends to be a process of drift as successive measures fail to prevent (or even exacerbate) conflict. A

| Box 7.2 | Explanations of why the UK participated in the Iraq War in 2003 |

The justification most used to convince those opposed to the war was that Iraq had 'weapons of mass destruction' nearly ready for use. At the time of writing, the evidence for this proposition has largely dissipated. It is then alternatively being seen as a justification used by those already committed to war, raising a whole range of issues about how questionable information derived from spying activities was packaged for the public.

A second kind of explanation for the UK role in the Iraq conflict is that Blair and some of his key supporters regarded it as essential to follow the American lead on international affairs. Here we have echoes of that version of globalist theory that sees American world dominance as a key factor in national decision making.

The third kind of explanation goes beyond the overt political positions in both the UK and the US to suggest the continuing importance of what an American President, Eisenhower (interestingly, an old soldier and on the Right of the political spectrum), many years ago called the 'military–industrial complex', an unrepresentative network that stands to benefit from military actions. There are here some key questions about the interests of the oil industry.

A fourth kind of explanation, much favoured by journalists, simply focuses on the personal psychology and choices of the key actors and on the relationships between them.

mid-twentieth-century war that provides a powerful example of this is the Vietnam War (see Box 7.3).

Box 7.3	The escalation of the Vietnam War – an incremental process

After France abandoned its Vietnamese colony in the late 1950s, the United States became involved in attempting to prevent Communist dominance of the whole country. It moved incrementally from a position of simply providing military advice to the regime ruling the south of the country to providing supporting troops. Then it gradually increased the number of troops in the country to the point where it was to all intents and purposes a war between America and North Vietnam, despite the fact that America never formally declared war. Eventually, the United States withdrew and allowed the North to take over the whole country. Much political recrimination followed, but it is very difficult to point to crucial decisions that precipitated action, as opposed to a process of drift and particular leaders who took significant decisions that escalated the conflict.

Overall, then, it may be argued that the making of war is a very peculiar policy process, both in terms of separating out the influences upon it and in terms of the stages it goes through.

Trying to control the economy

The comments in the last section about the way in which international relations are given little attention in the policy process literature also applies to some extent to issues about the management of the economy (though an important exception to this is Hall, 1986). Much analysis of alternative approaches to this issue comes, of course, from economists rather than political scientists, and the fusion between the disciplines tends to come in the form of a 'political economy' literature that is particularly interested in macrotrends in the political system and in the analysis of globalism. But in the modern world the processes involved in efforts to manage the economy are of fundamental importance, both because of the importance of the issue and because of the significance of this activity for other policy processes.

The evolution of stances on how to control the economy is an important feature of modern political history. The nineteenth-century ideal of minimal government in the United States and the United Kingdom rested upon the idea of *laissez-faire*. The role of government in this field was simply to ensure that nothing interfered with the working of the market. Government expenditure in this context should be kept under control by the 'balanced budget', trying to make income and expenditure balance and minimising government borrowing. The threat to laissez-faire that was most evident to politicians at this time came from the emergent trade unions, and the legislative response to this was generally repressive. At the end of the nineteenth century, as political participation increased, the maintenance of the status quo began also to suggest (a) a slightly more conciliatory attitude towards trade unions and (b) a recognition that the other side of industry might act in ways that damaged the market. It was for the latter reason that American legislators, in particular, developed anti-trust legislation to try to limit monopolistic tendencies in industry.

The laissez-faire view of public economic policy was not shared by many of the nations that formed and/or industrialised later than the United Kingdom. The origins of a more corporatist view of the role of government (see pp. 63–7) in various continental European nations stemmed from the recognition that government might play a more active role in the stimulation of economic development, in partnership with business (and perhaps labour).

The events that did most to challenge the laissez-faire view of the role of government were the two world wars. These forced governments into an active role in the control of the economy, into roles (which they expected to be temporary) as key managers of enterprises themselves and into the accumulation of high levels of debt. The Second World War had a particularly fundamental impact on the relationship between government and the economy. But even before it started, a search had begun for new ways in which governments might regulate economic activities. After the war a system was developed to try to stabilise relationships between national currencies. But in addition, nations began to develop new ways of managing their internal economics. In the long run the relationship between these two issues was to become critical.

Boxes 7.4 and 7.5 (see pp. 120 and 121) provide an abbreviated account of economic management in the United Kingdom between 1945 and the present day, but it should be noted that other countries developed similar measures and faced similar problems with them.

The discussion of UK economic policy in Boxes 7.4 and 7.5, whilst superficial in terms of the complexity of the issues, may seem to go a long way away from the central concerns of this book. It has been inserted to give some idea of the extent to which this crucial area of public policy involves largely centralised decision making, in which very specialised interest groups may be consulted (particularly from both sides of industry). What is involved is a variety of complex devices, under expert control and (in the case of the delegation of powers to central banks) partly outside direct political control. The participants will include key figures from other countries and from international organisations (the European Union, the International Monetary Fund, etc.). Against the background of a policy process literature that emphasises processes, and sometimes stages, we have here an activity that may be compared to driving a vehicle, in which a succession of specific (and often quick) adjustments have to be made by key central actors. As already stressed, these decisions may be very important to other aspects of the policy process. Arguments about the right way to take

| Box 7.4 | UK economic management, 1945–79 |

Economic management techniques (often called Keynesian) were developed in the 20 years after the Second World War, involving manipulation of levels of government expenditure and taxation to try to retain full employment without inflation. This generated a cyclical pattern of economic (and government expenditure) growth, regularly punctuated by curbs to prevent rapid inflation. In the 1960s, despite an increasing commitment to economic planning, the cyclical pattern worsened. Inflation increased, balance of payments crises forced strong restraints to be applied to public expenditure and private incomes on a number of occasions, and, at the depressed point of the cycle, quite marked increases in unemployment occurred. In the mid-1970s, the UK faced a more severe crisis, in which very high inflation, a balance of payments problem and continuing high unemployment occurred all at the same time. Measures to cope with the first two by traditional means worsened the third (Dell, 1991).

Different schools of economists preached different solutions to these problems. On the Right, the 'monetarist' school of thought became increasingly influential, arguing that governments must control the money supply and let economic forces bring the system under control (Friedman, 1962, 1977). This viewpoint had some influence over policies in the 1970s, but politicians were reluctant to let bankruptcies and redundancies occur on a sufficient scale to test the monetarist hypothesis properly. More influential, and more in conformity with Keynesian orthodoxy, were those economists who argued that income restraint was necessary to bring unemployment and inflation into balance, and to prevent the UK's balance of payments becoming unmanageable as rising wages led us to import goods we could ill afford, while making it more difficult to sell things. Incomes policies were seen as crucial to solving these problems, yet over and over again governments found that political pressures made these very difficult to sustain for any length of time. The whole picture was, however, complicated by changes in the pattern of trade in the world and, particularly, by rises in prices of primary commodities, especially oil.

them have lain at the centre of disputes between political ideologies, which may be seen as macro elements in the overall policy process.

Providing income maintenance

Turning to income maintenance, or what is often called social security or social protection policy, we come right into one of the mainstream government domestic issues and one to which a great deal of the policy process literature is seen to be applicable. Income maintenance dominates the

| Box 7.5 | UK economic management, 1979–2003 |

After 1979, the 'monetarist' theory mentioned in Box 7.4 was more boldly put into practice by the new Conservative government. It treated the money supply, and particularly the public sector borrowing rate, as the key phenomena to keep under control. It was prepared to let unemployment rise rapidly in the war against inflation. It abandoned incomes policy in the private sector, seeking only to keep pay increases to public employees tightly under control. Initially, it found the removal of pay controls and its own taxation adjustments produced severely inflationary effects. It was subsequently successful in bringing inflation under control, but achieved that at the expense of a rapid increase in unemployment.

Later in the 1980s, the government abandoned any rigorous attempt to keep the money supply under control, concentrating attention instead on the foreign exchange value of the pound (Stephens, 1996). At this stage the European Union was moving towards the idea of a common currency. This measure would obviously eliminate currency fluctuations between its member countries. The UK, while cautious about the idea of a common currency, saw the merit of at least using controls to shadow European currency movements. That effort then failed in the UK, when currency speculation forced a dramatic currency revaluation. Meanwhile, the arrival of the Euro imposed this sort of discipline on its members. The governments of those still outside, like the UK, continue to agonise about the case for going in.

An interesting feature of Labour's stance on the control of the economy since 1997 has been to give control over interest rates to a committee (appointed by the government) under the leadership of the nationalised Bank of England. That committee is charged to use interest rates to control inflation, an echo of monetarism but without the rigid and rather artificial element of control over the money supply. This is not a uniquely British idea – similar controls are exercised by central bankers in the United States and, most importantly for the UK, within the Euro zone by a European central bank. This measure leaves the government having to make decisions about public expenditure and about measures to prevent unemployment with a key economic regulator out of its hands. Active policies on either of these fronts may have an impact upon inflation, in which case the raising of interest rates could have a contrary effect inasmuch as private and/or public borrowing will be affected (Keegan, 2003).

public policy spending agendas of many states. But it is interesting to see how, when we look at all that is embraced under this rubric, we find a mixture of types of policy. Not surprisingly, there are very lively political controversies about the forms income maintenance policies should take.

Income maintenance policy emerged as a major issue on the public policy agenda at the beginning of the twentieth century. Before that there were limited efforts to relieve poverty, characterised by strict tests of need and high levels of local discretion. The new income maintenance agenda arose as societies urbanised, industrialised and democratised. The idea that income inadequacies should be addressed by public policy arose both from the recognition of demands of new members of the electorate and from an awareness of the threat to public order from an increasingly organised mass population. Mass mobilisation for war increased attention to this issue. Since that time the issues on the agenda have been very much a combination of a concern for income maintenance in general with more specific issues about the relief of poverty. It is interesting to note how concerns about the difficulties that voluntary or market-based efforts encountered in dealing with the income maintenance needs of the broad mass of workers played a big part in the evolution of the policy agenda, alongside concerns about poverty. It is not without significance that in many countries pensions for soldiers and for government employees were established well before any other regularised income maintenance provisions. Such policies – and particularly pensions – imply very long-term commitments. Hence there are four crucial issues about this part of the policy agenda:

1. Income maintenance does not necessarily imply redistribution: it is to a large extent ultimately redistributively neutral inasmuch as what is involved is a form of forced savings for predicted contingencies (particularly old age).

2. Inasmuch as income maintenance policies offer benefits for the well-off as well as the poor, they may have substantial and strong electoral and pressure group support coalitions.

3. Inasmuch as income maintenance policies offer strongly supported rights to future benefits, their construction involves a distinct, staged process from the placing of issues on the policy agenda, through the enactment of quite complex policies with elaborate rules about entitlements, to an implementation process in which officials are expected to honour claims based upon statutory rights.

4. Income maintenance structures (particularly pensions) imply long-run commitments and expectations. Hence this policy area is particularly one where pathways determined by past policies restrict opportunities for policy change.

Income maintenance benefits may be designed simply to relieve poverty, whatever its causes, but more typically income maintenance systems recognise a number of contingencies to which a response is provided, the main ones being: old age, sickness and disability, unemployment, or loss of a prime family breadwinner.

Income maintenance policy can take any of the following forms (indeed, a combination of these forms characterises most systems):

■ Contributory benefits

■ Non-contributory but contingent benefits

■ Selective, means-tested benefits

- Tax reliefs and tax credits
- Employer benefits mandated or regulated by the government.

We have already noted that income maintenance policies are not necessarily redistributive. This is particularly the case where contributory public or private pension schemes are in use. An extreme form of the non-distributive approach is offered by 'provident schemes' pioneered in Singapore, which simply involved state-enforced savings accounts.

A regulative approach to policy is directly visible where governments impose obligations upon private companies to provide schemes or expect private social security systems to abide by rules designed to protect their funds. But regulation is also in evidence in this policy area inasmuch as schemes impose obligations on claimants – to seek work or to undertake efforts to improve their health, for example.

Those last two examples highlight the fact that there are key policy issues that lie on the boundaries of income maintenance policy and other areas of public policy. Box 7.6 highlights the income maintenance policy/ employment policy interface and Box 7.7 sets out how income maintenance and health policy interact.

Box 7.6	The interface between income maintenance policy and employment policy

Cash benefits for unemployed people largely superseded relief policies that expected such people to do compulsory work for their maintenance. But that alternative has not altogether died out, indeed it has made something of a comeback in recent years. Beyond that, however, lie wider issues about responses to unemployment – as a problem to be addressed by measures to stimulate the economy, as an indicator of a need for more education and training, and so on.

The distinction between states in which contributory benefits (social insurance) dominate income maintenance rather than selective means-tested ones, together with one concerning the extent to which policies redistribute income, dominates the regime model described in Chapter 6 (see pp. 94–6). As was noted there, the regime model is seen to offer a route towards the interpretation of differences in access to the policy process. It also contributes to the explanation of why systems vary in their responses to cutbacks, and still diverge despite global influences which might have been expected to enhance homogeneity.

The fact that income maintenance policy is often costly for governments means policy change issues return to the agenda with great regularity. Pension provisions were developed when life expectancies were very much less than they are today. Fluctuations in unemployment pose unanticipated burdens from time to time. Changing patterns of family behaviours have

Box 7.7	The interface between income maintenance and health policies

Many health care systems are funded by social insurance policies that sit alongside income maintenance benefits. In the absence of public health provision, inability to pay for health care can be seen as equally a health provision problem or a problem arising from an income deficiency. While most modern systems do not address this issue in the latter way, a lot of other issues at the margins of the two systems raise hybrid policy problems. Noteworthy here is the issue of social care in old age, which is treated in various ways in different societies, involving varying mixtures of the following:

■ treating it as a family issue;

■ regarding it as an individual need problem to be covered through the purchase of services;

■ seeing it as evidence of a general income deficiency issue in old age;

■ seeing it as a health care problem;

■ seeing it as a problem to be tackled through forms of social insurance;

■ treating it as an issue to be remedied by targeted cash benefits to facilitate the purchase of care.

made the occurrence of single-parent families much more likely in some societies. In most countries current benefits are funded from current government income. Even most social insurance systems do not involve the accumulation of contributions in a fund but a 'pay as you go' approach, using current contributions. There are complicated reasons why this policy option was selected in the first place, which it would need a large digression to explore here. The point is that rising entitlements put pressure on income maintenance schemes, placing issues about the cutting of benefits very high on modern public policy agendas. This issue will be explored further in the next chapter, with particular reference to pensions.

This section has shown that income maintenance policy in many respects dominates the public policy scene. While many of the ideas used in the analysis of public policy can easily be applied to income maintenance policy, income maintenance policies are nevertheless very diverse.

Providing education

Education has been chosen as the next area of policy to consider. It is one where public provision has dominated for a long while. It is also a policy area in which the actual characteristics of policy are very likely to be considerably influenced at the point of delivery. In other words, in many respects education policy is determined by what teachers actually do. Education policy has quite a lot in common with health policy in this respect, and to a lesser extent with other services such as social care.

There are several ways in which the government may determine or influence education:

- as a direct provider;
- as a funder of services provided by other autonomous or partly autonomous organisations (local governments, school boards, schools, voluntary organisations, private organisations);
- as a regulator of privately provided services.

It is also important to recognise that there is a range of policy issues in a field like education, some of which may be given extensive attention in public policy whilst others are neglected or ignored. The following list highlights some key issues, but is surely not comprehensive:

- the funding of education
- the structuring of the system
- arrangements for control over the various parts of the system
- the content of the curriculum
- qualifications of teachers
- teaching quality
- the payment of teachers
- subsidies for students.

Comments here are based upon developments in the United Kingdom. Between the end of the Second World War and the early 1990s the government in the UK was the main funder of state schools and exercised a loose regulatory supervision of private schools. Education was free in the state schools. Central government delegated many of the issues about the structure of the education system to local government, but increasingly intervened towards the end of the period to try to influence the organisation of secondary education. It paid remarkably little attention to the content of the curriculum. It regulated the qualifications of teachers and their pay but operated a relatively light inspection system to scrutinise the quality of their work.

Over the same period, the level of government intervention in the higher education system was even lighter. Central government funded almost the whole system, providing free places for UK students and means-tested maintenance grants towards their living costs. The universities were self-governing institutions; many other colleges were run by local government. The content of higher education was totally in the hands of the institutions, except in a few special cases where education was providing a licence to practise a publicly supported profession like medicine or teaching (though in these cases control was largely in the hands of the professions themselves). There were no required qualifications for teachers in higher education and there was no inspection system.

Between these two sectors there is a further education sector; however, in order to keep the discussion simple, no observations are included on this.

Since the 1990s both sectors have experienced dramatic change driven by a strong political interest in education, with strong parental pressure for raising standards and opportunities, and a political ideology, shared by Right and Left, that education must serve the economy (see Tomlinson, 2001). Change in the system has consisted of a great deal of centralisation but also some decentralisation. Centralisation has involved a substantive increase in government control over the school curriculum, and the development of a testing system and a strong inspection system to go with it. In the higher education sector central government has exercised strong control over the way the system has expanded, has developed various inspection devices and has used its control over funding to steer the system. The school system has experienced decentralisation inasmuch as local authority control has been weakened, and there has been a sort of 'hollowing out process' (see Box 11.4 on p. 225) in which power has been delegated down to the schools and parents have been given more scope to choose schools for their children and to participate in the government of schools. In both sectors institutions have been given greater freedom to determine what individual teachers are paid.

While the state system has remained intact, various forms of what may be called 'quasi-marketisation' have occurred. In the school sector, funding depends on pupil numbers. Inasmuch as this interacts with parental choice (and how much the latter really exists depends upon geography), it has an impact upon whether schools succeed or fail. The publication of test results for individual schools can then further influence this process. In the higher education sector, similarly, funds follow students, and given the geographical mobility of students this can have a significant effect. A system which rations research money according to ratings of research performance, coupled with competition for other sources of funding, is contributing to the enhancement of the hierarchy within higher education institutions, with Oxbridge and some London colleges at the top and institutions recently promoted to university status at the bottom.

The overall, and necessarily simplified, objective of this brief account is to highlight the complexity of the politics of education policy. Governments come under a great deal of pressure on education policy and are engaged in much often ideologically driven change. There is a strong education policy community which is eager to influence policy, yet in the last few years this community has lost many battles against the government.

However, the complexity of the system and the subtlety of the teaching task mean that what actually happens cannot be 'read off' simply from the policy objectives that are set out by the key actors in the system. Thus Bowe and his colleagues, in their *Reforming Education and Changing Schools* (1992), have explored the complex way in which a strong, politically driven central initiative is translated into action. They describe the expression of policy as the production of a set of 'texts'. They go on to say:

texts are generalized, written in relation to idealizations of the 'real world', and can never be exhaustive, they cannot cover all eventualities. The texts can often be contradictory ..., they use key terms differently, and they are reactive as well as expository (that is to say, the representation of policy changes in the light of events and circumstances and feedback from arenas of practice). Policy is not done and finished at the legislative moment, it evolves in and through the texts that represent it, texts have to be read in relation to the time and the particular site of their production. They also have to be read with and against one another – intertextuality is important. Second, the texts themselves are the outcome of struggle and compromise. The control of the representation of policy is problematic. (Bowe, Ball and Gold, 1992, p. 21)

As noted above, for clarity of exposition the remarks above have been confined to the UK system, but similar developments can be seen elsewhere. At the same time there are, of course, many variations in the way in which the centralisation/localisation dynamic has been handled and in the forms that marketisation takes.

Trying to prevent pollution

Pollution policy is explored here not simply because it is a very good example of a policy area where public policy is primarily regulatory but also because pollution is an issue that literally spills over national boundaries, making it a salient concern for modern *governance* (see pp. 11–12).

Pollution comes about because of the abandonment of matter as waste and the discharge of effluents into water or air. Pollution problems are endemic in modern societies, a consequence of very many of the activities that create and sustain the levels of material prosperity enjoyed by advanced industrial societies. They need to be seen in the context of population growth, and the resultant pressure upon space and resources. They also need to be seen in relation to very high and complex levels of consumption.

In some respects pollution control policy may be regarded, particularly by those nations still struggling to raise material standards, as a luxury that is only available to those with high standards of living. If, further, the efforts of pollution policy are seen as directed towards the maintenance of an 'unspoilt' natural environment, this will particularly heighten the contrast between 'north' and 'south' (using those compass point expressions as shorthand for global conflicts of interest between developed and less developed nations). In the same way, where the problem is seen to be population growth, it will be pointed out by the nations of the 'south' that the amount of pollution generated per person is very much higher in rich countries than in poor ones. In still industrialising countries, these are bases for understandable hostility to some of the efforts to curb pollution that come from the nations whose earlier activities raised global levels of pollution to high levels in the first place.

This conflict also highlights the point that, whilst much of the attack upon environmental pollution involves a search for ways to eliminate the pollutants that are produced or to clean up after polluting activities, there is an alternative that is simpler – in the scientific if not in the political sense. This is to alter the way in which production or consumption occurs. Production techniques could be adopted that are slower and more extravagant in their use of human resources but produce fewer waste products (in particular, fewer waste products from energy use). Consumption patterns may involve simpler products, less well-packaged products, slower methods of travel and so on. There may even be a need to question whether certain forms of consumption are really necessary. These are the sort of considerations that enter into efforts to define 'sustainable growth' (see Weale, 1992 and Cahill, 2002 for good discussions of these issues).

Another factor in the increased interest in pollution control policies is the awareness that pollution cannot be a private matter – for nations any more than for individuals. The global economic interactions that sustain the prosperity of many nations, together with tourism, contribute to the recognition that pollution is an international issue. Ecological disasters with transnational implications – like the nuclear power station explosion at Chernobyl in 1986 – reinforce this awareness.

Pollution control policy development owes a great deal to scientific advances that have enabled people to perceive more clearly the damage that is being caused, and to understand how it is caused. This has also, through the contribution it makes to the understanding of long-range and long-term effects, assisted the process by which pollution has been put on the global political agenda (see Kormondy, 1989 and Brenton, 1994 for a discussion of the increasing international activity, starting largely from the Unesco conference on the biosphere of 1968 and the United Nations Stockholm conference of 1972 and carried forward by the Rio conference of 1992).

The importance of science also means that expertise is important for the identification of pollution problems. This contributes to complicated issues about the role of self-interest in relation to pollution control. In some cases democratic political participation has been seen to work against effective pollution control where actions against environmental hazards are seen as direct threats to jobs (Crenson, 1971; Blowers, 1984). In these cases it is not merely that there is the sort of insidious trade-off problem identified above, it is also the case that the trade-off is often perceived to be between a quite direct material threat and an uncertain health hazard. There are several factors which make the latter hard to perceive and interpret (these are outlined in Box 7.8).

Expertise is not only involved in identifying the presence of pollutants and in determining their effects, it is also involved in tracing pathways, interactions and long-term effects. Two good examples of this which have contributed to the evolution of the environmental policy agenda concern

| Box 7.8 | Issues concerning the detection and interpretation of pollution problems |

Some pollution problems are readily apparent to everyone – they can be smelt or seen or heard or even felt. But many pollution phenomena, including many of the most dangerous, are not open to straightforward sensory perception. This is the case with nuclear radiation hazards. It is also the case with many chemicals suspended in water or air, in particular metals like lead and asbestos. In these cases, measurements are needed to inform people that a pollution hazard is present. Methods may not be available to do this; but if they are, they are likely to involve the use of scientific techniques not usually available to the general public. Moreover, when such measurements are carried out, the evidence from them may not be made available to the public. The emitters are likely to want to conceal that evidence, and officials and governments may collude with this concealment.

Once measurements are taken, moreover, there may still be issues about the risks related to any particular form of pollution. Chemical suspensions in air and water are always present, and dangers exist when they are excessively concentrated. But what is an excessive concentration – how much over how long a period? The poisoning processes which occur from pollution are not generally dramatic. They occur over a long time span. The evidence that poisoning is occurring is accumulated gradually, and in circumstances in which there are reasons to argue that the resultant diseases have other causes. In the case of nuclear radiation, for example, there has been a long-standing controversy about whether a slightly raised incidence of comparatively rare diseases in particular places or amongst particular workforces is attributable to radiation exposure. The difficult policy issue that this raises concerns the extent to which a 'precautionary' approach is justified that curbs pollution just in case of long-run dangers or dangers that might emerge later (Barker and Peters, 1993).

acid rain and the ozone layer. Box 7.9 (overleaf) explores some key issues about the former. The issues about the impact of emissions on the ozone layer are even more complex. Here the potential problems are global and the adverse effects will take a long while to manifest themselves. There is still a great deal of controversy about them.

Another important issue about interaction, which is illustrated by the acid rain issue, concerns the relationships between the different strategies for disposing of pollutants. There are choices about whether to disperse pollutants into the air, into water (rivers or the sea), or to bury them in the ground. Yet chemicals in the air get carried into lakes and rivers, chemicals in rivers get deposited on the land, and chemicals from landfill sites leach out into water courses. Dispersal into air or water or land, which, in the past, has been seen to be unproblematical because of the capacity of these media to absorb (and ultimately dilute) pollutants, becomes less and less satisfactory over time. Now, not only is it recognised that many rivers are carrying

Box 7.9	Acid rain as a cross-national pollution issue

Initial concerns about emissions from combustion processes focused upon their impact on their immediate environment (Ashby and Anderson, 1981). Meteorological observations were necessary to identify the relationship between emissions from combustion processes and the subsequent precipitation of chemicals in rain at places separated often by considerable geographical distances. The relationship between British emissions on the one hand and tree loss and lake acidification in Scandinavia on the other, for example, had to be carefully established. Scientific complexity and national self-interest combined to make the debate about acid rain a difficult and long-drawn-out affair (Whetstone and Rosencranz, 1983).

more pollutants than they can absorb, but worries are also emerging about strategies which involve the disposing of pollutants at sea. Some seas in particular are vulnerable as 'sinks', where matter dispersed into them and into their feeder rivers is becoming concentrated (the Mediterranean and the Baltic, for example: see Kinnersley, 1994).

These interaction effects make the determination of pollution control policies difficult. First, they make it necessary for policy strategies to be holistic – concerns about reducing air pollution, keeping rivers clear or controlling landfill activities need to be integrated, despite the fact that very different agencies, interest groups and kinds of expertise are likely to be involved. Second, it is difficult to put effective geographical boundaries around policies and regulatory agencies. Pollutants travel from one administrative area to another; in many cases, indeed, they travel from one nation state to another. Seas like the Mediterranean obviously have many nation states around them. Air basins are even more complex, and an issue like ozone-layer depletion is a worldwide one.

All of this discussion makes it clear that pollution control policy involves some very complex collective action problems. Individuals with resources may be able to reduce the impact of pollution upon themselves, but such strategies may be limited and may fall foul of unexpected effects. Individuals can buy bottled water, but they may find it more difficult to get access to an unpolluted lake or beach. Hence part of the case for seeing pollution control as a collective action problem lies in the difficulty individuals have in adopting strategies which protect themselves satisfactorily. Perhaps what helps to put environmental policy on the modern political agenda is the increased difficulty elites have in escaping from pollution.

However, perhaps an even more important reason why pollution control policy is seen as a collective concern lies in the fact explored on p. 54 that the pursuit of economic self-interest generates pollution but rarely generates motives to do anything about it. Production processes generate unwanted by-products. If those by-products can be pumped out into rivers and seas, blown into the air or, perhaps less commonly, dumped on waste land they will be disposed of at minimal cost to the enterprise. The owners of the enterprise may suffer no ill effects from these actions, or if they do worsen the quality of their own environments, the effects of their own actions upon themselves may be marginal and shared with the rest of the 'community' they have polluted. The word 'community' is put in inverted commas here: it is used very loosely, as it should be evident from the earlier discussion that this could be a very large group indeed. The overall point is that issues of this kind seldom come in a simple form. This is illustrated in Box 7.10 using the example of the disposal of waste products into a river. (It could be added to this example that some rivers cross national boundaries – a point that highlights the even greater complexity involved when emissions are into the sea or the air: see Bennett, 1992, Chapters 3 and 4 for some good case study examples).

Box 7.10	Complexity in the case of river pollution

If a single enterprise pours waste products into a river, that river may well be able to absorb those products, diluting them and transforming them into less harmful forms with no danger to the wildlife of the river or to anyone seeking to take water from the river. Modern reality is often very different. There will be many potential polluters along the banks of this hypothetical river (and before readers start to think that the author only sees industry as a polluter, it should be said that human and animal waste, agricultural chemicals and pesticides are likely to be amongst the sources of damage to the river quality). All waste products have to go somewhere, hence the real political issue is not about how to stop emissions, it is about how to control and/or limit them in such a way that, in the above example, for instance, (a) the river quality is maintained to an acceptable standard, and (b) the people who wish to discard by-products into the river feel that they have been fairly treated relative to others.

At the national level, the most straightforward of the policy options involves direct state action to deal with the problem or clear it up afterwards. In the case of solid and liquid waste disposal there may exist government waste disposal services. These may simply be funded out of local or national taxation, like services to remove materials from homes and business premises. There may be charges if they have to deal with large or exceptional loads. In the case of liquid waste, the common device in urban societies is simply a drainage system. Again, arrangements have to be made to deal with the exceptional. There will be problems for sewage treatment and disposal systems both if there are enterprises putting exceptional pressure upon the system or if the material being discharged is toxic and requires special treatment. Government may regulate such discharges and impose charges. Solid and liquid waste disposal responsibilities may be subcontracted from government organisations to private firms.

Much environmental legislation gives central or local government regulatory powers. Two key distinctions concern the extent to which the powers are comprehensive ones determining the permissibility of the activity as a whole or specific ones relating to explicit activities (particularly emissions), and the extent to which powers relate solely to the start of an activity or impose continuous surveillance.

Implicit to this whole discussion are two key considerations for the policy process:

1. Pollution control is about treating collective interest as overriding individual interests.

2. Individual interests are likely to be strongly represented in the policy debate. Moreover, we are not talking here simply about some conflict between a small number of profit takers and a large public, since issues about threats to employment may be involved.

These considerations have a strong impact not merely upon the up-front politics of agenda setting but also on the way in which policy is formulated and implemented, since minimising conflict tends to involve a search for ways to tailor controls to individual situations. In pollution control policy in the UK, therefore, much attention has been given to the search for the 'best practical means' of dealing with problems while minimising their impact upon employment (Ashby and Anderson, 1981; Hill, 1983). Generalising about this issue, Hanf has written about pollution control policy as involving 'co-production' in which policy implementation is negotiated between officials and polluters (Hanf, 1993). This is a topic to which we will return in Chapter 12 (see pp. 254–6).

Overall, we may say that whilst the control of pollution offers a good example of regulatory policy, it entails some complex issues that affect how matters get on the agenda, complicated by the extent to which pollution control is today not simply a nation-state issue. Any one country has a strong interest in how other countries deal with the problem, not merely because of externalities but also because controls have an impact upon economic competitiveness.

Reorganising local government

In this discussion of different kinds of policy it is important not to disregard policy changes that shape institutional systems. Such changes may be massive – the establishment of devolved forms of government, for example – or they may be quite slight, such as the reframing of some quite specific policy delivery arrangements (like the delegation of elements of school management from local authorities to individual schools, as discussed in the section on education policy). Local government reorganisation has been chosen to illustrate this point though it may vary enormously in its impact.

In dealing with this example there is a danger of getting into complexities that are inappropriate here. In order to avoid that, this discussion will be rather shorter than has been the case with the other policy area examples.

Over the past 40 years, the United Kingdom has seen a rather frenetic succession of changes to the institutions of local government. In some societies the constraints upon organisational reform are much greater, particularly where arrangements for local government are embedded in the constitution. In the case of the United Kingdom there has been a strong tendency to see organisational reform as the key to securing more efficient policy delivery, delivering more to the public but at a lower cost. Box 7.11 provides a list of the kinds of changes that have been imposed on the English local government system *by central government* since 1970 (there have been related changes in the rest of the UK, but not necessarily at the same time).

Box 7.11	Main changes to English local government (with dates of the key legislation in brackets – not necessarily put into operation in that year)

- Alterations to the territorial areas covered (1972, 1985, 1992, 1998)
- Alterations to the functions performed (1972, 1988)
- Alterations to the way political representation is organised (2000)
- Alterations to internal management (1970, 1989)
- Alterations to the way taxes are raised (1988, 1992)
- Alterations to the formulae governing central subventions (1980, 1982, 1984, 1992)
- Alterations to the way activities are supervised or inspected (1970, 1999).

Changes of this kind, particularly when put together, can make – and, in the case of the UK, certainly have made – a great difference to (a) how local services are controlled, and (b) who benefits from local services. The policy processes that introduce change are thus often contested in terms of concerns about how local democracy should work and about the extent to which they do enhance efficiency, but also in terms of their distributive consequences. On the other hand, arguments about organisational arrangements are often obscure, and are recognised as important only by or to the key political and administrative players. The politics of organisational change lacks the popular appeal of political debates in which clear gainers and losers can be identified.

The suggestion here, therefore, is that there is an important category of policy processes, concerned with constituent policy, that may tend to be handled rather differently in the policy process than policy whose public impact is more direct (despite the fact that it does ultimately have an impact on 'who gets what'). This sort of policy has been called meta-policy (Dror, 1986, p. 102; see also Hupe, 1990).

Revisiting the stages issues

The next two sections will revisit the two issues set out at the beginning of this chapter, about stages in the policy process and about policy types, relating them to the six policy areas that have been discussed above.

As far as the stages approach to policy analysis is concerned, there are some significant contrasts to be made. The two extremes are perhaps economic policy and income maintenance policy. In the case of economic policy, in the use of the key instruments of influence in the modern world – the exchange rate and the rate of interest – there really is no staged process at all. Specific actions or specific decisions are often made and implemented simultaneously. While we should not, of course, assume that they will have the desired effect, there is really no more to the policy process *per se*. There will of course be some sort of agenda-setting process. Inasmuch as this may be expected to involve a public debate, political leaders may be reluctant to have one, since a debate about impending economic measures generates anticipatory actions by those likely to be affected.

As far as the device of leaving interest rate setting to a partly autonomous committee is concerned, it may be argued that such a body is merely an implementing agency working within strict parameters defined by 'policy'. But that is really playing with words, thereby illustrating the problematical nature of the policy formulation/implementation distinction. The decisions in question may have been quite closely pre-programmed, but their impact can be such that it seems inappropriate to describe them as merely implementation.

On the other hand, in the case of income maintenance policy there is likely to be not merely a prolonged, but almost certainly a public, agenda-setting process. During its later stages that agenda setting will generally take the form of the presentation of proposals to a legislature, which will then debate and perhaps amend them. Once that stage is completed (or nearing completion, as these parts of the process will overlap), work will be done to translate legislation into a rule structure that will enable individual entitlements to be identified. Once that is done the legislation will be brought into action in a form in which very explicit instructions will be given to implementers. Inasmuch as the legislation gives individuals rights, the concerns in the implementation process will be about managerial control and about ways in which people may ensure they secure those rights. Of course, discretions may be enshrined within the rules, but these will tend to be tightly structured by the legislation. Feedbacks will occur, but primarily in the interaction between legislation and more detailed formulation. Here simultaneous work on both will tend to save governments the embarrassment of having to introduce amending legislation soon after the initial legislation. Furthermore, as is the case in the UK, with what is known as the use of 'delegated legislation', flexibility for amendments based upon later experience will be built into the primary legislation. Feedbacks can often be seen as a clearly structured part of a structured process.

The only exceptions to these propositions about income maintenance policy will be some forms of means-tested benefits (with characteristics not dissimilar to the 'poor laws' of earlier ages), where high levels of policy choice have been delegated downwards (Eardley et al., 1996). On the other hand, in the cases of education policy and pollution control policy the delegation of policy choice is likely to be much more evident. Furthermore, in these two areas notions that are crucial for the characteristics of the policy are likely to be left to be settled at later stages. The UK National Curriculum for schools offers a good illustration. Beyond the specification of subjects to be studied, most of the detail of what should go into a specific curriculum has been left to officials within the education system, and even then the resulting documents leave many areas of choice for teachers. Reference was made to Bowe at al.'s (1992) notion of 'texts', in this case negotiated and debated up and down. Occasionally, politicians or the media have raised certain issues for national debate – such as the extent to which the history that is taught should be national history – but on the whole the detail is settled 'lower down' the system.

The equivalent to this in pollution control policy is the range of issues discussed above about different options for use of the planning system, about co-production and doctrines like 'best practical means'. These too need to be seen as matters not just for any particular level in a staged system but as the subject of interactions between the systems. A good approach to the exploration of these interactions involves seeing one level as engaged in 'mandating' others (May, 1993; and see the discussion in Chapter 11, pp. 225–6). An interesting characteristic of pollution control is the extent to which there is expectation of a tightening of control over time, using targets to be reached incrementally. Such targets even appear in international agreements. Hence there is an interesting contrast between the macro-politics of target setting (often involving supra-national bodies) and the very specific (and more local) micro-politics of determining implementation arrangements. If a stages model is used in this field of policy then it is at best going to be one in which feedback is particularly important.

The case of local government reorganisation fits less well into this discussion. A great deal depends upon the nature of the reorganisation. Also very relevant is the structural context in which it occurs, the distinction here being between the UK system, in which incremental changes are frequent, and systems in which legal constraints make change a matter for fundamental legislation, even constitutional change. In the UK, whilst legislation will be important, local government is likely to contribute to the modifications of 'bills' while they are before Parliament. Moreover, the implementation of some legislation has been made, formally speaking, subject to local referenda and other forms of public consultation.

Turning now to the making of war, here there is clearly a prolonged process which can be traced over time. But does it make any sense at all to describe, for example, the Vietnam War as involving agenda setting, formulation and then implementation, let alone to follow any even more elaborate version of the stages model? What was described above in relation to all the examples given was indeed agenda-setting processes, in which public participation was unwelcome and political elites sought (not necessarily successfully) to keep strong control over events. An interesting (dare I say sinister?) feature of the relationship between agenda setting and policy formulation is the fact that nations do not declare war until they have prepared for it. The author recalls American military supply ships massing off the shores of the United Kingdom long before war was declared on Iraq. To what extent does preparing for war make war inevitable? The evidence on the Cuban missile crisis suggests there can be a negative answer to that question, but that was a very closely run thing.

Going to war is therefore, perhaps, a very strong example of implementation as policy making. A great deal of the detail is settled incrementally in action. What makes this implementation very different from most of the examples of implementation discussed in the texts on this subject is the very high involvement of the 'top' of the political and administrative systems in the process. Once a war is in progress, policy change processes, affected by local intelligence and by local action, are likely to continue. It is an interesting paradox about military action that, whilst there is a high stress upon top-down authority and discipline, much of this is actually designed to preprogramme highly discretionary actions in situations in which those at the front have to react to unpredictable situations. This aspect of limits to control over the policy process is explored in parts of Chapters 10 and 12.

There are clearly other policy issues where a 'crisis' (in reality or as defined by the government) that requires rapid executive action creates a policy process in which separating the stages is problematical. Taylor's (2003) study of the response to the outbreak of foot and mouth disease amongst animals in the UK in 2001 provides a good example of this. What was involved was action that the Prime Minister and other politicians initiated quickly to supplement or replace an existing policy framework. In this case an animal disease emerged, foot and mouth, for which there was already an apparently coherent policy on the statute book, but the problem was that the disease had not manifested itself for nearly 40 years and in that time the organisation of both agriculture and the regulatory system had changed dramatically. Policy therefore had to be made 'on the hoof', as Taylor puns in his article, in a context in which very activist politicians needed quick results when a general election was pending (see Box 7.12).

It was suggested in the introduction to this chapter that there is a pragmatic case for using a simple form of the stages model as an approach to the discussion of the policy process, if only to divide up complex subjects. But the arguments against letting a stages model dominate analysis are very strong. This discussion reinforces that argument. It is thus contended that an examination of actual policy examples throws up cases where analysis can very readily follow a simple stages model, cases where recognising that a modified version of it that is very sensitive to the complexity of feedback may be applicable, and cases where its use makes very little sense.

However, even where stages are least in evidence, it is a fairly fundamental characteristic of the policy process that decisions that have to be

Box 7.12	Ian Taylor's (2003) account of the handling of the 2001 foot and mouth disease outbreak in the UK

The last serious outbreak of foot and mouth disease occurred in 1967–8. A sequence of recommendations was adopted after that to involve – in the UK as in the EU – the rapid diagnosis, slaughter and disposal of all animals that might have been exposed to the disease. The problem in 2001 was that agricultural and marketing arrangements had changed significantly, with very much more movement of animals around the country, hence the potential rate of spread of the disease was much increased. After such a long, almost disease free, period, few experts had any familiarity with the disease. Furthermore, there had been substantial changes to the veterinary service at the disposal of the government, so that it was very difficult to get services into action quickly. Evidence that the disease was likely to be located in several different parts of the country and that very large numbers of animals might have been exposed to it (in all, once the picture became clear, about 2000 cases were confirmed and 4 million animals needed to be slaughtered) made it difficult to implement the standard policy. The government were seen by some as acting too slowly, by others of making unnecessarily draconian decisions about slaughter and about the movement of both people and animals. 'From a policy-making and implementation perspective, the notion of "policy on the hoof" is appropriate because that was the way in which policy proceeded during the crisis' (ibid., p. 544). This is illustrated by:

> The proposal to vaccinate and the decision to base culling on contiguous contact culling rather than contiguous premises, the decisions to reprieve Phoenix [a pet calf featured in newspaper stories] . . ., bury instead of burn carcasses, make use of retired veterinary surgeons after initially rejecting the proposal, use the army later rather than immediately and transfer major decision making to . . . [the Prime Minister's office]. (Ibid.)

taken at any point in time will be influenced by those that preceded them. There are two sayings which can be applied in this discussion: that 'dead battles, like dead generals, hold the military mind in their dead grip' (Tuchman, 1962, Chapter 2), and that 'practical men . . . are usually the slaves of some defunct economist' (Keynes, 1947, Chapter 24). But, more seriously, as institutional theory stresses (see Chapter 5), earlier decisions structure subsequent ones.

Policy types

Some policy analysts have sought to develop policy typologies. The most influential approach to this has been the typology developed by Lowi, who argues that 'policy may determine politics' (1972, p. 298) and goes on to specify four kinds of policy:

1. distributive policy: the distribution of new resources;
2. redistributive policy: changing the distribution of existing resources;
3. regulatory policy: regulating activities;
4. constituent policy: establishing or reorganising institutions.

Amongst the examples discussed here, neither the waging of war nor controlling the economy has any place in that typology. Education also fits very awkwardly into it. Providing education gives social advantages, and education policies may be (but are also often not) designed to redistribute advantages by enhancing social mobility. Education policy also involves a great deal of regulation of both public and private actors. In some respects regulation is one of the functions of education. Children are required to be sent to school where they have to be taught effectively by (normally) qualified persons. But its most obvious characteristic is as a state-provided or state-supported service.

Income maintenance seems prima facie to be an example of redistributive policy but may also involve regulatory policy. What is most important about it, however, is that much of it is not redistributive, inasmuch as social insurance is premised – to varying degrees – upon the idea of forced saving. Pollution control policy is obviously regulatory but has a variety of redistributive effects. The same is true of the example of constituent policy.

There is a logical problem with Lowi's concept of 'distributive policy'. The notion of policies being distributive without having any redistributive effects is problematical inasmuch as expenditure has to be funded and any advantages conferred on one person implicitly confer disadvantages on another. Ripley and Franklin (1982), who use the Lowi typology, seem to rest their version of the distributive/redistributive divide on the extent to which the losers can readily identify themselves. Significantly, Ripley and Franklin partly acknowledge the illogicality of this by indicating that they confine their redistributive concept to shifts of resources from advantaged to disadvantaged groups, whilst acknowledging that the reverse does apply. They justify this in terms of ideological perceptions in the United States (perhaps better put as the 'dominant ideology').

Of course, what Lowi was concerned with in his original formulation of the typology (that is, before he added constituent policy) was identifying the extent to which policy initiatives encounter resistance. But if that is to be the case, then all the policies discussed here create winners and losers, though the mechanisms by which gains and losses may occur are subtle. Clearly, it is a crucial point about the politics of policy that a great deal depends upon whether these people (and particularly losers) can identify themselves and are organised to do something about it. Wilson (1973), for example, has distinguished between 'concentrated' and 'dispersed' costs and benefits, and Hogwood (1987) suggests that policies vary in the extent to which their benefits can be distinguished. On this issue, however, it is not clear that a policy typology is much help.

We are left then, perhaps, simply with the notion that, whilst we cannot necessarily develop a typology based on these differences, policy differences matter for the way in which the policy process works.

Before we leave this point entirely it is appropriate to mention one theorist who addresses this issue, albeit in a much simpler way. Matland (see Figure 7.1) suggests two distinguishing features of policies: the extent to which they are ambiguous and the extent to which they provoke conflict. In doing this he is trying to theorise about implementation, but equally this distinction may be as much an underlying feature of a whole policy area as a specific feature of any policy as enacted.

Figure 7.1 Matland's analysis of the impact of conflict and ambiguity upon implementation

	Low conflict	High conflict
Low ambiguity	1	3
High ambiguity	2	4

Source: Adapted from Matland, 1995, p. 160, Table 4.1. By permission of Oxford University Press.

While the whole policy areas discussed in this chapter cannot, then, be neatly fitted into Matland's boxes, the high ambiguity of both education and pollution control policies in practice are evident. The extent to which policies provoke conflict hinges on the extent to which they involve creating very explicit and evident losers (as equal opportunities policy does in education or the anti-pollution measures do that threaten the economic viability of enterprises). Local government reorganisation tends to fall into the high ambiguity but low conflict category, though we have noted situations where this will not be the case. Economic intervention measures (notwithstanding that their actual economic effects will be disputed) are both relatively unambiguous and relatively unlikely to provoke conflict. War would seem to sit fairly clearly in the low ambiguity, high conflict camp, but for two crucial difficulties: that many contemporary international policing activities are very ambiguous because they may be taking nations on a path that leads to war (the Vietnam case has already been cited), and that within nations there is a strong tendency for a closing of ranks, with the effect that international conflicts may occur with a minimum of conflict within the nation.

There are quite a lot of conditional clauses in that last paragraph. Where you put policy activities on the two axes may depend upon some very complex questions. In general, while Matland, like Lowi before him, helps to sensitise us to issues about differences between policy processes, he does not progress this subject very much. Moreover, Matland's distinction perhaps becomes more workable when attention is paid to much more specific policies.

Instrument choice

Closely related to Lowi's efforts to develop a typology of policies is a literature that examines the alternative 'policy instruments'. This term is used:

> To encompass the myriad techniques at the disposal of governments to implement their public policy objectives. Sometimes referred to as 'governing instruments', these techniques range in complexity and age . . . (Howlett, 1991, p. 2)

Issues about the choice of instruments have been seen to be influenced by concerns about costs and benefits. Hence, Howlett suggests, 'Instrument choice, from this perspective, is public policymaking' (ibid.).

However, efforts to specify the key instruments have involved the provision of a list that is often quite extensive. As an appendix to his 1991 article, Howlett provides a list from other work, which contains 63 items. However, in the textbook he produced with Ramesh in 2003 he commends an approach to the delineation of policy instruments based upon Hood's listing of 'tools of government'. Hood (1986) classifies these in terms of

- 'nodality' – meaning the use of information;
- 'authority' – meaning the legal power used;
- 'treasure' – that is the use of money;
- 'organisation' – the use of formal organisational arrangements.

It is unfortunate that Hood's fondness for acronyms leads him to use this rather odd terminology (added together they make NATO), but his approach is helpful. Howlett and Ramesh (2003) go on from this starting point to a valuable discussion of the strengths and weaknesses of various policy instruments. Key issues from their analyses are summarised in Box 7.13.

Policy making involves choices about instrument use. Linder and Peters (1991) see policy instruments as in principle substitutable but argue that in practice choice depends upon:

- resource intensiveness
- the extent to which precise targeting of policies is required
- levels of political risk
- constraints on state activity.

Doern, on the other hand, sees instrument choice as essentially ideological, but with governments choosing the least coercive instrument. In his work with Phidd (Doern and Phidd, 1983, p. 134) he portrays instruments along a continuum rather like that provided in Box 7.13, from 'exhortation' through 'expenditure' and 'regulation' to 'public ownership'.

| Box 7.13 | Howlett and Ramesh's (2003) analysis of policy instruments |

It is argued that instruments can be seen as within a spectrum involving increased levels of state involvement from low (at the voluntary instruments end) to high (at the compulsory instruments end). Decisions about instrument use will be influenced by the likelihood of resistance. Hence there will tend to be a preference for using low state involvement options. However, choices will be affected by the resources (as specified in Hood's list of tools) available to governments.

Howlett and Ramesh specify the following instruments (2003, p. 195):

Voluntary Instruments
Family and Community
Voluntary Organization
Private Markets

Mixed Instruments
Information and Exhortation
Subsidies
Auction of Property Rights
Tax and User Charges

Compulsory Instruments
Regulation
Public Enterprise
Direct Provision

Earlier in their book they offer a more complex formulation of this typology (p. 92).

What the literature on instruments has made very clear is that the factors that influence instrument choice are complex. Policy type comes into play here and the issues about resistance to policy (rather as in Matland's analysis set out on p. 139), but we may also see ideology influencing choice. In the examples discussed in this chapter we saw cases where policy types are obviously important (as for example in education or pollution control) but also ones where ideological influences on instrument choice seem likely to be very significant (for example in social security). In each specific case much depends on what is available, what has been done before, or what is already in use in a closely related policy area. Howlett argues that it is not feasible to 'develop a general theory of policy instrument types' (1991, p. 1). Rather, he suggests that issues of instrument choice need to be linked up with issues about national policy styles:

there are several areas in which much more work remains to be done. First, the relationship between policy styles and policy instruments needs to be elaborated more precisely. This involves not only additional work conceptualizing and clarifying theories of policy instrument choice, but also work clarifying the concept of national policy styles. Second, much more comparative work needs to be done to add to the number of cases of instrument choice available, thus contributing to the development of studies of national styles, whether these turn out to be truly national or sectoral in nature. (Ibid., p. 16)

These questions about instrument choice connect up with another theme in the discussion of the policy process, one which is widely used in association with analyses of modern approaches to public management and to governance. Various writers have developed typologies for the analysis of policy processes, stimulated by the issues on the agenda about the use of market mechanisms. Government has been seen to have choices between leaving matters to the market or imposing hierarchical systems. Then, with the development of network theory (see pp. 67–72) it has been suggested that networks offer a third alternative. Hence Thompson et al. (1991) speak of hierarchies, markets and networks as three general models of social coordination, while Ouchi (1980) distinguishes between bureaucracies, markets and clans. Bradach and Eccles (1991) and Colebatch and Larmour (1993) examine the organisation of policy action in terms of hierarchic authority (bureaucracy), individual exchanges (markets) and group activities (community). In work with Peter Hupe, the author's version of this is to propose the following distinctions for policy processes:

- 'authority' – where rules are laid down in advance;
- 'transaction' – where certain outputs are expected, often as specified in contracts;
- 'persuasion' – where the essential mode of operation involves collaboration or what may be called 'co-production'. (Hill and Hupe, 2003, pp. 180–1)

There are then questions about choices between the alternatives (just as explored in the policy instruments literature). These will depend on:

- considerations about the 'best' ways to organise any specific policy delivery process;
- the ideologies of those who make the crucial choices (for example the strong preference for markets amongst many politicians of the liberal Right).

Once these choices are made, they have a considerable impact upon the shape of the policy process, affecting participation in detailed policy formulation and more particularly influencing implementation processes (the concerns of the next two chapters).

CONCLUSIONS

This chapter has tried to prepare for the discussion in the rest of the book by exploring issues about differences between policies. This has been related to questions about the applicability of the stages model to the policy process and of policy types. Using a limited number of important policy areas, the limitations of the stages model and the weaknesses of simple policy typologies have been demonstrated.

The exploration of policy areas has also been designed to highlight the great diversity of policy processes. At various places in the rest of the book discussion will return to the policy examples outlined here. The exploration of the complexities embedded in these policy areas is offered in an effort to sensitise readers to some of the key issues to be explored in the discussion to follow, in which a very limited application of the stages approach will be used to separate out some key themes in policy process analysis.

A recognition of policy diversity helps to throw light upon some of the variations in the arguments about policy process theory. Propositions about the biases in the overall structure of power are much more easily illustrated (even possibly tested) by the big political issues about war and peace and about control over the economy than they are by some of the other issues. Pollution control is interesting as an issue that has both an international and a very local dimension. Global politics increasingly determines its broad parameters but networks and local institutional arrangements need to be looked at to explain what happens at 'street level'. The clash of interest groups is much in evidence in the making of both social security policy and education policy. Evidence from these policy areas is widely used to support both rational choice theory and network theory, but institutional constraints are also in evidence (particularly in a field like pension policy). Any examination of local government reform obviously takes us into issues about the roles of institutions. While, as stressed at the end of Chapter 6, choice between theories is bound to be influenced by our value biases, it may also be affected by the substantive policy area in which we are interested.

8 Policy formulation

SYNOPSIS

This chapter explores a variety of issues which some writers examine separately as agenda setting, policy formulation and decision making (see, for example, Howlett and Ramesh, 2003). In practice there are difficulties with separating these three. The case for ignoring this division was made in the discussion on policy stages in Chapter 1.

The starting point for the discussion here is a longstanding controversy about the way policy decisions *should* be made. The dispute about this has been between an approach that is distinctly prescriptive – rational decision-making theory – and alternatives of a more pragmatic kind which suggest that most decision making is 'incremental' in nature, and that this offers the most effective way to reach accommodations between interests. The arguments between proponents of the rational model and the incrementalists will be examined, as will some compromise positions between them.

This will be followed by considering an approach to this topic which can be said to come out of incrementalism but goes considerably further, in stressing more strongly the relative absence of a consistent or 'rational' process. This is Kingdon's model of the agenda-setting process. Kingdon's (1995) model will be described, and then (given that Kingdon's book only applies it to the United States) its use will be evaluated with reference to an issue that is on the agenda all over the world, pensions. The argument will be advanced that in some countries, including the United Kingdom, politics may have a bigger influence on the agenda than in Kingdon's model. This will be explored with reference to the importance of mandates in the United Kingdom.

The chapter ends with some examination of issues about the respective roles of politicians and civil servants in relation to the policy formulation process, contesting the view that these can be readily distinguished.

Introduction

Warnings about using the stages model have been included at various places in this book, whilst at the same time the necessity of cutting the discussion of elements in the policy process into parts that can be easily handled in analysis has also been acknowledged. The agenda setting/formulation distinction is a particularly difficult one to make, since in the modern world we very rarely see an issue that is entirely new appearing on the agenda. Moreover, where this does happen there is often a very strong and complex interaction between the initial stages of that process and those that immediately follow it as it is translated into a more concrete form. It is also important to bear in mind that in some circumstances policy may be initiated and changed without formal legislation. In the last chapter, the examples from foreign policy and economic policy both largely fell into this category.

Sometimes agenda-setting processes and further policy formulation can be distiguished, sometimes not. At the time of writing, the UK government is committed to legislation that changes how university education is funded. The most controversial element in this is a proposal to allow individual universities to increase student fees. This is facing opposition from both the other main political parties but also from many of the government's own supporters. There is no question that changing the fee arrangements is firmly on the agenda, and one aspect of this (making the fees payable after the education has been received, and then only gradually using a means-tested formula, which will not apply to people who do not achieve significant incomes) is clearly popular. It is a reasonable prediction at this time that some version of the changes will be enacted, but instead of an arrangement for variable fees, it is quite possible that there will be instead a simple across-the-board increase in fees. Moreover, whatever happens, there are a lot of minor details on which adjustments may occur – to the threshold income at which repayment begins to be required, for example. Hence it may be said that the basic structure of the new policy is firmly on the agenda, but the formulation of the details is still going on. But of course, since this is a comment on ongoing events, this may be wrong. The government could still decide simply to abandon the legislation in the face of opposition.

The rational model of policy decision making

Since the very beginnings of attempts to develop an academic approach to administration, efforts have been made to formulate guidance on how to secure the 'best' decisions. This discussion will take as its starting point a theorist, Herbert Simon, who is often portrayed as a key proponent of a 'rational' model for decision making but who saw himself as a realist modifying earlier theory. There is a danger of oversimplifying the positions of the contributors to the debate about rationality. Simon is by no means advocating a simplistic, politics- and pressure-free model of decision making. Nor is he unaware of the complexity of the ideal of 'rationality'.

In his book *Administrative Behaviour*, Simon argues that a theory of administration has to be concerned with 'the processes of decision as well as with the processes of action' (Simon, 1957, p. 1), and to this end he attempts to specify exactly what is involved in decision making. Beginning with a definition of a decision as a choice between alternatives, Simon states that rational choice involves selecting alternatives 'which are conducive to the achievement of goals or objectives within organisations', and that this is of fundamental importance in giving meaning to administrative behaviour. Rational decision making involves the selection of the alternative that will maximise the decision maker's values, the selection being made following a comprehensive analysis of all the alternatives and their consequences.

It should be noted that Simon is using the word 'rational' in a rather different way to the economic theorists whose work was discussed in Chapter 3. For him, being rational seems to equate with getting things 'right', if not in absolute terms then certainly in terms of the relationship between means and ends. But Simon acknowledges that there are various difficulties with his version of the rational approach. The first is: whose values and objectives are to be used in the decision-making process? Clearly, organisations are not homogeneous entities, and the values of the organisation as a whole may differ from those of individuals within the organisation. Simon's response to this point is to argue that 'a decision is "organisationally" rational if it is oriented to the organisation's goals; it is "personally" rational if it is oriented to the individual's goals' (ibid., pp. 76–7).

This leads on to a second difficulty with Simon's approach, namely that it may not make sense to refer to the goals of an organisation. A similar problem arises here as in the discussion of policy (see Chapter 1), namely that general statements of intention within organisations are implemented by individuals and groups who often have discretion in interpreting these statements. Goals in public organisations are 'policies', and are likely to be the continuing subject of dispute and modification. If, furthermore, policy is to some extent made, or at least reformulated, as it is implemented, then it may be less useful to refer to an organisation's goals than to the goals of the individuals and groups who make up the organisation.

The third major difficulty with Simon's model of rationality is that in practice decision making rarely proceeds in such a logical, comprehensive and purposive manner. Among the reasons for this are that it is almost impossible to consider all alternatives during the process of decision; that knowledge of the consequences of the various alternatives is necessarily incomplete; and that evaluating these consequences involves considerable uncertainties. But it is precisely because of these limits to human rationality, maintains Simon, that administrative theory is needed.

What Simon is arguing, then, is that there is a need to explore ways of enhancing organisational rationality. There is a fourth difficulty in achieving this, namely how to separate facts and values, and means and ends, in the decision-making process. The ideal rational model postulates the prior specification of ends (perhaps we may call this 'agenda setting') and the identification of means of reaching these ends. Simon notes a number of problems with the means–ends schema, including that of separating facts and values. As he argues, the means of achieving ends are not devoid of values, and a way of coping with this has to be found in decision making. Simon's proposed solution is 'A theory of decisions in terms of alternative behaviour possibilities and their consequences' (p. 66), in which 'The task of decision involves three steps: (1) the listing of all the alternative strategies; (2) the determination of all the consequences that follow upon each of these strategies; (3) the comparative evaluation of these sets of consequences' (ibid., p. 67). Rationality has a place in this model in that 'The task of rational decision is to select that one of the strategies which is followed by the preferred set of consequences' (ibid.).

It follows that the means–ends rational model is, as Simon always intended, an idealised view of decision making in organisations. Simon recognises this, and he notes various ways in which actual behaviour departs from the theory. Accordingly, he elaborates the idea of 'bounded rationality' in the preface to a later edition of his work (1957, p. xxiv) to describe decision making in practice. Bounded rationality involves the decision maker choosing an alternative that is intended not to maximise his or her values but to be satisfactory or good enough. The term 'satisficing' describes this process. Bounded rationality enables the administrator faced with a decision to simplify by not examining all possible alternatives. Rather, rules of thumb are adopted, and as a result important options and consequences may be ignored.

Through all this, as identified in relation to Simon's first and second areas of difficulty, policy decision making is an interactive process, involving individuals with often conflicting interests and goals. Simon has a tendency to offer rules for *the* decision maker – in the singular – when what is involved is a complex collective process. This is where the incrementalist theorists offer a superior model.

Incrementalism

If Simon is a complex thinker whose views tend to be oversimplified, that is even more true of the leading exponent of the incrementalist view, Charles Lindblom. His work is particularly confusing because he has revised his position several times.

Lindblom is critical of the rational-comprehensive method of decision making. In its place, he sets out an approach he calls 'successive limited comparisons' which starts from the existing situation and involves the changing of policy incrementally.

In describing decision making by successive limited comparisons, Lindblom reiterates many of Simon's reservations about the rational model. Braybrooke and Lindblom note eight ways in which the rational-comprehensive model fails to adapt to the real world of policy decision making (set out in Box 8.1).

Box 8.1	**Braybrooke and Lindblom's eight reasons why the rational approach fails to deal with real-world decision making**

1. limited human problem-solving capacities;

2. situations where there is inadequacy of information;

3. the costliness of analysis;

4. failures in constructing a satisfactory evaluative method;

5. the closeness of observed relationships between fact and value in policy making;

6. the openness of the system of variables with which it contends;

7. the analyst's need for strategic sequences of analytical moves;

8. the diverse forms in which policy problems actually arise.

(Summarised from Braybrooke and Lindblom, 1963)

Consequently, Braybrooke and Lindblom argue, decision making in practice proceeds by successive limited comparisons. This simplifies the decision-making process not only by limiting the number of alternatives considered to those that differ in small degrees from existing policies, but also by ignoring the consequences of possible policies. Further, deciding through successive limited comparisons involves simultaneous analysis of facts and values, means and ends. As Lindblom states, 'one chooses among values and among policies at one and the same time' (1959, p. 82). That is, instead of specifying objectives and then assessing what policies would fulfil these objectives, the decision maker reaches decisions by comparing specific policies and the extent to which these policies will result in the attainment of objectives.

Lindblom argues that incrementalism is both a good description of how policies are actually made, and a model for how decisions should be made. Prescriptively, one of the claimed advantages of what he calls 'muddling through' is that serious mistakes can be avoided if only incremental changes are made. By testing the water the decision maker can assess the wisdom of the moves he or she is undertaking and can decide whether to make further progress or to change direction. This is developed at some length by Lindblom and his collaborators. In *A Strategy of Decision* (1963), he and David Braybrooke describe in detail the strategy of disjointed incrementalism, which is a refinement of the successive limited comparisons method (see Box 8.2).

| Box 8.2 | The case for disjointed incrementalism as a decision strategy |

Disjointed incrementalism involves examining policies which differ from each other incrementally, and which differ incrementally from the status quo. Analysis is not comprehensive but is limited to comparisons of marginal differences in expected consequences. Using disjointed incrementalism, the decision maker keeps on returning to problems, and attempts to ameliorate those problems rather than to achieve some ideal future state. What is more, decision makers adjust objectives to available means instead of striving for a fixed set of objectives. Braybrooke and Lindblom note that disjointed incrementalism is characteristic of the United States, where 'policy-making proceeds through a series of approximations. A policy is directed at a problem; it is tried, altered, tried in its altered form, altered again, and so forth' (Braybrooke and Lindblom, 1963, p. 73).

This theme of coordination is taken up in Lindblom's *The Intelligence of Democracy* (1965). The problem addressed in this book is how to achieve coordination between people in the absence of a central coordinator. 'Partisan mutual adjustment' is the concept Lindblom develops to describe how coordination can be achieved in such a situation. Partisan mutual adjustment is the process by which independent decision makers coordinate their behaviour. It involves adaptive adjustments 'in which a decision-maker simply adapts to decisions around him', and manipulated adjustments 'in which he seeks to enlist a response desired from the other decision-maker' (ibid., p. 33). Each of these forms of adjustment is further divided into a variety of more specific behaviour, including negotiation and bargaining. In a later article, Lindblom (1979) notes that although there is no necessary connection between partisan mutual adjustment and political change by small steps, in practice the two are usually closely linked. This has been shown (by Harrison, Hunter and Pollitt, 1990, pp. 8–13) to be a weakness in Lindblom's argument since a sequence of essentially incremental changes may well occur in a context in which certain parties are dominating and therefore 'mutual adjustment' is not occurring. This, they contend, has been characteristic of change in British health policy, where medical interests have dominated.

Later, Lindblom altered his position, moving away from the rather optimistic pluralism of his earlier work. In *Politics and Markets* (1977), he accepts that pluralism is biased in favour of certain groups, particularly businesses and corporations. Yet he resists the argument that centralised planning would be a preferable means of making decisions. Rather, Lindblom argues that the veto powers so prevalent in the US political system, and which prevent even incremental change occurring in some policy areas, need to be challenged through a restructuring of 'mutual adjustment'. Specifically, he proposes that the role of planners in the policy-making process should be to help to give 'absentees' a voice. The overall aim should be 'greatly improved strategic policy-making, both analytical and inter-active' (1977, p. 346). This case is argued through fully in his work with Woodhouse (1993), where he reasserts his critique of 'bureaucratic intelligence' and speaks of 'the potential intelligence of democracy' which can be realised if the 'impairments' of the political process are remedied through measures to increase the influence of ordinary groups of citizens as opposed to that of business elites.

Lindblom also accepts, in his later work, that partisan mutual adjustment is only active on ordinary questions of policy. Certain grand issues such as the existence of private enterprise and private property and the distribution of income and wealth are not resolved through adjustment. Rather, because of 'a high degree of homogeneity of opinion' (1979, p. 523) grand issues are not included on the agenda. Lindblom adds that this homogeneity of opinion is heavily indoctrinated, and in *Politics and Markets* he explores the operation of ideology. Lindblom's argument is that in any stable society there is a unifying set of beliefs which are communicated to the population through the church, the media, the schools and other mechanisms (1977, Chapter 15). These beliefs appear to be spontaneous because they are so much taken for granted, but they favour, and to some extent emanate from, dominant social groups.

There is thus a shift in Lindblom's position from one in which bargaining is seen as both inevitable and desirable to one in which ideology is seen to play a role, though essentially the latter has a limited influence upon the range of actors and options going into the bargaining process.

Alternative perspectives on decision making

In the light of the carefully qualified position taken by Simon and the many modifications Lindblom has been prepared to make to his earliest statements of the incrementalist position, there might be thought to be little middle ground between them. That has not stopped scholars trying to occupy that ground. Key examples of this are found in the work of Dror (1964) and Etzioni (1967). Dror's concern is very much a prescriptive one. Thus, while he is prepared to accept the validity of incrementalism as a descriptive theory, he argues for an optimal method which combines rationalism and incrementalism as a means of strengthening and improving decision making. Such a method needs to draw a distinction between contexts of social stability, in which incrementalism is appropriate, and others where bolder social change strategies are needed. Hence he is concerned to explore ways of engineering the latter. One of the features of the method he proposes is the stress placed on meta-policy making, that is, 'policy-making on how to make policy' (Dror, 1968, p. 160), a useful concept that has been adapted to apply to the design of institutions.

Etzioni similarly has a prescriptive concern, accepting the force of the argument that a series of small steps could produce significant change, but adding that 'there is nothing in this approach to guide the accumulation; the steps may be circular – leading back to where they started, or dispersed – leading in many directions at once but leading nowhere' (1967, p. 387). In place of incrementalism, Etzioni outlines the mixed scanning model of decision making, a model he suggests is both a good description of how decisions are made in a number of fields and a strategy which can guide decision making.

Mixed scanning rests on the distinction between fundamental decisions and incremental or bit decisions. Etzioni suggests that fundamental decisions, such as the declaration of war and the initiation of the space programme, are recognised by the incrementalists but are not given sufficient emphasis. In Etzioni's view, fundamental decisions are important because they 'set basic directions' (1967, p. 388) and provide the context for incremental decisions. Mixed scanning is an appropriate method for arriving at fundamental decisions because it enables a range of alternatives to be explored. Essentially, mixed scanning involves the decision maker undertaking a broad review of the field of decision without engaging in the detailed exploration of options suggested by the rational model. This broad review enables longer-run alternatives to be examined and leads to fundamental decisions.

This search for compromise very much involves efforts to separate fundamental or important or strategic decisions from more routine ones. Is this feasible? As Smith and May note, 'fundamental decisions in one context are incremental in another and vice versa' (1980, p. 153). Etzioni's example of the declaration of war seems an obvious enough fundamental decision, yet as was argued in Chapter 7 (see pp. 115–18), wars have emerged from a succession of incremental decisions made with a minimum of open debate. Another example is the nuclear energy programme. Here the evidence is that nations drifted into this, developing scientific research in secret because of nuclear power's close links with defence, only gradually realising the dangers involved in the nuclear energy programme and then tending to play these down in order not to cause public alarm.

The most significant attack upon the instrumentalist position comes not from the advocates of closed, administrator-dominated, 'rational' decision processes but from those whose ideological commitments lead them to demand bold steps. A very old ideological argument, influential in the 1950s and 1960s, led to a peculiar distortion of the arguments about incrementalism. Incremental decision making was seen as a characteristic of pluralistic societies, whilst comprehensive planning was seen as a feature of totalitarian societies (Popper, 1966).

We now know that the so-called 'planning' of communist societies was often a very haphazard process. Those societies seldom engaged in holistic planning, despite their claims and rhetoric; rather, they tended to lock themselves into bureaucratic allocation systems which were hard to change. Furthermore, when there were great leaps forward in policy, these were ideologically driven, not the product of the kinds of planning processes described by Simon (see, for example, various analyses of the 'great leap forward' and the 'cultural revolution' in China, in Brugger and Reglar, 1994, Chapter 1). Whilst today dramatic policy changes motivated by socialist ideology have become rare, if not extinct, on the other political 'wing' ideologues of the 'liberal' Right seem prepared to disregard Popper's endorsement of the desirability of 'piecemeal social engineering' in their endeavours to eliminate the collectivist state altogether or to enforce their concept of the ideal family. In other words, the clearest recent examples of policy makers disregarding the warnings of the 'incrementalist' school come from ideologically driven politicians of the 'Right' committed, as Margaret Thatcher was, to eliminating 'socialism' in the institutions of the central and local state and restoring 'Victorian values'.

The rationalism/incrementalism debate is beside the point when it is party-political commitment or ideology rather than either rational planning or 'partisan mutual adjustment' that drives the policy debate. The following scenario is surely by no means unlikely:

1. A problem arises on which it is difficult for government to develop an effective response – its causes are unknown, or beyond the reach of government action, or are phenomena with which the government is reluctant to deal (for example, economic influences upon crime).

2. Nevertheless, the key policy actors want to be seen to be 'in control', or at least doing something (they have made claims that they can manage the economy, combat crime, solve international conflicts).

3. In addition, some of the actors are driven by strong ideologies (particularly important as far as politicians are concerned).

4. The result is a series of actions that are presented as problem-solving but which may equally be the thrashing around of a system that needs to be seen as active but does not really know what to do (in these circumstances it is important not to be deceived by the rational action language politicians are likely to use).

It is also vital to see agenda-setting processes in their institutional contexts. Such constraints make both 'rational' policy planning and 'partisan mutual adjustment' difficult. March and Olsen argue that 'Insofar as political actors act by making choices, they act within definitions of alternatives, consequences, preferences (interests), and strategic options that are strongly affected by the institutional context in which the actors find themselves' (March and Olsen, 1996, p. 251). We also saw that in some of their work March and Olsen seem to go even further, seeing the way policies emerge as being similar to the way rubbish accumulates in a 'garbage can' (see pp. 89–90). An alternative, institutional theory-linked approach to this issue which picks up on all the points emphasised in this paragraph is Kingdon's analysis of agenda setting.

Kingdon's model of the agenda-setting process

Kingdon originally set out his model in a book published in 1984. He updated that book in 1995. This discussion is based upon the latter book. Kingdon's work is a study of policy agenda setting in the United States. Kingdon describes his approach to the analysis of agenda setting as follows:

> Comprehensive, rational policy making is portrayed as impractical for the most part, although there are occasions where it is found. Incrementalism describes parts of the process, particularly the gradual evolution of proposals or policy changes, but does not describe the more discontinuous or sudden agenda change. Instead of these approaches, we use a revised version of the Cohen–March–Olsen garbage can model of organizational choice to understand agenda setting and alternative generation. We conceive of three process streams flowing through the system – streams of problems, policies, and politics. They are largely independent of one another, and each develops according to its own dynamics and rules. But at some critical junctures the three streams are joined, and the greatest policy changes grow out of that coupling of problems, policy proposals, and politics. (Kingdon, 1995, p. 19)

It is important to note the way in which Kingdon associates his analysis with the 'garbage can' model. He thus dissociates himself from traditional positivist American political science, which searches for universal testable propositions and sees the policy process instead as in many respects chaotic and unpredictable. Despite that, he aims to offer an approach that helps us to understand what goes on even if we cannot easily predict outcomes.

An aspect of Kingdon's approach that is widely quoted is his alternative metaphor to the 'garbage can', 'primeval soup'. This is a reference to the way in which modern explanations of the early stages of biological evolution see change occurring because genetic combinations occurred in the shapeless, soup-like environment, then only some of them proved successful and thus led on to subsequent developments. But this is just an analogy, and one which should be treated with caution.

Rather more important for his theory is the notion that in the soup-like environment that is the modern policy process there are three streams: problems, policies and politics. Simpler explanations of the policy process have seen policies as designed to solve problems, but the weakness of such approaches is that problems themselves are socially constructed (Berger and Luckman, 1975). Kingdon suggests it can often be the case that there are policies looking for problems, that it is things key actors want to do that need justifications. He identifies the presence of what he calls 'policy entrepreneurs' who do this. These people may be politicians or civil servants or pressure group leaders with issues they want to put on the public agenda. They are, he says, like 'surfers waiting for the big wave' (Kingdon, 1995,

p. 225), on the look-out for a combination of public concern about a problem and political interest in doing something about it.

Kingdon's primeval soup image is intended to convey the way in which the policy process environment is forever changing, hence opportunities for agenda setting come and go with shifting attention to issues, influenced by the short attention span of the media and the changing needs of politicians in the course of the electoral cycle (this observation echoes earlier work by Downs suggesting that there is an 'issue-attention cycle' in politics, 1972, p. 38). Kingdon shifts into another image here, of windows that open briefly and then close. He recognises the importance of something to which a lot of emphasis is given in this book: feedback from existing policies into the agenda-setting process. He also identifies what he calls 'spillovers', the impact of one policy change on other policies. These two elements – feedback and spillovers – may be important for the problem identified with regard to both network theory and institutional theory: that despite evidence of the existence of strong forces towards stability in the policy process, there are spells of quite intense change in many systems. What may appear to involve marginal change can have major consequences.

Birkland's research on 'focusing events' offers support for this perspective (see Box 8.3). When the 'big wave' comes problems, policies and politics may be coupled to form the policy agenda. This is not necessarily a simple process. Kingdon makes a distinction between 'agendas' and 'alternatives', recognising that there is competition at this time.

Another approach to events which create opportunities for policy change involves an emphasis on policy fiascos (Bovens and 't Hart, 1996; Gray and 't Hart (eds.), 1998). Here, of course, the problems that force their attention on policy makers are the consequences of earlier policies. In this case, then, we see feedback cycles in the policy process as emphasised on p. 21, and also a variation on Kingdon's theme of the impact of 'feedback and spillovers' on the policy process.

A related concern is with the impact of crises. Bovens, 't Hart and Peters' comparative study (2001; see pp. 103–5) emphasises ways in which crises force attention to be given to problems, looking then at different ways in which governments respond to problems.

Box 8.3	Birkland's (1998) analysis of the impact of focusing events

Birkland studied the impact of disasters (hurricanes and earthquakes) and industrial accidents (oil spills and nuclear power disasters) on the policy agenda in the United States. Interestingly, he links Kingdon's analysis of 'problems' with the network and policy communities perspective (explored in Chapter 4). He shows that focusing events may serve to bring attention to problems on the agenda, but that

> An event is more likely to be focal if an interest group or groups are available to exploit the event . . . (Birkland, 1998, p.72)

Kingdon sees his approach to the agenda-setting process as building on incrementalist theory in its rejection of the 'rational' problem-solving model. But he argues that not all change is incremental and that incrementalist theory tends to disregard issues about the way streams join and policy windows open. He sees his approach as superior to a pluralist perspective inasmuch as he is interested in the way key actors both inside and outside government come together. Similarly, for him network theory and the work on policy communities neglect issues about coupling and about variations in the extent to which behaviour is unified. His perspective can be seen as institutionalist in approach, in the light of its emphasis on the significance of actors both inside and outside government and its recognition of the impact of earlier decisions on current ones. Indeed, in his second edition he recognises the parallels between his approach and that of Baumgartner and Jones (1993) in their analysis of punctuated equilibrium (see the discussion on pp. 85–6).

It has been stressed that Kingdon's book is only about the United States (and in practice only about the federal government). It seems amazing that a book that offers a general approach to the analysis of agenda setting should have no references whatsoever to the process outside the United States. It is desirable to explore the theory further using material from elsewhere before launching into a discussion of whether Kingdon's ethnocentrism matters. This will be done in the next section.

An agenda-setting example: pensions policy

In many countries (and particularly in Europe) there have been three phases in pension policy making:

- A first phase, in which, in most countries, relatively rudimentary public pensions were provided for only some groups in the population.
- A second phase of consolidation, involving either the development of comprehensive public schemes or the formation of combinations of public and private provisions.
- A third phase, in which, while development and consolidation issues are still on the agenda, a key policy preoccupation is with cutting public pension commitments.

Tables 8.1 to 8.3 (see next page) summarise the issues that influence the prospects of pension issues getting on the public policy agenda using Kingdon's key concepts.

The explanation given for the first phase in policy pension making (see Table 8.1) seems to offer a more political approach to agenda setting than there is in Kingdon's model. This seems to be dominant in historical accounts of the evolution of pension policies, though there are differences

Table 8.1   Phase 1: Initial moves towards pension policies

Problems	An ageing population and increasing reluctance on the part of employers to keep older workers.
Politics	The emergence of democracy, a readiness to see poverty in old age as not the fault of the individual.
Policies	Either ideas derived from insurance or more universal models of public assistance for the elderly.
Policy entrepreneurs	Politicians on the Left; friendly society leaders recognising increased problems with voluntary initiatives.
Windows of opportunity	Electoral shifts to the Left.

of view on the importance of the political Left (Heclo, 1974; Ashford, 1986; Baldwin, 1990). But the demographic aspect of the emergence of the problem has also been widely emphasised (Pampel and Williamson, 1989), and detailed accounts suggest the importance of policy entrepreneurs other than politicians (Gilbert, 1966; Baldwin, 1990). Furthermore, accounts of European developments make a great deal of the activities of one politician of the Right, Bismarck, who perceived an opportunity to tie the new industrial working class into the support of the state as the collector of their contributions and the guarantor of their pensions.

In the consolidation period (see Table 8.2) the divergences that are a key concern of modern comparative studies really emerged (see the discussion of Esping-Andersen's regime theory on p. 94) between those countries that adopted more or less universal public schemes (Sweden, Norway, Denmark, for example), those that developed a more divided version of the universalist approach (Germany and France, for example) and those that settled for provisions that were a mix of public and private (the UK and Australia, for example). The key explanatory variables were perhaps concerns about inconsistencies and a strong universalist drive from the left of the political spectrum. But the emergence of a variety of private pension initiatives

Table 8.2   Phase 2: Consolidation

Problems	Poverty amongst those not in schemes; equity problems because of mixtures of different schemes; insolvency of some private schemes.
Politics	Championing of universalist solutions by the political Left.
Policies	Universal models; models involving public/private combinations.
Policy entrepreneurs	Politicians of the Left; private companies eager to secure new business or protect existing business.
Windows of opportunity	Electoral shifts to the Left; scandals about private schemes.

meant that the Left faced a rival agenda, with the more sophisticated of the advocates of the private model recognising the case for partnership (inasmuch as they were reluctant to take on the provision of pensions for low-income workers) and the need to secure private schemes against scandals that could discredit them.

Table 8.3   Pension cutting

Problems	Substantial increases in the elderly population; threats of insolvency for both public and private schemes.
Politics	Championing of privatised solutions by the political Right.
Policies	Cuts to promised entitlements; ways to increase pre-funding.
Policy entrepreneurs	Private pension providers: international organisations.
Windows of opportunity	Electoral shifts to the Right; fiscal crises.

The interesting thing about the third phase (see Table 8.3) is not so much successful agenda setting as considerable difficulties in getting cuts on the agenda (see the discussion on p. 96) because of the strength of the support coalition for the status quo. A peculiarity of any pension scheme is that it embodies promises made to people a long while before they reach the age of entitlement. Furthermore, if a scheme is contributory, which it is in most countries with large comprehensive schemes, then those promises for the future are being paid for in the present. The problem that prompts action is very often an expected future one rather than a current one. Policy entrepreneurs have to persuade politicians, whose time frames are short, that they should worry about long-term trends. Here the so-called 'demographic time bomb' is a good example of a socially defined problem exaggerating the implications of demographic change (see Hill, 1996, pp. 300–6). Moreover, funded pension schemes, particularly if that funding is through investment in the stock market, themselves offer uncertain promises for the future. Nevertheless, a combination of the recognition of emergent fiscal problems by governments only too aware of difficulties in raising revenues, increased commitment to privatisation, and, perhaps above all, hard selling by private pension providers has succeeded in getting the case for changes onto the agenda.

This discussion has explored the issue in the group of countries that went into pension provision early in the twentieth century and consolidated schemes soon after the Second World War. The politics of pensions is very much more complicated in countries where pension provision or consolidation has only recently got onto the agenda. In these cases the conflict between the case for pension development and recognition of the strong case against open-ended and unfunded commitments made by bodies like the World Bank (1994) seriously complicates the agenda. In the case of the UK, summarised in Box 8.4, efforts at consolidation came relatively late and therefore we see complications of this kind in the agenda-setting process.

Box 8.4	Pension development in the UK

Pension schemes were set up for some citizens in the period before the First World War. Then, following the recommendations of the Beveridge Report (Beveridge, 1942), a scheme of low-level, flat rate social insurance pensions was set up which survives to this day. Beveridge expected that many people would also contribute to additional private schemes to provide more than subsistence incomes in old age. By 1963 about 48 per cent of employees were enrolled in occupational pension schemes.

In the 1950s a political debate emerged about the need for additional pensions for those not in private schemes. A complex policy-making process ensued in which concerns to improve future pensions competed with concerns about current pensions. The measure that eventually emerged was the Social Security Pensions Act of 1975, which provided an earnings related superannuation scheme, the State Earnings Related Pension Scheme (SERPS). This allowed individuals in adequate private schemes to opt out of the state scheme, but provided an enhanced inflation-proofed state superannuation scheme for all other working people. This scheme, whilst it appeared to involve funding, was, like the flat rate scheme upon which it was built, a scheme managed on a 'pay as you go' basis. By the early 1980s it was beginning to have some effect upon the number of pensioners requiring supplements from social assistance.

After 1979, the Conservative government sought to cut social security expenditure. The value of the original flat rate pension was significantly reduced. SERPS was deemed to involve rising costs and to impose excessive burdens on future generations. The government's initial idea was to replace it by a funded scheme, but then they recognised what heavy short-term costs the government would impose upon itself since it would lose the use of contributions to fund current benefits. Instead, they cut sharply the benefits guaranteed under SERPS. The government also gave further encouragement to the private pensions industry through tax relief and insurance contribution rebates. They abolished the requirement that any approved private scheme should be as good as SERPS. These measures unleashed a massive sales campaign by the private pensions industry which contributed to subsequent scandals about inadequate protection for some people.

By 1997, three classes of pensioners could be identified. One group, about a third of all retirees, and including public servants, had well-funded private pensions to supplement the basic Beveridge pension. At the other extreme was another group – including particularly many women and older pensioners – whose main provision came from the flat rate Beveridge scheme, which (since it remained low) they might need to supplement with means-tested benefits. In the middle there were people with modest sums from either SERPS or limited (and often fragile) private schemes to supplement the flat rate pension. The Labour government then enacted pension reforms that provided:

- maintenance of the basic, flat rate contributory pension;
- voluntary 'stakeholder' pension schemes designed to offer an alternative to entirely private pensions for those on middle incomes;
- a state second pension for those unable to get into private or stakeholder schemes;
- a means-test-based 'guarantee credit' for pensioners on low incomes;
- a 'savings credit scheme' to supplement the incomes of those with relatively low private pensions but above the level to qualify for the full 'guarantee credit'.

Controversy continues, however, in the face of a growing elderly population and difficulties facing market-based private pensions.

Box 8.4 explores what has been going on in the UK, particularly since 1960. What has occurred has been an effort to reach a compromise between the conflicting concerns about the pension system:

- the high levels of current pensioner poverty;
- the future balance between the generations;
- the recognition that the favourable situation of many contributors to good private pension schemes is one that should be shared more widely;
- the desire of the financial market to sell pensions;
- a recognition that some marketised pensions may not be a good buy for their contributors in the long run.

What the examination of the British case highlights for an understanding of agenda setting is:

- the way in which current agendas emerge as consequences of past decisions;
- the way alternative agendas come into conflict;
- the way those alternative agendas do not just arise out of conflicting interests and ideologies but also out of interrelated problems (in this case particularly the differences between the issues about current pensioner poverty and those about future comprehensive provisions).

Issues about applying Kingdon's model

Kingdon's model depicts the policy process as disorganised or haphazard. The pensions case discussed here suggests a need to question that. What has been suggested in the exploration of that issue is that it has been regularly on the agendas of many nations over a long period of time, that there has been a distinct 'politics' theme running through it and that there has been a comparative similarity, or at least a clustering, of ultimate policy responses. However, there is a case for caution about the case chosen. It is perhaps a rather 'mainstream' policy issue, bound to get considerable attention and to appear regularly on policy agendas.

Nevertheless, there is a need to ask whether Kingdon's American perspective leads him to underemphasise the factors that may give agenda setting a rather clearer shape, bringing it closer to the notion of a rational search for solutions to problems that he has criticised. The view that there may be differences in the way the agenda is set is explored by Cobb, Ross and Ross (1976), who distinguish between the 'outside initiation model' of liberal pluralist societies, the 'mobilisation model' of totalitarian regimes and the 'inside initiation model' where influential groups have easy access to decision makers. But that approach seems still to accept the relevance of the Kingdon model for open systems. In a book in which the emphasis is on the policy process in the United Kingdom and Europe, it seems important to consider whether the Kingdon model pays sufficient attention to party politics. This will be done in the next section.

Politicians as agenda setters

Essentially, the theory of representative democracy involves a model of the political process in which political parties compete to win elections, presenting manifestos between which the public may choose. There is then some expectation that the winners will implement the policies set out in their manifestos, on the basis that they have a 'mandate' for those policies. However, studies of electoral behaviour suggest that our voting choices are largely not determined in the rational way embodied in that model, and that fact may give politicians an excuse to disregard their commitments. That is, however, beside the point for this discussion, which aims to explore to what extent the 'mandate' model operates as an important influence upon the formation of the policy agenda.

There are, then, clearly differences in the extent to which a coherent mandate can be expected. It is in the division that exists in the United States between President and Congress, and in the relatively loose programmatic bonds within parties, that we may find the basis for the relative underplaying of 'politics' in the Kingdon model. But within systems that are in formal terms more unified there may be another problem with identifying a coherent mandate: the fact that the government emerges not from the decisive victory of one party over another but from a compromise between more than one party. Notwithstanding this, it is interesting to note the continuing importance of the notion of a mandate in the very divided system in the Netherlands. A crucial stage in negotiations about the formation of a government there involves the drawing up of a *regeeraccoord* embodying an agreed policy programme.

Our exploration here of the impact of a mandate upon agenda setting will take a case where a very strong effect of this kind could be expected, after a decisive victory by a single party in the 'first past the post' UK system. We will examine the record of the Labour government headed by Tony Blair between the 1997 and 2001 elections. Tables 8.4 and 8.5 itemise:

- manifesto pledges and what had happened by 2001;
- key policies adopted which were absent from the manifesto.

Table 8.4   Manifesto pledges by the UK Labour Party in 1997 and the extent to which they were fulfilled by the end of 2001

Measures	Outcome by 2001
Introduce a minimum wage	Yes
Welfare to work programme funded by tax on utilities	Yes
10p starting rate of income tax	Yes
Reform of Bank of England to provide for open monetary control free from political manipulation	Yes (see note 1)
Reform the structure of the NHS	Yes
Promote choice in pension provision	Yes
Right to roam in countryside	Yes
Devolve power to Scotland and Wales	Yes
New government system for London	Yes
Incorporate European Convention on Human Rights into UK law	Yes
Free nursery places for all 4-year-olds instead of the voucher system	Yes
Abolish the hereditary element in the House of Lords	Incomplete
Pension reform	Incomplete
Public/private partnership for London Underground	Incomplete
Referendum on Euro	No

Note 1: What happened was a good bit more radical than this general pledge: the delegation of control over interest rates to a Bank of England committee (with appointed outside members).

There are problems with an exercise like this. Much in the manifesto was vague and general. In order to compile a manageable list of the activities of a very active government, the author has had to make difficult judgements about (a) the importance of the issues and (b) the specificity of the pledges in the manifesto. The focus is confined to items that seemed to imply specific policy changes as opposed to improvements in administration.

The list of manifesto pledges in Table 8.4 indicates a strong adherence to the mandate. While there were some items of unfinished business, the only outright failure to do what had been promised was the absence of a referendum on the Euro, but even this may be claimed to be simply unfinished business since the pledge was translated into one that a referendum would be held when the Chancellor of the Exchequer judged the economic conditions to be right.

Perhaps more important for any analysis of agenda setting in the UK is the way in which new items appeared on the agenda. Several reasons why the combination of a strong executive with decisive electoral support may mean that certain kinds of items will not appear in a political manifesto can be suggested (the numbers in brackets indicate the items in Table 8.5 to which these may apply):

■ those items might benefit unpopular minorities (5)

■ those items might be particularly likely to anger the party faithful (4)

■ those items might depend upon developments elsewhere in the world (3 and 6)

■ those items might be affected by unpredicted economic developments (none in the table, but this partly applies to the one unenacted pledge, that on the Euro).

Table 8.5   Key policies adopted by the UK Labour Government 1997–2001 that were not in the Labour Party 1997 Manifesto

1. Cuts to benefits provided to single-parent families
2. Introduction of tax credits
3. War over Kosovo
4. Privatisation of the air traffic control system
5. Liberalisation of the law relating to homosexuality
6. Agreement to the enlargement of the European Union

Clearly, the two social security items (1 and 2) do not figure in this list. Commentators on government change in the past have suggested that incoming ministers encounter items on the official policy agenda that they had not learnt about before. The comparative absence of surprises for the incoming government in 1997 seems to have had a lot to do with the fact that Labour when in opposition took a great deal of care to make sure they were well informed, assisted by the fact that it had become very obvious to the civil service that there would be a change of government (Keegan, 2003). The exception was in the field of social security, where the Labour Party was in the awkward position of wanting to adopt a more liberal stance on benefits and attack poverty more effectively than its predecessor, but having promised that there would be no tax increases and no spending increases. Right from the outset it was evident that there were internal divisions in the government on social security (Hill, 2001). Then a cut already planned under the previous government was pushed by civil servants (item 1, Table 8.5). A conflict then developed between the idea of new approaches to targeting benefits through tax credits (item 2) and approaches that laid a stronger emphasis on contributory benefits but would be more costly. The powerful Treasury, backed by a powerful Chancellor, then largely took over the social security agenda, pushing tax credits both as a recipe for combining work and welfare and as a solution for one of the dilemmas of pension reform.

The analysis above seems to offer support for the view that, if applied to the UK, the Kingdon model rather underplays the politics dimension of agenda setting. However, there are questions to be asked about the extent to which it is the presence of a strong executive rather than a strong party system that explains the particularly good correspondence between policy pledges and the policy agenda in the period 1997–2001 in the UK. That then takes us on to a key aspect of that kind of explanation, the role of the civil service. This topic will be explored further in the next section.

Civil servants and policy formulation

We saw in Chapter 4 that a combination of politicians, civil servants and interest group representatives is implicit in the policy networks and policy communities theories. Much of the discussion of the roles of civil servants outside that framework, however, has tended to involve seeing them as alternative, even subversive, decision makers to politicians rather than as partners in a shared system (see Box 8.5 overleaf). Such a perspective has been strongly influenced by the traditional preoccupation with the relationship between politics and administration. This discussion will start from that issue but aim to move away from it to a more balanced account of how these two groups interact in the policy process. In doing so it will consider, first, some of the issues about the respective roles of politicians and civil servants and then some of the issues about the compatibility of values, or ideologies, between them.

If permanent civil servants play a key role in the policy process they may tend to give continuity to the policy agenda, pursuing a departmental line regardless of political leadership. The power of the civil service and the importance of departmental agendas was emphasised in many past studies of British public administration. A particular concern of politicians and of some of the small number of outsiders brought in to support them during the Labour government of 1964–70 was civil service control over the agenda. The 'Whitehall model' has been seen as firmly established in Britain. Even though, as will be shown below, they suggest change is occurring, Campbell and Wilson say:

Box 8.5	Why civil servants subvert political agendas

- 'The conspiracy theory' – they 'have agendas of their own'.
- 'The bureaucracy theory' – they are trapped in bureaucratic routines (see more on this in Chapter 13).
- 'The wise counsellors theory' – they are needed to prevent policy being flawed.

(Based on the discussion in Pollitt, 2003, pp. 86–7)

The first two of those perspectives can be found illustrated (and of course exaggerated) in the very successful TV comedy series *Yes, Minister* and its sequel, *Yes, Prime Minister*. That particularly featured a key civil servant, the Permanent Secretary (Sir Humphrey), who could be seen controlling the system and resisting change in the face of demands from a naïve politician. But the role of the more junior civil servant who looked after the minister's private office (Bernard) was also interesting: he was the person responsible for day-to-day routines and was of course ultimately more concerned to satisfy his civil service boss than his political boss. The series owed a great deal to revelations from politicians' memoirs, particularly those of Richard Crossman, who served in the Wilson governments of 1964–70.

The notion of the British civil service as a 'community' with a life, and agendas, of its own was well explored in Heclo and Wildavsky's study of the dominance of the British Treasury, where they speak of a 'Whitehall village' (1981).

In favour of the 'wise counsellors theory' it is appropriate to raise questions about the extent to which there is a civil service 'ethic' of responsibility. There have been efforts by senior British civil servants to develop an explicit ethical code. The issue has also been highlighted in situations in which civil servants have been 'whistle blowers', breaking their normal commitment to confidentiality because of what they have seen as unethical demands or even demands not in the national interest. In any case, there are obvious questions of job satisfaction at stake here which make it unlikely that senior staff will simply carry out political instructions mindlessly.

politicians in few countries place as much faith in bureaucrats as do the British. The British system contrasts not only with the patronage system at the top of the executive branch in the United States but also with the continental European practice (as in Germany) of placing senior civil servants in temporary retirement if a governing party loses power. . . . [t]he dependence of elected politicians on the non-partisan, permanent civil service was the core of the system that has been exported to other countries and admired by many non-British scholars. (Campbell and Wilson, 1995, p. 293)

Nevertheless, we see similar features in some other European systems. Anderweg and Irwin's (2002) account of policy making in the Netherlands suggests the importance of departmental agendas, with civil servants as the key advisers for their ministers. In respect of France, Knapp and Wright speak of 'the colonisation by the civil service of areas beyond the confines of mere administration' (2001, p. 276). Knapp and Wright's discussion of this phenomenon indicates that this came under attack but that the situation has not been changed significantly.

Beyond this recognition of the prominence of the civil service role in general, a great deal of the discussion of the roles of civil servants seems to have got locked into a very dated debate about the possibility of distinguishing policy making from administration, concerning itself, as in the quotation from Knapp and Wright above, with the extent to which civil servants are involved beyond 'mere administration'.

There have been attempts to define appropriate roles for politicians and civil servants. Simon's 'rational model' (1957) envisages politicians making the value choices that will form 'premises' for the more detailed decision processes to be carried out by officials. In this he echoes the influential early work of Wilson (1887), which tried to delineate the respective territories of 'politics' and 'administration'. Wilson's dichotomy has been widely attacked, not so much for its prescriptive aspirations as for its impact on the way policy processes are described. It is seen as a 'hindrance to accurate scholarship' (Skok, 1995). It still emerges, however, in contemporary discussions of the policy process. For example, Huber and Shipan's *Deliberate Discretion* (2002) explores why 'politicians sometimes allow substantial discretion and at other times tell bureaucrats precisely what to do' (p. 9).

Campbell and Wilson's analysis of the changing role of the UK civil service seems to use a similar dichotomy, speaking of 'civil servants increasingly defining their role as policy implementers rather than policy analysts' (1995, p. 60). But surely that disregards the very substantial task between agenda setting and implementation, translating relatively agreed goals into action. This can involve a whole sequence of activities: filling out and explaining the meaning of a new law, establishing the funding arrangements the measure requires, setting up organisational arrangements for putting it into effect, and so on.

There is, as we have already acknowledged, a difficulty about drawing a line between agenda setting and formulation of policy. An interesting illustration of this comes from an apparently trivial argument between the British political parties in later 2003 and is set out in Box 8.6 overleaf.

The long-standing concern to distinguish politics (or policy making) from administration, though it has its roots in an obvious issue about representative democracy, manifests itself often as a naïve demand to take politics out of medicine, or education, or whatever. In practice, these issues matter too much either for politicians to be prepared to leave them alone or for the 'administrators' (including many professional staff, a point we return to on pp. 249–52) to abdicate what they see as their responsibilities for doing the right thing. Hence there are large parts of the policy process in which political and administrative roles are inextricably mixed.

| Box 8.6 | A 'new policy' or strengthening an old one? |

The British government announced, in summer 2003, a new initiative to reduce cross-infection in hospital. The opposition argued that a 'new' policy should be brought before Parliament. The government response to this was that it was merely strengthening existing procedures. At this the opposition claimed that the government was 'spinning' news again, dressing up old initiatives as new to try to strengthen its image. An interesting further feature of the argument was that the crucial 'new' steps were being taken by a civil servant, the Chief Medical Officer, who had issued the guidance on actions that should be taken by hospitals. Here, then, is an issue about 'what is a new policy?' In the end, except to the politicians trying to score points, the answer to that question does not matter; we have here a small part of the continuous flow of activity involved in managing a system that is continually in the eye of political conflict, the National Health Service.

This discussion of administrative roles in the policy formulation process involves an exploration of what is perhaps the most ambiguous part of the initial policy process. It is certainly the most difficult to research, because so much of the action is private (in the UK we have to wait 30 years for the publication of official papers, and even then some items are protected for longer, some are purged, and many were never committed to paper records in the first place). The fact that there have been so many attempts to draw the politics/administration distinction or to delimit the political roles and interests of permanent officials indicates the complexity of this issue. The achievement of the ideal – that civil servants should be just 'managers' or just concerned with 'means' – is fraught with difficulty. Furthermore, it has been very evident that many politicians *want* civil servants to play central policy-making roles (see Campbell and Wilson, 1995). Indeed, they often even want them to play 'political' roles – anticipating political risks and handling controversial issues.

A valuable modern exploration of these issues, where interviews with civil servants involved with legislation has lifted the veil a little on the way in which they work on policy formulation, is Page's (2003) study of recent British legislation. Box 8.7 explores Page's findings. He is in no doubt that British civil servants, largely drawn from the middle ranks of the service, play important roles in preparing legislation. He suggests that the division of labour between politicians and civil servants may be partly characterised in terms of a distinction between 'abstract' and 'applied' policy work, but that this should not be seen to mean simply a distinction between adopting a policy and then filling in its details. Feedbacks between the two processes are complex.

The assumption that top administrators are problem solvers, likely to want to make improvements in policy (some of which entail much more than adjustments at the implementation stage), is built into much of the

| Box 8.7 | Page's (2003) examination of the role of the British 'civil servant as legislator' |

British civil servants are drafted into 'bill teams' to work on the preparation of legislation. Such teams are typically led by civil servants drawn from the lowest grade of the 'senior' civil service. The teams tend to be formed early in the process of preparing a new policy, before it has been agreed that there will be a place for legislation in the parliamentary timetable. The decision to legislate will be a political one. However, Page shows that in some of the cases he studied during Blair's second term in government, the identification of a need for legislation was as much a civil service activity as a political one.

Once a decision to legislate is made, teams will work on the detailed drafting of legislation. Drafting will involve the team, joined or assisted by lawyers employed by the civil service. Before being put before Parliament a draft bill will be submitted to the relevant minister or ministers, who will be responsible for steering the legislation through Parliament. To assist ministers, large briefing documents will be compiled. During the legislation process any suggested amendments will be carefully scrutinised by the team. Many will be the product of further thoughts about the legislation from within the department. Some will be inspired by pressure groups and some will come from within Parliament, but very often the aim will be to accept these in principle and secure their withdrawal so that they can be replaced by amendments compatible with the bill as a whole. Once the legislation has been steered through Parliament, the bill team is likely to move on to drafting implementing amendments and guidance on the legislation.

Page summarises the process as follows (p. 651):

These teams work with considerable autonomy in developing legislation, but it cannot be assumed that they operate outside ministerial control. Teams see themselves as reflecting the priorities of the government in general and their ministers in particular. Yet ministers typically know relatively little about the law they are bringing in until they receive the submissions and briefings from their officials. Perhaps the biggest danger for democracy is not a civil service putting forward proposals which a minister feels forced to accept, but rather that ministers do not notice or fully appreciate what is being proposed in their name despite having the political authority to change it and a civil service which bends over backwards to consult and accommodate them.

prescriptive literature on the policy process. The 'rational model' discussed above is largely founded on this assumption. In this case it is the expertise of the permanent officials that is seen as providing the justification for their role in policy making. But the way in which value issues and factual issues are intertwined makes it difficult to draw lines to determine limits to their participation.

Dunleavy and O'Leary refer to the 'professionalisation' of government to suggest that in areas where expertise is important, issues are pulled out of the general political arena into the more private politics of 'policy communities':

In the professionalized state the grassroots implementation of policy, and major shifts in the overall climate of debate in each issue area, are both influenced chiefly by individual occupational groups. Professional communities act as a key forum for developing and testing knowledge, setting standards and policing the behaviour of individual policy-makers and policy implementers. Knowledge elites are crucial sources of innovations in public policy-making ... in areas where professions directly control service delivery the whole policy formulation process may be 'implementation skewed'. (Dunleavy and O'Leary, 1987, pp. 302–3)

A modern twist to all the issues about the way the politician/administrator boundary is organised comes with two approaches to government which, while they have echoes in the past and particularly in pre-democratic regimes, are currently assuming increasing importance: public/private partnerships and the delegation of public tasks to quasi-independent or independent organisations. In many respects this is a subject for the discussion of implementation. Certainly this is how governments tend to present these developments – emphasising Woodrow Wilson's politics/administration distinction or stressing that 'we' still make the 'policy', 'they' are responsible for 'operations'. Invoking the already criticised Wilson distinction indicates that this should be viewed with caution. Leaving aside the new ways in which this now brings politicians into concerns about 'implementation', it will be seen that any 'agent' with responsibilities to implement a policy is likely to develop very real concerns about the way in which the policy it operates is constructed. If confronted with something unexpectedly expensive or something unworkable, the agent is likely to lobby (probably covertly) for policy change. The 'agent' with a contract to carry out a specific task with a specific sum of money is a politically interested party (a new actor in the bargaining part of the game), and perhaps particularly likely to behave in the way predicted by public choice theory.

Obviously there will be differences between societies in how these roles are distributed. Dyson's analysis of 'strong' and 'weak' states discussed in Chapter 6 suggested that in the 'strong' state civil servants are carriers of a tradition of service to the state, which is seen as providing a context for the more temporary concerns of politicians (see pp. 99–101). Much depends here upon other aspects of the constitution. If electoral systems tend to produce unified programmatic parties then there is a potential tension between the two elements in the policy-making process. Here differences between the early (agenda-setting) and later parts of the policy process are likely to be relevant. But much will depend upon the extent to which either one party is largely dominant (as in Sweden until recently) or where there is a relatively low level of conflict between the parties (as in Germany). France is an interesting case because the constitution of the Fifth Republic gives administrators considerable autonomy. Commentators on France suggest that the period in which Mitterrand came to presidential power with innovatory socialist policies but was then forced first to water them down and then to accept 'cohabitation' with a prime minister of a different political persuasion was a crucial testing time for French democracy (Ritchie in Harrop, 1992; see also Knapp and Wright, 2001).

An alternative perspective on strong states is supplied by those where multi-party systems dominate or have dominated (the Netherlands, Belgium, the French Fourth Republic). In these the party-political input is largely seen very early in the policy process – in the issues that are contested in elections and in the compromises that occur between the elements in a coalition – after which a kind of administrator/politician accommodation seems to apply.

One of the reasons for the preoccupation in much earlier literature with questions about whether politicians or administrators dominate in the policy process arises from a concern that civil servants 'subvert' policy because they do not share the ideologies or value commitments of democratically elected politicians. One possible way of dealing with this concern, the idea that civil servants should be 'representative' in a social sense, is explored in Box 8.8. The extent to which it is seen as a problem is influenced by the extent to which there are significant political or ideological divisions with regard to the policy agenda. Earlier writers on the British civil service (for example, Chapman, 1970) suggested that

| Box 8.8 | Representative bureaucracy |

One response to ideological differences between politicians and civil servants has been to argue that civil servants should be, as far as possible, representative of the societies from which they are drawn. Kingsley's (1944) pioneering work on this topic looked at the British civil service, arguing that it was transformed from an aristocratic into a bourgeois organisation during that period in the nineteenth century when the commercial middle class were becoming politically dominant. The British bureaucracy was thus made representative of the dominant political class, but not, of course, of the people as a whole. To work effectively the democratic state requires a 'representative bureaucracy', Kingsley argues, thus taking up the theme, developed also by Friedrich (1940), that the power of the civil service is such that formal constitutional controls upon its activities are insufficient. Kingsley sees the recruitment of the civil service from all sectors of the population as one means of ensuring that it is a 'responsible bureaucracy'.

This issue has traditionally been explored very much in class terms (see Aberbach, Putman and Rockman, 1981). More recent work has added attention to issues about gender and about ethnic, regional or religious origins or background (Meier, Stewart and England, 1991; Selden, 1997).

civil servants in Britain have strong reservations about party politics while at the same time possessing commitments to particular policies. The implication is that these officials find changes in their political masters easy to adjust to so long as they do not involve violent ideological shifts. Officials can operate most easily in a situation of political consensus. Where consensus does not exist, however, their role may become one of trying to create it. Graham Wallas (1948) sums this up most neatly:

> The real 'Second Chamber', the real 'constitutional check' in England, is provided, not by the House of Lords or the Monarchy, but by the existence of a permanent Civil Service, appointed on a system independent of the opinion or desires of any politician and holding office during good behaviour. (Wallas, 1948, p. 262)

In the 1960s, discontent developed on the political Left about this comfortable consensual doctrine (Thomas, 1968). A response to it was to appoint temporary political advisers to ministers. But it was on the political Right that the most robust response developed during the governments led by Margaret Thatcher in the 1980s. As a consequence, Campbell and Wilson suggest that the traditional 'Whitehall model' is being destroyed by:

- the breaking of the monopoly of the civil service as advisers to ministers;
- the development of systems to help the Prime Minister contest civil service advice;
- most importantly, 'whole generations of bureaucrats and politicians have been socialised since the 1970s into very different professional norms . . . enthusiasm for government policies has been rewarded more than honest criticism' (Campbell and Wilson, 1995, p. 296);
- 'the erosion of the belief that the civil service is an established profession, like all professions delineated from society as a whole by clear boundaries' (ibid., p. 297).

That argument was developed before Tony Blair came to power. Despite the fact that he has altered the institutions at the centre, his obsessive desire to control policy and to control the way policy is presented has done much to further these developments. This is leading to a very different attitude to the organisation of the upper reaches of the civil service, with many more temporary civil servants being recruited and much more attention being paid to the commitments of candidates for top jobs. It is interesting to note that this approach to filling top offices is now also well established in the German federal government:

> Administrative state secretaries, who are civil servants, occupy the highest grade in the Federal administration, and are regularly amongst the key figures in the ministerial policy process. They deputize for the minister in

running the department, and they operate directly at the interface between politics and administration. Their special position is recognized in their status as 'political civil servants' as defined by Article 36 of the Federal Civil Service Law. It is acknowledged that they need to be in permanent basic agreement with the government's views and objectives in order to perform their task of helping to transform the government's political will into administrative action. Political civil servants, who also include heads of division, need not be recruited from amongst career civil servants. (Goetz, 2003, pp. 27–8)

Campbell and Wilson chart some similar developments in other systems close to the 'Whitehall model' in Australia, New Zealand and Canada. In Australia, Pusey has, however, raised a rather different issue. He has explored the way in which a new ideological agenda has been pursued from within the civil service. He argues that alternative ways of managing the economy have been advanced systematically by 'economic rationalisers' who have come to dominate key roles within the civil service (Pusey, 1991). An interesting ambiguity in Pusey's analysis concerns the extent to which this has been tacitly encouraged by elected politicians, on the Labor side as much as the Liberal. A similar phenomenon has been observed in New Zealand, where a determined group of 'economic rationalisers' closely linked with the Treasury secured the support of first a Labour finance minister and later a National Party one. In respect of this case, Wallis writes of a 'conspiracy', in which the change of the agenda depended upon a concerted effort to win support in the civil service and the political parties (1997).

The evidence marshalled by Pusey and Wallis suggests that there may be a need, alongside interest in the way in which the relationship between political values and a permanent administration is managed, to look at how new ideological consensuses may be developed within a ruling elite. If, in fact, it is the case in the more unified systems, particularly those following the Westminster model, that the policy process is more controlled than Kingdon's analysis suggests, it may be beside the point to ask whether this control comes from the politicians' agenda or from a civil service-dominated policy agenda. We may, particularly when one party is in government for a long while (as in Sweden) or when the differences between the two parties are quite slight (as in the UK between 1951 and 1979) or when political changes often involve slight shifts within a coalition (as in the Netherlands), be looking at control over the agenda exercised by a relatively unified community of politicians and civil servants.

The implication of the above discussion is that it may be inappropriate to polarise the distinction between politician and civil service domination. In addition, it may be important to see interest groups as part of this organised community. These issues were explored in Chapter 4, where it was suggested that some theorists, particularly those who have seen 'corporatism' as important, may have exaggerated the unification of the whole system. However, while it may be unhelpful to exaggerate the sources of policy community unification, there is a need to recognise that there may be situations in which this unification is much in evidence.

In relation to the above discussion of politics and ideology it is important to bear in mind that political parties may not be the driving forces with regard to the injection of ideological elements into the political process. Furthermore, when ideologies become dominant they may fuse all aspects of the policy process. Many writers at the end of the twentieth century gave attention to the way in which economic belief systems, stressing a need to restore market processes to a more central position in the determination of policy, secured acceptance beyond the ranks of the political 'new Right'. The case of New Zealand has attracted particular attention in this respect, since there it was a Labour government that took the crucial first steps (Kelsey, 1995; Massey, 1995). It was noted above that Wallis (1997) describes the New Zealand case as involving a 'conspiracy', inasmuch as 'an exclusive social network of policy participants' worked together to change policy (p. 1). Clearly, where 'policy communities' are able to dominate the policy process, shared ideologies may be important for this domination.

But equally important may be a commitment to collaborative working in government regardless of ideology. The political system of the Netherlands has been seen as characterised by 'consociational democracy' (Lijphart, 1975) with extensive collaboration between opposed social 'pillars' (Catholic, Protestant, secular liberal and social democratic) in both politics and administration. While there is extensive evidence that the era of pillarisation has passed (see Anderweg and Irwin, 2002), corporatist characteristics remain very persistent in the Netherlands. Success in dealing with the need for industrial restructuring has been seen as attributable to the continuation of a weak form of corporatism which has been called the 'polder model' (Visser and Hemerijk, 1997).

CONCLUSIONS

It has been stressed that agenda setting and further aspects of policy formation need to be seen as closely related. Theories about the former are likely to embody propositions about the latter. This is clearly the case with the 'rational' model put forward by Simon, which embraces an overall view of the way in which policy *should* be constructed. That model offers not so much an approach that helps us interpret how policy is actually made but rather an 'ideal type' against which more realistic models may be measured. The dominant approach to this realism is 'incrementalism', offered as an account of what is, but also as a more 'democratic' model for the messy world of pluralistic politics. But the analyst who really gets away from the prescriptive preoccupations of the rationalism/incrementalism debate is Kingdon.

Kingdon is not a dogmatic theorist. He speaks of himself as aiming to make progress 'in understanding . . . vague and imprecise phenomena', but finding that 'vision is still obscured' (ibid., p. 208) and that he is 'trying to weave a rich tapestry' (1995, p. 230). In this sense the fact that he gives no attention to agenda setting anywhere other than the US federal government should not be held against him. Rather, he has given us an approach – we may even say a 'toolkit' – which we can use to explore agenda setting anywhere.

Embodied in Kingdon's notion that three streams – problems, policies and politics – mingle in the 'soup' is an interesting challenge to do two related things. These are to ask questions about the extent to which agenda setting may be stabilised in practice, and thus in a sense come closer to the more considered, 'rational' model advocated by those who want to prescribe ways to analyse policy options. The discussion above, conducted by means of the example of pensions policy, where in some respects stability or shaping comes from the long-run continuity of the 'problem', has suggested that 'politics' makes a difference to national responses. From there it proceeded to look at the role of politics as a source of agenda shaping in societies that are less institutionally fragmented than the United States.

But it is not only political party mandates that may shape the policy agenda. There may also be civil service domination of the agenda, and it may be the case that stable 'policy communities' shape it. However, as will be shown in the next chapter, this topic is further complicated by issues about the extent to which policy is made during the implementation process.

The three main approaches to the exploration of policy formulation – the rational model of decision making, incrementalism, and Kingdon's agenda-setting model – are interesting for the way in which they reflect different policy process theories. The rational model has much in common with the traditional approach to representative government, seeing policy formulation as a systematic response to authoritatively set goals. While there is not much discussion of how these may be set, the presumption is that they emerge from the democratic political process. Incrementalism's links with pluralist thinking are very evident in the writings of Lindblom. Furthermore, Lindblom's shift in perspective through his career can be seen as a response to the challenge posed to pluralism by those who stressed power inequalities. Finally, the way in which Kingdon was influenced by March and Olsen's emphasis upon system unpredictability in an institutional context shows itself in his explicit use of the concept of the 'garbage can'. Furthermore, the challenge to Kingdon's model offered by evidence that systems may be more organised than he suggests emphasises institutional arrangements and the stability of some policy networks and communities.

Implementation: an overview

SYNOPSIS

This chapter starts by noting how a very distinctive vein of 'implementation' studies developed towards the end of the twentieth century. It goes on to explore briefly how that work was concerned to make a clear distinction between policy formulation and implementation, and suggests that this is now a source of difficulties. This leads naturally into a consideration of the 'top-down' studies that particularly emphasised that distinction. It is followed by an exposition of the 'bottom-up' evaluation of these studies. The next section, headed 'Beyond the top-down/bottom-up debate', provides an approach which then dominates the rest of the chapter. It suggests a need for an awareness that there is a complex mix of issues to be understood about the different ways actual policies are developed, about how they may best be studied, and about the normative arguments about who should be in charge which often dominate (and obscure) discussions about implementation. Subsequent sections then highlight issues about variations in the 'policy rule framework' and about 'variations in the administrative system'.

In this chapter the focus will be very much upon introducing issues about what happens during the implementation process. The chapters that follow it explore aspects of the organisation of the policy process that need to be looked at in any account of that process as a whole, but in which issues about implementation loom large.

Introduction

In the United States in the early 1970s and in Europe later in that decade there emerged a wave of studies examining the implementation of public policy. Their rationale was that there had been, in the study of public policy, a 'missing link' (Hargrove, 1975) between concern with policy making and the evaluation of policy outcomes. We should perhaps be wary when academics claim to have discovered a new topic or a 'missing link', as they are very good at dressing up old concerns in new language and thereby claiming originality. The absence of theory and literature on implementation before Pressman and Wildavsky's seminal work (1973) on that topic has been exaggerated: for example, many organisational studies are de facto concerned with this phenomenon. Furthermore, a concern with the relationship between policy making and administration is as old as democratic politics (Wilson, 1887). Nevertheless, as empirical research in political science developed in the first half of the twentieth century there was perhaps a relative neglect of the study of the processes by which policies are translated into action. They were regarded as mundane and taken for granted. As Gunn (1978) argues, 'Academics have often seemed obsessed with policy formation while leaving the "practical details" of policy implementation to administrators' (p. 1).

The explosion of implementation studies therefore represents an important advance in policy analysis. Yet, like so many paradigm shifts in the social sciences, this new intellectual development has come to be seen to have its own limitations. At various places in this book warnings have been sounded about the stages model of the policy process. The distinction between policy formulation (often, indeed, called 'making') and implementation is almost certainly the division within the policy process that has been most highlighted in stagist approaches to policy analysis. As stressed earlier (see p. 21), there are pragmatic reasons for breaking the analysis of the process into stages, and this is particularly relevant when we reach the topic of implementation.

The strength of the case for stressing the importance of implementation as distinct from the policy formulation process, and as deserving of attention in its own right, has tended to lead to an overemphasis on the distinctiveness of the two processes. There has been a tendency to treat policies as clear-cut, uncontroversial entities whose implementation can be studied quite separately. This has raised both methodological problems and problems about the extent to which the very practical concerns of implementation studies may involve, explicitly or implicitly, identification with some actors' views of what should happen.

This difficulty has been compounded by the extent to which actors regard it as important to make this distinction. We have here an argument that may be taken in two possible ways. One is to say that inasmuch as people regard a distinction as important, then in all sorts of respects it will be evident in their activities, and the empirical study of their activities must have regard to that. The other is to say that there is a need to be sceptical about a distinction that is so widely used in policy rhetoric, closely linked as it is with the notion that some actors have responsibilities to be leading decision makers (a notion often embedded in versions of democratic theory) whilst others have duties to carry out the policies of their 'masters'. There is in this latter case a situation in which there will be powerful people who want us to believe that the reality corresponds with the rhetoric, or will want to blame the 'implementers' when events do not correspond with original expectations.

In this book the aim is to try to have it both ways – that is, both to reflect the importance of the formulation/implementation distinction in the policy process, and to be aware of how confused it may be in practice.

The top-down model for the study of implementation

In the course of the evolution of work on implementation in the later part of the twentieth century, a debate developed between the 'top-down' and the 'bottom-up' perspectives. As in all such debates, a later resolution has been reached in which most scholars will want to avoid taking either of the extreme positions, but it is nevertheless helpful to examine this debate for the insights it gives us into some of the key issues about the study of implementation.

The top-down perspective is deeply rooted in the stages model, and involves making a clear distinction between policy formulation and policy implementation. Hence, Van Meter and Van Horn (1975) define the implementation process as 'Those actions by public or private individuals (or groups) that are directed at the achievement of objectives set forth in prior policy decisions' (p. 445).

Pressman and Wildavsky go on in a similar vein:

> Implementation to us, means just what [dictionary definitions] . . . say it does: to carry out, accomplish, fulfill, produce, complete. But what is it being implemented? A policy, naturally. There must be something out there prior to implementation; otherwise there would be nothing to move toward in the process of implementation. A verb like 'implement' must have an object like 'policy'. But policies normally contain both goals and the means for achieving them. How, then, do we distinguish between a policy and its implementation? (Pressman and Wildavsky, 1973; 1984 edition: xxi)

Pressman and Wildavsky thus highlight a question that is for them of more than linguistic relevance:

> We can work neither with a definition of policy that excludes any implementation nor one that includes all implementation. There must be a starting point. If no action is begun, implementation cannot take place. There must be also an end point. Implementation cannot succeed or fail without a goal against which to judge it. (Ibid., p. xxii)

There is an issue of logic here. The act of 'implementation' presupposes a prior act, particularly the act of formulating what needs to be done. Various questions follow from this: Who is the formulator? Who is the decision maker? Who is the implementer? If they are not integrated as a single actor, there is a need to identify the variety of actors involved. Then there are questions about whether the formulator or decision maker has more power, or a role that is more legitimised, than the implementer. The act of formulation and decision making may take place anywhere in the policy process. There is no necessary assumption that formulators are always at the 'top' in a political or hierarchical sense, but there is embodied in this perspective a view of the prior nature of the formulation process. This may be called the *implementation follows formulation and decision theorem*' (Hill and Hupe, 2002, p. 4).

The pioneering implementation studies therefore highlighted the need to examine the process of putting policy into action. Their concern was to challenge those who, at that time, took it for granted that this process would be smooth and straightforward. Hence Pressman and Wildavsky gave their book a very long and often quoted subtitle: 'How Great Expectations in Washington are Dashed in Oakland; or Why It's Amazing that Federal Programs Work At All, This Being a Saga of the Economic Development Administration as told by Two Sympathetic Observers who Seek to Build Morals on a Foundation of Ruined Hopes'!

One senses here some of the frustration felt by many Americans about the failure, or limited success, of the war on poverty and the great society programmes of the late 1960s. Pressman and Wildavsky were not the first to observe this apparent gap between federal aspirations and local reality: there was a similar body of literature on the limitations of Roosevelt's reformist interventions in American society in the 1930s (see, in particular, Selznick, 1949). An important preoccupation in this work is clearly the concern with the problem of intervention from the top of a federal system; it comes through similarly in other analyses of American social policy which have less of an emphasis on implementation *per se* (see Marris and Rein, 1967; Moynihan, 1969).

However, the focus on American federalism does not destroy the value of this approach for the study of implementation in other societies. Indeed, if analysed in this manner it raises important questions about the ways in which policy transmission occurs, or fails to occur, through multi-government systems. Certainly, a great deal of the analysis in Pressman and Wildavsky's book is concerned with the extent to which successful implementation depends upon linkages between different organisations and departments at the local level. They argue that if action depends upon a number of links in an implementation chain, then the degree of cooperation required between agencies to make those links has to be very close to 100 per cent if a situation is not to occur in which a number of small deficits cumulatively create a large shortfall. They thus introduce the idea of 'implementation deficit' and suggest that implementation may be analysed mathematically in this way. This is an important idea, but it is perhaps stated too strongly in this formulation. Bowen (1982) points out that such a formulation disregards the extent to which the interactions between these actors occur in contexts in which they rarely concern simply 'one-off' affairs; rather, these interactions are repeated and accompanied by others, in which case it can be seen that collaboration becomes much more likely.

The notion of cumulative deficit if cooperation is less than perfect has similarities to the approach to the study of administration developed in Britain by Christopher Hood (1976). He suggests:

One way of analysing implementation problems is to begin by thinking about what 'perfect administration' would be like, comparable to the way in which economists employ the model of perfect competition. Perfect administration could be defined as a condition in which 'external' elements of resource availability and political acceptability combine with 'administration' to produce perfect policy implementation. (Hood, 1976, p. 6)

Hood goes on to develop an argument about the 'limits of administration' (his book title) which focuses not so much on the political processes that occur within the administrative system as on the inherent limits to control in complex systems. This is similarly the concern of a two-volume contribution to the subject by another British writer, Andrew Dunsire (1978a, 1978b). Hood and Dunsire, although they use examples from real situations, are concerned to link organisation theory with the study of implementation to provide an abstract model of the problems to be faced by persons attempting top-down control over the administrative system.

All of this work embodies notions of implementation gaps – shifts of policy between initial objectives and final outputs. There are obviously hypotheses about why these gaps may occur, and propositions about the extent to which such gaps should be expected. But the main way in which this work has been taken up has been in a literature that is quite explicitly *prescriptive*, seeing gaps as 'deficits', as problems for those who 'made' policy, and offering advice on the way such gaps may be prevented (Gunn, 1978; Sabatier and Mazmanian, 1979; Hogwood and Gunn, 1984). Policy is taken to be the property of policy makers at the 'top', who are then given advice on how to secure more effective implementation involving versions, of varying degrees of sophistication, of propositions like those in Box 9.1.

Box 9.1	Typical advice to policy makers at the top on how to ensure effective implementation

- Keep policy unambiguous.
- Devise simple implementation structures, with as few links in the implementation chain as possible.
- Effectively control implementing actors.
- Prevent outside interference with the policy process.

Criticisms of the top-down approach

The argument in this section will be complicated, since there are a number of different kinds of criticism of the top-down approach which apply differently to different representatives of that school of thought. Broadly, the arguments separate out into those about the nature of policy, those about the interrelationship between policy formulation and the implementation process, and those about the normative stance adopted by students of implementation (particularly when this is implicit rather than explicit).

Pressman and Wildavsky were quoted earlier as approaching their definition of implementation by asserting that 'implement' is a verb that must have an object: policy. In arguing in this way they surely run the risk of catching themselves in a linguistic trap of their own making. As was recognised in the third edition of their book (1984), published after Pressman's death, it is dangerous to regard it as self-evident that implementers are working with a recognisable entity that may be called a policy. In Chapter 1 it was shown that policy is indeed an extremely slippery concept. It may really only emerge through an elaborate process that is likely to include those stages that are conventionally described as implementation.

The definitions of policy quoted in Chapter 1 (see pp. 6–10) referred to its different characteristics. The two particularly different approaches to identifying policy described there – as a general stance and a rather more concrete formulation – both entail problems for implementation studies, however. These problems are, in a sense, mirror images of each other. Policies as defined as stances (Friend, Power and Yewlett, 1974) may be relatively clear-cut, political commitments to specific action. The difficulty is that they are made much more complex as they are translated into action. Policies as defined in more concrete terms are, as the definitions of Easton (1953) and Jenkins (1978) suggest, often so complex that we are unlikely to be able to identify simple goals within them. Friend's definition is really closer to the concept of policy as used in everyday speech. It refers to the goals embodied in the 'Queen's speeches' or the President's 'messages to Congress', not to the complex phenomena that emerge at the end of the legislative process. Yet it is surely the latter with which students of implementation work.

The argument so far has been that implementation studies face problems in identifying what is being implemented because policies are complex phenomena. This needs now to be taken a stage further. Perhaps policies are quite deliberately made complex, obscure, ambiguous or even meaningless. As was suggested in Chapter 1 (p. 9) with particular reference to the work of Edelman, in the most extreme case the policies that are the concern of politicians may be no more than symbolic, formulated without any intention to secure implementation. Politicians may want to be seen to be in favour of certain ideals or goals while actually doing nothing about them. Any system in which policy making and implementation are clearly separated, either by a division between legislature and executive (as in the United States) or by a division between levels of government or ministries and implementing agencies (present in most systems but most clear in federal ones), provides opportunities for the promulgation of symbolic policies. In Britain, for example, many regulatory policies require parliamentary enactment but local authority implementation. Parliament may relatively easily pass laws allowing the control of certain activities or the provision of certain services whilst not providing the resources to make action possible. Relatively small teams of local environmental health officials, for example, have to cope with a mountain of legislation designed to protect the public from many potential health hazards in restaurants, shops, etc.

Even when policies are not simply symbolic it is important to recognise that the phenomena upon which action must be based are products of negotiation and compromise. Hence, as Barrett and Hill (1981) argue, many policies:

- represent compromises between conflicting values;
- involve compromises with key interests within the implementation structure;
- involve compromises with key interests upon whom implementation will have an impact;
- are framed without attention being given to the way in which underlying forces (particularly economic ones) will undermine them. (Barrett and Hill, 1981, p. 89)

It must, then, be recognised, first, that this compromise is not a once-and-for-all process but one that may continue throughout the history of the translation of that policy into action. Second, the initial 'policy makers' may be happy to let this occur as it enables them to evade decision problems. If, then, the implementers are distanced from the original policy-framing process, and indeed perhaps even belong to separate, 'subordinate' organisations, they may be perceived as responsible for problems and inconsistencies and for unpopular resolutions of these. Thus, in Britain, local authorities are responsible for supporting the rents of people on low incomes because central government has failed to resolve a conflict between its desire to deregulate the housing market and its concern not to let increases in the cost of benefits to low-income rent payers escalate too rapidly. It has left it to local authorities to use their discretion, at their own expense, to decide which high rents should be fully reimbursed.

A further complication for the analysis of policies is that many government actions do not involve the promulgation of explicit programmes requiring new activities. They involve adjustments to the way existing activities are to be carried out. The most common and obvious interventions of this kind are increases or decreases in the resources available for specific activities. In this way programmes are stimulated or allowed to wither away. What, however, makes implementation studies even more complex is that the relationship between resource adjustment and substantive programmes may be an indirect one. This is particularly a feature of central–local government relations in Britain where, generally, central government does not explicitly fund programmes but makes resources available to multi-purpose authorities (see Box 9.2).

Box 9.2	Implementation of central initiatives by local government in the UK

Indirect funding of UK local government means that the study of the relationship between policy and implementation is by no means straightforward. Bramley and Stewart have shown how varied was the actual effect of public expenditure cuts in Britain in the late 1970s (in Barrett and Fudge, 1981). A study by Webb and Wistow (1982) looks at personal social services policy and demonstrates apparent implementation deficits because local governments chose to disregard central guidelines and preserve social services expenditure, letting the impact of a reduction of central grants fall on other services. They refer to the central government minister subsequently boasting of his success in protecting social services from cuts. Yet Webb and Wistow's way of presenting these events, with its deference to the top-down approach, makes this appear more inconsistent than it really was since they treat the initial cutting decisions as rational top-down policy formulation. The reality was a government committed to cutting public expenditure, a bargaining process in which different spending ministers were forced to deliver specific shares in the cuts, and a cash supply control process in which lower level actors (local governments) were able to do their own separate priority exercises. The ministry at the top did not have a *policy for social services spending* in any very substantive sense.

While Webb and Wistow's is now a rather dated study, the issues they highlight continue to be significant. Central to a debate about local council tax levels that is going on at the time of writing is the fact that at one and the same time central government is imposing high performance expectations upon local government and constraining the funds available to it.

Adjustments to the context in which decisions are made do not only come in the form of resource change, they may also come in the form of structure change. These structure changes may or may not carry implications for substantive outputs. Hence services may be transferred from one agency to another, new rules may be made on how services are to be administered, or new arrangements may be made for policy delivery. These changes to the 'programme shell' (Knoepfel and Weidner, 1982; Whitmore, 1984) are common top-down interventions in public policy, but the analysis of their effects must rest upon an elaborate study of the way in which the balance of power is changed within the implementation system. In purposive language they are concerned with means, not ends, therefore explicit goals cannot be identified, yet they may be of fundamental importance for outcomes and may embody implicit goals. The developments in Britain and elsewhere that are transforming the way policies are delivered – replacing large, bureaucratic departments by hived-off agencies, units that are placed in a quasi-market situation, or even private organisations operating as contractors for public services – must be seen not merely as restructuring the policy delivery system but also as often transforming the policies themselves.

When the 'stance' definition of policy was contrasted with the 'interrelated decisions' definition (see p. 7), it was suggested that a process of concretising goes on. It was also implied that it may be difficult to determine where policy formulation stops and implementation begins. That point should be emphasised further:

> to say that some policies are easier to implement than others one has to be able to identify the point at which they are packaged up ready for implementation. We may be able to say some commitments in party manifestos are easier to implement than others. We may equally be able to say that some Acts of Parliament are easier to implement than others. But in both cases such generalisation may be heavily dependent upon the extent to which aspirations have been concretised. (Hill, in Barrett and Fudge, 1981, p. 208)

The concretisation of policy continues way beyond the legislative process. There is something of a seamless web here, though it may be that it is possible to identify some decisions that are more fundamental for determining the major 'policy' issues than others. There is, however, no reason why we should always expect to find such decisions, nor is it the case that these decisions, when they exist, are invariably taken during what we conventionally define as the policy formulation process. There are, on the contrary, a number of reasons why they may be left to the implementation process, of which the following is by no means an exhaustive list:

- because conflicts cannot be resolved during the policy formulation stage;
- because it is regarded as necessary to let key decisions be made when all the facts are available to implementers;
- because it is believed that implementers (professionals, for example) are better equipped to make the key decisions than anyone else;
- because little is known in advance about the actual impact of the new measures;
- because it is recognised that day-to-day decisions will have to involve negotiation and compromise with powerful groups;
- because it is considered politically inexpedient to try to resolve the conflicts.

Considerations of this kind must lead us to regard the policy-making process as something which often continues during the so-called implementation phase. It may involve continuing flexibility, it may involve the concretisation of policy in action, or it may involve a process of movement back and forth between policy and action. Barrett and Fudge (1981) have stressed the need, therefore, 'to consider implementation as a policy/action continuum in which an interactive and negotiative process is taking place over time between those seeking to put policy into effect and those upon whom action depends' (p. 25).

Lane (1987) highlights some of the key issues here in a paper in which, amongst a variety of approaches to implementation, he identifies it as 'evolution' (p. 532; see also Majone and Wildavsky, 1978), as 'learning' (p. 534; see also Browne and Wildavsky, 1984), as 'coalition' (p. 539, with important references to the essentially collaborative implementation implicit in corporatist relationships – see Chapter 4 above), and as 'responsibility and trust' (p. 541; this is a theme which we will explore further in later chapters in relation to organisational life). All of these imply a system in which a close collaborative relationship characterises relations within the policy system, allowing policy to emerge in action.

The bottom-up alternative

These arguments lead us on to the view that a model of the policy implementation relationship in which the policy formulation process can be seen as setting 'goals', the extent of whose realisation can be measured, provides an insufficient foundation for studies of implementation. It is this that has led various students of implementation to argue for a bottom-up rather than a top-down stance for the study of implementation. Elmore has coined the term 'backward mapping', which he defines as

> 'backward reasoning' from the individual and organisational choices that are the hub of the problem to which policy is addressed, to the rules, procedures and structures that have the closest proximity to those choices, to the policy instruments available to affect those things, and hence to feasible policy objectives. (Elmore, 1981, p. 1; see also Elmore, 1980)

Focusing on individual actions as a starting point enables actions to be seen as responses to problems or issues in the form of choices between alternatives. One of Elmore's justifications for this approach derives not so much from the concern explored here about the difficulty in separating policy formulation and implementation, as from a recognition that in many policy areas in the United States (youth employment policy is Elmore's particular interest) implementation actors are forced to make choices between programmes which conflict or interact with each other.

The proponents of the bottom-up approach argue that it is, by comparison with the top-down model, relatively free of predetermining assumptions. It is less likely to imply assumptions about cause and effect, about hierarchical or any other structural relations between actors and agencies, or about what should be going on between them.

The approach is expounded even more forcefully by Hjern and his associates (Hjern and Porter, 1981; Hjern and Hull, 1982), who argue for a methodology in which researchers construct empirically the networks within which field-level, decision-making actors carry out their activities without predetermining assumptions about the structures within which these occur. The present author, in his work with Susan Barrett, has added his own support to the methodological argument for this perspective, arguing as follows:

> to understand the policy–action relationship we must get away from a single perspective of the process that reflects a normative administrative or managerial view of how the process should be, and try to find a conceptualisation that reflects better the empirical evidence of the complexity and dynamics of the interactions between individuals and groups seeking to put policy into effect, those upon whom action depends and those whose interests are affected when change is proposed. To do this, we have argued for an alternative perspective to be adopted – one that focuses on the actors and agencies themselves and their interactions, and for an action-centred or 'bottom-up' mode of analysis as a method of identifying more clearly who seems to be influencing what, how and why. (Barrett and Hill, 1981, p. 19)

These are to a large extent arguments about methodology, about how to study implementation. But they also suggest a more realistic approach to the discussion of how implementation occurs than do those propositions rooted in a concern about how implementation should be controlled. What, in many respects, is being emphasised in this more action-centred mode of analysis is that the very things that top-down theorists like Gunn (as exemplified in Box 9.1) urge must be controlled are the elements that are difficult to bring under control. The reality, therefore, is not of imperfect control but of action as a continuous process of interaction with a *changing and changeable policy*, a *complex interaction structure*, an *outside world which must interfere* with implementation because government action does, and is designed to, impinge upon it, and implementing actors who are *inherently difficult to control*. Analysis is best focused upon the levels at which this is occurring, since it is not so much creating implementation deficiency as recreating policy.

This emphasis, in the bottom-up critique, upon the complexities in the concept of policy and the way it is made also suggests that implementation may itself be an ambiguous concept. Lane has argued that there is some confusion in the implementation literature between 'implementation and successful implementation as an outcome, and the implementation process or how implementation comes about' (Lane, 1987, p. 528). The classical top-down studies are principally concerned with explaining why a successful outcome does or does not occur, and to do this they need clear goal statements to work with. These may be supplied by the policy makers or imputed by the researchers. Without such yardsticks we may still study processes, but our activity is rather different. Sabatier, in an attempt to fuse the best ideas from both top-down and bottom-up processes, rightly suggests that the presence or absence of a 'dominant piece of legislation structuring the situation' (1986, p. 37) may help to determine which approach is appropriate. However, that may involve starting with a question begging the assumption that this structuring has in fact occurred. One can obviously treat a piece of legislation as dominant, but if one does so the problems for explanation, in cases of implementation failure, tend to be either what others have done to subvert it, or what is wrong with it. Both of these may be oversimplified questions about both policy and its implementation context, and particularly about the relationship between the two.

Beyond the top-down/bottom-up debate

The methodological argument that surfaces in the discussion above can be resolved relatively simply. It may be possible to examine an implementation process in terms of what happens to goals proclaimed early in the policy process (or even in terms of imputed goals) and then look at what happened. It may also be possible to start at the output end and engage in 'backward mapping'. Both approaches will have strengths and weaknesses; both may be biased by the prejudices of the actors, the researchers or the research funders; and choices between them need to be determined by empirical factors and contingencies. As with Allison's alternative approaches to explaining the Cuban missile crisis (see p. 115), mixed approaches, with triangulation between them, may be desirable. As this is not a textbook on methodology, this topic will be left there (but see Hill and Hupe, 2003, Chapters 6 and 7 for further discussion of this).

The case for trying to ensure that normative preoccupations do not interfere with a clear analysis of the implementation process has been emphasised throughout the discussion. The issue, then, for discussion here about ways to move beyond the top-down/bottom-up debate is about recognising that there will be various ways in which actors will attempt to exercise prior control over the implementation process. The concern is with a variety of issues about the extent to which actors impose rules upon others. The other side of this is about how discretion is structured, about how easily actors can exercise autonomy. In the last analysis these are questions about hierarchies and their legitimacy, but we want to leave these out of the discussion at this stage (we will come back to some of these points in Chapter 13). At the risk of overdoing the warnings about the ease with which discourse in this area slips from 'is' into 'ought', it must be pointed out that in the following discussion we use two words much used by lawyers and legal philosophers – 'rules' and 'discretion' – to distinguish between legitimate and illegitimate action, but that the concern here is with the basic sociological processes involved when actors attempt to structure the actions of others. Box 9.3 uses a homely example to set out the core issues here.

Box 9.3	Alternative ways in which discretionary elements occur in implementation: a homely example

Imagine a two-person household in which one person undertakes to cook a meal to be shared with the other. There are then a variety of possibilities, of which the following are the main ones:

1. That the cook is quite free to choose what to do.

2. That the cook is free to choose what to do within constraints such as the size of the budget, the availability of ingredients, the amount of time available and some knowledge of the likes and dislikes of the other.

3. That the ingredients were chosen in advance but that the cook then still has considerable latitude about how to use them.

4. That the recipe was chosen in advance, which means that what is to be done is closely prescribed (but following a recipe may still involve judgements about when elements are sufficiently well cooked, about seasoning 'to taste', etc.).

5. Variants of the above but with negotiations during the process – 'Would you like this?', 'How do you think I should deal with that?', 'Taste this and tell me what you think of it' and so on.

In the author's own household versions of all those five options occur, with the last very common.

In the world of public policy we find a similar range of options to those set out in Box 9.3. The discussion in Chapter 7 of types of policy suggested various ways in which decisions may be structured. It also suggested that the quest for some simple policy typology that would help with the interpretation of when different structuring will occur has been fruitless. It was suggested that the nearest to a successful effort to do this is Matland's use of 'ambiguity' and 'conflict' to typify policy issues (see p. 139). Clearly, ambiguity tends to make the delegation of discretion likely (the need to make judgements during the process highlighted in the cookery example in Box 9.3). In the absence of conflicting goals, experimentation will be feasible. Conflict, on the other hand, implies a desire to control. Actors claiming hierarchical rights will seek to assert them, and this will be particularly evident in the absence of consensus. If low ambiguity is involved then rules will be formulated (the cookery book approach to implementation). High conflict and high ambiguity is a difficult combination. Matland, in his original analysis, called this 'symbolic implementation', implying not merely unpredictability but also, perhaps, situations in which those attempting to dictate policy could merely claim to have tried!

Matland's approach is still rather static, however, and his model of conflict rather a simple dichotomy. Many of the most controversial (and perhaps most interesting) implementation stories involve prolonged interactions in situations of considerable and very complicated multi-party conflicts, a somewhat tempestuous version of the last of the meal preparation models in Box 9.3.

This leads us on to two crucial issues for the examination of the implementation process:

■ the fact that policy processes vary greatly in the extent to which there is an attempt to prescribe a rule framework;

■ the importance of variations in the administrative framework within which the process occurs.

In the terms of the cooking analogy in Box 9.3 the issues can be said to be about the extent to which there is a cookbook containing clear prescriptions, and about the relational frameworks in which that will be used (not just two persons in a household but something much more complex).

The nature of the policy rule framework

The issues about the policy rule framework are best explored through the use of examples. It has already been argued that the policy/implementation distinction largely rests upon the capacity – present in many policy systems – to distinguish stages in the translation of policy into action. It has been stressed that to identify stages as real phenomena is not to regard them as essential or inevitable elements. The sorts of stages that may be identified involve increasing concretisation of policy – from a general commitment to action through the formal enactment of a law to the establishment of a series of guidelines to implementers, 'street-level' interpretations and thus eventually an 'output'. These stages may be recognised institutionally, in terms of formal rules and practices about the roles of various organisations in the process. The products of these stages may have specific legal forms, to which reference will be made in disputes about the meaning and impact of the policy. Constitutions – of varying degrees of formality and rigidity – will be likely to embody assumptions about these products and the legitimacy of the participants who shape them. One way to model these structuring processes was suggested in the discussion of Kiser and Ostrom's work in Chapter 5 (see p. 87). Box 9.4 illustrates these propositions using elements that are likely to give structure to policies in the UK.

The central problem is that whilst some policies pass out of the legislative stages like the British ones with very clear rule structures, enabling implementation deficits to be easily identified, others are much less fully formed. A related issue – once we get into any comparative discussion of the policy process – is that national systems differ in their formal stages and in the extent to which these are regarded as crucial for the policy process. But before we go on to that complication, some British examples will be used to highlight the issues. Box 9.5 outlines a very well-known policy failure where nevertheless great efforts were made to minimise implementation problems by actors often hostile to the legislation.

Box 9.4	Possible elements in the features of UK policies

UK policies may include:

- political manifesto commitments;
- proposals in the 'Queen's speech' at the beginning of a parliamentary session;
- 'green' and 'white' papers, which set out policy objectives in general terms;
- commitments expressed during parliamentary debates and questions;
- the Bill and subsequent Act which gives the policy its primary legal shape;
- regulations enacted after the passing of the Bill;
- circulars, codes and other instructions to officials;
- detailed notes, reports and accounts of working practice.

Implementation is, of course, conventionally seen as involving the last two or three of the items on this list, but the stress in this discussion has been upon the recognition of the complex interactions between parts of the policy process.

Box 9.5	The poll tax: a policy 'failure' yet a very explicit implementation task

Perhaps the best-known British policy 'failure' in the 1980s was the attempt to transform the local taxation system, replacing a system of property taxation by a poll tax (Butler, Adonis and Travers, 1994). This policy was abandoned after widespread protest. Local authorities faced considerable implementation difficulties – in registering all those liable to pay the tax, in enforcing payment and in administering rebates from full tax liability. Yet there was little ambiguity about the implementation task and no local authority attempted to evade its implementation responsibilities or to reinterpret the tax to suit local circumstances. The intentions of central government were too explicit and the consequences for local government-elected members and staff of non-compliance – both legal (suspension and prosecution) and practical (a serious cash deficiency) – were quite clear. Here, then is a case where implementation problems can be analysed in a clear-cut, 'top-down' way – policy objectives were quite specific – and practical implementation problems can be explored in terms of the difficulties those objectives imposed. Implementation 'deficit' came about from public resistance to the operation of the policy in practice.

It can generally be argued that in modern Britain taxation initiatives will reach the implementation stage with comparatively clear rule structures. Those rules may be hard to implement and may be the subject of formal disputes in the courts, hence implementation deficit may be analysed, but political and social forces in British society have taken taxation a long way from the vague 'tax farming' that characterised such policies in early medieval Britain when implementers were charged to bring in money – to profit if they were good at it and to be punished if they were not – by rulers who cared little about how it was done.

Similar points may be made about cash benefit systems. British income maintenance policy has evolved a long way from the decentralised 'poor law', in which a great deal of discretion was vested in local 'boards of guardians', to a modern situation in which all the main benefit systems (including the means-tested ones) have strong rule-based structures which facilitate computerised calculation and the operation of formal appeal mechanisms. A widely discussed 'policy failure' from the 1990s – the Child Support Act of 1991, explained in Box 9.6 – has many features in common with the 'poll tax', though this time with a central agency charged with a difficult and unpopular task. Students of implementation in this case can find their evidence in official auditing studies of error rates and delay and in complaints to the 'ombudsman' about administrative inefficiency.

Box 9.6	An unworkable policy: the UK Child Support Act, 1991

The government decided to tackle the issue of contributions from absent parents by means of a comprehensive, formula-driven scheme to replace both the assessments made as part of the administration of the existing means-tested benefits and the assessments made by the courts in determining maintenance on the breakdown of a relationship. It enacted the Child Support Act in 1991, setting up an agency to administer it. That legislation ran into severe implementation problems because:

- it was retrospective in effect – agreements, including court settlements, made in the past were overturned;
- where the absent parent had obligations to a second family, these were given relatively low weight in the calculations;
- the parent with care of the child had nothing to gain from collaborating with the agency if she (it is nearly always she in this situation) was being supported by state benefits;
- the operation of a rigid formula was unfair when there were regular contacts with the absent parent and a variety of connected expenses.

The enforcement of the Act was not helped by the income targets imposed on the agency and a programme of work which meant that it started with families on 'income support' and had incentives to tackle the easier cases (that is, the more compliant absent parents).

Implementation difficulties led first to the sacking of the first chief executive of the agency, but then the system accumulated evidence on the problems with the process that led to amending legislation, inspired more by the problems within the system than by political initiatives. Incremental changes did not eliminate the problems, hence further amending legislation followed.

These examples from taxation and social security may be contrasted with policies where there is a complex and dynamic relationship between rule structures and their interpretation. Two British examples, both involving what have been regarded as controversial policy changes driven by political commitments, illustrate this. They are set out in Boxes 9.7 and 9.8.

Box 9.7	Trial and error implementation: general practice fundholding in the UK

Glennerster, Matsaganis and Owens (1994) studied the early history of a health policy initiative designed to enable primary health care doctors to secure hospital services for their own patients by entering into contracts without reference to health authorities. These 'general practitioner fund-holders' were allocated budgets based upon the size of their lists and past referral practices. The initial setting of those budgets was very much a matter of 'trial and error'. Similarly the establishment of rules to regulate this activity – to prevent possible abuses of autonomy and to cope with unexpected problems – was an evolutionary process, involving collaboration between the health authorities, the national Department of Health and the 'fundholders' themselves.

Glennerster and his colleagues describe this as 'Lewis and Clark planning' (adapting an idea from Schultze, 1968). They say:

> The American explorers, Lewis and Clark, were merely told to find a route to the Pacific. They did so by finding the watershed, following the rivers to the sea using their wits as they went.
>
> The implementation of fundholding can be seen as a Lewis and Clark adventure – but in this instance there was telephonic contact between the field explorers and the equivalent of Washington and regular flights back to discuss progress with other explorers. (Glennerster, Matsaganis and Owens, 1994, p. 30)

A similar process has occurred more recently when, during 2002, before the enactment of legislation, hospitals were encouraged to explore ways of enacting a new proposal to give them greater autonomy (by becoming foundation trusts). Issues from this process were fed back into the formulation of the policy.

The two examples set out in Boxes 9.7 and 9.8 were selected because in both cases the authors were using new ways to try to capture the complexity of the policy/implementation relationship. Many others could have been chosen from areas where policy implementation involves complex service activities. In both cases issues about the way policy was realised during implementation are emphasised. There is a clear contrast here with the poll tax and the child support examples, where the policy was clear but hard to implement in practice.

Similar issues arise in many areas of regulatory policy. In this area of policy, alongside the problems of complexity there may be other features

| Box 9.8 | The National Curriculum in England and Wales: interactions in making policy aspirations a reality |

Here the issue is the development, under the 1988 Education Act, of a 'national curriculum' setting parameters for teaching in schools. In this case the legislation does little more than prescribe broad subjects to be included (Maths, English, Science, etc.) and organisations and procedures have been set up to determine more detailed content and to enforce compliance. Then, even within the implementation process there is – not surprisingly, given the complexity of the issues – considerable latitude to enable individual schools and teachers to select topics to emphasise, approaches to teaching and so on. Bowe, Ball and Gold (1992) use a concept from sociology and linguistics, 'texts' (Atkinson, 1985), to explain what is here being described as an implementation process. They argue:

> Texts carry with them both possibilities and constraints, contradictions and spaces. The reality of policy in practice depends upon the compromises and accommodations to these in particular settings. ... [o]ur conception of policy has to be set against the idea that policy is something that is simply done to people ... (Bowe, Ball and Gold, 1992, p. 15)

They go on to highlight the peculiar combination of 'Thatcherite policy-making which rides roughshod over the sensibilities of teachers', lack of public confidence in teachers and low morale on the one hand with the fact that it has depended upon a very complex interaction between education officials, advisory bodies and teachers themselves to make the National Curriculum 'work'. Thus Bowe and his colleagues argue:

> Policies ... are textual interventions but they also carry with them material constraints and possibilities. The responses to these texts have 'real' consequences. These consequences are experienced in ... the arena of practice to which policy refers ... policy is not simply received and implemented within this arena, rather it is subject to interpretation and then recreated. (Ibid., pp. 21–2)

which complicate implementation: in particular, the fact that the regulatee often understands the process better than the regulators, that there are difficult trade-off judgements to be made about the costs of compliance and that the ability of the regulatee to evade control puts willing compliance at a premium. This has led Hanf to see much regulatory activity as involving 'co-production' between regulator and regulatee (Hanf, 1993).

At its extreme – and this probably characterised much British pollution control until very recently – policy is essentially no more than the terms that the regulator is able to reach with the regulatee (this issue was explored a little in Chapter 7, on p. 132). In industrial air pollution control the statutory concept of the use of the 'best practicable means' to limit emissions had little meaning except in the context of such an agreement (Hill in Downing and Hanf, 1983). It certainly could not in any realistic sense be described as defined in the policy-making process. Since then, under pressure from the European Community for a more precise approach, this 'policy' has moved on a little, but the policy emphasis is still rather more upon ambient air quality targets than upon specific control over what goes up individual chimneys.

There are very important areas of policy where the policy/implementation distinction is even more blurred than in these examples from service provision and regulation. Oddly, these do not seem to have been given much attention in the implementation literature, perhaps because they concern issues at the very centre of national politics – economic and foreign policy. These issues were discussed in Chapter 7.

If your primary aim is to understand the implementation process, a great deal is going to depend upon what activity you are interested in. If you are looking at one in which there is a quite explicit 'top'-initiated, goal-directed activity, it may be justifiable to use a 'top-down' methodology and work with a notion such as 'implementation deficit'. This may be particularly the case where a quantifiable output is available and explicit inputs can be measured. The British experience with the Thatcher governments was of a number of examples where government goals were very clear. There were cases of very determined top-down pursuit of clearly specified objectives (the sale of local authority-owned homes to their occupiers, for example – see Forrest and Murie, 1991), cases where clear evidence of implementation problems ahead pulled the government back (the strange case of an identity cards scheme to prevent football hooliganism) and dramatic cases of implementation difficulty leading to yet further policy innovation (the cases of the 'poll tax' and the Child Support Act mentioned above).

Yet many other events in the policy process do not involve such clarity. Examples can be taken, even from the Thatcher years in Britain, of complex and confusing cases where central goals were not nearly so clear, or where central goal statements should be received with great scepticism – in fields like community care, employment policy, urban renewal or the prevention of crime, for example. Yet if this is true of unified, centralised, one-party-dominated Britain, how much more true is it of societies where politics is dominated by compromises between federal units or coalition governments? Furthermore, as suggested above, concern may be with an ongoing process where explicit change is not initiated from above, or where there are grounds for scepticism about whether efforts to bring about change will carry through to the 'bottom'.

The importance of variations in the administrative system

The discussion in the last section has drawn distinctions between situations in which rules for implementation are very much in evidence, situations in which implementation is very much a process of developing and elaborating initial policy frameworks and situations in which either we need to say that the implementation process *is* the policy-making process or to regard this distinction as meaningless. This variation may, of course, be influenced by the characteristics of governmental systems and by political or administrative culture, as discussed on pp. 98–105 and pp. 168–72. Nearly all the examples in the discussion above come from Britain. They therefore come from a system which is a peculiar mixture of extreme centralisation and considerable ambiguity about the 'hidden wiring' (Hennessy, 1995) of an unwritten constitution. There is thus considerable variation in control over implementation processes from issue to issue, where matters like centrality to the commitments of the government of the day or the capacity of outsiders to compel or prevent rule making may have a considerable influence.

Contrastingly, it is perhaps not surprising that issues about the capacity of policy makers to influence implementation have been given particular attention in the United States, because of the ways in which federalism, the division of executive, legislative and judicial powers and the written constitution complicate executive action. As suggested above, ever since the New Deal in the 1930s the exploration of ways to increase Washington's influence in Oakland, or wherever, has been a key preoccupation of those Americans who regard active federal government as important for their society. In the 1960s the struggle against racial segregation in the Deep South and the efforts to develop new initiatives in welfare policy and in urban policy offered particularly salient examples.

Alternatively, the combination of quite complex and often decentralised administrative arrangements in small consensual societies – like Sweden, Norway and the Netherlands – contributes perhaps to a relaxed view of delegated implementation in which the centre expects to play a 'steering' role in a context of trust. See, for example, Gustafsson (1991) on central local relations in Sweden.

A realistic approach to the examination of implementation in its administrative context therefore needs to give attention to the facts:

- that implementation involves complex intra-organisational interactions;
- that the analysis of those interactions must take us into issues about negotiations between actors who are at least quasi-autonomous;
- that this autonomy may be linked with claims of legitimacy which render beside the point those analyses that emphasise recalcitrance, shortfalls and deficits;
- that these complexities need to be seen as contained within different national or transnational political systems which influence the games played and the legitimacies claimed.

We will come back to some of the issues about inter-organisational interactions in Chapter 11.

CONCLUSIONS

This chapter started with the arguments between top-down and bottom-up approaches to the study of implementation. Like all such dialectical debates in the social sciences, this one is more important in illuminating the many facets of the subject than in leading the reader to a conclusion on one side or the other.

The aim in this discussion has been first to draw attention to the importance of the top-down school of implementation studies initiated by Pressman and Wildavsky, stressing their role in opening up the analysis of an important, and previously rather neglected, part of the policy process. But then, second, it has sought to demonstrate the blind spots in such a perspective – which may be corrected by considering the alternative bottom-up approach. Whether you favour one or the other approach, some combination of the two, or one that tries to avoid either, depends very much on what you are trying to do. Clearly, they can be integrated.

Any effort to develop implementation theory – once it moves away from the attempt to develop checklists of pitfalls for the implementation process in the way described and criticised above – must face the difficulty of becoming involved with the wide range of questions that have been raised in relation to policy making and in the study of organisations. If we substitute the word 'doing' for 'implementation' we see how we are confronted by an attempt to develop a 'theory of doing' – or of action. Perhaps, therefore, that is not a very helpful way to proceed. Rather, as Susan Barrett and the present author have suggested, it is hard to go beyond the identification of the key elements that must be analysed in the study of implementation, and the recognition of the overwhelming importance of the negotiation and bargaining that occur throughout the policy process. Barrett and Hill (1981) argue:

> many so-called implementation problems arise precisely because there is a tension between the normative assumptions of government – what ought to be done and how it should happen – and the struggle and conflict between interests – the need to bargain and compromise – that represent the reality of the process by which power/influence is gained and held in order to pursue ideological goals. (Barrett and Hill, 1981, p. 145)

This general exploration of implementation – with its emphasis upon the significance of organisational complexity and upon the sources of variation in discretion in the implementation process – is now followed by chapters which look at some of these issues more fully.

At the end of the last chapter it was noted how approaches to the exploration of policy formulation reflected policy process theories. A similar pattern can also be seen, though perhaps less clearly, with implementation theory. The top-down approach to implementation has much in common with the rational model of policy formulation, with here a concern about conformity to authoritatively set goals. Running through critiques of that model is a recognition that either the games implicit in pluralist politics or the biases within the structure of power will continue to manifest themselves during implementation. Finally, the more detailed analysis of implementation, fusing earlier approaches, lays much stress on the need to give attention to institutional context alongside policy content.

10 The importance of organisational processes

SYNOPSIS

The public policy process, particularly that part of it concerned with implementation, is very largely an organisational process. It involves work within (intra-) and between (inter-) organisations. This chapter looks at the former, the next at the latter. An introductory section to this chapter shows that the pragmatic distinction between phenomena that are intra-organisational and those that are inter-organisational may at times be problematic.

Public organisations are often described as bureaucracies. A brief discussion explores the implications of the use of the word 'bureaucracy' in light of the fact that it is often given a pejorative sense. This leads into an examination of the most influential theoretical analysis of public bureaucracy, that provided by the German sociologist Max Weber, and an exploration of the way his ideas have been used by others. A brief account is provided of some other key work on the sociology of organisations that is important for understanding public sector organisations.

The section on 'rules and discretion' seems to involve a distinct change of emphasis, particularly as some of the important work analysing this has been done within academic law. However, the aim in that section, and the one that follows it on the treatment of the same theme in organisational sociology, is to show how issues about possibilities of and limits to control are of fundamental importance for understanding how policy process decision making is handled in many contexts.

Introduction

In order to determine the contents of this chapter and the next, a distinction is being drawn here between those issues about the policy process that can be seen as occurring within a single organisation and those that concern relationships between organisations.

In most respects this distinction can be understood in common-sense terms. Distinctions between what goes on, for example, within a government department and between departments are often made, and need no explanation. However, at the margins it may be difficult to make this distinction. Some sociological analyses of organisations draw attention to the way in which the boundaries between them are social constructions that may vary and may be disputed. Boundaries may be permeable and changing. This issue has become more important in the modern world of governance, two of the characteristics of which are the abandonment of simple hierarchical arrangements and the creation of hybrid organisational forms in which tasks may be subcontracted and shared. Hence, individuals may work for more than one organisation and services may depend upon collaborative arrangements. Inasmuch as this is the case, the distinction drawn here may be a misleading one. It is important, therefore, to bear this in mind as we take as our starting point a literature that has some theory about the analysis of the unitary and hierarchical nature of organisations at its very heart.

Organisation as bureaucracy

The issues about the policy process as an organisational process are empha-sised in discussions of the role of bureaucracy. In the first part of the book it was shown that some of the key theories of the state – particularly elitist theories, rational choice theories and institutional theories – concern them-selves with issues about bureaucratic power, often seeing it as involving the domination of the policy process by those inside the organisational system. The word 'bureaucracy' is a neutral term used to describe a complex organis-ation, particularly a governmental one. But it is also used in a pejorative sense to denote an impenetrable, ponderous and unimaginative organisation.

In many discussions of the role of organisations in the modern world these complex 'bureaucracies' are seen as necessary evils. As Perrow puts it, 'Without this form of social technology, the industrialized countries of the West could not have reached the heights of extravagance, wealth and pol-lution that they currently enjoy' (Perrow, 1972, p. 5). The emphasis upon bureaucracy as a potentially problematical form of organisation, highlighted by the frequency with which the term is used pejoratively, has two separate key concerns which can be described simply as concerns about (a) account-ability and (b) efficiency and effectiveness. One tendency of critiques of bureaucracy is to stress problems with making government organisations accountable to the people. Another is to emphasise the extent to which they are unsatisfactory 'instruments' for the carrying out of policy – they are seen as increasing costs and distorting outputs.

Protagonists at both ends of the political spectrum offer solutions to the alleged problem of 'bureaucracy' in public policy. For the extreme 'Right' the solution is the allocation of goods and services by way of the market, with the role of government kept to a minimum. The market offers a mechanism which is accountable, because the public are then consumers and are able to make choices about what they purchase, and efficient, because providers are in continuous competition with each other. The extreme 'Left' alternatively sees a world in which capitalist power is overthrown as offering the possibility of free collaboration between equal citizens in meeting their needs. Both extremes embody a utopian element – in the case of the 'Right', a belief in the feasibility of a really competitive market rather than an economy in which there is a tendency for monopoly to develop and for choices to be limited and manipulated, in the case of the 'Left', a world in which big government is as unnecessary as big capitalism.

The utopianism of the 'Right' is more important for the modern political agenda than that of the 'Left', partly because of the dominance of capitalist ideology and partly because the history of communism has offered so dramatic a betrayal of its idealistic roots. Yet nearer the centre of the political debate the idealistic assertions of both camps offer key poles for debate about public policy – concerning the extent to which there are problems about organising the public sector and regulating the market sector. This takes us back to Perrow's neat aphorism. Complex organisations are needed to meet the needs of modern society because governments are engaged in a complicated combination of direct provision and market regulation. Moreover, they have to cope with trade-offs between the two. In most of the twentieth century the tendency was for governments – at least in western Europe – to see direct provision as preferable to regulation in many areas of social and economic life. This forced attention to focus on issues about the control of their own large, bureaucratic organisations. In the final quarter of the century there was something of a reaction against this approach. But that heightens the need for attention to regulation, essentially an issue about the relationships between government organisations and private or quasi-autonomous ones. The worries about 'bureaucracy' have not been dispelled, as many within the 'New Right' had hoped – rather, they take new forms, forcing us to reconceptualise bureaucracy in a more complex way. This reconceptualisation has been a key concern of work which sees late twentieth-century innovations in the public sector as a 'new public management' movement (Pollitt, 1990; Hood, 1991). New public management is discussed further in Chapter 13, pp. 267–71.

These normative and prescriptive arguments are not the main concerns of this book. However, some of them will emerge again in the analysis of the issues about accountability in Chapter 13. They have also coloured much theorising and research about organisational behaviour. And, as the last paragraph suggests, they have had an impact upon innovation in public policy and particularly on efforts to influence the implementation process.

Max Weber and the theory of bureaucracy

The work of a German theorist, Max Weber, active at the end of the nine-teenth century and in the early years of the twentieth, was particularly important for the development of the theory of organisations. Furthermore, it was the organisation of government in the modern state that particularly concerned him. He observed the development of a powerful unified civil service in Germany, recognising its potential as an instrument of govern-ment and worrying about its implications for democratic accountability.

Weber embedded his theory of bureaucracy in a wider theory of social power. His discussion of bureaucracy is linked to an analysis of types of auth-ority. He postulates three basic authority types: charismatic, traditional and rational–legal (see Box 10.1). He sees the last-named as characteristic of the modern state.

Box 10.1	Max Weber's analysis of types of authority

Charismatic authority is based upon 'devotion to the specific and exceptional sanctity, heroism or exemplary character of an individual person' (1947, p. 328). It is a transitory phenomenon associated with periods of social turmoil; the essentially personal nature of the relationship between leader and follower makes the development of permanent institutions impossible and accordingly it succumbs to processes of 'routinisation' which transform it into one of the other types of authority.

Traditional authority, on the other hand, rests upon 'an established belief in the sanctity of immemorial traditions and the legitimacy of the status of those exercising authority under them' (ibid.). While charismatic authority's weakness lies in its instability, the weakness of traditional authority is its static nature. It is thus argued to be the case that the rational–legal type of authority is superior to either of the other two types.

Weber states that *rational-legal authority* rests upon 'a belief in the legality of patterns of normative rules, and the right of those elevated to authority under such rules to issue commands' (ibid.). The maintenance of such a system of authority rests upon the development of a bureaucratic system of administration in which permanent officials administer, and are bound by, rules.

Weber regards the development of bureaucratic administration as inti-mately associated with the evolution of modern industrialised society. Bureaucratisation is seen as a consequence of the development of a complex economic and political system, and also as a phenomenon that has helped to make these developments possible.

Students of Weber have differed in the extent to which they regard him as a theorist who believed that bureaucracy can be subjected to democratic control. He was clearly ambivalent on that topic. Whilst the use of 'bureaucracy' as a pejorative term (see the discussion above) clearly predates Weber, he must be seen as the theorist who effectively poses the dilemma: here is an instrument that enables much to be done that could not otherwise be done, but there is a need to be concerned about how it is used, how it is controlled and who controls it (Albrow, 1970; Beetham, 1987).

The strength of the bureaucratic form of administration, according to Weber, rests upon its formal rationality, a notion which a number of modern students of organisations have equated with efficiency. This translation of Weber's concept has led to some useful discussions of the relationship between formalism and efficiency but has also given currency to a rather unsubtle characterisation of Weber's theory. Albrow (1970) shows how this confusion arose and provides the following clarification of Weber's position:

> The real relation between formal rationality and efficiency can best be understood by considering the means by which efficiency is commonly measured, through the calculation of cost in money terms, or in time, or in energy expended. Such calculations are formal procedures which do not in themselves guarantee efficiency, but are among the conditions for determining what level of efficiency has been reached. At the heart of Weber's idea of formal rationality was the idea of correct calculation, in either numerical terms, as with the accountant, or in logical terms, as with the lawyer. This was normally a necessary though not sufficient condition for the attainment of goals; it could even conflict with material rationality. (Albrow, 1970, p. 65)

Weber's theory is seen as providing a number of simple propositions about the formal structure of organisations, a misconception that has contributed to his usefulness to students of organisations but which does not do justice to the depth of his understanding of the critical issues in organisational sociology. As he outlines the characteristics of an organisational type that is important in complex societies because of its formal rationality, he naturally stresses the strength of that type rather than its weakness. Weber's aim is to define a widespread kind of organisation and explain why it is growing in importance, offering thereby sociological analysis rather than political polemic.

Weber lists a number of characteristics which, taken together, define bureaucracy. These characteristics are set out in Box 10.2. While Weber does not see these characteristics as prescriptions for organisation, many subsequent writers have seized upon their similarity to the model prescribed by others who were searching for the best way to organise. Pundits like Fayol (1916), a Frenchman writing around the time of the First World War, and Urwick (1943), an Englishman who was influential in both private and public organisations in the inter-war period, seek to set out rules and maxims for successful administration.

However, perhaps the most influential figure in the search for principles of organisation before the First World War was F. W. Taylor (1911). He was

| Box 10.2 | Max Weber's delineation of the characteristics of bureaucracy |

1. A continuous organisation with a specified function, or functions, its operation bound by rules. Continuity and consistency within the organisation are ensured by the use of writing to record acts, decisions and rules.

2. The organisation of personnel is on the basis of hierarchy. The scope of authority within the hierarchy is clearly defined, and the rights and duties of the officials at each level are specified.

3. The staff are separated from ownership of the means of administration or production. They are personally free, 'subject to authority only with respect to their impersonal official obligations'.

4. Staff are appointed, not elected, on the basis of impersonal qualifications, and are promoted on the basis of merit.

5. Staff are paid fixed salaries and have fixed terms of employment. The salary scale is normally graded according to rank in the hierarchy. Employment is permanent with a certain security of tenure, and pensions are usually paid on retirement.

Based on Weber, 1947, pp. 329-41

an American who tried to develop scientific principles for industrial management based upon a series of generalisations which he claimed to be of universal application. His importance for this account is that he has been widely seen as the leading exponent of methods of organisation which rest upon treating human beings as units of labour to be used 'efficiently' without regard to their needs, attitudes and emotions (Braverman, 1974). Hence a great deal of the subsequent concern about human relations in organisations emerged from the exposure of the limitations of 'Taylorism'. Despite that exposure the influence of Taylorism lives on. Pollitt (1990) has described much modern managerialism in the public services as 'neo-Taylorism'. He argues:

> Taylorism was centrally concerned with the 'processes of determining and fixing effort levels' and can be seen as 'the bureaucratization of the structure of control but *not* the employment relationship' (Littler, 1978, pp. 199 and 185 respectively). It proceeded on the basis that ... the work process could and should be measured by management, and then used as a basis for rewarding and controlling effort. ... This is not far, in principle, from the recent epidemic of electronically-mediated public-service systems of performance indicators, individual performance review and merit pay. (Pollitt, 1990, p. 16)

Taylor was working for the Ford motor company, a pioneer in mass production methods. Hence other theorists have spoken of 'Fordism' (Sabel,

1982) to describe an approach to organisation in which Taylorist methods are used to try to reduce workers to commodities, performing limited tasks in tightly regulated conditions for the lowest possible rewards. Whilst public policy implementation is seen as less likely to embody circumstances in which such mass production is feasible, Taylorism or Fordism can be seen to offer one model for the public bureaucracy (see Pollitt, 1990). It is one model, moreover, which may be seen as solving the dilemma of accountability – at least as far as routine tasks like social benefit administration are concerned – by ensuring a rigid adherence to hierarchically (and thus perhaps ultimately democratically) determined rules. This is an issue to which we will return below when we explore the relationship between rules and discretion.

But that is only one way to take the Weberian model, seeking to make it simply a compliant instrument. Other ways suggested that there were problems with this, and observed some of the tensions and contradictions in the 'ideal type'. In the 1920s and 1930s, management theory gradually began to move away from a concern with the development of formal prescriptions for organisational structure towards a better understanding of organisational life (see Box 10.3). This development, while still firmly preoccupied with the question of how to control subordinates within the industrial enterprise, nevertheless eventually contributed to a transformation of the way organisations are understood.

The development of the sociology of organisations

As the social sciences began to grow in importance in the United States in the 1940s and 1950s, two developments in organisation theory – one stimulated by the work of Max Weber, the other influenced by the more obviously relevant findings of the Hawthorne research – began to come together. Sociologists, using Weber's work (or their understanding of it) as their starting point, set out to show the importance of patterns of informal relationships alongside formal ones. Social psychologists, on the other hand, sought to explore the conflict between human needs and the apparent requirements of formal organisations. Drawing on this work, administrative theorists sought to update the old formal prescriptive models with more flexible propositions based upon this new understanding of organisational life (Argyris, 1964; McGregor, 1960; Herzberg, 1966).

Once Weber's work became available to sociologists in the United States in the 1940s and 1950s, it was applied to organisational studies as a kind of model against which real situations might be measured. By treating it in this way sociologists began to identify problems with the rational model of bureaucracy, often unjustly alleging that Weber had not been aware of them but nevertheless usefully advancing organisational theory.

In some of this work it is suggested that there is likely to be a conflict within a bureaucratic organisation between the principle of hierarchy and

Box 10.3	The role of the Hawthorne research programme for an understanding of the importance of human relationships in organisational life

An important contribution to understanding the importance of human relationships in organisational life came from research carried out under Elton Mayo at the Hawthorne Works in Chicago during the late 1920s and early 1930s (Roethlisberger and Dickson, 1939). The researchers were influenced by research on morale carried out during the First World War. They were also well aware of the progress being made in social psychology between the wars, and in particular they were influenced by the more sophisticated approach to human motivation that Freudian psychology helped to produce. The development of a more complex approach to social structure at this time, by sociologists and anthropologists, also had an impact on their work.

The main importance of the Hawthorne researchers lies in the way they shifted the emphasis in organisation theory from a mechanical concern to discover the 'one best way' to organise work tasks to a recognition of the importance of human relationships for organisational performance. Their early research draws attention to the relevance of managerial interest in workers' activities for motivation and morale, while their later work throws light upon relationships within the work group.

The Hawthorne researchers demonstrate the need to analyse organisations as living social structures. They indicate that, just as to discover that there are such and such a number of farmers, shopkeepers and labourers living in a village and that 'x' works for 'y' and so on is not to find out a great deal of significance about the social structure of that village, so to regard an organisation as merely a pattern of formal roles is likely to make it impossible to understand fully the determinants of behaviour, even formally prescribed behaviour, within that organisation.

Although these findings relate to the shop floor, to the lowest level in an organisation's hierarchy, subsequent research has demonstrated the validity of these findings for all levels. Inter-personal relationships within groups of office workers or within management have equally been found to determine work behaviour in a way that formal organisational rules in no way anticipate.

the need to maximise the use of expertise. Gouldner (1954) makes this point in the following way:

> Weber, then, thought of bureaucracy as a Janus-faced organisation, looking two ways at once. On the one side, it was administration based on expertise: while on the other, it was administration based on discipline. (Gouldner, 1954, p. 22)

Bureaucratic organisation is founded upon the need to make the maximum use of the division of labour. Such division is based upon the need to subdivide a task either because of its size or because it is impossible for a single individual to master all its aspects. In fact, in most cases both of these reasons apply. The principle of hierarchy rests upon the notion of the delegation of responsibility to subordinates. If the superior could perform the whole of the task that is delegated, there would be no need to have subordinates. He or she will delegate part of the task either because of a lack of time to do it alone, or because he or she has neither the time nor the knowledge to perform certain parts of the task. Inasmuch as the latter is the case, it is obvious that in respect of at least part of the task the superior is less expert than the subordinate. But even in the former case this may also be true, since, particularly as far as tasks that require decision making are concerned, the subordinate will be in possession of detailed information which, in delegating responsibility, the superior has chosen not to receive. We are back here, of course, to the issues about the likelihood of discretion in action (explored in the cookery example in Box 9.3).

It is for these reasons that, as far as the detailed functioning of any organisation with complex tasks to perform is concerned, it must be recognised that expertise resides to a large extent in the lower ranks of a hierarchy. And it is for these reasons that it is inevitable that there tends to be conflict between authority based upon expertise and authority based upon hierarchy in bureaucratic organisations.

The apparent inconsistency in Weber's theory identified by Gouldner has helped to provoke several valuable studies of conflict between experts and administrators within organisations. An allied topic that has also been explored is the conflict that exists for experts between professional orientation and organisational orientation in their attitudes to their work (Gouldner, 1957–8; Reissman, 1949).

A second important theme deriving from Weber's work concerns the relationship between rationality and rigidity. One of the earliest essays on this theme was Merton's (1957) discussion of bureaucratic structure and personality. This emphasis fits with the arguments about expertise within organisations. Its implications for the behaviour of bureaucratic employees will be explored further in Chapter 12.

All this sociological work led to an exploration of the relationship between organisational structure and organisational tasks. Thus, the question raised was whether the 'rational' structure may be well adapted to some tasks but ill adapted to others. Two British researchers, Burns and Stalker (1961), made one of the most important contributions on this theme. They drew a distinction between 'mechanistic' and 'organic' management systems (see Box 10.4). Other sociologists began, however, to raise wider questions about the fit between organisational task and structure by examining a wide range of work situations. Some other British research played a seminal role in this development. First, Woodward (1965) developed a typology of industrial organisations based upon differences in technology. Then, later sociologists, notably a group working together at Aston

University, began to argue that the varied and multi-dimensional nature of organisational arrangements is determined by a variety of 'contingencies' (see Greenwood, Hinings and Ranson, 1975 for an application of this work in public organisations). These include variables which are external to the organisation in its 'environment', variables determined by the power structure in which it operates, and variables which will depend upon 'ideology', or what Child (1972) describes as 'strategic choice'.

Box 10.4	Burns and Stalker's distinction between mechanistic and organic management systems

Mechanistic systems, involving formal structures broadly comparable to the Weberian model, are, their research suggests, most suitable for stable, unchanging tasks. Organic ones are, by contrast, best

> adapted to unstable conditions, when problems and requirements for action arise which cannot be broken down and distributed among specialist rules within a clearly defined hierarchy. Individuals have to perform their special tasks in the light of their knowledge of the tasks of the firm as a whole. Jobs lose much of their formal definition in terms of methods, duties, and powers, which have to be redefined continually by interaction with others participating in a task. Interaction runs laterally as much as vertically. Communication between people of different ranks tends to resemble lateral consultation rather than vertical command. Omniscience can no longer be imputed to the head of the concern. (Burns and Stalker, 1961, pp. 5–6)

Burns and Stalker base their dichotomy on experience of research into two contrasting industrial situations.

Organisations have thus to be recognised as being power systems in which structural features interact with, and are affected by, factors which make some participants within them more powerful than others. Hence Salaman argues:

> What occurs within organisations, the ways in which work is designed, control applied, rewards and deprivations distributed, decisions made, must be seen in terms of a constant conflict of interests, now apparent, now disguised, now overt, often implicit, which lies behind, and informs, the nature of work organisations within capitalist societies. (Salaman, 1979, p. 216; see also Clegg, 1990 for more on these modern contributions to organisational theory)

These power relations within organisations are in various respects related to others outside the organisation. This issue was explored in the discussion of institutional theory in Chapter 5 (particularly pp. 79–80). We will return to this theme in the next chapter.

Rules and discretion

A key issue in respect of the hierarchical model of public organisation is the relationship between rules, which specify the duties and obligations of officials, and discretion, which allows them freedom of choice of action. This topic, clearly very central to the accountability concerns of the top-down model of implementation, is, not surprisingly, also a preoccupation of a body of literature on public law. However, these legal preoccupations tend to involve an approach to these concepts which sees rules very much in a statutory context and discretionary actions as involving not so much individual choice of courses of action (which many will take for granted as inevitable) but as particular cases of legitimate departure from action prescribed by a legal rule structure. This is a theme to which we return in Chapter 13.

In any administrative system regulated by law, discretion will be embedded in a rule structure – at the very least in a form that will make it clear that only in a very specific set of circumstances can officials do what they like (probably the laws which come nearest to this form are those that give certain officials very strong powers to act in the interests of public safety or to prevent entry to the country of foreigners deemed to be a threat to the regime). This embedded character of discretion leads to a rather confusing argument between those who use broad and those who use narrow definitions of the concept. Perhaps the most influential definition of discretion is Davis's: 'A public officer has discretion wherever the effective limits on his power leave him free to make a choice among possible courses of action and inaction' (1969, p. 4). Others have used quite restrictive definitions, reserving the concept for only some of the phenomena embraced by Davis's definition. For example, Bull (1980) and Donnison (1977), in their separate discussions of social security discretion, draw a distinction between judgement, where the simple interpretation of rules is required, and discretion, where the rules give specific functionaries in particular situations the responsibility to make such decisions as they think fit. This seems to be drawing an unnecessary distinction. If all discretion is embedded to some extent in a rule structure (being what Dworkin has called 'the hole in the donut', 1977), then Bull and Donnison are merely drawing a distinction between more and less structured discretion, or between what Dworkin has called weak and strong forms (ibid., p. 31).

The approach in this book is to use the concept of discretion in the wide sense embodied in Davis's definition. This is partly influenced by a belief that social scientists should try to avoid imposing their own restrictive definitions of concepts used in everyday speech. But it is also justified by the fact that this discussion is concerned to see to what extent discretion is a useful concept with which to explore delegated decision-making processes.

The use of a wide definition like Davis's implies a concern with almost all decision-making situations since, as Jacques (1967) points out, almost all delegated tasks involve some degree of discretion. This, of course, was the point made in Box 9.3, with particular reference to cookery books. The study of discretion must involve, by implication, the study of rules, and may alternatively be defined as being concerned with the extent to which actions are determined by rules. This also means that students of discretion must be concerned with rule breaking since in real-life situations the interpretation of the extent to which rule following allows discretion merges imperceptibly into the witting or unwitting disregard of rules.

Davis's definition comes from a book in which he argues for any rule structure within which discretion is exercised to be drawn as tightly as possible. He argues: 'Our governmental and legal systems are saturated with excessive discretionary power which needs to be confined, structured and checked' (1969, p. 27). Later in the same book he argues that:

> we have to open our eyes to the reality that justice to individual parties is administered more outside courts than in them, and we have to penetrate the unpleasant areas of discretionary determinations by police and prosecutors and other administrators, where huge concentrations of injustice invite drastic reforms. (Davis, 1969, p. 215)

Davis argues that citizens' rights to procedural justice can best be achieved through earlier and more elaborate administrative rule making and in better structuring and checking of discretionary power (ibid., p. 219). He is thus concerned with the need for the public organisation to control the discretionary power of the individual public officer, and he feels this should be primarily attempted through rules that are open to public inspection.

In Britain, Jeffrey Jowell carried forward the kind of concern about discretion shown by Davis in the United States. Jowell's definition of discretion is similar to Davis's. He defines it as 'the room for decisional manoeuvre possessed by a decision maker' (Jowell, 1973, p. 179), and argues that the key need is to ensure that decision makers cannot make arbitrary decisions. However, Jowell lays a far greater stress than Davis upon difficulties with reducing administrative discretion. In particular, he shows how many of the considerations with which decisions must be concerned are inherently difficult to specify in rules. Legislators are concerned to prevent *dangerous* driving, for example, to ensure that food is *pure*, and that factories are *safe*. The provision of clear-cut rules to define what is safe or dangerous, pure or polluted, is often difficult. It may be that legislators need the help of the experts who are to enforce the law to provide some specific rules. In this sense discretion may be limited at a later date when experience of enforcement enables explicit rules to be devised. It may be that conflict over the legislation has led to a blurring of the issues, and that legislators have evaded their responsibility to make more explicit rules. But it may be the case that the translation of standards into explicit rules is so difficult as to be practically impossible.

Jowell provides a valuable discussion of the problems of fettering discretion where concern is with the enforcement of standards. He argues that standards may be rendered more precise by criteria, facts that are to be taken into account. However, he argues that 'the feature of standards that distinguishes them from rules is their flexibility and susceptibility to change over time' (Jowell, 1973, p. 204). Box 10.5 shows how Jowell develops this point.

Box 10.5	Jowell's (1973) analysis of the issues about standards

Very often standards involve questions of individual taste or values. Jowell quotes with reference to this point an appeal court case in which the judge was unable 'to enforce a covenant restricting the erection of "any building of unseemly description"'. Jowell similarly suggests that situations in which unlike things have to be compared, or which are unique and non-recurring, cannot be regulated by reference to a clearly specified standard. He argues:

It is not difficult to appreciate that it would be asking too much of the English football selectors to decide after a public hearing and with due representation, to state reasons why the national interest would be served by having X rather than Y or Z to play centre forward in the coming match. (Jowell, 1973, p. 206)

This issue about standards has been taken up in other legal writing on discretion – hence Dworkin's (1977) distinction between strong discretion, where the decision maker creates the standards, and weak discretion, where standards set by a prior authority have to be interpreted. Galligan (1986) is similarly concerned to analyse discretion in this way, pointing out that decision makers have to apply standards to the interpretation of facts. These distinctions may seem very academic, but they are important in administrative law for drawing distinctions between decisions that are within an official's powers and ones that are not, and therefore for determining whether intervention by an appeal body is appropriate.

Issues about conflicting facts arise where evidence is ambiguous, or where individuals present different versions of the same events. One of the surprising aspects of some of the less sophisticated attacks on discretionary administration by lawyers is that, while in practising their own profession they talk of facts and law and of proof and disproof, they very often require judges and juries to decide between conflicting evidence. The proper distinction to make here is not between the precision of judicial decision making and the imprecision of much administration, but between the extent to which procedural safeguards for the individual, or due process, exist in each situation. Here again Jowell's work is helpful since he distinguishes between two approaches to the control of discretion: 'legalisation', the 'process of subjecting official decisions to predetermined rules' and thus, of course, the elimination of discretion; and 'judicialisation', involving 'submitting official decisions to adjudicative procedures' (1973, p. 178).

Jowell does not accept a simple dichotomy between rules and discretion as suggested by Davis, but rather argues that discretion 'is a matter of degree, and ranges along a continuum between high and low' (1973, p. 179). At first glance, rules may appear to abolish such discretion, 'but since rules are purposively devised ... and because language is largely uncertain in its application to situations that cannot be foreseen, the applier of a rule will frequently be possessed of some degree of discretion to interpret its scope' (ibid., p. 201). This last comment suggests that any study of discretionary decision making requires a consideration of social processes internal to the organisation and a study of the attitudes and beliefs of those who have to interpret the rules.

Jowell's arguments quoted above suggest a need to relate any evaluation of discretion to the substantive issue involved. He suggests some reasons why discretion may be inevitable. His football selection example highlights not merely the issue of standards but also the relevance of expertise and the significance of 'polycentric' issues where many factors interact (Baldwin, 1995, p. 29). This suggests a need to identify types of decision situations in which discretion is more likely. That is a topic to which we return in the discussions of street-level work in Chapter 12 and of accountability in Chapter 13.

Rules and discretion in organisational sociology

It has been argued that all work, however closely controlled and supervised, essentially involves some degree of discretion. Wherever work is delegated, the person who delegates it loses a certain amount of control. To approach the concept in this way is, of course, to examine it from the perspective of superordinate authority. Viewed the other way round, the equivalent phenomenon is rules which apparently guarantee benefits or services but nevertheless have to be interpreted by intermediaries. It is in the twin contexts of task complexity and the delegation of responsibility that the phenomenon of discretion becomes of salient importance. In complex organisational situations gaps readily emerge between intentions and outcomes. People running one-person businesses exercise discretion, of course, but the concern here is with it as a relational phenomenon. The problems about discretion are perceived, not surprisingly, as arising when one person's discretionary freedom may subvert the intentions of another.

Running through much organisation theory, and in particular through the work of those writers who are seeking to help those they see as in control of organisations to determine the right way to approach the delegation of tasks, is therefore a concern about the balance between rules and discretion, even when different words are used. Hence Simon, in his classic work *Administrative Behaviour* (1957), emphasises the importance of the various premises upon which decisions are based. Rule making and control within organisations is concerned with the specification of premises for subordinates. Simon argues:

The behaviour of a rational person can be controlled, therefore, if the value and factual premises upon which he bases his decisions are specified for him. This control can be complete or partial – all premises can be specified, or some can be left to his discretion. Influence, then, is exercised through control over the premises of decision. (Simon, 1957, p. 223)

One reservation must be made about this statement (in addition to objecting to its gendered nature), namely that, as suggested above, the notion of total control in an organisational context is unrealistic. Otherwise this is a valuable statement of the place of discretion in a hierarchical relationship. Simon goes on to suggest that what occurs within an organisational system is that a series of areas of discretion are created in which individuals have freedom to interpret their tasks within general frameworks provided by their superiors. He quotes a military example relevant to the 'modern battlefield' (see Box 10.6), recognising the prevalence of discretion even in the most hierarchical and authoritarian of organisations. Dunsire (1978a) has seized upon the interesting reference to the 'province' of the subordinate in this context. He portrays organisational activities as involving 'programmes within programmes'. In a hierarchy subordinate programmes are dependent upon superior ones, but they may involve very different kinds of activities. Dunsire elaborates an example of a railway closure to show that while activities such as the rerouting of trains, the selling of railway property and, at the very end of the chain, the removal of ballast from abandoned tracks are necessarily dependent upon superior decisions about the closure of the line, the way they are carried out is not predetermined by the decisions taken at the top of the hierarchy. He argues that decisions at the higher level are of high generality, those at the bottom of high specificity. This does not mean, however, 'that a worker at a high specificity level necessarily has a smaller amount of discretion (in any of its

| Box 10.6 | Simon's example of the rules/discretion relationship on a battlefield |

Simon writes:

how does the authority of the commander extend to the soldiers in the ranks? How does he limit and guide their behaviour? He does this by specifying the general mission and objective of each unit on the next level below, and by determining such elements of time and place as will assure a proper coordination among units. The colonel assigns to each battalion in his regiment its task; the major, to each company in his battalion; the captain, to each platoon in his company. Beyond this, the officer does not ordinarily go. The internal arrangements of Army Field Services Regulations specify that 'an order should not trespass upon the province of a subordinate. It should contain everything beyond the independent authority of the subordinate, but nothing more'. (Simon, 1957, p. 224) senses) than a worker at a high generality level' (Dunsire, 1978a, p. 221). This approach helps us to make sense of the use of the concept of discretion in relation to professional hierarchies such as education or medicine. The organisational or planning activities at the top of such hierarchies set contexts for, but do not necessarily predetermine, decision making at field level, where very different tasks are performed and very different problems have to be solved.

All the writers who have been concerned with the complexity of organisations have acknowledged that there are related problems of control, coordination and communication between these different 'provinces' and linking these programmes within programmes (see Dunsire, 1978b). Attention has been drawn to the interdependence involved, and therefore to the fact that in a hierarchical situation superiors may be dependent upon subordinates. This is taken further by Gouldner (1954), who shows that the top-down presentation of hierarchical relationships with superiors promulgating rules to restrict the discretion of subordinates may sometimes be turned on its head. He draws attention to the development of rules which limit the discretionary freedom of superiors in the interests of their subordinates. The classical discussion of this occurs in Gouldner's *Patterns of Industrial Bureaucracy* (1954), in which he shows the part that workers may play in securing rules to protect their interests. Overall his emphasis is upon the appeal to rules, by either party, in a situation in which a previously obtaining relationship breaks down:

> Efforts are made to install new bureaucratic rules, or enforce old ones, when people in a given social position (i.e. management or workers) perceive those in a reciprocal position (i.e. workers or management) as failing to perform their role obligations. (Gouldner, 1954, p. 232)

Gouldner explores the many functions of rules in situations of social conflict. He draws our attention, therefore, to the extent to which rules and discretion must be studied in the context of relationships in which the parties on either side seek to influence the freedom of movement of the other.

It is important to move away from the older emphasis in organisation theory which saw the rules/discretion relationship from the perspective of superiors concerned to limit discretion, as far as acceptable, in the interests of rational management. Instead, attention should be directed towards the extent to which both rules and discretion are manipulated and bargained over within hierarchies. Fox (1974), coming to the examination of this issue from a concern with industrial relations, has interestingly related rule imposition to low-trust relationships. He picks up the top-down concern with detailed prescription and shows how this creates or reinforces low-trust relations:

> The role occupant perceives superordinates as behaving as if they believe he cannot be trusted, of his own volition, to deliver a work performance

which fully accords with the goals they wish to see pursued or the values they wish to see observed. (Fox, 1974, p. 26)

A vicious circle may be expected to ensue. The subordinate who perceives that he or she is not trusted feels little commitment to the effective performance of work. This particularly affects the way the remaining discretionary parts of the work are carried out. The superior's response is to try to tighten control and further reduce the discretionary elements. The irreducible minimum of discretion that is left leaves the subordinate with some weapons against the superior: the prescribed task is performed in a rigid, unimaginative and slow way.

This means that some rather similar phenomena may emerge by different routes. One may be defined as discretion, the other as rule breaking. The former emerges from a recognition of the power and status of implementers (this word is used deliberately instead of subordinates). This is the high-trust situation described by Fox, and applies to much professional discretion within public administration. The latter is seized by low-level staff regarded as subordinates rather than implementers who, in practice, superiors fail to control. One is legitimised, the other is regarded – by the dominant elements in the hierarchy – as illegitimate. To the member of the public on the receiving end they may be indistinguishable.

Much of the organisation theory explored here indicates that discretion and rule breaking cannot be simply contrasted. Actors may be faced with situations in which rules conflict, in which rules are ambiguous, or in which so many rules are imposed that effective action becomes impossible. In these situations choices are made between rules, or about how they are to be respected. Hence occasions arise in which subordinates can paralyse the organisation by working to rule, by obsessively following rules which under normal operating conditions everyone would tacitly recognise as only to be applied in unusual situations.

The author has discussed elsewhere (Hill, 1969) the way in which social security officials may operate when they suspect fraud. They are able to operate rules and procedures in a heavy-handed way to ensure that claims are fully investigated and claimants are made fully aware of the consequences of detection. If, however, they operate like this in more normal situations they will severely slow down the processing of claims and deter genuine applicants.

Alternatively, Blau (1955) shows how front-line bureaucrats disregard rules to enable them to relate more effectively to their peers and to the members of the public with whom they deal. In this sense rule bending or breaking operates as a substitute for discretion to generate a responsive organisation. However, there are issues here about the legitimacy of such adaptation, and the extent to which it may be used to favour some clients but not others. In Chapter 12 the discussion of Merton's (1957) portrayal of 'over-conforming' bureaucrats who create problems because they apply the letter and not the spirit of the law, and of Lipsky's (1980) work on 'street-level bureaucracy', returns to this theme.

This excursion into the treatment of discretion in organisation theory suggests, therefore, that there are a number of reasons why discretion is likely to be an important phenomenon in bureaucracies. At times, confusion arises between notions of organisation flexibility in which discretion, particularly professional discretion, is accepted as an inherent feature and notions of conflict between formal requirements and informal behaviour (or more explicitly between rule making or enforcement and rule breaking). This confusion may be a reflection of the fact that in reality these phenomena cannot be easily separated. Organisations are not simply fixed entities within which informal behaviour may develop. They are in a permanent state of change with both new rules and new forms of rule breaking occurring as conflicting interests interact. The granting of discretion may be a conscious ingredient of the formal design at one extreme, or a reluctant concession to organisational realities at the other. Conversely, new limitations upon discretion may stem from attempts by superiors to assert their hierarchical rights, or from aspirations of subordinates to introduce greater certainty for their activities. In this last sense, therefore, there is no simple equation between rule making and hierarchical control or between the preservation of discretion and subordinate freedom.

This final point needs emphasising further. Baumgartner (1992) criticises the legal concern that discretionary behaviour is unpredictable and argues that 'social laws' make it predictable. Her essay analyses the impact of a variety of sociological features of official encounters upon their outcomes. In some respects she caricatures the legal approach – the preoccupation of people like Davis with the regulation of discretion is based as much upon a concern about the social biases that enter into it as upon its unpredictability. However, this sociological perspective is important in reminding us that 'rules' in a sociological sense may be as readily 'made' in the course of official behaviour as promulgated by policy makers and managers. These 'rules', moreover, may have characteristics which give them a power that is difficult to resist. Feldman, in an essay in the same volume as Baumgartner's offers a clever analogy:

> The difference between the formal limits and the social context limits to discretion can be likened to the difference between a wall and a rushing stream of water. The wall is firm, clearly delineated, and it hurts when you run into it. The rushing stream ... moves; its speed varies; it is more powerful in the middle than on the edges. It does not always hurt to go into the stream; indeed it may at times be pleasurable. The wall, however, can be assaulted and broken down while the stream rushes on creating a path for itself against the mightiest resistance. (Feldman, 1992, p. 183)

Summing up on rules and discretion

In examining rules and discretion, several issues need to be given attention. First, the complex interaction of the two concepts must be emphasised. Issues about rigid rule frameworks are implicitly issues about the absence of discretion. Concerns about excessive discretion are concerns about the limitation of the rule systems within which it is embedded. Hardly ever, in the discussion of public policy, is there either absolute rule dominance or unstructured discretion.

Second, therefore, as stressed throughout this book, policy (in which rules and discretion are mixed together) must be seen in a wider social and political context, which is likely to affect the way discretion manifests itself and the attempts that are made to control it. Discretion may arise from ambiguity, sometimes deliberate, in public policy.

Third, while acknowledging political reasons why discretionary power may be conferred, the discussion has not disregarded the extent to which this phenomenon arises as a consequence of inherent *limits* to control. As Prottas (1979) argues:

> A general rule in the analysis of power is that an actor with low 'compliance observability' is relatively autonomous. If it is difficult or costly to determine how an actor behaves and the actor knows this, then he is under less compulsion to comply. (Prottas, 1979, p. 298)

Fourth, as this last observation reminds us, there is a need to analyse discretion as a facet of organisational life in a complex relationship to rule breaking. It is important to relate discretion to issues about organisational complexity, reward systems, motivation and morale.

Fifth, we should not disregard the extent to which the concern about discretion is a normative one. Under what circumstances may discretion be said to be a problem, and for whom? To what extent does the balance established between discretion and rules distribute differential advantages and disadvantages to the parties involved, and particularly to the members of the public affected by the policy?

Finally, in noting that discretion has been regarded as a problem, we should recognise that a variety of strategies of organisational control have developed to try to deal with it. The traditional approach has been to try to control it through tighter rules and procedures. More recently, identification of the ubiquitous nature of the phenomenon has led rather to attempts to structure it. This is one of the key preoccupations of the 'new public management' movement, which is explored further in Chapter 13 (see pp. 267–71).

CONCLUSIONS

This chapter started by examining the way in which Max Weber's theory of bureaucracy has been seen as defining a model for organisational control that has been widely adopted. We are again, as in so much of any discussion of the policy process, in a literature where issues about what *does* happen and issues about what *should* happen are often confused. The Weberian model is seen both as a way of conveying the essential character of hierarchical admin-istration and as an ideal widely espoused by the architects of administrative systems. Organisational sociologists came along somewhat later to suggest that the reality of organisational life may be rather different. It was also the case that many of them indicated that they thought it *should* be rather dif-ferent.

Nevertheless, the Weberian model was attractive to those who wanted to stress that public servants should administer impartially policies devised by politicians. In taking that view they were supported by a legal view of the desir-ability of rule following and a hostility to administrative discretion. The discussion of this then indicates a fascinating parallel literature to both the implementation debate and evaluation of the bureaucratic model, seeing the issues about the relationship between rules and discretion to be very complex and some forms of discretion as inevitable. All three debates can be seen as taking place against a background of controversy about the validity of the model of government also embodied in Simon's rational decision-making model.

11 Inter-organisational processes

SYNOPSIS

This chapter explores the importance of inter-organisational relationships for the policy process. After an initial examination of why this subject is important the discussion is divided into two sections. The first of these looks at inter-organisational relationships in 'vertical' terms, examining the extent to which such relationships have 'top-down' characteristics. It explores the particular complications where the apparently 'lower'-tier organisations have substantial policy-making autonomy, which is particularly the case in federal or quasi-federal situations. The second section examines 'horizontal' relationships where collaboration is required by organisations which have no hierarchical relationship. Finally, it is noted that very often there are complex inter-organisational 'networks' which have both vertical and horizontal dimensions.

Introduction

In Chapter 9 one of the main contributions from Pressman and Wildavsky's influential analysis of implementation was shown to be the argument that the number of links in an implementation chain can be shown, logically, to have an impact on the effectiveness of a policy transmission process. The starting point for this argument is a version of the old children's game in which a message is whispered from one end of a line to the other. Inaccuracies arise in transmission and new constructions are fabricated to try to retain the sense of the message. But of course, in the implementation process, as was noted in Chapter 9, this is not just a matter of communication. The chain or transmission line image is very often too great a simplification of the inter-organisational arrangements. Some of the links in the chain may be more complex. Imagine a complication to the children's game in which at various points in the chain two or more children had to listen to the message and then decide what its content was before passing it on. But then again, recognise that we are talking about more than mere

216

communication when we explore inter-organisational communication in the real world, hence making sense will be influenced by roles and interests. This implies (sticking with the children's game analogy) negotiation about what they would like the message to be! There are differences of roles and interests along the 'line' and negotiations between parties. At the same time there are institutional links which may contribute to minimising dissent, or indeed in some circumstances to increasing it. In short, implementation, and indeed all aspects of the policy process, very often involves inter-organisational systems. This has been noted as a pervasive feature of modern governance (see Chapter 1, pp. 11–12).

Some efforts to solve inter-organisational collaboration problems involve integration, so that the coordination issues are contained within single organisations. Since this often involves the creation of organisations that are large and complex, it may be argued that internalising the issues makes little difference: inter-organisational problems are merely turned into intra-organisational ones. Furthermore, since collaboration issues are ubiquitous, any specific integrated arrangements may leave some coordination problems unresolved. Box 11.1 describes an ongoing English saga about efforts to coordinate personal social services which highlights these issues.

Box 11.1	Efforts to integrate social services in England

Between the 1940s and the 1960s social care services for children were supervised nationally by the Home Office and organised locally in local authority children's departments. Adult care services were the national responsibility of the Department of Health and were organised separately at the local authority level. The Seebohm Committee (1968) argued for the unification of social services in the following terms:

> a unified department will provide better services for those in need because it will ensure a more co-ordinated and comprehensive approach to the problems of individuals and families and the community in which they live. (Seebohm Report, 1968, para. 140, p. 44)

These recommendations were put into effect in 1971, with the Department of Health (actually at this time in its history the Department of Health and Social Security, though that additional complexity will not be explored here) responsible at central government level and local authorities required to set up integrated social services departments.

Once the institutional change was in place effort was put, for several years, into ways to ensure service integration within departments, through integrated teams. However, two things quite soon began to disrupt this development. One was experiments with 'one-stop shops' for all local government services. The other was concerns about the lack of coordination between the National Health Service (NHS) and the social care services.

The latter concern then came to play the major role in generating change. A variety of devices, often finance-led, were tried to facilitate collaboration, particularly in respect of adult services (where the social aftercare of people discharged from hospital has been perhaps the dominant issue). The Health Act 1999 imposed partnership 'duties' and allowed arrangements whereby health and social services authorities could operate 'pooled budgets', transfer funds between organisations and even create new integrated organisations combining parts of both health and social care services.

As adult care services became more integrated with the NHS so they began to be split away from services for children. Then the government began to permit organisational arrangements in which local authorities broke up their social services departments. The most widely favoured arrangement involved closer integration of children's services with local education departments.

In 2003 there was a crucial change at central government level. A 'Minister of State for Children' was appointed, to belong within the Department for Education and Skills. After this the government indicated that it expected education and child protection policy to be brought together at local level too. It announced that it proposed to legislate to require local authorities to create posts of Directors of Children's Services 'accountable for local authority education and children's social services'.

We see here, then, a belief in an ideal of departmental integration becoming unpicked later as alternative links between services were emphasised. By 2003 the 'Seebohm' model had been undermined. At the same time we see the search for the ideal single organisation being accompanied by alternative concerns about the best ways to achieve inter-organisational collaboration. Hudson and Henwood (2002), exploring this issue, argue that the contemporary restructuring does not necessarily offer the best way forward; rather, they suggest, issues about collaboration are essentially about behaviour at the 'street level' and are not necessarily solved by large structures.

Many writers have sought to offer advice to governments on the best ways to achieve service delivery integration. Alongside the questions about where the organisational boundaries should be drawn, there are many prescriptions for inter-organisational collaboration. O'Toole summed up the problems about making policy recommendations on these issues in an article published in 1986, but the situation has not changed since then. He noted:

> The field is complex, without much cumulation or convergence. Few well-developed recommendations have been put forward by researchers, and a number of proposals are contradictory. Almost no evidence or analysis of utilization in this field has been produced. (O'Toole, 1986, p. 181)

O'Toole goes on to attribute the lack of progress to (a) 'normative disagreement' and (b) 'the state of the field's empirical theory'.

Since this book is not designed to offer recommendations but rather to explore the working of the policy process, it is tempting to leave this subject there. But it is important to try to explore some of the ways in which issues about inter-organisational collaboration are important for an understanding of the policy process.

It is appropriate to talk about inter-organisational links that are both horizontal and vertical. This is the obvious way to talk about this subject, as shown in Figure 11.1. Figure 11.1 assumes a national organisation passing policy recommendations through two regional ones to local ones. The chart shows hierarchical links. However, the development of policy may require horizontal links. For example, even if the organisations at each level are all-embracing, multi-purpose ones, there may be activities for which collaboration is essential. A simple example of this would be the management of a river which passes through both regions and all four local areas.

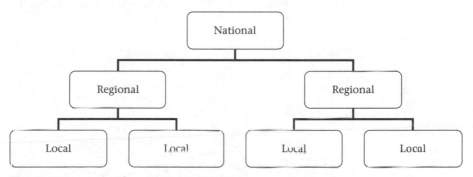

Figure 11.1   A simple organisation chart

In the real world of public policy the range of possible permutations on this simple design is considerable. There may be any one of the following, singly or in combination:

- many more organisations;
- organisations with overlapping jurisdictions;
- differences of function between organisations (health/social care/education, etc.);
- organisations with cross-cutting authority relationships (local organisations required to cooperate at the local level but accountable to different national organisations).

In addition, a chart like Figure 11.1, derived as it is from a computer package designed to help people draw organisational charts, embodies assumptions about hierarchy. Power equalities are normally implied along the horizontal dimension but not along the vertical one. The vertical dimension is normally used to convey the notion of hierarchy. In the complex world of modern governance there is a danger of falling too easily into assumptions about the existence of hierarchy. There may be various respects in which the bodies at either regional or local level in that diagram claim autonomy from central control. Conversely, whilst the bodies at the same level may be notional 'equals' there may be power inequalities. Hence even in the simple example given above of control over a river, one local authority may be a large and rich one that is reluctant to modify its policies to satisfy the demands of smaller and poorer ones.

The complexity of the topic of inter-organisational relationships is powerfully conveyed by a bold attempt by Patrick Ainley (2001) to capture the complexity of the English (not British or UK, note, since the complexities would then have been even greater) system for the administration of education and training. His chart of the situation at the end of 2000 is set out as Figure 11.2. The article from which this is derived examines the changing administrative system. Change in the system is so frequent that the chart in question was probably out of date by the time the article was published, and it certainly is now.

Figure 11.2 encapsulates the complexity of the modern world of governance, highlighting the need to identify some very complex inter-organisational relationships: the following discussion can do no more

Figure 11.2 The English education and training system, 2000
Source: Ainley, 2001, p. 469.

than explain some of the aspects of this complexity. It will do so first by separating the 'vertical' dimension from the 'horizontal' to help to organise the discussion, notwithstanding the warning about this above. It will go on to some ideas, particularly derived from organisation theory, that help with the analysis of the issues.

The vertical dimension

Clearly, analysis of the vertical dimension owes a great deal to the contribution of Pressman and Wildavsky, noted above, with their subtitle highlighting the 'distance' between Washington and Oakland and emphasising the links in the implementation chain. This is a theme that has been taken up in several important American contributions to the study of implementation. In their joint book *Implementation Theory and Practice: Toward a Third Generation* (1990), Goggin, Bowman, Lester and O'Toole set out what they call a *'communications model'* for the analysis of implementation which has a very strong emphasis upon what affects the acceptance or rejection of messages between layers of government. They set out a large number of hypotheses in which 'inducements and constraints' between federal and state level and between the latter and the local level figure prominently.

Stoker (1991) identifies as a crucial flaw in the American top-down literature the extent to which it is concerned with failures to exert federal authority in a system of government that was designed to limit that authority (see also Ferman, 1990 on this theme). Stoker therefore contrasts two alternative approaches to the solution of implementation problems, and, taking his lead from Lindblom (1977), he labels these approaches 'authority' and 'exchange'. The authority approach involves suggesting ways to simplify or circumvent the barriers to compliance. The exchange approach requires the achievement of cooperation. There are problems with the exchange approach, however, since this takes us back into questions about how to distinguish policy formulation and implementation in situations in which both (or all) of the partners in the exchange relationship have the right or power to create policy. This leads him to formulate a third alternative in which there is a 'governance' role to 'manipulate the conditions of the implementation process to encourage co-operative responses to conflicts of interest' (Stoker, 1991, p. 50). This is an activity in which 'reluctant partners' are induced to collaborate. In this sense Stoker takes up an argument from C. Stone (1989) that it is important to give attention to 'power to' accomplish collective goals as opposed to 'power over' recalcitrant others. This leads him on to an exploration of the extent to which different 'implementation regimes' can arise, or be created. Here Stoker uses game theory, drawing particularly upon scholars who have developed this to explore relationships between nations (Axelrod, 1984; Axelrod and

Keohane, 1985; Oye, 1985). What is important for Stoker is the extent to which games are repeated, and occur in contexts in which there is a 'history of interaction between participants' and 'the expectation of future interaction' (Stoker, 1991, p. 74).

Cline (2000) contrasts the theoretical contribution from Goggin and his associates with that from Stoker. Exaggerating their emphases a little, he characterises the former as seeing action as involving solving communication problems between agencies, while the latter is seen as solving collaboration problems. In the first case the issue is about how to get the 'messages' right, in the second it is about the management of a bargaining process. It is clearly both.

Hence, we see an emergent concern in the implementation literature to highlight situations in which there is participation in the policy formation process by actors who, in the initial top-down formulation of the problem, were seen simply as implementers whose recalcitrance explicitly or implicitly might be the problem.

The present author and Peter Hupe (Hill and Hupe, 2003), starting from a view that the American preoccupation with federalism was perhaps distorting the analysis of implementation, have sought to develop a way of distinguishing issues about divergence in a complex system of governance deriving from distinct autonomies from issues about transmission between links in a chain highlighted by Pressman and Wildavsky. It was noted on pp. 11–12 that the development of the modern notion of governance is connected with observations about the supercession of the nation state (and about the development of federalism in Europe). But it seems confusing to mix the issues about policy or political coordination with the traditional concerns of implementation analysis. Box 11.2 identifies some studies that do this.

Box 11.2	Confusing issues about implementation with issues about inter-governmental collaboration in the context of the European Union

- Lampinen and Uusikyla have published an article called 'Implementation deficit: Why member states do not comply with EU directives' (1998).

- Knill and Lenschow (1998) say of one of their articles (1998) that it 'analyses the roots of the widely recognized "implementation gap" of European legislation'. They go on to say:

  We define implementation effectiveness as the degree to which both the formal transposition and the practical application of supranational measures at the national level correspond to the objectives specified in the European legislation. (Knill and Lenschow, 1998, p. 1350)

- Cram also uses 'implementation failure' language in her discussion of national adoption of European Union policy (1997, p. 84).

The new language of implementation highlighted in Box 11.2 tends to replace earlier analyses using an inter-governmental perspective which can be seen as deriving from international relations theory (Jordan, 1997, 2001). Surely it is rather early to abandon the international relations approach, and it is problematical to be speaking of deficits when the crucial issue is the explicit undermining of the policy thrust of an EU directive by a national government with a substantial measure of autonomy which enables it to do so.

Knill's work, notwithstanding the criticism of his use of the term 'implementation', offers an interesting perspective on the factors that influence the adoption of European Union directives by nation states. Drawing upon institutional theory he suggests that reception of new initiatives will be affected by the extent to which they are compatible with 'embedded' national administrative traditions. This can be seen as a useful contribution both to the problem of explaining change in institutional contexts and to the understanding of vertical intra-organisational relationships of all kinds. The way Knill applies his approach to issues about the adoption of European environment policy initiatives is set out in Box 11.3.

Box 11.3	Knill's (1998) analysis of the reasons for the effective adoption of EU directives by nation states

Knill explores the extent to which three states – Britain, Germany and France – have fully complied with four EU environment policy directives. The interesting feature of his analysis is his contrast between Britain and Germany (France fell between the two extremes). Given the strong German commitment to environment policy he is surprised to note poor compliance. By contrast, Britain, allegedly with a poor record of environment policy, was largely compliant. He explains this as follows:

> The distinctive characteristics of different national administrative traditions have an important impact on a country's general ability to comply with EU requirements within the national 'logic of appropriateness'. Thus, the low adaptation capability found in Germany is the result of a thick institutional core combined with low structural capacity for administrative reform. This constellation increases the potential that European legislation contradicts core administrative arrangements, which cannot effectively comply within the scope of 'appropriateness'. By contrast, adaptation capability is much higher in Britain where the general capacity for national reforms creates a potential for changing the 'logic of appropriateness' hence allowing for effective adaptation to initial core challenges. (Knill, 1998, p. 25)

In essence, the reforms challenged deeply embedded German practices whilst in the UK they benefited from the lack of formal restrictions upon government action and also from the fact that the ongoing privatisation of the water industry was stimulating regulatory reform.

However, while it is easy to highlight the special autonomies built into American federalism, and even easier to identify how far the European

Union still falls short of being a federal system, it is not so easy to determine how to draw a line between federal arrangements and others that involve a strong measure of local autonomy.

Lane and Ersson (2000), when trying to identify a classification of states in terms of whether they are federal or not, note that while power sharing between layers of government is seen to be a key identifying characteristic of a federation, it also occurs outside federations. Hence 'one cannot simply equate federalism with a decentralized state structure, because unitary states could also harbour considerable decentralization' (p. 87). Geographical decentralisation may be seen as a continuum running from strong federalism through weak federalism, to countries where local governments have clearly entrenched autonomy, to those where it is very much weaker.

Given all that, it is relevant to raise questions about the extent to which, even in apparently unitary systems, local governments are to some degree autonomous originators of policy. Some efforts have been made to distinguish local government systems in different countries, exploring issues about levels of autonomy (see, for example, Page and Goldsmith, 1987; John, 2001). But the issues here are very complex, and are becoming more so as forms of 'governance' are developed which blur hierarchical lines and bring new actors from 'civil society' into the policy process.

Many observers of British central/local government relations have observed reductions in local autonomy, charting the increasing distrust of local government by the centre across the period of Conservative rule between 1979 and 1997 (see, for example, Lansley, Goss and Wollmar, 1989). The election of a Labour government might have been expected to make a difference, yet in many respects controls over local government since 1997 have if anything increased. Janet Newman explores this theme, drawing attention to the conflicts in policy between strong central commitments and a belief in the case for decentralisation. But this is made more complicated by a desire to bring new participants and new forms of participation into the policy process. Hence she notes that 'many of the policy changes being introduced speak "over the heads" of local governments direct to neighbourhoods and communities' (Newman, 2001, p. 78). Box 11.4 provides an illustration of this point.

The example of the school system given in Box 11.4 highlights a further complication. When looking at potential autonomies in the policy process there are other organisational layers that need to be taken into account below local governments. There may be delegation of autonomies to schools and hospitals, for example. And 'below' that we are perforce into some of the questions about discretionary powers amongst street-level staff which will be addressed in the next chapter.

As an approach to this problem which does not altogether solve it, but which may help with its analysis, Peter Hupe and the present author have drawn a distinction between 'layers' in the administrative system and 'levels' within policy-making activities. We refer to layers as 'separate co-governments exercising authority, with a certain territorial competence and a relative autonomy' (Hill and Hupe, 2003, p. 479). But then there are levels

Box 11.4	Developments in the governance of education in England

Bache (2003) shows how since 1997 UK central government has enhanced its control over education, suggesting that the shift from government to governance in this case involves strengthening schools and bringing new actors (including private companies) into education policy in such a way that local authorities have been weakened. Of key importance here are two things:

- first, central government have modified the complex formulae governing the funding of education in ways which force increasing proportions of the money going to local government to be passed on in predetermined ways to schools;

- second, the scrutiny of the performance of local authorities as managers of the school system, which includes powers – which have been used – to take functions away from them.

in the policy-making systems. These were discussed on p. 87 with reference to the work of Kiser and Ostrom as 'constitutional', 'collective choice' and 'operational' levels. The notion here is that policy processes involve nesting decisions which set quasi-institutional contexts for each other. The confusion that we want to avoid by highlighting the *layers/levels* distinction is that these should not be expected to be the same. Hence whilst in some situations it will be true that responsibility for policy structuration is delegated through a sequence of layers – nation state governments setting the main policy parameters, regional governments designing organisational arrangements and local governments dealing with policy delivery – it is fallacious to expect this neat equation to apply as a matter of course. Rather, the dynamic of relations between layers in many systems involves a succession of struggles for control over action running up and down Kiser and Ostrom's levels.

Some of the most interesting research on the issues about relationships between layers in the policy process has been done by Peter May on environment policy, in which the nature of the 'mandates' between layers of government are explored. May had done a range of work comparing local government responses in the United States (1993), but then he extended his work to Australia and New Zealand (1995). May and Burby (1996) compared intergovernmental policy mandates designed to prevent environmental hazards in Florida (USA) and New South Wales (Australia). The Florida mandate involved detailed prescriptions for local planning and regulation and imposed severe sanctions on governments that disregarded the law. The New South Wales mandate used what May and Burby describe as a cooperative approach, requiring local governments to engage in a planning process and offering inducements, including promises of future funding, to encourage them to do so.

May and Burby found that the approach adopted in Florida had several advantages: it

proved to be much more successful in securing the compliance of local governments with procedural requirements ... [and] it seems to have an edge – at least in the short run – in building commitment of elected officials to state policy objectives.

But they go on to argue that:

The scorecard ... is not uniformly in favor of coercive intergovernmental mandates. The cooperative policy as implemented in New South Wales had the advantage of securing strong substantive compliance once different risk levels and other factors were taken into account. Stated differently, amongst the more committed and higher risk jurisdictions, the cooperative policy is at least as effective in motivating local actions in support of state policy goals. Moreover, among those complying with the prescribed processes, the quality of substantive compliance appears to be higher under cooperative policies. (May and Burby, 1996, pp. 193–4)

This sort of approach starts to tease out some of the complexities in the processes under which authorities relate to each other in a (broadly speaking) superordinate system. There are some intriguing unanswered questions with this research, about the extent to which there is in play here also unmeasured institutional or cultural differences between the countries. In another article produced at around the same time May reflected on the translatability of Australian and New Zealand systems of intergovernmental cooperation to the United States:

These settings share many commonalities with the United States in terms of government roles, assignment of property rights, and other factors governing land use and environmental management. However, the American system is exceptional for its procedural and legal complexity with respect to intergovernmental regulatory programs. Breaking through these complexities and associated adversarial climate would seem to be additional challenges for success. (May, 1995, p. 113)

This exploration of the cooperation/coercion dimension is interesting since questions about the nature of central/local government relationships have been widely explored in these terms.

The policy communities literature is also relevant here, in analysing if not in explaining some of these relationships. Clearly, when disparate actors are linked together on some relatively continuous basis this may affect the likelihood of cooperation. As far as central local relationships are concerned, where there are organisations to represent local governments in their negotiations with central government they may contribute to policy coordination (Rhodes, 1981; Blom-Hansen, 1999). This point is clearly also pertinent to the issues about horizontal collaboration discussed in the next section.

The horizontal dimension

Recognising the importance of collaboration between organisations, governments have been prone to argue the case for greater cooperation and tried to set up devices to facilitate joint planning. Theorists have sought to assist this task, in the process generating some very complex attempts to model the factors that affect inter-organisational collaboration. This discussion will identify some of the key themes in this literature.

It is important to recognise that collaborative relationships run along a continuum from very detached interactions to arrangements that come close to integration. In making that point it is appropriate to reiterate the one made in the introduction to this chapter, that collaboration issues occur within organisations as well as between them. Choices about organisational arrangements for policy processes need to consider what 'boundaries' there are, and what effects they have. Some writers on organisations have stressed that the very use of the concept of 'organisation' can involve an arbitrary drawing of boundaries. There are many situations in which distinctions between organisations are unclear or in which individuals belong to more than one organisation.

There is, then, a second set of issues about what collaboration may entail. Drawing upon the work of Thompson (1967), Perri 6 (2004) has suggested the taxonomy of relationships set out overleaf in Box 11.5. But he goes on to supplement these with another approach to classification that distinguishes collaboration over policy formulation, programme coordination, integration of service relationships and integration of services to individual clients (ibid., table 3, p. 109). These distinctions remind us of two key points: (1) the danger of letting stagist thinking get in the way of understanding the complexities of intra-organisational relationships, and (2) the extent to which this subject is complicated (as analysed in relation to vertical collaboration in the last section, pp. 221–5) by issues about autonomies.

Organisation theories which focus upon the internal concerns of organisations naturally suggest that these will inhibit collaboration with others. The focus is then upon situations in which 'exchanges' are likely to be in the interest of organisations (Levine and White, 1961; for a wider discussion see Hudson, 1987). It is possible to postulate a variety of situations in which exchanges will be seen to be of mutual benefit to separate organisations. Conversely, situations can be identified in which suggested exchanges will be rejected as offering no mutual benefit or as benefiting one party and not the other. Policy systems may be set up to try to increase incentives to engage in exchange relationships.

Box 11.5	A taxonomy of types of relationship

Category of relationship	Type of relationship between entities	Definition
Coordination	Taking into account	Strategy development considers the impact of/on others
	Dialogue	Exchange of information
	Joint planning	Temporary joint planning or joint working
Integration	Joint working	Temporary collaboration
	Joint venture	Long-term joint planning and joint working on major project core to the mission of at least one participating entity
	Satellite	Separate entity, jointly owned, created to serve as integrative mechanism
Increasing closeness and mutual involvement (but not necessarily greater efficacy or collective action)	Strategic alliance	Long-term joint planning and working on issues core to the mission of at least one participating entity
	Union	Formal administrative unification, maintaining some distinct identities
	Merger	Fusion to create a new structure with a single new identity

Source: 6, P., 2004, p. 108. By permission of Oxford University Press.

Very many organisational activities intrinsically involve relationships with others, including other organisations. Often even key public organisations are weak and need to engage with others to perform tasks. While the UK has remarkably large local authorities, in countries such as the Netherlands and France there are many small authorities (particularly outside the main towns) that need to work with other local governments or with private organisations to secure quite basic services. Without exchanges many such organisations will fail. In this sense a narrow concern with internal relationships is likely to be self-defeating.

Theory on this topic tends to have been developed in relation to manu-facturing firms, which need exchange relationships to provide inputs of raw materials, etc. and to secure the successful sale of outputs, or produced goods. Economic 'market' theory deals with these relationships, with price systems governing the relevant exchanges. Organisational theorists have inevitably explored the extent to which organisational exchanges in non-market situations can be seen to involve activities in which, even if money transactions are not concerned, there can be seen to be a kind of 'trading' (of power, prestige, etc.).

The criticism of public sector organisations particularly associated with the 'public choice' theory focuses on the extent to which inefficiency and a lack of accountability arise because of a lack of 'market'-type constraints (see pp. 58–60). Organisations can be inward looking and get away with it, or they may have monopoly power which enables them to control their exchange activities in their own interests.

In the exploration of market exchanges it has been recognised that one of the problems faced by emergent capitalist enterprises was control over the input and output relationships discussed above. In, for example, the emer-gent oil industry in the United States in the late nineteenth century, any company engaged in refining faced problems from the instabilities associ-ated with erratic crude oil extraction on the one side and from difficulties in organising distribution on the other. The result was efforts to integrate and extend control in both directions. The classic success story in this respect was Rockefeller's Standard Oil Company. Indeed, it was such a success that the US government was pressured into breaking it up, in the interests of the enhancement of competition (Yergin, 1991). This is an example of a market organisation trying to control its environment. Notwithstanding liberal economic theory's hostility to monopoly or oligopoly, this is 'rational' behaviour from the organisation's point of view. Furthermore, even from a wider perspective the stability that monopoly imposes upon a production system may be in the public interest, reducing uncertainties and costs (see Chandler, 1977 for an economic historian's perspective on these issues).

These costs have been described as 'transaction costs' (Coase, 1937; Williamson, 1975, 1985). When separate organisations trade with each other the process of finding the best bargain is not cost free. Furthermore, when that trading needs to be on a regular basis there is likely to be a need for a 'contract' that sets out obligations on either side, lasts for a period of time and is ultimately renegotiable. Making, monitoring and revising con-tracts entails costs. Both sides are likely to seek long-run stability. One way of doing this is through amalgamation. That may be by agreement or, as in the case of the build-up of the Standard Oil empire, one organisation may have the market power to be able to acquire others.

Williamson has gone on to analyse these issues in terms of a contrast between 'markets' and 'hierarchies' (1975). His supposition is that whilst in general market relationships are superior because of their flexibility and because of the role competition can play in keeping down costs, this may not apply if 'transaction costs' are high. When these are high the incorporation of suppliers, distributors, etc. into hierarchies may become a desirable strategy.

Williamson's dichotomy relates to another dichotomy, that between Fordism and post-Fordism (Piore and Sabel, 1984; Aglietta, 1987; Elam, 1990; Jessop, 1992). The heyday of the Ford motor company involved routinised production on an assembly line. It also involved the incorporation of many elements of the production and distribution processes into a single hierarchical organisation. Post-Fordism entails either or both of (a) fragmentation of activities within an organisation and (b) the hiving-off of parts of the process into separate organisations. In the business world today choices are not simple ones between 'market' and 'hierarchy', rather they are about a range of alternative ways of controlling exchange relationships – internal markets, franchising, subcontracting, etc. Williamson's work has been generalised into forms of contingency theory (Donaldson, 1985) and has been challenged by writers who see issues of power and of control over environmental uncertainties as of greater explanatory value than Williamson's original approach (see, for example, Minzberg, 1983).

The literature on 'markets and hierarchies' suggests answers to questions about the design of systems of interacting public policy organisations. The reasons for exploring it here are thus:

1. that there are significant attempts by governments to take note of the public choice criticism of bureaucracy and to try to transform some hierarchies into markets; contracts between public organisations or between public and private organisations are becoming an increasing feature of the public policy process (these are discussed on pp. 267–71);

2. that even without contracts the issues about transaction costs are relevant to the exchange relations between public organisations, and there are issues about the consequences of choices between forms of organisation which incorporate many functions under one department and forms which leave them in separate bodies (see Flynn, 1993; Walsh, 1995).

However, Thelen and Steinmo, amongst others, argue that seeing 'institutions as efficient solutions to collective action problems, reducing transaction costs ... in order to enhance efficiency' begs 'the important questions about how political power figures into the creation and maintenance of these institutions' ... (Thelen and Steinmo, 1992, p. 10).

A general problem with the use of the concept of 'exchange' is that it tends to direct attention to comparatively equal transactions. The Standard Oil story outlined above is one of the growing capacity of one organisation to control its transactions with other organisations. Similarly, as intraorganisational relationships involve power inequalities, so too do interorganisational ones. There is therefore a need to explore the inequalities and 'power dependencies' in organisational interactions (Kochan, 1975; Aldrich, 1976). It will be noted that, inasmuch as power inequalities are involved here, the issues to be discussed may be about relationships that are in some respects vertical rather than horizontal.

Analysis of this subject needs to be sited within an overall analysis of social power, as explored earlier in this book. One writer who has done this, Benson (1983), has criticised writers who concentrate on the problems of securing the coordination of public services and neglect the broader influences that affect coordination. Benson maintains that inter-organisational analysis is at one level concerned with examining the dependency of organisations on each other for resources such as money and authority, but that at another level it must focus on the interests built into the structure of a particular policy sector. Benson defines a policy sector as 'a cluster or complex of organisations connected to each other by resource dependencies and distinguished from other clusters or complexes by breaks in the structure of resource dependencies' (ibid., p. 3). Defined in this way, the concept of policy sectors has similarities to the policy communities discussed in Chapter 4. As well as examining the interests built into a policy sector, Benson suggests that it is necessary to examine the system of rules that governs relationships between these interests. In essence, then, there is a need to explicate the interaction between the surface level and the 'deep structure which determines within limits the range of variation of the surface levels' (ibid., p. 5).

Thus, according to Benson, a complete analysis of inter-organisational relationships needs to explore three levels in the structure of policy sectors (1983, p. 6). First, there is the administrative structure – that is, the surface level of linkages and networks between agencies held together by resource dependencies. On this Benson argues elsewhere:

> interactions at the level of service delivery are ultimately dependent upon resource acquisition. . . . It is assumed that organizational decision-makers are typically oriented to the acquisition and defence of an adequate supply of resources. Two basic types of resources are central to the political economy of inter-organisational networks. These are money and authority. (Benson, 1975, p. 231)

Second, there is the interest structure – that is, the set of groups whose interests are built into the sector either positively or negatively. These groups comprise demand groups, support groups, administrative groups, provider groups and coordinating groups. The interest structure is important because it provides the context for the administrative structure, which cannot be adequately understood except in terms of the underlying power relations manifested within the interest structure.

In turn, the interest structure has to be located within the third level – that is, 'the rules of structure formation'. In advanced societies, Benson argues, these rules are principally those that relate to the maintenance of capital accumulation. In this context we may interpret that in a slightly less Marxist way, to mean having regard to the competitiveness of business and the requirement to keep public sector costs under tight control.

Summing up these aspects of Benson's work, Ranade and Hudson say:

The implications of his analysis are that organisational life is marked by a constant struggle for survival and domain control, and collaboration will only be entered into where there is some mutual benefit to be derived from doing so. (Ranade and Hudson, 2003, p. 39)

But Benson also puts his argument in a more structuralist form:

For each policy sector, then, it would be necessary to explore the impact of deep rules of structure formation. These would not determine the structure of the sector in every detail. It is reasonable to assume some measure of autonomy for the other levels – administrative organisation and structural interests. In broad terms, however, the events at those levels are to be explained at the level of rules of structure formation. The rules limit and enable action at other levels. Social science accounts which do not consider these deeper rules are to varying degrees incomplete. (Benson, 1983, p. 31)

One of the issues this raises is: what precisely is the relationship between Benson's three levels? While the main thrust of Benson's argument is that action at the surface level cannot be understood without reference to the interest structure and the rules of structure formation, he is careful not to suggest that the relationship between levels is simply deterministic. Indeed, in discussing how changes might occur within sectors, he notes the possibility that the administrative structure might become independent of the structural underpinnings and that bureaucracies might develop a life and logic of their own.

Benson's theory clearly takes us back to some of the ideas about structural determinism explored in Chapter 2, particularly those ideas that derive from Marxist theory. A somewhat similar position is reached, in a way which is less determinist and draws less upon the concept of 'interests', by the institutionalist theorists discussed in Chapter 5. Thus March and Olsen argue:

Institutional theories supplement exchange theories of political action in two primary ways: first, they emphasise the role of institutions in defining the terms of rational exchange ... Second, without denying the reality of calculations and anticipations of consequences, institutional conceptions see such ... as occurring within a broader framework of rules, roles and identities. (March and Olsen, 1996, p. 250)

Institutional theory is clearly relevant for the exploration of the barriers to change that are erected when efforts are made to get separate organisations to work together in new ways. If traditional bureaucratic organisations have well-established, complex institutional arrangements that include standard operating procedures, organisational cultures and value systems, then there will be resistance to ways of working with others that threaten these. There have been many efforts since 1997 to get British government departments to work together better on cross-cutting issues and problems (Flynn, 1993; Kavanagh and Richards, 2001). It has become commonplace to emphasise the 'silo' approach to government which makes inter-departmental collaboration difficult. In relation to efforts to form partnerships, 'delivering on the core business will obviously take precedence' (Ranade and Hudson, 2003, p. 41). Questions then arise, from the efforts of the institutional theorists to explain change (see pp. 81–4), about how 'access points' or 'critical junctions' may occur, to be seized upon by those who want to create more 'joined up government'. Inasmuch as these changes to the arrangements for 'governance' occur against a background of externally generated change or the evolution of international organisations, for example, these critical change opportunities may be occurring. Equally, success in generating change, for example devolution to Scotland, may create a platform for further change.

DiMaggio and Powell (1983) explore – in a way which rejects 'functionalist or Marxist' explanations of organisational change (p. 156) – what they call 'isomorphic processes' which tend to make organisations similar to one another. They offer a series of hypotheses on this topic – including factors like internal organisational uncertainties and external resource dependencies – to explain this convergence.

Another way into this issue without using structuralist theory is to recognise that individual members of organisations also have other affiliations. They belong to families, voluntary organisations, political parties, churches, etc. This may mean that they have commitments to other organisations which interact with the organisation that employs them. That may seem a rather trivial point, but there are circumstances in which it is definitely not. The most significant of these for public policy is where individuals are members of professional groups that extend across a number of organisations. The impact of this is then further enhanced by intra-organisational divisions, with different professional groups in separate sections or hierarchical systems. To describe this phenomenon Ouchi has added 'clans' as a third element to be looked at within organisational relationships alongside markets and bureaucracies (1980). Degeling, analysing hospitals as organisations, writes of them as often

> locales in which members of distinct authority structures are loosely linked in the provisions of services. The separateness of medicine, nursing, allied health and hotel services, recognised in the formal structure of most hospitals, attests to the past capacity of these occupational groups to stake out and preserve their control over particular aspects of treatment provision. (Degeling, 1993, p. 33)

Laffin (1986) identifies how these professional communities may have an influence upon relations between organisations, and DiMaggio and Powell (1983) argue that professional communities are important in generating convergence in organisational structures.

A related issue is the need to recognise that individual participants in organisations have careers which may spread across more than one organisation.

Studies of the British civil service have suggested that Treasury dominance over the system stems, amongst other things, from that body's capacity to control career moves and in particular from its tendency to take promising young civil servants from other departments for a period and to bring the most successful back into its ranks later in their careers (Heclo and Wildavsky, 1981; Campbell and Wilson, 1995). That is perhaps a comparatively simple case of organisational dominance.

A less explored example, but one that is particularly pertinent to this discussion, concerns the dramatic personnel changes that occur in some of the organisations particularly affected by the establishment of a quasi-market system in Britain which may involve fairly rapid moves between purchasers and providers or between local government and the health service. Where individuals come from and where they hope to go to must surely influence their willingness to engage with others.

Those who have explored ways to enhance inter-organisational cooperation have explicitly suggested a need for the fostering of roles which help individuals to look outwards from their own organisation (Hudson, 1987; Huxham and Macdonald, 1992). Such individuals have been described as 'reticulists' (Friend, Power and Yewlett, 1974) or 'boundary spanners' (Ranade, 1998). Questions then arise about the extent to which, given the dominant impact of intra-organisational concerns for individual careers, such roles may be created or encouraged. A variety of devices may be adopted to this end: the setting up of special joint units, the designation of collaboration as a key ingredient of a work task, the temporary secondment of staff and so on. The success of these ventures depends upon some of the considerations already discussed – the feasibility of meaningful exchanges, the overall power context, the extent to which there are shared values. But inasmuch as they must be seen in terms of individual motivation as well as organisational motivation there are key considerations to take into account about the extent to which they yield rewards – explicit or implicit, financial or psychic – for the persons involved or for the organisations from which they originate. A concern of a number of writers on this subject has been the conflict between hierarchical intra-organisational pressures and the search for inter-organisational linkages. Pollitt thus argues:

> It would not be difficult to slide into the worst of both worlds – a combination of traditional 'vertical' organizations, still carrying the principal legal responsibilities and means of delivery, and an overlay of fashionable new units or teams, which cream off the most talented staff but lack either clear lines of accountability or the implementation capacity to get things done. (Pollitt, 2003, p. 72; see also Powell, Exworthy and Berney, 2001)

A book edited by Glendinning, Powell and Rummery, *Partnerships, New Labour and the Governance of Welfare* (2002), explores contemporary evidence on many of the current issues about inter-organisational cooperation. Partnership ideas are shown to be used in a wide range of ways. In her concluding chapter, Kirstein Rummery suggests that partnerships may be characterised as involving 'interdependence' and 'trust'. The case study examples in the book show that alongside partnerships involving a great deal of reciprocity there are others that are very unequal and some that involve some very reluctant partners making minimal contributions. Since many partnerships are encouraged, supported or required by central government, elements of power and hierarchy loom large in many situations. Networks and partnerships are likely to be steered, often from above, and involve transactions and mutual exchanges characteristic of markets. Notions of voluntary compacts often have little substance without some devices, both statutory and financial, to give them substance.

In one of the essays in Glendinning et al. (2002), Hudson and Hardy, drawing particularly on their work on health and social care, ask 'What is a "successful" partnership and how can it be measured?' They make a case for the specification of six 'principles' for a successful partnership. While they claim that their principles derive from 'an extensive and extensively validated research base' (p. 62), they are perhaps more appropriately described as intuitively plausible hypotheses, supported by modest evidence, that need to be tested much more rigorously in further, more extensive empirical studies of partnerships. Their six principles are:

1. Acknowledgement of the need for partnership
2. Clarity and realism of purpose
3. Commitment and ownership
4. Development and maintenance of trust
5. Establishment of clear and robust partnership arrangements
6. Monitoring, review and organisational learning.

Networks

It has already been acknowledged that the vertical/horizontal distinction is very often not at all clear cut. In particular, in many situations both vertical and horizontal interactions between organisations are involved. In this context it is perhaps more appropriate to speak of networks, the 'net' notion here implying both directions. The contemporary importance of network theory was explored on pp. 67–72. Rhodes describes governance as 'governing with and through networks, or, to employ shorthand, it refers to steering networks' (Rhodes in Hayward and Menon, 2003, p. 67). There is an interesting bringing together of potentially conflicting ideas here. Earlier, we saw network theory used to characterise the whole policy process. But to talk of 'steering' networks suggests a coordinating role for someone or something that steers. In relation to policy implementation, clearly the notion is that there is an element of hierarchical steering *from the government*.

Hence we have two alternatives here. One is to talk of networks as informally coordinated systems, in which case the general organisational theory issues discussed in the last section are sufficient for our analysis and propositions like those set out in Hudson and Hardy's list need to guide the discussion. Alternatively, there are questions to be considered about the relationship between any efforts to pull the network from 'above' and the way in which the parties relate to each other.

These issues are explored well in research by Exworthy, Berney and Powell (2002) (see Box 11.6). They show how action depends upon horizontal linkages at national level (between government departments) and vertical linkages between those departments and local agencies and then also horizontal linkages at the local level. In one discussion of this issue they make use of Kingdon's streams model, suggesting that problem identification, political organisation and policy coordination need to occur at both levels. This perspective offers an interesting slant upon two issues which have been given much attention earlier in this book, namely the extent to which policy making cannot be seen as a 'staged' process and the limitations of the top-down model of implementation.

Box 11.6	Exworthy, Berney and Powell's (2002) analysis of the relevance of network linkages in British health inequalities policy

Health inequalities policy is the kind of policy that can easily become merely symbolic if it is not firmly endorsed by key actors at all levels. It can easily be seen as an optional extra when there are mainstream policy delivery goals. The fact that action to eliminate health inequalities competes with other policy goals is significant here both in inhibiting horizontal collaboration and in blunting policy transmission between levels. Exworthy and his colleagues echo Pressman and Wildavsky's famous subtitle in one of their articles, 'How great expectations in Westminster may be dashed locally'. But in fact they do not simply endorse the top-down implications of that title. They argue:

> many local practitioners have been disappointed that, although the government had emphasised health inequalities, they had not put in place the range of initiatives that (they thought) would be necessary to effect demonstrable change. . . . [t]hey claimed that joined-up government centrally (and partnerships locally) had not been translated into better policy-making processes. The rhetoric of tackling health inequalities had not yet matched the reality for these individuals. It is not just *national* expectations that have foundered locally but also *local* expectations that have foundered centrally. (Exworthy, Berney and Powell, 2002, p. 92)

Similar observations could be made about anti-discrimination policy.

CONCLUSIONS

Perri 6 comments that 'Coordination is an eternal and ubiquitous problem in public administration' (2004, p. 131). However, whilst not dissenting from 6's generalisation, it is important to recognise the extent to which it is a characteristic of modern governance that inter-organisational collaboration issues are very salient. The definition of governance was explored in Chapter 1 (see pp. 11–12). Writers vary in the way they stress the elements in the definition, but in the context of this chapter the gloss John puts on the terms is particularly relevant:

> Governance is a flexible pattern of public decision-making based on loose networks of individuals. The concept conveys the idea that public decisions rest less within hierarchically organized bureaucracies, but take place more in long-term relationships between key individuals located in a diverse set of organizations located at various territorial levels. (John, 2001, 9)

Clearly, inasmuch as that is true then – unless we are to engage in a reductionist approach of simply focusing on those 'key individuals' – the exploration of inter-organisational relationships is important for an understanding of the policy process.

A recognition of the importance of inter-organisational relationships can be seen not just as arising from the pragmatic concerns of practioners but also from the recognition in policy process theory of the importance of networks and policy communities, and of the way in which institutional configurations influence action. It may even, as Benson argues, extend to issues about the wider structural context.

The next chapter focuses rather more on individuals, and tends in the first place to see their behaviour in the context of a single organisation, but it will be important not to lose sight of the extent to which 'street-level bureaucrats' are not just located *in* organisations but are essentially located *at their boundaries.*

12 The policy process at the street level

SYNOPSIS

Earlier chapters have paid relatively little attention to the roles of middle- and lower-level employees in public policy systems. They have presented them as working within complex, partially controlled organisations, granted various degrees of discretion and required to collaborate with others, but there has been no examination of the implications of their own dispositions and motivational structures for these situations. This chapter explores this issue. First, it examines some rather old but still relevant theory, developed by sociologists influenced by the work of Max Weber, which stresses the way in which work in bureaucratic organisations may involve the selection of (or the creation of) people who will be rigid rule followers and tend to give more attention to the means by which policy is enacted than to its ends. This will then be contrasted with the 'street-level bureaucracy' perspective of Michael Lipsky, with its particular implications for those working with relatively unroutinised service and professional roles, which stresses the many ways in which officials may actually create policy. This leads on to an examination of the issues about the roles of professionals in public sector bureaucracies. The chapter finishes with a discussion of Mashaw's analysis of issues about professional autonomy, a topic which leads towards the issues about accountability that will be examined in Chapter 13.

Bureaucratic behaviour and the bureaucratic personality

It was suggested in Chapter 10 that the administrative organisation has typically a complex structure of a kind which many writers have described as bureaucratic. For a number of commentators, however bureaucracy implies something more than a complex organisation. For them, bureaucracies are characterised as rigid and slow, with effective action hampered by red tape. Although the main arguments on this topic are concerned with the inherent limitations of elaborate formal procedures, several writers have sought to show that bureaucratic rigidity is in some respects a consequence either of the impact of working in a rule-bound context upon the personalities of individuals, or of a tendency for bureaucracies to recruit people with inflexible personalities.

In the study of public bureaucracy, the organisation personality theory links up with a theme that has had a place in popular mythology for many centuries, a theme which several European novelists have developed most effectively: the portrayal of the clerk in public service as an individual whose life becomes dominated by the complex rules that have to be followed in dealings with the public. A pioneering essay on organisational sociology by Merton (1957) takes up this theme and attempts to explain the conditions under which bureaucratic personalities are likely to be found. Merton argues as follows:

1. An effective bureaucracy demands reliability of response and strict devotion to regulations.
2. Such devotion to the rules leads to their transformation into absolutes; they are no longer conceived as relative to a set of purposes.
3. This interferes with ready adaptation under special conditions not clearly envisaged by those who drew up the general rules.
4. Thus, the very elements which conduce towards efficiency in general produce inefficiency in specific instances. (Merton, 1957, p. 200)

The position of those in authority is markedly simplified if subordinates are submissive individuals conditioned to follow their superiors uncritically. Moreover, the implication of much managerial training is that the successful operation of a system of authority will depend upon creating bureaucratic personalities.

In his essay, Merton argues that in Weber's analysis of bureaucracy 'the positive attainments and functions of bureaucratic organisation are emphasised and the internal stresses and strains of such structures are almost wholly neglected' (1957, p. 197). He contrasts this with the popular emphasis upon the imperfections of bureaucracy. Merton argues that bureaucrats are likely to show particular attachment to rules that protect the internal system of social relationships, enhance their status by enabling them to take on the status of the organisation and protect them from conflict with clients by emphasising impersonality. Because of their function in providing security, rules of this kind are particularly likely to be transformed into absolutes. Policy goals are then distorted as means are treated as ends.

Merton's essay is applied to bureaucratic organisations in general, but there are reasons why it may be particularly applicable to public administration. First, public officials are placed in a particularly difficult position vis-à-vis their clients. They may be putting into practice political decisions with which they disagree; they are facing a public who cannot normally go elsewhere if their demands are unsatisfied, as they often can with private enterprise; and the justice of their acts is open to public scrutiny, by politicians and sometimes by courts of law. They are thus under particular pressure to ensure that their acts are in conformity with rules. Rules are bound to play a major part in their working lives.

Second, the careers of public officials are normally organised very much along the lines of Weber's bureaucratic model. Indeed, in this respect at least, state bureaucracies often come very close to Weber's ideal type. The demand for fairness in selection and promotion leads to the development of highly regularised career structures. It tends to be very difficult to justify dramatic or unconventional promotions, and therefore public service careers are likely to be oriented towards what F. Morstein Marx (1957) has called 'the economics of small chances'. Marx explains this expression in the following way:

> In the first place, the ideology of service itself minimises the unabashed display of consuming ambition. In some respects, indeed, service is its own reward. Moreover, the mass conditions to which personnel policy and procedure must be addressed in large-scale organisations cry out for recognition of the normal rather than the exceptional. Meteoric rise of the outstandingly able individual is therefore discouraged quite in the same way as favouritism and disregard of rules are discouraged. Advancement, if it is not to attract suspicious or unfriendly eyes, must generally stay in line with the 'normal'. Exceptions call for too much explaining. All this tends to make reward for accomplishment something that comes in small packages at fairly long intervals. (Marx, 1957, p. 97)

Such a career structure obviously puts an onus upon conformity, and will tend to create a situation in which if a public official becomes conspicuous for disregarding rules it will be more likely to hamper than enhance his or her career.

Marx's book is interesting in developing the picture of the public official as a bureaucratic personality as a result of the factors discussed above. He therefore characterises the public service as 'the settled life' in which security is valued above high rewards (ibid., p. 102). He says: 'the merit bureaucracy is not the place for those who want to make money, to rise fast, to venture far, or to stand on their own'. Marx concedes that senior public officials are usually required to be of a reasonably high calibre, but suggests that those who compete for entry will be mostly the 'solid – as contrasted with the brilliant but restive, for instance' (ibid.).

Marx goes on to suggest that the career structure he describes reinforces the pressure for uniformity within a government bureaucracy which arises from the political need for equity and consistency. Thus he claims: 'When the common rule and the common mind combine, the natural consequence is a narrowness of perspective – a weakness more aggravating than mediocrity in administrative performance' (ibid., p. 103).

Marx suggests, then, that the bureaucratic personality will be both a product of the fact that only certain types of people choose to join the public service, or indeed the fact that selection procedures may pick out certain types of people, and a product of the bureaucratic environment. The two influences upon personality operate to reinforce each other. Merton (1957) also recognises this interaction as a key problem for research. He asks:

> To what extent are particular personality types selected and modified by the various bureaucracies (private enterprise, public service, the quasi-legal political machine, religious orders)? Inasmuch as ascendancy and submission are held to be traits of personality, despite their variability in different stimulus situations, do bureaucracies select personalities of particularly submissive or ascendant tendencies? And since various studies have shown that these traits can be modified, does participation in bureaucratic office tend to increase ascendant tendencies? Do various systems of recruitment (e.g. patronage, open competition involving specialised knowledge or general mental capacity, practical experience) select different personality types? (Merton, 1957, p. 205)

There are, therefore, a number of related issues to consider here: (1) to what extent certain types of people choose to embark on bureaucratic careers; (2) the impact of selection processes in selecting certain types from amongst those who seek to enter bureaucratic careers; (3) the extent to which personalities who do not fit the organisational environment drop out in the course of their careers; and (4) the extent to which success or failure in climbing a career ladder is associated with personality characteristics.

Merton and Marx are, of course, attempting to analyse systematically the widely accepted stereotype of the bureaucratic official. But because it deals with a stereotype the bureaucratic personality theory runs into difficulties. On the most superficial level, the public official's role is difficult to distinguish from the role played by a very high proportion of the employed persons in a modern complex society – in which case there is nothing very special about the role of the public official. On the other hand, if an attempt is made to analyse roles more deeply it will be found that distinctions can be made both between the many different roles in a public bureaucracy, and also between alternative adjustments to formally similar roles. The bureaucratic personality theory is both too specific, in trying to single out certain kinds of organisational roles in a context in which most people are organisational employees, and too general, in implying the existence of uniformity of roles in organisations where such uniformity does not exist.

An important contribution to organisation theory that modern management training has taken seriously recognises that there are problems about creating over-submissive subordinates, and that there are advantages to be gained from having bureaucrats who are unwilling to be excessively bound by formal rules (McGregor, 1960; Argyris, 1964). This was noted in Chapter 10 (see pp. 211–12). Moreover, subordinates will resist over-formalisation, and so it may be said that they will try to avoid becoming bureaucratic personalities. This tendency may be reinforced by the fact that public sector employment is less secure in the modern world.

There is a secondary criticism of the theory which can be made that suggests that there is a tendency to assume the existence of a bureaucratic personality when in practice such behaviour may be a means of protecting the individual from total involvement in the work situation. On this theme a more recent vein of writing is more relevant. It focuses on the pressures upon bureaucrats, and helps to explore, more effectively than the bureaucratic personality theory, how policies become reshaped as public officials seek to bring some order into their own lives. This is the work on street-level bureaucracy by Michael Lipsky (1980) and his associates. For these writers the issue is not the apparent total rule conformity suggested by Merton but rather the way in which officials make choices to enforce some rules, particularly those which protect them, while disregarding others.

Street-level bureaucracy

The theory of street-level bureaucracy is set out in Lipsky's book of that title. It is further developed in work by two of his former research students, Weatherley (1979) and Prottas (1979). Lipsky says of his book:

> I argue that the decisions of street-level bureaucrats, the routines they establish, and the devices they invent to cope with uncertainties and work pressures, effectively become the public policies they carry out. (Lipsky, 1980, p. xii)

He argues that this process of street-level policy making does not involve, as might be hoped, the advancement of the ideals many bring to personal service work but rather the development of practices that enable officials to cope with the pressures they face. He says:

> people often enter public employment with at least some commitment to service. Yet the very nature of this work prevents them from coming close to the ideal conception of their jobs. Large classes or huge caseloads and inadequate resources combine with the uncertainties of method and the unpredictability of clients to defeat their aspirations as service workers. (Ibid.)

Lipsky argues that street-level bureaucrats develop methods of processing people in a relatively routine and stereotyped way. They adjust their work habits to reflect lower expectations of themselves and their clients. They

> often spend their work lives in a corrupted world of service. They believe themselves to be doing the best they can under adverse circumstances and they develop techniques to salvage service and decision-making values within the limits imposed upon them by the structure of work. They develop conceptions of their work and of their clients that narrow the gap between their personal and work limitations and the service ideal. (Ibid., p. xii)

Thus Lipsky handles one of the paradoxes of street-level work. Such workers see themselves as cogs in a system, as oppressed by the bureaucracy within which they work. Yet they often seem to the researcher, and perhaps to their clients, to have a great deal of discretionary freedom and autonomy. This is particularly true of the many publicly employed semi-professionals – people like teachers and social workers who secure a degree of that autonomy allowed to professional workers. These are the people whose roles Lipsky and his colleagues are particularly interested in.

Lipsky analyses the paradox suggested above in the following way. He outlines the many ways in which street-level bureaucrats are able to manipulate their clients. He stresses the non-voluntary status of clients, suggesting that they only have limited resources inasmuch as the street-level bureaucrat needs their compliance for effective action (ibid., p. 57). This is a view supported by two other American writers, Hasenfeld and Steinmetz (1981), who argue that it is appropriate to see bureaucrat–client relationships as exchanges, but that in social services agencies serving low-status clients the latter have little to offer except deference. They point out, as does Lipsky, that 'clients have a very high need for services while the availability of alternatives is exceedingly limited' (Hasenfeld and Steinmetz, 1981, pp. 84–5). Accordingly, 'the power advantage social services agencies have enables them to exercise considerable control over the lives of the recipients of their services' (ibid., p. 85). Clients have to wait for help, experience 'status degradation', have problems in securing access to information, and are taught ways to behave (ibid., pp. 89–92). They possess a generally weaker range of tactics with which to respond.

Lipsky also stresses that the street-level bureaucrat cannot readily be brought under the control of a superior. He argues:

> The essence of street-level bureaucracies is that they require people to make decisions about other people. Street-level bureaucrats have discretion because the nature of service provision calls for human judgement that cannot be programmed and for which machines cannot substitute. (Lipsky, 1980, p. 161)

In this sense Lipsky portrays the street-level bureaucrat as making policy, carrying out a political role that determines 'the allocation of particular goods and services in the society' (ibid., p. 84). Weatherley summarises this view as follows:

> a view of policy as determining frontline behaviour is insufficient for explaining what workers actually do and why, and how their activities affect clients. Of course, teachers do teach, caseworkers dispense public assistance, public defenders defend indigent clients, and doctors treat patients, and their work activities are certainly responsive to public policy. But their activities are also responsive to a number of other influences over which the policy-maker and administrator may only have limited or no control. The pyramid-shaped organisation chart depicting

at the bottom the front-line worker as passively receiving and carrying out policies and procedures dispensed from above is a gross oversimplification. A more realistic model would place the front-line worker in the center of an irregularly shaped sphere with vectors of differing size directed inward. (Weatherley, 1980, p. 9)

Elsewhere in Lipsky's book the street-level bureaucrat's role is portrayed very differently. He speaks of it as an 'alienated role' (Lipsky, 1980, p. 76), stressing such classic features of alienation as that work is only on 'segments of the product', that there is no control over outcomes or over 'raw materials' (clients' circumstances), and that there is no control over the pace of work. Lipsky also emphasises the 'problem of resources': street-level bureaucrats face uncertainty about just what personal resources are necessary for their jobs, they find that work situations and outcomes are unpredictable, and they face great pressures of inadequate time in relation to limitless needs.

Is there in Lipsky's work, therefore, an element of inconsistency, or can the contradictions in his analysis be explained? Perhaps he is providing a new variant on the Marxist dictum, 'Man makes his own history, even though he does not do so under conditions of his own choosing'. This is certainly partly the case. Street-level bureaucrats make choices about the use of scarce resources under pressure; contemporary fiscal pressure upon human services makes it much easier for officials to emphasise control than to try to put into practice service ideals.

But Lipsky does not really try to link his analysis to a macro-sociological perspective which would enable him to claim that the illusory freedom of street-level bureaucrats only operates as an instrument of class oppression and manipulation, and not in any other direction. His analysis, perhaps even more pessimistically, tends to show that the street-level bureaucrat's *freedom* to make *policy* is largely used to provide a more manageable task and environment. He talks of 'defenses against discretion', emphasising, as Smith (1981) and Zimmerman (1971) have, the extent to which street-level bureaucrats develop rigid practices which may be described by the observer as involving rule conformity even though the rules are imposed upon themselves. He stresses patterns of practice as 'survival mechanisms', a perspective that is echoed in a British study of social workers which, using older American theoretical work on organisational roles by Everett Hughes (1958), has a great deal in common with Lipsky's work. This is Satyamurti's (1981) study of English urban social work teams. There she speaks of the use of 'strategies of survival' by social workers under pressure which nearly always led people with the 'best of intentions' to do 'less for clients than they might have' and often behave in 'ways that were positively damaging' (Satyamurti, 1981, p. 82). The conclusion this literature comes to is that difficult work environments lead to the abandonment of ideals and to the adoption of techniques that enable clients to be 'managed'.

Lipsky argues that there is a problem about matching limited resources to apparently much greater needs that is recognised by all sensitive members of social services agencies. Accordingly, therefore, considerable efforts are made to prioritise need and to develop rational ways to allocate resources. The problem is that 'theoretically there is no limit to the demand for free public goods' (Lipsky, 1980, p. 81). Therefore it is important to accept that welfare agencies will always feel under pressure. Lipsky says that the resource problem for street-level bureaucrats is often irresolvable 'either because the number of people treated ... is only a fraction of the number that could be treated, or because their theoretical obligations call for higher quality treatment than it is possible to provide to individual clients' (ibid., p. 37). Adjustments to caseloads further the quality of work but leave the worry about quantity, and vice versa. It is always possible to make out a case for new resources. Marginal changes in those resources will not necessarily result in visible changes in stress for individual workers.

This equally seems to provide support for the cynical cutting of caseloads. Certainly Lipsky suggests that this is how it is sometimes seen. An agency that has great difficulty in measuring success or providing data on quantity of 'output' is inevitably vulnerable to cutting. Lipsky cogently shows how this response heightens the feeling of stress for individual workers and thus intensifies recourse to the manipulation of clients. Retrenchment and redundancy are particularly threatening to the remaining vestiges of altruism in the human services. In this sense it may be suggested that incremental growth does little to relieve stress, but incremental decline intensifies it considerably.

A substantial section of Lipsky's analysis is concerned with the way in which street-level bureaucrats categorise their clients and respond in stereotyped ways to their needs. Lipsky speaks of these as 'psychological coping mechanisms' and elaborates the importance of simplified views of the client, of his or her situation and of responsibility for his or her plight and how this enables him or her to act (Lipsky, 1980, Chapter 10). Many studies of the police have been made; distinctions are made there between different kinds of citizen, which enable officers to develop responses in uncertain situations. Such stereotyping offers short-cuts to decision making on how to act, how to determine whether to act on suspicion and so on (see Brown, 1981). Lipsky argues that such is the need for street-level bureaucrats to differentiate clients 'that it seems as useful to assume the equality of treatment (however modest) and ask why it sometimes does not occur, than to assume its absence and ask why it is regularly abridged' (Lipsky, 1980, p. 111). Giller and Morris (1981) offer evidence of similar stereotyping in British social work in their essay 'What type of case is this?' An issue that is related to simplifying assumptions in categorising different kinds of clients is the adoption of stereotyped responses to clients in general. The need to stereotype in order to cope may enhance tendencies towards racist and other prejudiced behaviour. This 'management' of complex decision situations can, depending of course on your point of view, have both benign and malign effects. Box 12.1 (overleaf) highlights some examples.

Richard Weatherley (1979) specifically applies the street-level bureaucracy perspective to the study of the implementation of special education reform

Box 12.1	Policy evolution in the hands of street-level bureaucrats

Chaney and Saltzstein (1998) show that female representation in police forces is positively correlated with active responses to domestic violence. A (1994) study by Weissert of Medicaid spending in the United States shows that office managers' 'activism' in the community influences the generosity of local spending decisions.

A Californian study shows that policy reforms requiring 'welfare' recipients to increase their labour market participation were largely ignored by workers who were primarily concerned with carrying out normal eligibility interviews. We see here a point emphasised by Elmore (1980) that the implementation of a new policy often needs to be seen as a demand which people may have difficulty in accommodating with their existing view about how their work should be done.

Another interesting example of street-level bureaucrat modification of policies they find difficult to put into practice comes from two studies of the ineffectiveness of a new provision in the US AFDC ('welfare') law that expected beneficiaries to be penalised if their children did not attend school regularly. Ethridge and Percy (1993) show that the policy was premised upon a 'rational actor' theory in which quite complex linkages were expected. They set this out in terms of steps in a logical chain: parents want to maximise AFDC payments, parents are able to monitor the school attendance behaviour of their children and interpret messages about this, parents are able to control the behaviour of their children, and the threat of sanctions will lead parents to take action. They go on to show how difficult it was for staff to operationalise these in practice. Stoker and Wilson (1998) focus more precisely upon flaws in the verification process for this policy. They explore how staff encountered weaknesses with the two alternatives, one at least of which was essential for verification: the transfer of administrative information from other agencies or the production of evidence from clients that they had complied with the requirements of the legislation. Clearly, whilst from one point of view these phenomena may be seen as 'disobedience' at the street level, from another they can be regarded as the refinement of a flawed policy.

in the state of Massachusetts. A new law, enacted in 1974, required schools to operate much more sophisticated procedures for assessing needs for special education and to develop individualised programmes for children. The problem for staff was that they were required to do this without significantly more resources. 'Administrators were caught between the requirements to comply with the law, which they took quite seriously ... and the certainty that their school committees would rebel against expenditures that led to increased taxes' (Weatherley and Lipsky, 1977, p. 193). Accordingly, a response to the reform was developed which accommodated the new requirements without substantially disrupting established ways of working. Implementation involved the adjustment of the law to local needs and requirements (see also Hudson, 1989 for a discussion of the applicability of Lipsky's theory to similar policy contexts in Britain).

In many situations the notions that (a) laws need to be adapted to local needs and circumstances and (b) new laws are superimposed upon already established tasks can be taken further with the recognition that much action at the street level involves trying to integrate conflicting requirements. This point was made in general terms in Chapter 9, in exploring the case for the bottom-up perspective on implementation. Box 12.2 provides an illustration of this.

Box 12.2	Conflicting policy objectives in the management of public housing at the local level

The way in which staff involved in the management of public housing have to fashion practice in ways which accommodate conflicting policies is well explored by Chris Allen (2001) in a study of a public agency, Scottish Homes. The title of Allen's article sums up the issue very well: '"They just don't live and breathe the policy like we do . . .": Policy intentions and prac-tice dilemmas in modern social policy and implementation networks'. The article described Scottish Homes as a 'multi-functional social policy institu-tion' which has to pursue 'community care policy goals and regeneration policy goals in relation to disadvantaged communities' (p. 150) whilst, at the same time, having to have regard to 'value for money' considerations in the management of the housing stock. Allen does not then arrive at the sim-plistic conventional view that business goals will drive out social goals, but rather argues that progress towards the latter can be achieved insofar as 'sympathetic individuals' secure key positions in the system.

Notwithstanding the continuing importance of Lipsky's analysis of street-level behaviour, it must be recognised that public administration is changing with the development of new technology (see Hudson and Lowe, 2004 for a discussion of this). This issue has been explored by Bovens and Zouridis (2002). They suggest that issues about discretion may be transformed as

> Public servants can no longer freely take to the streets, but are always con-nected with the organization via the computer. Client data must be filled in, with the help of fixed templates, in electronic forms. Knowledge man-agement systems and digital decision trees have strongly reduced the scope of administrative discretion. (Bovens and Zouridis, 2002, p. 177)

But their analysis suggests that there may be a complex shift going on here, first to what they call the 'screen level' and subsequently to the 'system level'. Box 12.3 (overleaf) describes their illustration of this process using the example of student grants in the Netherlands. At 'screen level' there are issues about how data is interpreted and how special cases and complaints are handled. At 'system level' discretionary power is located in system design.

Box 12.3	From street-level discretion, through screen level to system level: a summary of Bovens and Zouridis's (2002) analysis of the development of the administration of the system of student grants and loans in the Netherlands

In the Netherlands a system of scholarships was established early in the twentieth century to assist 'gifted young people lacking financial means'. That system was very personalised, with officials interviewing applicants and following their progress through higher education. Decisions could depend upon comparatively arbitrary views of deservingness.

In the 1960s the system was 'mechanised' and gradually computers were more and more used for processing applications. 'By the early 1980s, the leeway available to the allocating officer had largely been reduced to accepting or rejecting the decisions proposed by the computer.' Later in that decade, 'form processors replaced allocating officers'. Discretionary elements only remained when there were appeals or complaints.

In the later 1990s the system changed again, to involve a wholly automated process of form completion and decision making. This is described as the shift to 'system level'. Bovens and Zouridis note, however, that what is disputed at this stage of policy evolution is the algorithms used for this process, which brings onto the agenda issues about public access to these and the right to contest them.

This is clearly an important development. While (as was suggested in the discussion of the cookery example in Chapter 9, on p. 186) it may be questioned whether discretion can be entirely eliminated, these developments may be making the analyses of Merton and Morstein Marx more relevant for our understanding of the work of bored officials sitting behind computer screens or in call centres. At the same time, rather more attention needs to be given to a group of bureaucrats whose work has been comparatively neglected: the junior management staff who supervise street-level work, since much of the responsibility for decisions about how detailed data collection should occur lies with them. It should also be noted that system design is often in the hands of private companies working under contract to public authorities (for example, in the UK in respect of local administration of housing benefit).

The points made by the analysts of routine work were rather different to Lipsky's concerns about people offering human services. It is important not to lose sight here of the comments made in Chapter 7 on different types of policy. In terms of the policies discussed there, the contrast here is between social security and education. Of course there is a middle ground, where social security services may be personalised or where education may be routinised. But the phenomena analysed by Bovens and Zouridis are much more likely to arise in respect of the former than the latter policy area.

In his last chapter Lipsky connects his analysis of street-level bureaucracy with some of the discussion of professionalism in bureaucracy. Are professionals different, and can the enhancement of professionalism provide a corrective to the forms of bureaucratic behaviour outlined in Lipsky's analysis? The next section will suggest that the presence of professionals in bureaucracy can make some difference to the ways in which policy is implemented, but this does not imply that the answer to the normative question posed by Lipsky is a clear 'yes'. Professional power is a sub-category of bureaucratic power in this context, with some distinctive characteristics of its own which raise equally important value questions.

Professionalism in the bureaucracy

Modern emphases upon flexibility within organisations seem to offer solutions to the problems about bureaucracy outlined by Merton, Morstein Marx and Lipsky. They suggest that organisational employees should be expected to have and use expertise, and be trusted by their managers to use discretion to tackle their work tasks in an adaptive way. In short, they should be 'professionals'. The paradox in this solution is that it conflicts both with that other modern theme, rooted in public choice theory (see Chapter 3), which sees public employees as untrustworthy and professionals as the most likely of all to distort the organisation in their own interests, and with a wider body of literature (from the Left as well as the Right) which has warned against professional power. Before we look at some more specific aspects of this issue we need to look at the standard analysis of professionalism.

Sociologists have made many attempts to define professions. An influential essay by Greenwood (1957) suggests that 'all professions seem to possess: (1) systematic theory, (2) authority, (3) community sanction, (4) ethical codes, and (5) a culture' (p. 45). However, this list of the attributes of a profession mixes occupational characteristics with societal treatment of that occupation. Systematic theory, ethical codes and culture fall into the former category, authority and community sanction into the latter. An analysis of professions needs at the very least to separate the occupational characteristics that give some groups high prestige (and corresponding power if they possess scarce and needed skills) from the way in which the state and society treat them. In practice there is a very complex interaction between these two groups of factors. It is more fruitful, therefore, to see a profession as an occupation whose members have had some success in defining 'the conditions and methods of their work ...' and in establishing 'a cognitive base and legitimation for their occupational autonomy' (DiMaggio and Powell, 1983, p. 152).

This can be explained better by exploring the issues about one particularly powerful profession: medicine. Of course it is true that doctors possess expertise, and that the public, in its quest for good health, values that expertise. But much medical knowledge is accessible to all. What is therefore also important about the position of the medical profession today is that the state has given that profession a monopoly over many forms of care, allowed it to control its own education and socialisation process, and in many countries created a health service or health insurance system in which its decision-making prerogatives are protected (Harrison, Hunter and Pollitt, 1990; Moran and Wood, 1993).

There is a vein of writing on professions within organisations which sees professional power and autonomy as threatened by bureaucratic employment (see Wilensky, 1964). This is misleading, since professionals may secure dominant roles within organisations. Professionalism is often a source of power *within* organisations. The core of that argument is contained in the example of the doctors quoted above. They have succeeded in persuading politicians and administrators that the public will receive the best service if their discretionary freedom is maximised, and if they are given powerful positions in the organisations that run the health services.

The arguments about expertise, linked with the emotive nature of our concerns about health and the social status that the profession acquired before medical services were provided on any large scale by the state, have reinforced that professional claim to dominance. Other, later established, professions with a weaker base in either expertise or social status have claimed similar privileges – teachers and social workers, for example.

Ironically, the argument about the role professions may play in bureaucracy has been fuelled by the contrast popularly drawn between the concepts of bureaucracy and professionalism. As Friedson (1970) has argued:

> In contrast to the negative word 'bureaucracy' we have the word 'profession'. This word is almost always positive in its connotation, and is frequently used to represent a superior alternative to bureaucracy. Unlike 'bureaucracy' which is disclaimed by every organisation concerned with its public relations, 'profession' is claimed by virtually every occupation seeking to improve its public image. When the two terms are brought together, the discussion is almost always at the expense of bureaucracy and to the advantage of profession. (Friedson, 1970, pp. 129–30)

Hence, professionals stress their altruism, arguing that they are motivated by an ethic of service which would be undermined if their activities were rigidly controlled. In some respects this is a question-begging argument. If public servants are given a high degree of autonomy their actions need to be motivated by ideals of service. The maintenance of ethical standards is important if a group of people have extensive influence on the welfare of individuals. However, the ethical codes of the major professions are often more concerned with protecting members of the group from unfair competition from their colleagues, or from 'unlicensed outsiders', than with service to the public. Moreover, even the public concept of 'good health' is to a considerable extent defined for us by the medical profession: in particular, the measures necessary to sustain it, or restore it when it is absent, are largely set out in terms of the activities of the medical profession when in practice many other aspects of our lifestyles and forms of social organisation are also important (Kennedy, 1981; Illich, 1977).

We trust and respect doctors, and ask them to take responsibilities far beyond those justifiable in terms of expertise. They are allowed to take decisions on when life-support systems may be withdrawn, to ration kidney machines and abortions, to advise on where the limits of criminal responsibility may lie and so on. Such powers have emerged gradually as a complex relationship has developed between the state, society and the profession. That relationship has been legitimated partly as a result of the evolution of the medical profession's ethics and culture and partly because those with power in our society have been willing to devolve authority to it (see Johnson, 1972). The two phenomena, moreover, are closely interrelated – internal professional control has made feasible the delegation of responsibility, but equally the latter has made the former more necessary to protect professional autonomy.

Occupations like medicine are not simply accorded the status of profession by virtue of their own characteristics. Professional status cannot simply be won, as some of the aspirant occupations seem to assume, by becoming more expert and devising an ethical code. It depends upon the delegation of power, and on the legitimisation process in society. In the case of doctors that legitimisation process may well owe a great deal to our fears concerning ill health and to their special expertise; nevertheless, some theorists have argued that it must also be explained in class terms. Johnson (1972) and Parry and Parry (1976) have analysed the way in which medical power was established during the nineteenth century through a developing relationship with other powerful groups in society. It is clearly relevant, therefore, to ask questions about the comparable autonomy enjoyed by other established professions whose expertise is much more accessible (lawyers, for example). Dunleavy (1981) has provided an interesting analysis of the influence on public policy of one such group, architects, tracing the close connections between conventional professional wisdom and economic interests within the building industry.

The argument in defence of professional autonomy, that they possess inaccessible expertise, is not sufficient on its own. We need to look at the situations in which that expertise is used. There are two key issues here.

The first of these is *indeterminacy*, the extent to which it is impossible to predetermine the situations in which expertise will be needed. The complexity of the situations that doctors have to face, and solutions to medical problems, are not always of a kind that can be programmed automatically. If they were we would merely have to enter our symptoms into a computer and it could offer solutions. Of course, in very many situations this is possible. The difficulty is that judgements may be needed where the solution is not obvious or there are reasons to distrust the obvious. Paradoxically, of course, indeterminacy is most evident when expertise does not offer ready solutions.

The second issue is *invisibility*, the extent to which detailed surveillance of work is impossible. Under an anaesthetic we have to trust the surgeon to react quickly to the unexpected. We cannot debate the implications of what has been found. It is equally inappropriate to have a manager looking over the surgeon's shoulder asking for an account of what is happening, or a medical committee waiting to be convened to debate the next step.

These two issues of indeterminacy and invisibility are not peculiar to the classic cases of professional decision making, as in medicine. They apply also to the police officer alone on the beat who comes upon the unexpected around a corner. Whilst the police are not seen as 'expert' in the medical sense, there is a similar issue here about ensuring that they are as well trained as possible, to enable them to deal with the unexpected. But the case of the police reminds us of the need to go back to the issue of community sanction. Despite all that the sociologists have reminded us about the potential for collusion between powerful groups, there needs to be a sort of social contract in which the decision maker is trusted to exercise discretion in situations that are indeterminate and invisible.

This concept of 'trust' is crucial – it was explored on pp. 211–12 in relation to Fox's (1974) analysis of discretion in organisations. The argument against Fordism within organisations rests fundamentally upon the idea that desired creative responses to exceptional situations occur when individuals have been trusted to exercise discretion. Where it is hoped that public officials will play an active role in developing new approaches to their tasks and more sophisticated service to the public, there may be a strong case for granting them a high degree of autonomy. In individual services there is a need to make a choice between the case for a reliable service which can only be changed by initiative from the top and a less predictable service which may nevertheless be flexible in practice. The organisation that makes extensive use of professionals is one in which there is high expertise in the lower ranks, a complex task to perform, difficulties in developing effective patterns of supervision and a need for flexibility and openness to change. A strong group of arguments for autonomy come together. In this sense professionals are street-level bureaucrats who have been able to develop special claims to autonomy. But, as suggested above, they claim to differ from other public officials in that their relationships with their clients are governed by ethical codes and by altruistic values which others lack.

Analysing professional autonomy: Mashaw's approach

These questions about autonomy are important for accountability (which will be examined in the next chapter). These themes are linked together by Mashaw's work, in which he advances the notion of three 'models' of justice (1983, Chapter 2):

- the *bureaucratic rationality* model, which demands that decisions should accurately reflect the original policy makers' objectives;

- the *professional treatment* model, which calls for the application of specialist skills in complex situations and where intuitive judgements are likely to be needed;

- the *moral judgement* model, where fairness and independence matter.

The features of these three models are set out in Table 12.1.

Table 12.1   Task diversity and models of discretionary justice

Model	Primary goal	Organisation	Example
Bureaucratic rationality	Programme implementation	Hierarchical	Income maintenance
Professional treatment	Client satisfaction	Interpersonal	Medicine
Moral judgement	Conflict resolution	Independent	Pollution control

Source: Adapted from Mashaw, 1983, p. 31.

Both the 'professional treatment' model and the 'moral judgement' model are offered as justifications for high discretion; in so doing they raise issues about alternative modes of accountability to that posed by 'bureaucratic rationality', where a combination of political and legal accountability can be deemed broadly applicable. It is Mashaw's second and third models that will therefore be discussed here.

The case for regarding professional treatment – particularly medical treatment – as a special kind of public policy process has been set out above in terms of the issues of expertise, indeterminacy, invisibility and trust. The case against this is that these issues are used to obscure professional power, and used to deliver a protected work environment, occupational control and high rewards. This is a long-running argument. To what extent is its configuration changing in favour of those who seek to exercise control over professionalism?

We have seen that it is possible to show that a high percentage of professional work situations do not involve indeterminacy and do not have to be invisible. The rare and unexpected diagnostic situations, the medical or surgical emergencies where it is not possible to stop to debate or to consult a protocol, form but a small percentage of many doctors' work. Television hospital dramas give us a distorted view of a profession that is much more routine much of the time. Protocols are increasingly being developed to govern medical decision making, offering rules for many situations and yardsticks against which actions can subsequently be judged. Computerised decision models are being developed for many conditions.

The consequence is that, as has already been stressed in the discussion of discretion in Chapter 10, professional treatment involves discretion within some sort of framework of what may loosely be called 'guidance'. It is important to see guidance as a continuum, with rules at the strong end and advice at the weak end. Concepts like 'codes' and 'directives' can be found towards the strong end and ones like 'pathways' and 'protocols' towards the weak end. There are issues, then, about determinacy or indeterminacy in relation to any activity which guidance seeks to structure. Thus, in medicine there are distinctions to be drawn between the relatively strong guidelines in relation to the administering of anaesthetics or the performance of some orthopaedic operations on the one hand, and the much weaker ones in relation to much psychiatric medicine on the other.

An important aspect to consider when looking at the impact of guidance is where the guidance comes from. The top-down model of public policy sees such guidance as structured through a sequence of measures with an Act of Parliament at its apex. But guidance may be simply ministerial advice about 'best practice'. Then within the professional treatment model the interesting thing about notions of best practice is that the source of guidance will often be from within the profession. Guidance may thus come from either the current professional consensus on practice or from research evidence. However, since the governance arrangements for public service professionals involve professional practitioners as staff within, or advisers to, government departments, a distinction cannot necessarily be easily drawn between guidance from government and guidance from the profession.

On looking at how guidelines affect occupational practice, there is also a need to give attention to the sanctions that follow from disregarding them. We have to recognise that there is a variety of possibilities about how adherence to guidelines may be enforced:

- requirements for immediate reporting back to a superior;
- regular collection of monitoring data;
- intermittent inspections;
- attention to whether practice followed guidelines when something has gone wrong or complaints arise.

That is surely not an exhaustive list. Enforcement of guidelines may involve all of these phenomena, or just some of them, or of course none at all. To make sense of the impact of a guidance these issues need attention alongside issues about what the guidance is trying to regulate.

There are also issues about who enforces guidance. The argument about self-regulation by professions concerns the extent to which enforcement of good practice can be delegated to the profession. However, alongside this there are issues (particularly evident in relation to the last of the items in the list above) about either the extent to which enforcement comes through a legal process and/or about the extent to which the public customers/consumers/beneficiaries of the service may have a role in the enforcement process.

Turning now to Mashaw's third model, while there may be doubts about his label for this model, 'the moral judgement model', it draws attention to many situations where the key official role involves regulation – a form of law enforcement where the state has prescribed or is seeking to control certain activities. Much that has been said about the professional treatment model also applies to this one. These activities may in general terms be described as 'professional' but they also have much in common with criminal law enforcement. Law enforcement is particularly difficult where there is an absence of unambiguous support for the enforcing agency. Studies of the police have drawn attention to particular difficulties where there is an absence of people who regard themselves as victims (drug and alcohol offences, prostitution and traffic offences where no one is injured) or where there are groups in the community that will try to protect the criminal. Public health inspectors, pollution control officials and factory inspectors, as law enforcement agents, have to operate in a similar way to the police. The difficulties that beset the police are even more likely to apply in relation to the wide range of civil law regulatory tasks that concern officials like this – where the 'offenders' see themselves as engaged in carrying out their legitimate business, not as polluters or producers of impure food, etc.

This model particularly highlights two other conditions which often apply to these regulatory situations. First, what is being enforced by the regulator is a standard – about unreasonably high levels of pollution, etc. – that is likely to be disputed. Second, there are likely to be conflicts of interest between those who are the source of the alleged problem and those who are affected by it. On top of all this, the second alleged 'interest' is often a latent one, because:

- either the 'victims' the regulators have a duty to protect do not know they have a problem (when, for example, pollution cannot be detected by the sense of smell, etc.);
- or they regard the problem as the lesser of two evils (when they perceive it as a choice between a polluted environment and employment – see Crenson, 1971; Blowers, 1984);
- or they are quite satisfied with a situation that others consider unsatisfactory (residents suffering from dementia in a poor-quality care home, for example).

The discussion of pollution control policy in Chapter 7 explored some aspects of these issues. In some cases the conflict is between a quite specific individual interest and a very general public interest. In all these situations enforcement is likely to be controversial and the enforcers may lack clear-cut forms of public support. In many systems professionals with regulatory responsibilities therefore work not with absolute rules but with principles about best practice established by expert officials and operationalised using discretionary powers (see Hill in Downing and Hanf, eds, 1983). The relationship between rules and discretion in these situations may involve 'framework laws', with officials and regulatees negotiating to fill in the details so that gradually the law becomes more codified.

What is often involved in these cases, given that officials need to work very closely with the objects of their regulatory activities, is a process of bargaining between regulator and regulatee (Peacock, 1984; Hawkins, 1984). Such bargaining will not merely deal with costs and consequences, but will also be likely to take into account past behaviour (has the compliance record of the regulatee been satisfactory?) and the likely impact of any outcome on the behaviour of others. Hanf has described this process as one of 'co-production' in which the determinants of regulatory behaviour need to be seen as 'embedded in the social worlds within and outside the regulatory agency' (Hanf in Hill, ed., 1993, p.109; Hanf in Moran and Prosser, eds, 1994). Whilst the field of pollution control provides particularly good examples of this 'co-production', it is also evident in other cases where complex activities are being regulated – the running of a private residential care home or nursing home, for example.

It is appropriate to recapitulate briefly what have been the central concerns of this section. The argument is that in both the professional treatment and the moral judgement cases there are reasons why systems are likely to have sought to find some sort of balance between rules and discretion in which both are significant. Key issues have been stressed which tip the balance in the discretion direction: indeterminacy, standards, trust, enforcement difficulties. Against the arguments for discretion are counterpoised arguments for rules. There is a search for balance between rules and discretion which must involve some more complex approaches to holding officials to account than those embodied in either the political or the legal models. In both cases there are complex issues of co-production; crucially, there are sensitive relationships between 'officials' and clients or regulatees, with at the same time a wider public interest (involving 'third parties' who are not necessarily simply to be subsumed into some wider category of the general public interest).

CONCLUSIONS

Since the purpose of this book is to explore how public policy is made rather than to advance propositions about alternative ways of making or controlling it, to go beyond noting the phenomenon of professional power to the exploration of the extent to which it can be seen as a 'problem' would be beyond its brief. However, in the next chapter issues about ways in which attempts are made to secure accountability in public policy are explored, and there it will be necessary to return to these particular issues about professional power.

In this chapter street-level officials (of all kinds) have been identified as key influences upon policy outputs. The main reasons why this is the case were, of course, explored in the examination of rules and discretion in Chapter 10. But it has also been shown that these need to be analysed within their institutional contexts. This chapter has highlighted two rather different analyses of the phenomena, one which emphasises the passivity of officials and one which emphasises their active roles. There is no necessary contradiction here. Individuals, as Selznick has stressed (see pp. 79–80), are both constrained by the structures in which they work and shape their work roles in various ways in conformity with their needs and values. An examination of the roles of street-level bureaucrats can be seen as involving an exploration of the strengths and weaknesses of institutional theory. Action at the street level makes manifest institutional constraints whilst also demonstrating ways in which actors who seem to be in weak roles as organisational change agents can (and sometimes have to) nevertheless operate creatively.

13 Holding to account

SYNOPSIS

This chapter explores issues about accountability, not by moving from the descriptive approach this book has adopted to a prescriptive one but by exploring what is involved in processes of holding public officials to account and the ways in which this is an area of dispute. The introductory section shows that there are many forms of accountability, including ones that supplement or challenge traditional top-down approaches. Attention is given to the traditional political model of accountability and the related legal one. Then issues about the way professionalism poses problems for these models are explored, picking up on themes developed in the last chapter. This takes the discussion on first to the extent to which new modes of accountability are embodied in the New Public Management (NPM) movement and second to some important ideas about direct accountability to the public.

A final section explores 'accountability and governance today', recognising the way in which mixed modes of accountability often co-exist and pose questions of choice for public policy decision makers. The concluding point, like so much in this book, will be a stress on diversity: that is, the diversity of policy issues and of policy process contexts, which leaves issues about accountability very much areas of dispute. It is on this note that the book ends.

Introduction

At the end of the first chapter of this book it was noted that much writing on the policy process mixes *description* and *prescription*. It was also noted that a particularly important feature of the way in which they are mixed is that concerns about accountability, managerial or democratic, have been seen to be of overriding importance in policy analysis. A return to this theme was promised in this, the last chapter. That return does not imply a shift of emphasis from description to prescription but rather an examination of the way in which that key prescriptive concern with accountability manifests itself in efforts to control the policy process.

This raises an essential question about what is meant by accountability. It has been described as 'probably one of the most basic yet most intractable of political concepts' (Uhr, 1993, p. 13). Thomas, in a review of its use, argues for its restriction to describe situations 'where an authoritative relationship exists in a formal sense' (Thomas, 2003, p. 555). Yet he recognises that there is a much wider usage:

> The meaning of accountability has consistently widened over the years. The term is now frequently used to describe situations where the core features of an authoritative relationship and a formal process of enforcement are not necessarily present. Certainly, the public no longer sees accountability in strictly legal and organizational terms. For them, accountability is a broader professional, ethical and moral construct that is achieved only when public officials, both elected and appointed, serve with a commitment to do the right things. (Thomas, 2003, p. 550)

This widening involves two things. One of these is a recognition of the complexity of the accountability relationship in the context of modern governance, with the range of intra- and inter-organisational complexities that have been explored in earlier chapters. This is therefore something that cannot be disregarded in this discussion. The other is a confusion of 'accountability' and 'responsibility'. Criticising this confusion, Gregory says: 'accountability is a matter of political and organizational housekeeping, whereas responsibility is often about moral conflict and issues of life and death' (2003, p. 558). While Gregory goes on to suggest that there are problems with accountability systems that disregard these wider issues, it is appropriate to adopt the perspective embodied in that quotation for this chapter since the concern here is with ways in which actors in the policy process are held to account, not with those wider ethical issues.

If one's starting point is a narrow rather than a wide definition of accountability, it must be recognised that 'accountability is an unapologetic bureaucratic concept' (Kearns, 2003, p. 583) which is particularly enshrined in traditional notions of representative government. In the study of public administration the accountability theme emerged early on in the efforts to separate politics and administration, rooted in the idea that in a democratic state politics should set the goals for administration to put into practice. That idea lives on, despite all the evidence that this distinction is difficult to make in practice. Hence, there is one approach to accountability, which we may still call the dominant one, which places politics, in the form of 'top-down' representative government, in the driving seat.

That approach to accountability then secures support from a slightly different source, a legalistic view of what gives policy action legitimacy, that it should be within the framework of the 'rule of law'. This can involve, in some of the more philosophical approaches to this topic, notions like principles of 'natural' or 'common' law which derive from universal principles independent of the actions of governments (a view that features significantly in discussion of human rights and international legal principles). But in most more mundane debates about accountability, legitimacy is seen as lying in the extent to which action is authorised by either constitutional rules or specific legislation. Both of these are in the last resort 'top-down' mandates, the product of what are seen as legitimate political processes.

Therefore, the dominant approach to accountability can be seen as a 'top-down' one, normally buttressed by some notion of representative democracy. However, if representative democracy is to be really meaningful it needs to be recognised that the ultimate accountability of governments is to the people. In the face of deficiencies in the doctrines of representative government there are claims that people should have direct control over policy processes in ways other than, or additional to, representative democracy. Embodied in those propositions is a great deal of complexity, which could take us into issues in political philosophy well beyond the brief of this book. What is clear is that as far as policy processes are concerned, claims that functionaries should be accountable to *the government* are still very much in evidence.

Alongside the democratic challenge to top-down accountability will be found two other forms of accountability: bureaucratic and professional. Pollitt defines the former as 'accountability to the codes and norms within the bureaucratic context' and the latter as 'accountability to the standards laid down by one's professional body' (Pollitt, 2003, p. 93). Both of these have come under attack as involving a rejection of the democratic forms of accountability. The defence to this charge involves arguing that they embody apolitical notions of direct duty of service to the public. In that sense doctors, for example, may argue that they are accountable to their patients for the service they provide and to their peers who monitor those standards of service. But that brings us close to the widening of the concept of accountability to embrace responsibility as well, a moral responsibility that overrides ordinary accountability.

It is not proposed to evaluate here the justifications on offer for the various forms of accountability – the point here is to acknowledge that accountability is a complex and contested concept. Box 13.1 summarises the various forms of accountability.

All of the forms of accountability, including the direct democratic one, are often expressed in relatively simplistic top-down forms. What is meant by that is that executive bodies – prime ministers and cabinets, elected representatives of parents, etc., supreme courts, professional governing bodies, bureau chiefs – demand that others are accountable to them. The very complexity of the policy process and of modern governance makes the achievement of any simple form of accountability difficult.

Box 13.1	Forms of accountability

- **Political** – direct accountability to elected representatives (recognising that these arrangements may be complex since often there are alternatives – presidents and parliaments, central and local governments, etc.).

- **Hierarchical** – accountability to the 'head' of an organisation, a version of accountability that is often embodied in the political concept of accountability; but since the one does not logically embrace the other this should not be taken for granted.

- **Direct democratic** – direct accountability to the public (complicated by issues about who the public are in particular cases: patients, parents, pupils, tenants, etc. or everyone, and by the fact that these will be in specifically defined geographical areas).

- **Legal** – forms of accountability that may be secured through the courts. But is this just political accountability in another form or are there situations in which legal legitimacy overrides political legitimacy?

- **Professional** – governed by profession-related principles which, like some legal ones, may be considered to override political accountability.

- **Bureaucratic** – normally a derivative from political, hierarchical or legal accountability but may be seen in some cases to involve overriding 'responsibilities' similar to those embodied in some versions of professional accountability.

Accountability to the top: the political model

Brown sets out the importance of the top-down perspective for public administration in Britain in the following way:

> The formal characteristic of any public service is that in the last resort a lay politician carries responsibility for it to an elected assembly. There is a chain of command leading from the bedside and the local insurance office to the front bench in the House of Commons. In the personal social services the chain leads first to the committee room in county hall and then, because of his overall duty to guide the development of the service, to the secretary of state.
>
> These lines of accountability give the public, through its elected representatives, the opportunity to question and influence the operation of public services. They provide constitutional channels through which grievances can be ventilated. In the very last resort they provide a means through which the electorate can withdraw support from an administration whose policies it dislikes, and substitute one more to its liking. This is the ultimate sanction in public administration ... (Brown, 1975, p. 247)

Brown is right to emphasise how this is the starting point for most discussions of accountability. He then, of course, goes on to recognise the limitations to this approach, saying: 'A moment's reflection, however, suggests that this needs to be supplemented in some directions and perhaps qualified in others if services are to be efficiently administered in the public interest' (ibid.). Day and Klein similarly, in an exploration of the 'career' of the concept of accountability, chart a progression from 'simple to complex models' (1987, Chapter 1).

A recognition of these complexities has characterised the analysis of public administration at least since Woodrow Wilson's classical essay (1887) on the distinction between politics and administration. While that has been seen as supporting the view that administration must be subordinate to politics, it in fact sought to prescribe a way of separating the two in the context of the realities of American politics. Wilson sought thus to combine democratic accountability with efficient administration. Wilson was both identifying an important problem about administrative accountability and recognising that the United States faced great difficulties in coming to terms with a set of institutional arrangements that made political problem solving very difficult.

The alternative view on his politics/administration dichotomy is that this is a distinction that bears little relation to the reality of political and administrative behaviour. Evidence for this has been explored in various places in this book. But what is important about Woodrow Wilson's perspective is the way his ideal division influenced thinking about the management of government. It finds resonances not just in discussion of representative democracy but also in arguments about the 'rule of law', the concern of the next section.

The legal model of accountability and the problem of discretion

Two key ingredients in the 'rule of law' according to Wade (1982, p. 22) are:

1. 'that everything must be done according to the law', which when applied to the powers of government means that 'every act which affects the legal rights, duties or liberties of any person must be shown to have a strictly legal pedigree. The affected person may always resort to the courts of law, and if the legal pedigree is not found to be perfectly in order the court will invalidate the act, which he can then safely disregard';

2. 'that government should be conducted within a framework of recognized rules and principles which restrict discretionary power'.

The particular way those principles are enunciated by Wade may have characteristics that are peculiar to Anglo-Saxon countries, but the general thrust of the principles is accepted wherever it is claimed that governments operate within the 'rule of law'.

The importance of the 'rule of law' as a basis for legitimate rule is explored in Weber's third type of authority: 'rational-legal'. This was examined on p. 199. Weber argues (in a text originally put together in the early years of the twentieth century):

> Today the most usual basis of legitimacy is the belief in legality, the readiness to conform with rules which are formally correct and have been imposed by accepted procedure. (Weber, 1947, p. 131)

Weber goes on to distinguish a social order derived from voluntary agreement from one that is imposed – but he calls this distinction 'only relative'. The first of the ideas which he sees as central to the 'effectiveness' of legal authority is:

> That any given legal norm may be established by agreement or by imposition, on grounds of expediency or rational values or both, with a claim to obedience at least on the part of the members of the corporate group. This is, however, usually extended to include all persons within the sphere of authority or of power in question – which in the case of territorial bodies is the territorial area – who stand in certain social relationships or carry out forms of social action which in the order governing the corporate group have been declared to be relevant. (Ibid., p. 329)

In that rather convoluted argument, of course, lies the concept of the state. The second idea is that:

> every body of law consists essentially in a consistent system of abstract rules which have been intentionally established. (Ibid., p. 330)

Thus issues about the legitimacy of official rules, and the related discretions they may explicitly or implicitly convey, may be disputed with reference to their specific source, to their constitutional context or to wider principles. However, this is not a simple matter.

In Britain the absence of a written constitution gives debate about public law a peculiar shape which derives from the fact that the primary source of law is Parliament. The main source of arguments about the limits to parliamentary power rest upon a peculiar body of legal tradition known as 'common law', and the main remedies for the citizen have emerged out of an arcane procedure under which the Crown was petitioned to consider remedies against the excesses of its own officials. The central concern is with whether the rules applied by public officials have the formal sanction of Parliament and whether departures from those rules (discretion) are formally authorised (or not formally proscribed) by statute. A secondary concern is with the capacity of the court system – as supplemented in the modern world by simpler grievance procedures such as tribunals and ombudsmen – to respond in situations in which citizens (singly or in organised groups) regard official behaviour as falling outside those statutorily determined boundaries.

The peculiarities of the British system (shared of course by some Commonwealth countries) contrast with those of countries with written constitutions and a supreme adjudicative body entrusted with the protection and interpretation of that constitution. In such countries, an additional test of the legitimacy of any policy process-related action will be its compatibility with the constitution.

A constitution like the American one is, of course, a product of political action, and can be amended by political action. In Europe there are also potentially wider ways of testing the legitimacy of action, in relation to broad principles setting out human rights and limitations upon governmental action. These are set out in various supra-national declarations which, although also created by political decision-making processes in the first place, may offer – if there are usable enforcement mechanisms (such as the European Court) – another avenue of redress to the aggrieved citizen.

But much of the detailed role of the law in dealing with accountability concerns questions about the extent to which powers exercised by administrators have been formally authorised by government. It thus particularly deals with administrative discretion. Hence what the law textbooks provide is a portrait of the law as trying to keep administrative discretion under control. In so doing the law is presented as the defender of the citizen against the arbitrary exercise of power. Wade (1982) perceives administrative law as an attempt to ensure that the 'whole new empires of executive power' conform to the principles of liberty and fair dealing. This perspective leads Wade to argue that the key issue is ensuring that the law can control 'the exercise of the innumerable discretionary powers which Parliament has conferred on the various authorities' (p. 4). His emphasis is on ensuring that such authorities do not act *ultra vires* by exceeding their statutory power or following the wrong procedures. Authorities cannot escape such control by being offered statutes that give them unlimited power, since 'in practice all statutory powers have statutory limits, and where the expressed limits are indefinite, the courts are all the more inclined to find that limits are implied. The notion of unlimited power has no place in the system' (ibid., p. 50). While it is clearly possible to see in this view of the rule of law a control over arbitrary government, it is largely transformed into a notion of control over arbitrary administration.

Two things further complicate this boldly stated application of the model of the 'rule of law'. One is the difficulties citizens experience in using the law to protect themselves from the executive. The other, very much within our terms of reference, is that these so-called statutory powers are very complicated. One view, abandoned by any realistic critic of the British legislative system at least 50 years ago, was that all rules should be embodied in formal Acts of Parliament. The reality is that there is a great deal of subordinate rule making – not only in 'regulations' which are hypothetically open to parliamentary scrutiny, but also in a variety of departmental guidance circulars, codes and working instructions to officials.

The very institutional complexity of the policy system means that there is a wide range of bodies which have responsibilities to interpret and perhaps amplify their statutory mandates. Hence, it is not possible to draw a simple distinction between statutory rules deriving from the legislature and the discretion of officials. The intermediary departments, agencies, local governments and so on, which, from the old-fashioned perspective, can be seen as discretionary actors themselves, engage in subordinate rule-making processes. A considerable body of case law governs these processes.

Traditionally, British administrative law textbooks give attention to administrative discretion as a 'taken for granted' phenomenon within the political system. They point out that the concern of the courts has been with (a) whether or not the discretionary powers that are exercised have been clearly delegated by statute; (b) whether the exercise of those powers is within the boundaries of natural justice (are they exercised reasonably and with regard to due process?); and (c) the principle that if a statute grants discretionary powers then the officials using them should not devise rules which in practice fetter that discretion.

So the 'rule of law' approach to the issue of accountability primarily reinforces the top-down model of accountability, embodied in the notion of the primacy of politics in a context of representative democracy, but it may suggest that there should be wider principles to which citizens can appeal. It sets up a tension between accountability to 'Parliament' and accountability to the 'courts', which takes its most clear form in the way in which the American constitution gives the Supreme Court a superordinate role. It has led to recognition that the Supreme Court can be in some circumstances a 'policy maker'. A corresponding interesting feature in Europe is the role of the European Court, which is reinforced by an international search for ways of specifying and enforcing universal human rights.

This excursion into issues about legal control over policy introduces something else: concerns about the extent to which law may be comparatively impotent in the face of the complex issues of administrative discretion. A recognition of the limits to legal control over administration as well as the limits to top-down political control stimulates a search for other models of accountability. The debate about that has particularly centred on issues about professionalism.

Accountability, discretion and professionalism

The last chapter explored the arguments about professional discretion, showing how a case for professional autonomy has been made. That case tends to be most strongly made in relation to the role of medical doctors. That role will therefore be given particular attention here. Medical autonomy is traditionally defended in terms of the sanctity of the doctor/patient relationship and the needs of good medical practice. In this argument the most important form of accountability is seen as being to the patient, but it takes the paternalistic form of suggesting that the doctor's expertise enables him or her to determine what is in the patient's best interests. That is reinforced by arguments about indeterminacy in many situations and about the need for a relationship of 'trust'. A wider protection is then alleged to be offered by the fact that the doctor's behaviour is subject to scrutiny by his or her professional 'peers', who were given responsibility (by the state) for training and accreditation, and have the power to take disciplinary action against malpractice.

However, individual clinical decisions are not merely the concern of the practitioner, the profession and the patient, at least as far as publicly financed medicine is concerned. In a situation of resource constraints (which must be regarded as a normal situation for a publicly financed health service) a response to the needs of any patient involves claims on scarce resources. It must thus – taking an overall view – be to some extent at the expense of a response to others. That issue comes to the fore most poignantly where there is manifestly a lack of resources relative to an identified need – as is the case with various forms of treatment for kidney disease, or in a hard-pressed emergency unit. It is also present inasmuch as there are cost differences between professionals who carry out ostensibly the same practices. Concerns about these issues are then heightened by the fact that there are often waiting lists for treatments and operations. Overall, it may be contended that there is a ubiquitous requirement for all clinical work to be planned and organised against a backcloth of resource issues, which are surely public concerns.

If the need for wider public control is conceded, the question then becomes: who is to do the controlling? Here we find, alongside straightforward top-down arguments for political and legal control, some alternatives (or some combination of them): lay managers, professionally qualified managers, other professional colleagues and patients. There are problems with accountability in respect to each of these groups.

Clearly, the standard control model for the policy process involves appointed managers working within a remit supplied by politicians. The intense need for cost control over services like health has increased the propensity to see lay managers as having a key role to play. That view has been reinforced by the availability of new technologies (computerised medical records, systems to identify the costs of 'normal' medical procedures like those offered by the identification of 'diagnosis related groups' (DRGs), etc.).

This approach to the management of professional activity is opposed by two alternatives. One is control by managers who are drawn from the ranks of the service professionals themselves. There has been a long-standing argument about this approach to the management of professionals: do these managers retain their old professional loyalties or become co-opted to the ranks of the lay managers? There seems good reason to believe, confirmed by research led by Degeling (Degeling et al., 1998, 2003) that the truth lies somewhere between these two positions. These 'managers' obviously offer scope for the development of a more sophisticated, shared accountability, but they do not, of course, open up the system to public accountability in the widest sense.

The other alternatives are variations of this. These are either the creation of a cadre of people who are involved in management but still practising their profession, or collective self-management through collegial shared participation. This is a managerial model widely favoured by professionals. However, there are well-founded suspicions that – particularly when review processes are not shared outside the professional group (medical audit, for example: Harrison and Pollitt, 1994) – this approach to management preserves traditional professional domination. There are also questions about whether this is an efficient use of members of an expert workforce.

This discussion has deliberately explored the doctor/patient relationship, but the arguments explored are also applicable to other, similar, relationships, such as those between teacher and pupil. A view that the case of professional autonomy is weaker outside the medical profession has been embodied in arguments that in many cases it is more appropriate to speak of semi-professions rather than professions (Etzioni, 1969).

All the managerial approaches to increasing the accountability of professional service groups involve the development of performance indicators. The use of these can be seen as a particular feature of modern approaches to accountability, embodied in concepts of new public management. These will be explored next (we return to issues of direct accountability to patients, etc. later).

The impact of 'new public management'

It has been difficult to decide where to include a discussion of 'new public management' (NPM) in this book. Inasmuch as the NPM movement has been motivated by concerns about accountability, this is the appropriate place. However, whilst issues like control over professional autonomy have been one of the movement's preoccupations, this has been accompanied by a concern that the obvious alternative to this autonomy, top-down control of a bureaucratic kind, is also inadequate. In this respect, this discussion might have been included in Chapter 10, where the sociological work on the deficiencies of the top-down model was outlined, or in Chapter 12 where issues about street-level autonomy were examined. NPM is a response to dilemmas about public bureaucracy that go back at least as far as Max Weber's time, and it draws upon the sociological analysis of organisations stimulated by Weber's work and by the arguments about Taylorism or Fordism as well as the rational choice critique (examined in Chapter 3). In discussing it here, then, it is important to recognise the potential contradiction within NPM between a strong stress on accountability and a rejection of traditional forms of top-down control.

Hood (1995) identifies seven 'doctrines' to which 'Over the last decade, a "typical" public sector policy delivery unit in the UK, Australia, New Zealand and many other OECD [Organization for Economic Cooperation and Development] countries would be likely to have had some exposure' (p. 4). These ideas have travelled quickly from country to country, promoted by fashionable 'gurus'. Hood does not mention the United States, but perhaps the most influential of all the NPM tracts, a book by Osborne and Gaebler (1992), comes from that country. The seven doctrines Hood identifies are set out in Box 13.2.

Box 13.2	Hood's summary of NPM 'doctrines'

1. 'Hands-on professional management in the public sector'
2. 'Explicit standards and measures of performance'
3. 'Greater emphasis on output controls'
4. '. . . disaggregation of units in the public sector'
5. '. . . greater competition in the public sector' (to this may be added actual privatisation)
6. '. . . private sector styles of management'
7. '. . . greater discipline and parsimony in resource use'.

Source: adapted from Table 1 in Hood, 1995, pp. 4-5.

In some respects the expression NPM is simply useful shorthand for a variety of innovations, widespread across the world, which are 'dominating the bureaucratic reform agenda' (Hood, 1991, p. 3). There is a danger that the use of this shorthand expression may convey the sense of a unified and compatible set of initiatives. In a later essay (1995), despite having established himself as the leading analyst of the phenomenon, Hood attacks the view that NPM is a 'new global paradigm' and highlights some of the inconsistencies within the work of its leading exponents.

Hood indicates that NPM has been attacked for its concern to place issues about efficiency before equity (Pollitt, 1990), but he argues that NPM advocates would assert that efficiency 'can be conceived in ways which do not fundamentally conflict with equity' (Hood, 1995, p. 20, citing Wilenski, 1986). That takes us into value issues which are not the concern of this discussion.

However, the issues about the relationship between efficiency and accountability *are* relevant here. Some of the NPM movement's concerns come directly from the rational choice attack (see Chapter 3, pp. 58–61) upon traditional public bureaucracy which links the two. But others – notably (1) and (4) in Hood's list – have their roots in Peters and Waterman's (1982) concerns about human relations in the organisation and the desire to create organisations where 'excellence' can be achieved by a committed workforce left to perform delegated tasks without undue surveillance. This seems to conflict with the rational choice view that public sector managers cannot be trusted to operate autonomously. A particular feature of NPM in practice has been an attack upon the traditional autonomy claims of the established professions – medicine, teaching, etc. Interestingly, the new 'hands-on professional' managers are seen as a countervailing force to the traditional professionals (Hoggett, 1996).

If the ideas are taken together as a package, these conflicts may be resolved to the satisfaction of the New Right perspective by stressing that market discipline imposes its own accountability. Managerial autonomy does not enable managers to 'buck the market'. Others, like the 'aristocratic' old professions, it is argued, must also learn to come to terms with market discipline. But that presumes that real market discipline can be established in a public service.

Hence for others not wedded to the New Right perspective or unconvinced about the feasibility of creating a market, this mixture of measures seems to preserve the autonomy of those 'hands-on' managers at the top whilst ensuring the efficiency of response by lower-level workers to their demands through the increased insecurity entailed in the combination of strict standards and competition from alternative providers (Hoggett, 1996). Relevant here is Pollitt's summary of the impact of NPM (2003, Chapter 2), in which what is particularly stressed is its emphasis upon the use of performance targets to impose accountability. In that sense NPM can be seen as an effort to secure tight controls over public organisations without recourse to traditional bureaucracy.

A characteristic of NPM in the United Kingdom (and probably in Australia and New Zealand too) is that it has been very much a 'top-down' movement. Reform of central administration has not involved decentralisation. The 'disaggregated units' Hood refers to have been subject to tight controls. There are grounds for arguing – with respect to the development of quasi-autonomous agencies – that the operational freedom here consists merely of a freedom to take the blame. At the lower levels British local government experienced over the decade 1985–95 steadily tightening financial control, strong steering to ensure that its interpretation of NPM was compatible with that of the government and requirements to accept and stimulate competition that weakened its capacity to respond to local political forces (Walsh, 1995; Butcher, 2002; Hoggett, 1996; Deakin and Walsh, 1996).

Research evaluations of the key developments have been slow to emerge and have produced equivocal findings (see Pollitt, 2003, Chapter 2). There are grounds for believing that the achievements of NPM will be limited. Realistic competitive 'markets' are hard to create. The evidence for this comes from studies of the behaviour of the private sector – here the discussion of transaction costs (pp. 229–30) is relevant. There are strong reasons why actors will try to secure long-run, stable, non-competitive relationships.

The 'search for excellence', or 'reinvented government', has involved an attempt to put a 'post-Fordist' form of administrative organisation into place to combat the bureaucratic 'diseases' associated with traditional hierarchies. Yet there is a conflict between this remedy for inefficient government and 'rational choice' theory, which sees bureaucratic autonomy as a key cause of the uncontrollable growth of government. It is also necessary to note the conflict between the case for the flexible organisation in which staff have high discretion and the use of rules to secure accountability.

The solution to this dilemma has been seen to involve two ideas. One of these is that control should deal with broad general parameters, leaving much detail to be settled at the 'street level'. This is the idea of the loose/tight organisation of 'steering' not 'rowing' (Osborne and Gaebler, 1992). Steering is seen as involving the setting of the financial framework and the specification of a range of incentives (Kickert, 1995, pp. 149–50). It must be questioned how much this is really new, and how much it is merely another approach to analysing the hierarchical structure of discretion emphasised in the points quoted from Simon and from Dunsire above (pp. 209–10) (see also Hoggett's criticism of Kickert, 1996). Nevertheless it does suggest the need for the co-existence of two forms of accountability (an issue to which we will return).

The other approach to control involves emphasis upon retrospective controls requiring the collection of information on performance. Rewards or sanctions are applied on the basis of such data. The crucial sanction may be the termination of a contract if a quasi-market system is operating. Some commentators on British public policy in the 1990s have seen developments of this kind as a retreat from accountable public administration (Baldwin, 1995). Others have seen it as a rather bogus loosening of control – taking out some actors who might have played a role in accountability such as local government (see Glennerster, Power and Travers, 1991) – whilst financial constraints and fear of sanctions reinforce strong central control (Deakin and Walsh, 1996). Some forms of managerial control have been enhanced at the expense of professional autonomy, particularly where those managers hold values compatible with the pro-market 'right' (Hoggett, 1996). Clarke and Newman (1997) have seen 'new managerial regimes as producing a field of tensions', an 'unstable settlement between bureau-professional power and the new managerialism' (Newman, 2001, p. 31).

At the same time it is still necessary to draw another lesson about the use of rational devices in the control of administrative behaviour, for example management by objectives and quantitative staff assessment, from Blau's old study (1955). He demonstrates how performance indicators used in the evaluation of work may distort bureaucratic behaviour. Individuals not only set out to cook their own performance statistics but choose to emphasise those activities that will maximise the score achieved by themselves and their agency. Quantitative rather than qualitative performance becomes emphasised. It is through the use of output rather than outcome measures, whose collection and analysis is facilitated by computer technologies, that much retrospective control over discretion is sought. This is one of the ingredients in the curious mix of apparent neo-Fordism with a reversion to Fordism in the public sector (Pollitt, 1990; Hoggett, 1996).

Some activities are much more easily measured than others, hence performance indicators that offer a distorting impression of a public service activity as a whole may come to have an excessive influence. Allied to this issue is the fact that some of those measurements most likely to impress are those that embody data on costs or can be translated into money terms. Therefore issues about effectiveness in education have often been translated quite spuriously into indicators of 'value added' for individuals and/or the national economy (Wolf, 2002).

Measurement activities may empower another group of people: experts in measurement and other forms of auditing. Such people may be every bit as difficult to bring under accountability systems as the people whose activities they measure. Hence Power has exposed some of the problems with auditing, raising questions about how auditors are audited (or more often, how they are not audited) (Power, 1997). Overall, what may be occurring is the enhancement, at the expense of professional service staff, of the power of those who monitor and measure their work, creating new kinds of 'professional dominance' among accountants, lawyers and managers (see Alford, 1975 and Ham 1992, on 'corporate rationalisers', and developments of this theme in Harrison, Hunter and Pollitt, 1990 and in Flynn, 1991).

The NPM movement claims to have ways to deal with these issues, but the discussion of their complexity suggests reasons to be sceptical about those claims. This is supported by Hood's analysis of the extent to which management changes under the influence of NPM produce 'side-effects and even reverse effects'. He borrows Sieber's (1981) notion of 'fatal remedies' – 'producing the opposite of the intended effect' – to analyse these (Hood, 1995, pp. 112–16). Amongst them the erosion of trust and the adverse effects of elaborate rule structures and reporting requirements loom large (see also Power's attack on 'the audit explosion', 1994). The next section explores an alternative way to increase sensitivity to the issues about accountability options.

Consumer control as an alternative

A set of alternative ways of conceptualising NPM have been put forward which recognise the force of the Peters and Waterman (1982) critique of bureaucracy and accept the importance of performance measures as indices to be shared with the public but reject the market orientation of much of the rest of the thinking. This approach tackles the issue of accountability not by the adoption of market devices but by trying to put bottom-up notions of accountability in place of the traditional top-down ones (Stewart and Clarke, 1987; Hoggett, 1991).

A good approach to exploring this issue is offered by Hirschman's (1970) analysis of the options available to consumers (in both public and private systems) as being 'exit, voice or loyalty'. This approach, which can be seen as related to ideas about the use of 'rational choices' by people (see Chapter 3), suggests that the first and last of Hirschman's trilogy are the easiest to use. Then, of course, the crucial issue is about the alternative opportunities for consumers to secure 'accountability' either by the simple method of 'exit' – causing a service producer to think again as business begins to disappear – or by the more complex method of getting one's 'voice' heard.

A feature of NPM that has been noted is the development of competition within public services, either through competitive arrangements within these or by allowing private providers to offer public services. Box 13.3 gives a potted history of British initiatives in this respect. It is important to note that the exit option depends not just upon the availability of alternatives but also on information about what these alternatives actually offer. Constraints are also imposed by the fact that exit carries 'transaction' costs for consumers (getting appropriate information, negotiating changes and adapting to new arrangements). Market systems operate better when people start consuming a service – choose a doctor, a hospital or a school, for example – rather than when they are already consuming it. In that sense it is not so much 'exit' options that people have in systems of public choice as 'entry' options. These points are particularly pertinent as far as health and social care services are concerned.

Box 13.3	*Accountability to consumers in the UK*

In the UK in the 1980s and 1990s there was considerable effort to avoid situations in which one agency was the sole provider of a publicly required service. In education, the Conservatives tried to increase the range of providers and to use parental choice to produce a 'quasi-market' system. In health and the personal social services, ways of splitting purchasers from providers were developed which, while they did little to empower the ultimate 'customers', seemed to offer the possibility of greater controls over providers. This model also allowed for the possibility that the providers might be private bodies, even profit-making bodies. The Conservative hope, largely unrealised, was that competition would emerge between providers.

After the fall of Margaret Thatcher, the Conservative regime led by John Major put a strong emphasis on consumerism. Major's approach to consumerism entailed stressing the importance of information about service outputs to enable people to exercise choice and exploring ways to provide financial compensation when services failed to deliver outputs or to deal with problems within a specific time span. This was central to Major's 'citizens' charter'.

The Blair government has continued to emphasise consumer control but has been rather more reluctant to use market-mimicking devices. An important aspect of the evaluation of services has become the use of surveys of consumer satisfaction. These are used – alongside devices that stress performance indicators and central inspection – to influence resource allocation to public agencies and in the last resort to give the government power to take away service provision responsibilities.

'Voice', the alternative to exit, involves seeking ways to increase 'grass-roots' public accountability through forms of participation. Perhaps the chief characteristic of this approach has been to seek to establish ways of decentralising decision making to the local government level or below it (particularly where, as in the UK, local authorities are large).

This leads us to an approach to professional accountability that has been widely canvassed, one which offers a combination of political accountability and accountability to consumers by stressing localised 'political' control mechanisms. Thus Lipsky argues for a new approach to professional accountability in which there is more emphasis upon client-based evaluation of their work (Lipsky, 1980, final chapter). Similarly, Wilding (1982) writes of the need to realise 'a new relationship between professions, clients and society' (p. 149), precisely because others have so little control over them. Stewart and Clarke (1987) offer a related approach in terms of the idea of a 'public service' orientation committed to accountability to local citizens' groups.

The main, perhaps rather dismissive, point to make here is that it represents more an aspiration than a properly tried form of accountability. It comes into direct conflict with concerns about territorial justice, which emphasise the need for uniformity of services. It can also be seen as difficult to integrate with concerns about interactions between services – the demand for 'joined-up government' explored in Chapter 11 (see Newman, 2001 for an analysis of these tensions in the UK). However, as indicated at the beginning of this chapter, if accountability ultimately means accountability to citizens, then the issues about how to do this other than through representative government are bound to be on the agenda. We come back to this theme in the next section.

Accountability and governance today

While academics may dismiss the political preoccupation with top-down accountability, the issue remains very much alive. It has, however, to confront the reality that new approaches to public administration – what has been described as the shift from *government* to *governance* – make the issues about control over implementation much more complicated. Central to this development was, first, the exploration of public policy delivery through private organisations using market mechanisms and public–private partnerships, followed by recognition of the importance of networks for policy delivery. This is summed up by Pollitt as follows:

> there are two sets of reasons why a simple, single accountor and single accountee model of accountability is an inadequate description of reality. First, many public managers find themselves working in partnerships or contractual relationships, where different parties are accountable for

different aspects of a joint activity (multiple accountors). Second, even where a public manager is working within a single institution they will often have several lines of accountability – political, legal, professional, bureaucratic (multiple accountees). (Pollitt, 2003, p. 94)

What is the implication of the new world of *governance* for the old issues about control over the policy process? One of the virtues of the work of the early top-down theorists was that they emphasised issues about purposive action and control over policy processes. Those issues remain important regardless of the stance one takes on who should be in control.

Appropriate answers to the question in the last paragraph in the new world of governance have to be framed without clear privileging of specific actors. Control over administrative activities is just as much an issue for citizens at the grass roots as it is for politicians who think that their policies are being subverted.

Alongside the question of *to whom* actors should be accountable, there are issues about *what* those actors should be accountable for. Some theorists have struggled with ways to situate action advice with reference to policy issues or policy contexts. The problem with these is the difficulty of achieving generalisations that hold across varying cultural and institutional contexts. Pollitt challenges the view, in much of the discourse about accountability, that 'the criteria for judging the accountor's performance are (a) reasonably clear and (b) agreed in advance by all those concerned' (Pollitt, 2003, p. 91). He goes on to illustrate this by emphasising how vague politicians' specifications of goals often are and how their accountability expectations are influenced by (often unanticipated) events that cause them to call officials to account. But he might equally have emphasised how complicated policies are. It is pertinent here to bear in mind the picture of the role of the 'street-level bureaucrat' described in the last chapter, as one subject to multiple demands and having to choose what to respond to and what to ignore. When the author started work many years ago as an administrator in a local public assistance office, his manager advised him that it was 'better to satisfy the coroner than the auditor'. That advice remains appropriate for officials today faced by very complex auditing processes, and not only for its powerful moral message. Officials are concerned not only with how they spend public money but also with a wide range of performance goals, but they still need to ask themselves which mistakes will most readily attract public or political attention. Hence accountability is complex because tasks are complex just as much as because governance is complex.

Drawing on work with Peter Hupe (Hill and Hupe, 2002, 2003) it is suggested that there are three crucial ideas that need to be used when trying to suggest ways to solve some of the dilemmas about accountability:

1. There are various alternative forms of governance, which may be chosen or used in some combination.

2. As policies evolve and become more complex, decisions are nested in such a way that some decisions structure or influence subsequent ones.

3. Choices about those forms of governance, whilst needing to be tailored to specific types of policies and contingencies, will also be matters of value or ideological choice.

On p. 142 it was suggested that alternative modes of governance might be identified. Three such modes were identified:

1. authority – associated with traditional notions of government by hierarchy;

2. transaction – involving particularly market mechanisms and contracting;

3. persuasion – involving collaboration within policy networks.

Embodied in these are alternative approaches to accountability, but not in any very explicit way. In developing them we were influenced by Etzioni's (1961) analysis of kinds of power, suggesting in the first row in Table 13.1 the kinds of activities for which the different modes of accountability may be appropriate.

Table 13.1   Three kinds of governance

	Authority	**Transaction**	**Persuasion**
Core activity of government	Imposing Regulating Delivering goods and services	Creating frameworks Assessing results	Inviting participation Showing direction
Appropriate perspective on managing implementation	Enforcement	Performance	Co-production
Management via	Inputs	Outputs	Outcomes as shared results

In the second row of Table 13.1 the alternative perspectives on the management of implementation draw a distinction between top-down authority in the first column, issues about the extent to which there has been conformity with a contract in the second one, and a very mixed mode of accountability in the third column called 'co-production'. In the final row the way the actual management of the system is likely to be carried out is highlighted. This is seen in the 'Authority' column as particularly concerned with inputs, that is, questions about the extent to which resources have been appropriately applied to the performance of a task. In the 'Transaction' column it is suggested that crucial for this mode is a concern with outputs – have contractual obligations been fulfilled? By contrast with these two, the concern within the 'Persuasion' mode is with success in achieving shared goals – health or education improvement, for example – where it is real results as opposed to formally specified outputs that is crucial.

However, as has been asserted at various places in this book, it is important to acknowledge that the production of policy is a complex process. Policies generally go through a process of elaboration in which initial objectives are gradually concretised into action. This is shown in Table 13.2 by making a distinction between policy formation, the determination of institutional arrangements and the management of operational activities (distinctions set out on pp. 87 and 225). The relationships between these and the modes of governance from Table 13.1 are then brought together.

Table 13.2 Summarising characterisations of settings

Policy formation	Distinct policy formation	Framework policy formation	Ongoing policy formation
Institutional arrangements	System of command	Market place	Network
Operational management	Rule application	Service	Consultation and consensus
Fitting label for mode of governance	Authority	Transaction	Persuasion

Source: used by permission of Sage Publications Ltd. A modification of Table 8.5 from Hill and Hupe, 2002.

It has been noted that Etzioni's idea that modes of authority need to be fitted to modes of action influenced this formulation. That is a very prescriptive perspective. It leads Etzioni to speak of 'congruent' and 'incongruent' forms of authority (and thus in this context congruent and incongruent forms of accountability). What he means by this, in short, is that how authority is exercised needs to depend upon the context. His examples are that authority in a church will need to be exercised rather differently from that in a business or a prison, and so on. Since the perspective adopted in this book is to describe policy processes but to be reluctant to prescribe, this analysis may seem to be a marked departure from that. However, the point here is that governance of policy processes in the modern world involves, in practice, the making of choices between 'authority', 'transaction' and persuasion'. Furthermore, these choices do seem likely to be influenced by policy substance (that elusive distinction between types of policy which – as was suggested in Chapter 7 – has a common-sense validity but cannot be reduced to any simple typology). There is a sense, therefore, in which actors recognise congruencies and incongruencies, even if they do not analyse them in those terms. Intuitively it is much easier to devise a top-down-controlled, input-driven system if the aim is to provide a simple categorical benefit, like child benefit, to which rights have been established by statute, than if it is to control a complex form of pollution or to develop a system of health care or education. However, there are a lot of areas where the issues that might determine choice of delivery system are not so clear. Furthermore, political ideology influences choice. We are back here, therefore, to some of the issues considered by those scholars who concern themselves with issues of instrument choice (see pp. 140–2).

Furthermore, a crucial point about bringing together the issues about kinds of governance and what has been called 'settings' is that accountability issues emerge at various places in the system, and it may well be that they may be explored not just by reading down the columns in Table 13.2 but by reading across as well. A policy system involves a nested sequence of

Box 13.4	Disputed accountability in a complex policy system: the British National Health Service

The British National Health Service (NHS) has experienced turbulent, top-down-driven change through most of its history, and certainly since the later 1980s. Issues about striving for top-down control have been much in evidence, contracting (the transaction mode) has been tried and largely (but not entirely) discarded, and a great deal of attention has been paid to ways of steering the work of professional staff. Perhaps the greatest area of turbulence has been around the basic organisational arrangements, with an incessant search for the best regional and local arrangements for operational management. Quite evidently there are contested accountability models in play: about the prerogatives of the Secretary of State at the central level, about the responsibilities of local managerial bodies and about how much they can and should consult patients and the public, about the autonomy of staff, particularly doctors, and about the roles to be played by bodies representing the professions. It is interesting to note how this mixed pattern of accountability is acknowledged by central government. A crucial element in the development of the accountability of doctors is the notion of 'clinical governance'. The government sees this as 'a partnership between the Government and the clinical professions. In that partnership, the Government does what only the Government can do and the professions do what only they can do' (Department of Health, 1998, para 1.13). In the same document the government goes on to argue (para 3.9):

> Clinical governance requires partnerships within health care teams, between health professionals (including academic staff) and managers, between individuals and the organizations in which they work and between the NHS, patients and the public.

At the same time the government has been tinkering with the ways in which patients may be consulted and their grievances dealt with. There has been a move away from the use of local government-appointed representatives, via a now discarded device called Community Health Councils, to new arrangements for Patients' Forums and for dealing with complaints. New advisory and auditing bodies – the National Institute of Clinical Excellence and the Commission for Healthcare Audit and Inspection – have also been developed.

The point here is, of course, not whether the government has got the accountability arrangements right but that they have shown an increasing awareness of multiple and complex accountability.

decisions – about structure, about financing and about the management of outputs – for which different actors may be accountable, perhaps in different ways. It is instructive to look at a policy area where the issues about accountability are very highly contested in these terms. Box 13.4 does that.

Does the description of the NHS in Box 13.4 describe a network with accountability fitting neatly into the persuasion mode? Surely it does not: rather, it describes contested territory in which, pragmatically speaking, accountability is very mixed and a great deal of experimentation is going on.

CONCLUSIONS

Accountability is inevitably a subject that attracts considerable controversy in discussions of public policy. In conformity with this book's concern with examining the policy process, this chapter has tried to steer clear of the debate about who should be in control and how they should do it. It has noted that the view that, in a system of representative government, the administration of public policy should be hierarchically controlled by elected representatives has dominated the literature. When a traditional top-down view of the system has been challenged, that challenge has involved either the assertion that the complexity of modern government requires that it should be supplemented by other forms of accountability or efforts to establish alternative 'democratic' legitimacy for a bottom-up perspective.

However, identification of the complexity of accountability has long involved a recognition of forms of legal accountability (normally reinforcing hierarchical political accountability but occasionally challenging it). More complexity has then been added by a recognition of ways in which the elaborate nature of many public activities involves extensive discretionary decision making. Consideration therefore needs to be given to the roles of professional groups and to the way in which forms of co-production occur. An alternative approach to these issues, coming particularly from the 'rational choice' school of thought, suggests that in various respects consumer participation can be enhanced to deal with these issues through market and quasi-market mechanisms. An alternative is to try to strengthen 'voice' at the 'street level'.

All of this adds up to recognising that accountability in modern governance is bound to be complex. It will often be mixed, involving multiple forms of accountability to multiple groups. In examining it, attention needs to be given to the very different ways in which different public policies are made manifest, a theme that has recurred throughout this book.

It is not proposed to add a concluding chapter to this book. Many of the key themes in the book as a whole have surfaced again in this chapter. The traditional approach to accountability has been seen as part of that consensus about representative government within which the rational model of decision making and the top-down model of implementation also belong. This has been challenged both by an ideological pluralism which sees the need for multiple 'accountabilities' and by those who see networks and complex institutional arrangements as making any simple form of accountability difficult. In the background, and perhaps not analysed much in this chapter, lies another view – one which sees the structure of power as imposing severe limits on any form of popular accountability.

Throughout the book it has been stressed that there is a need to think about the policy process as a whole, even when analysis requires parts of the process to be separated out. It has also been stressed that it is important to see that the policy process is embedded in the structure of power in society. At the same time there is a need to recognise that it is not easy to generalise about the policy process, inasmuch as different policy issues emerge in different ways in different institutional contexts. The art of policy process analysis needs to involve a capacity to see connections, and to compare and contrast, whilst being sceptical about all-encompassing generalisations.

References

6, P. (2004) 'Joined-up government in the Western world in comparative perspective: A preliminary literature review and exploration'. *Journal of Public Administration, Research and Theory*, **14** (1), pp. 103–38.

Aberbach, J.D., Putman, R.D. and Rockman, B.A. (1981) *Bureaucrats and Politicians in Western Democracies*. Cambridge, Mass.: Harvard University Press.

Aglietta, M. (1987) *A Theory of Capitalist Regulation: The US Experience*. London: Verso.

Ainley, P. (2001) 'From a national system locally administered to a national system nationally administered: The new Leviathan in education and training in England'. *Journal of Social Policy*, **30** (3), pp. 457–76.

Albrow, M. (1970) *Bureaucracy*. London: Pall Mall.

Aldrich, H.E. (1976) 'Resource dependence and inter-organizational relations: Local employment service offices and social services sector organizations'. *Administration and Society*, **7** (4), pp. 419–54.

Alford, R. (1975) *Health Care Politics*. Chicago: University of Chicago Press.

Allen, C. (2001) '"They just don't live and breathe the policy like we do . . .": Policy intentions and practice dilemmas in modern social policy and implementation networks'. *Policy Studies*, **22** (3/4), pp. 149–66.

Allison, G.T. (1971) *Essence of Decision*. Boston, Mass.: Little Brown.

Almond, G.A., Powell, G.B., Jr, Strøm, K. and Dalton, R.J. (2004) *Comparative Politics Today*, 8th edn. New York: Pearson, Longman.

Anderweg, R.B. and Irwin, G.A. (2002) *Governance and Politics in the Netherlands*, 2nd edn. Basingstoke: Palgrave Macmillan.

Anttonen, A., Baldock, J. and Sipila, J. (eds) (2003) *The Young, the Old and the State: Social Care Systems in Five Industrial Nations*. Cheltenham: Edward Elgar.

Argyris, C. (1964) *Integrating the Individual and the Organisation*. New York: Wiley.

Ashby, E. and Anderson, M. (1981) *The Politics of Clean Air*. Oxford: Clarendon Press.

Ashford, D.E. (1986) *The Emergence of the Welfare States*. Oxford: Blackwell.

Atkinson, M.M. and Coleman, W.D. (1989) 'Strong states and weak states: Sectoral policy networks in advanced capitalist economies'. *British Journal of Political Science*, **19**, pp. 747–67.

Atkinson, P. (1985) *Language, Structure and Reproduction*. London: Methuen.

Auster, R.D. and Silver, M. (1979) *The State as a Firm: Economic Forces in Political Development.* The Hague: Martinus Nijhoff.

Axelrod, R. (1984) *The Evolution of Cooperation.* New York: Basic Books.

Axelrod, R. and Keohane, R. (1985) 'Achieving cooperation under anarchy: Strategies and institutions'. *World Politics*, **39** (1), pp. 226–54.

Bache, I. (2003) 'Governing through governance: Education policy control under New Labour'. *Political Studies*, **51** (2), pp. 300–14.

Bachrach, P. (1969) *The Theory of Democratic Elitism.* London: University of London Press.

Bachrach, P. and Baratz, M.S. (1962) 'Two faces of power'. *American Political Science Review*, **56**, pp. 641–51.

Bachrach, P. and Baratz, M.S. (1963) 'Decisions and nondecisions: An analytical framework'. *American Political Science Review*, **57**, pp. 1947–52.

Bachrach, P. and Baratz, M.S. (1970) *Power and Poverty.* New York: Oxford University Press.

Baldwin, P. (1990) *The Politics of Social Solidarity.* Cambridge: Cambridge University Press.

Baldwin, R. (1995) *Rules and Government.* Oxford: Oxford University Press.

Barker, A. and Peters, B.G. (eds) (1993) *The Politics of Expert Advice.* Edinburgh: Edinburgh University Press.

Barnard, C. (1938) *The Functions of the Executive.* Cambridge, Mass.: Harvard University Press.

Barrett, M. (1980) *Women's Oppression Today.* London: Verso.

Barrett, S. and Fudge, C. (eds) (1981) *Policy and Action.* London: Methuen.

Barrett, S. and Hill, M.J. (1981) 'Report to the SSRC Central London: Methuen. Local Government Relations Panel on the "core" or theoretical component of the research on implementation' (unpublished).

Baumgartner, F. and Jones, B. (1993) *Agendas and Instability in American Politics.* Chicago: University of Chicago Press.

Baumgartner, M.P. (1992) 'The myth of discretion', in Hawkins, K. (ed.) *The Uses of Discretion.* Oxford: Clarendon Press.

Beer, S.H. (1965) *Modern British Politics.* London: Faber & Faber.

Beetham, D. (1987) *Bureaucracy.* Milton Keynes: Open University Press.

Béland, D. (2001) 'Does labor matter? Institutions, labor unions and pension reform in France and the United States'. *Journal of Public Policy*, **21** (2), pp. 153–72.

Bell, D. (1960) *The End of Ideology.* New York: Free Press.

Bendor, J. and Hammond, T. (1992) 'Rethinking Allison's models'. *American Political Science Review*, **86** (2), pp. 301–22.

Bennett, G. (1992) *Dilemmas: Coping with Environmental Problems.* London: Earthscan.

Benson, J.K. (1975) 'The inter-organizational network as a political economy'. *Administrative Science Quarterly*, **20** (June), pp. 229–49.

Benson, J.K. (1983) 'Interorganizational networks and policy sectors', in D. Rogers and D. Whetten (eds) *Interorganizational Coordination.* Iowa: Iowa State University Press.

Bentley, A.F. (1967) *The Process of Government*. Cambridge, Mass.: Belknap Press.

Berger, P.L. and Luckman, T. (1975) *The Social Construction of Reality*. Harmondsworth: Penguin Books.

Beveridge, W. (1942) *Social Insurance and Allied Services*. London: HMSO, Cmd. 6404.

Birkland, T.A. (1998) 'Focusing events, mobilization, and agenda setting'. *Journal of Public Policy*, **18** (1), pp. 53–74.

Blau, P.M. (1955) *The Dynamics of Bureaucracy*. Chicago: University of Chicago Press.

Blom-Hansen, J. (1999) 'Policy-making in central–local government relations: Balancing local autonomy, macroecnomic control and sectoral policy goals'. *Journal of Public Policy*, **19** (3), pp. 237–64.

Blowers, A. (1984) *Something in the Air: Corporate Power and the Environment*. London: Harper and Row.

Boase, J.P. (1996) 'Institutions, institutionalized networks and policy choices: Health policy in the US and Canada'. *Governance*, **9** (3), pp. 287–310.

Bogason, P. (2000) *Public Policy and Local Governance*. Cheltenham: Edward Elgar.

Booth, T. (1988) *Developing Policy Research*. Aldershot: Avebury.

Bottomore, T.B. (1966) *Elites and Society*. Harmondsworth: Penguin.

Bovens, M. and 't Hart, P. (1996) *Understanding Policy Fiascos*. Brunswick, NJ: Transaction Publishers.

Bovens, M., 't Hart, P. and Peters, B.G. (eds) (2001) *Success and Failure in Public Governance*. Cheltenham: Edward Elgar.

Bovens, M. and Zouridis, S. (2002) 'From street-level to system-level bureaucracies: How information and communication technology is transforming administrative discretion and constitutional control'. *Public Administration Review*, **62** (2), pp. 174–84.

Bowe, R., Ball, S.J. and Gold, A. (1992) *Reforming Education and Changing Schools*. London: Routledge.

Bowen, E.R. (1982) 'The Pressman–Wildavsky paradox'. *Journal of Public Policy*, **2** (1), pp. 1–21.

Bradach, J.L. and Eccles, R.G. (1991) 'Price, authority and trust: From ideal types to plural forms', in Thompson, G., Frances, J., Levacic, R. and Mitchell, J. (eds), *Markets, Hierarchies and Networks: The Coordination of Social Life*. London: Sage, pp. 277–92.

Braverman, H. (1974) *Labor and Monopoly Capital*. New York: Monthly Review Press.

Braybrooke, D. and Lindblom, C.E. (1963) *A Strategy of Decision*. New York: The Free Press.

Brenton, T. (1994) *The Greening of Machiavelli*. London: Earthscan.

Brittan, S. (1977) *The Economic Consequences of Democracy*. London: Temple Smith.

Brown, M.K. (1981) 'The allocation of justice and police–citizen encounters', in Goodsell, C.T. (ed.) *The Public Encounter*. Bloomington: Indiana University Press.

Brown, R. (1975) *The Management of Welfare*. Glasgow: Fontana/Collins.

Browne, A. and Wildavsky, A. (1984) 'Should evaluation become implementation', in Pressman, J. and Wildavsky, A., *Implementation*, 3rd edn. Berkeley: University of California Press.

Brugger, B. and Reglar, S. (1994) *Politics, Economy and Society in Contemporary China.* Basingstoke: Macmillan.

Buchanan, J.M. and Tullock, G. (1962) *The Calculus of Consent.* Ann Arbor, Mich.: University of Michigan Press.

Bull, D. (1980) 'The anti-discretion movement in Britain: Fact or phantom?' *Journal of Social Welfare Law*, pp. 65–83.

Bulmer, M. (ed.) (1987) *Social Science Research and Government.* Cambridge: Cambridge University Press.

Burns, T. and Stalker, G.M. (1961) *The Management of Innovation.* London: Tavistock.

Butcher, T. (2002) *Delivering Welfare*, 2nd edn. Buckingham: Open University Press.

Butler, D., Adonis, A. and Travers, T. (1994) *Failure in British Government: The Politics of the Poll Tax.* Oxford: Oxford University Press.

Cahill, M. (2002) *The Environment and Social Policy.* London: Routledge.

Campbell, C. and Wilson, G.K. (1995) *The End of Whitehall: Death of a Paradigm?* Oxford: Blackwell.

Castles, F. (1985) *The Working Class and Welfare.* Sydney: Allen and Unwin.

Castles, F. and Mitchell, D. (1992) 'Identifying welfare state regimes: The links between politics, instruments and outcomes'. *Governance*, **5** (1), pp. 1–26.

Chadwick, A. (2000) 'Studying political ideas: A public political discourse approach', *Political Studies*, **48**, pp. 283–301.

Chandler, A.D. (1977) *The Visible Hand: The Managerial Revolution in American Business.* Cambridge, Mass.: Harvard University Press.

Chaney, C.K. and Saltzstein, G.H. (1998) 'Democratic control and bureaucratic responsiveness: The police and domestic violence'. *American Journal of Political Science*, **42** (3), pp. 745–68.

Chapman, R.A. (1970) *The Higher Civil Service in Britain.* London: Constable.

Child, J. (1972) 'Organization structure, environment and performance: The role of strategic choice'. *Sociology*, **6**, pp. 1–22.

Clarke, J. and Newman, J. (1997) *The Managerial State: Power, Politics and Ideology in the Remaking of Social Welfare.* London: Sage.

Clegg, S. (1990) *Modern Organizations.* London: Sage.

Cline, K.D. (2000) 'Defining the implementation problem: Organizational management versus cooperation'. *Journal of Public Administration Research and Theory*, **10** (3), pp. 551–71.

Coase, R.H. (1937) 'The nature of the firm'. *Economica*, **4**, pp. 386–405.

Cobb, R.W., Ross, J.K. and Ross M.H. (1976) 'Agenda building as a comparative political process'. *American Political Science Review*, **70** (1), pp. 126–38.

Cohen, J. and Rogers, J. (1995) *Associations and Democracy.* London: Verso.

Cohen, M.D., March, J.G. and Olsen, J.P. (1972) 'A garbage can model of organizational choice'. *Administrative Science Quarterly*, **17**, pp. 1–25.

Cohen, R. (1987) *The New Helots: Migrants in the International Division of Labour.* Aldershot: Avebury.

Colebatch, H. and Larmour, P. (1993) *Market, Bureaucracy and Community*. London: Pluto.

Coleman, W.D. and Perl, A. (1999) 'Internationalized policy environments and policy network analysis'. *Political Studies*, **47**, pp. 691–709.

Collier, R.B. and Collier, D. (1991) *Shaping the Political Arena: Critical Junctures, the Labour Movement and Regime Dynamics in Latin America*. Princeton, NJ: Princeton University Press.

Cox, R. (1987) *Production, Power and World Order*. New York: Columbia University Press.

Cram, L. (1997) *Policy-making in the EU*. London: Routledge.

Crenson, M.A. (1971) *The Unpolitics of Air Pollution*. Baltimore, Md.: Johns Hopkins University Press.

Cunningham, G. (1963) 'Policy and practice'. *Public Administration*, **41**, pp. 229–38.

Dahl, R.A. (1947) 'The science of public administration: Three problems'. *Public Administration Review*, **7** (1), pp. 1–11.

Dahl, R.A. (1957) 'The concept of power'. *Behavioural Science*, **2**, pp. 201–15.

Dahl, R.A. (1958) 'A critique of the ruling-elite model'. *American Political Science Review*, **52**, pp. 463–9.

Dahl, R.A. (1961) *Who Governs?* New Haven, Conn.: Yale University Press.

Dahl, R.A. and Lindblom, C.E. (1953) *Politics, Economics and Welfare* (2nd edn 1976). Chicago: Chicago University Press.

Dallek, R. (2003) *John F. Kennedy: An Unfinished Life*. London: Allen Lane.

Daly, M. (2000) *The Gender Division of Welfare*. Cambridge: Cambridge University Press.

Davies, H.T.O., Nutley, S.M. and Smith, P.C. (2000) (eds) *What Works?* Bristol: Policy Press.

Davis, K.C. (1969) *Discretionary Justice*. Baton Rouge: Louisiana State University Press.

Dawkins, R. (2003) *A Devil's Chaplain*. London: Weidenfeld and Nicolson.

Day, P. and Klein, R. (1987) *Accountabilities*. London: Tavistock.

Deakin, N. and Walsh, K. (1996) 'The enabling state: The role of markets and contracts'. *Public Administration*, **74**, pp. 33–48.

Dearlove, J. and Saunders, P. (1991) *Introduction to British Politics*. Cambridge: Polity Press.

Degeling, P. (1993) 'Policy as the accomplishment of an implementation structure: Hospital restructuring in Australia', in Hill, M. (ed.) *New Agendas in the Study of the Policy Process*. Hemel Hempstead: Harvester Wheatsheaf.

Degeling, P. and Colebatch, H.K. (1984) 'Structure and action as constructs in the practice of public administration'. *Australian Journal of Public Administration*, **43** (4), pp. 320–31.

Degeling, P., Kennedy, J., Hill, M., Carnegie, M. and Holt, J. (1998) *Professional Sub-Cultures and Hospital Reform*. Centre for Hospital Management and Information Systems Research, University of New South Wales.

Degeling, P., Maxwell, S., Kennedy, J. and Coyle, B. (2003) 'Medicine, management and modernisation: A "danse macabre"?' *British Medical Journal*, **326**, pp. 649–52.

Dell, E. (1991) *A Hard Pounding: Politics and the Economic Crisis*. Oxford: Oxford University Press.

Delphy, C. (1984) *Close to Home: A Materialist Analysis of Women's Oppression*. London: Hutchinson.

Department of Health (1998) *A First Class Service: Quality in the NHS*. Consultation Document. London: HMSO.

Dery, D. (1999) 'Policy by the way: When policy is incidental to making other policies'. *Journal of Public Policy*, **18** (2), pp. 163–76.

DiMaggio, P.J. and Powell, W. (1983) 'The iron cage revisited: Institutional isomorphism and collective rationality in organizational fields'. *American Sociological Review*, **48**, pp. 147–60.

Doern, G.B. and Phidd, R.W. (1983) *Canadian Public Policy*. Agincourt, Ontario: Methuen.

Dolowicz, D. and Marsh, D. (1996) 'Who learns what from whom: A review of the policy transfer literature'. *Political Studies*, **44**, pp. 343–57.

Dolowicz, D. and Marsh, D. (2000) 'Learning from abroad: The role of policy transfer in contemporary policy making'. *Governance*, **13** (1), pp. 5–24.

Dolowitz, D.P., Hulme, R., Nellis, M. and O'Neill, F. (2002) *Policy Transfer and British Social Policy: Learning from the USA?* Buckingham: Open University Press.

Donaldson, L. (1985) *In Defence of Organization Theory: A Response to the Critics*. Cambridge: Cambridge University Press.

Donnison, D.V. (1977) 'Against discretion'. *New Society*, 15 September, pp. 534–6.

Dowding, K. (1995) 'Model or metaphor? A critical review of the policy network approach'. *Political Studies*, **43**, pp. 451–63.

Downing, P.B. and Hanf, K. (eds) (1983) *International Comparisons in Implementing Pollution Laws*. Boston, Mass.: Kluwer Nijhoff.

Downs, A. (1957) *An Economic Theory of Democracy*. New York: Harper and Row.

Downs, A. (1972) 'Up and down with ecology – the "issue-attention cycle"'. *The Public Interest*, **28**, pp. 38–50.

Dror, Y. (1964) 'Muddling through: "Science" or inertia?' *Public Administration Review*, **24**, pp. 153–7.

Dror, Y. (1968) *Public Policymaking Re-examined*. San Francisco, Cal.: Chandler.

Dror, Y. (1986) *Policymaking under Adversity*. New Brunswick, NJ: Transaction Books.

Drysek, J.S. (1990) *Discursive Democracy*. Cambridge: Cambridge University Press.

Dudley, G. and Richardson, J. (1999) 'Competing advocacy coalitions and the process of "frame reflection": a longitudinal study of EU steel policy'. *Journal of European Public Policy*, **6** (2), pp. 225–48.

Dunleavy, P. (1981) 'Professions and policy change: notes towards a model of ideological corporatism'. *Public Administration Bulletin*, **36**, pp. 3–16.

Dunleavy, P. (1985) 'Bureaucrats, budgets and the growth of the state: Reconstructing an instrumental model'. *British Journal of Political Science*, **15**, pp. 299–328.

Dunleavy, P. (1986) 'Explaining the privatization boom: Public choice versus radical approaches'. *Public Administration*, **64** (1), pp. 13–34.

Dunleavy, P. (1991) *Democracy, Bureaucracy and Public Choice*. Hemel Hempstead: Harvester Wheatsheaf.

Dunleavy, P. (1995) 'Policy disasters: Explaining the UK's record'. *Public Policy and Administration*, **10** (2), pp. 52–69.

Dunleavy, P. and O'Leary, B. (1987) *Theories of the State*. London: Macmillan.

Dunsire, A. (1978a) *Implementation in a Bureaucracy*. Oxford: Martin Robertson.

Dunsire, A. (1978b) *Control in a Bureaucracy*. Oxford: Martin Robertson.

Dworkin, R. (1977) *Taking Rights Seriously*. London: Duckworth.

Dyson, K. (1980) *The State Tradition in Western Europe*. Oxford: Martin Robertson.

Eardley, T., Bradshaw, J., Ditch, J., Gough, I. and Whiteford, P. (1996) *Social Assistance in OECD Countries: Synthesis Report*. Department of Social Security Research Report No. 46, London: HMSO.

Easton, D. (1953) *The Political System*. New York: Knopf.

Easton, D. (1965a) *A Systems Analysis of Political Life*. New York: Wiley.

Easton, D. (1965b) *A Framework for Political Analysis*. Englewood Cliffs, NJ: Prentice Hall.

Edelman, M. (1971) *Politics as Symbolic Action*. Chicago: Markham.

Edelman, M. (1977) *Political Language: Words that Succeed and Policies that Fail*. New York: Institute for the Study of Poverty.

Edelman, M. (1988) *Constructing the Political Spectacle*. Chicago: University of Chicago Press.

Edelman, M. (2001) *The Politics of Misinformation*. Cambridge: Cambridge University Press.

Elam, M.J. (1990) 'Puzzling out the post-Fordist debate: Technology, markets and institutions'. *Economic and Industrial Democracy*, **11**, pp. 9–38.

Ellul, J. (1964) *The Technological Society*. New York: Vintage Books.

Elmore, R. (1980) 'Backward mapping: Implementation research and policy decisions'. *Political Science Quarterly*, **94**, pp. 601–16.

Elmore, R. (1981) 'Backward mapping and youth employment', (unpublished paper prepared for the third meeting of the International Working Group on Policy Implementation).

Enthoven, A.C. (1985) *Reflections on the Management of the NHS*. London: Nuffield Provincial Hospitals Trust.

Esping-Andersen, G. (1990) *Three Worlds of Welfare Capitalism*. Cambridge: Polity Press.

Esping-Andersen, G. (ed.) (1996) *Welfare States in Transition*. London: Sage.

Esping-Andersen, G. (1999) *Social Foundations of Post-Industrial Economies*. Oxford: Oxford University Press.

Ethridge, M.E. and Percy, S.L. (1993) 'A new kind of public policy encounters disappointing results: Implementing learnfare in Wisconsin'. *Public Administration Review*, **53** (4), pp. 340–7.

Etzioni, A. (1961) *A Comparative Analysis of Complex Organisations*. New York: Free Press.

Etzioni, A. (1967) 'Mixed-scanning: A "third" approach to decision-making', *Public Administration Review*, **27**, pp. 385–92.

Etzioni, A. (1969) *The Semi Professions and Their Organization*. New York: Free Press.

Evans, P.B., Rueschemeyer, D. and Skocpol, T. (eds) (1985) *Bringing the State Back In*. Cambridge: Cambridge University Press.

Evans, R. (2001) *In Defence of History*. Cambridge: Granta Books.

Exworthy, M., Berney, L. and Powell, M. (2002) '"How great expectations in Westminster may be dashed locally": The implementation of national policy on health inequalities'. *Policy and Politics*, **30** (1), pp. 79–96.

Farmer, D.J. (1995) *The Language of Public Administration: Bureaucracy, Modernity and Post-modernity*. Tuscaloosa, Ala.: University of Alabama Press.

Fayol, H. (1916) *Administration Industrielle et Generale*. London: Pitman.

Feldman, M. (1992) 'Social limits to discretion: An organizational perspective', in Hawkins, K. (ed.) *The Uses of Discretion*. Oxford: Clarendon Press.

Ferman, B. (1990) 'When failure is success: Implementation and Madisonian government', in Palumbo, D.J. and Calista, D.J. (eds), *Implementation and the Policy Process: Opening Up the Black Box*. New York: Greenwood Press, pp. 39–50.

Ferrara, M. (1996) 'The "southern model" of welfare in social Europe'. *Journal of European Social Policy*, **6**, pp. 17–37.

Fischer, F. (2003) *Reframing Public Policy*. Oxford: Oxford University Press.

Flynn, R. (1993) 'Coping with cutbacks and managing retrenchment in health'. *Journal of Social Policy*, **20** (2), pp. 215–36.

Forrest, R. and Murie, A. (1991) *Selling the Welfare State*. London: Routledge.

Foucault, M. (1980) *Power/Knowledge: Selected Interviews and Other Writings, 1972–77*. Brighton: Harvester.

Fox, A. (1974) *Beyond Contract: Work, Power and Trust Relations*. London: Faber.

Fox, C.J. and Miller, H.T. (1995) *Postmodern Public Administration: Toward Discourse*. Thousand Oaks, Cal.: Sage.

Frederickson, H.G. and Smith, K.B. (2003) *The Public Adminstration Theory Primer*. Boulder, Col.: Westview Press.

Friedman, M. (1962) *Capitalism and Freedom*. Chicago: University of Chicago Press.

Friedman, M. (1977) *Inflation and Unemployment: A New Dimension of Politics*. London: Institute of Economic Affairs.

Friedrich, C.J. (1940) 'The nature of administrative responsibility'. *Public Policy*, **1**, pp. 3–24.

Friedson, E. (1970) *Professional Dominance*. New York: Atherton.

Friend, J.K., Power, J.M. and Yewlett, C.J.L (1974) *Public Planning: The Inter-Corporate Dimension*. London: Tavistock.

Fukuyama, F. (1992) *The End of History and the Last Man*. New York: Free Press.

Galligan, D.J. (1986) *Discretionary Powers*. Oxford: Clarendon Press.

Gamble, A. (1994) *The Free Economy and the Strong State*, 2nd edn. Basingstoke: Macmillan.

Gamble, A. (2003) *Between Europe and America: The Future of British Politics*. Basingstoke: Palgrave Macmillan.

Gaventa, J. (1980) *Power and Powerlessness, Quiescence and Rebellion in an Appalachian Valley*. Oxford: Clarendon Press.

George, V. and Wilding, P. (2002) *Globalisation and Human Welfare*. Basingstoke: Palgrave.

Giddens, A. (1976) *New Rules of Sociological Method*. London: Hutchinson.

Giddens, A. (1984) *The Constitution of Society*. Cambridge: Polity Press.

Gilbert, B.B. (1966) *The Evolution of National Insurance in Great Britain*. London: Michael Joseph.

Gilbert, M. and Gott, R. (2000) *The Appeasers*. London: Weidenfeld & Nicolson.

Giller, H. and Morris, A. (1981) 'What type of case is this? Social workers' decisions about children who offend', in Adler, M. and Asquith, S. (eds) *Discretion and Welfare*. London: Heinemann.

Glendinning, C., Powell, M. and Rummery, K. (eds) (2002) *Partnerships, New Labour and the Governance of Welfare*. Bristol: The Policy Press.

Glennerster, H., Matsaganis, M. and Owens, P. (1994) *Implementing Fundholding*. Buckingham: Open University Press.

Glennerster, H., Power, A. and Travers, T. (1991) 'A new era for social policy: A new Enlightenment or a new Leviathan?' *Journal of Social Policy*, **20** (3), pp. 389–414.

Goetz, K.H. (2003) 'Government at the centre', in Padgett, S., Paterson, W.E. and Smith, G. (eds) *Developments in German Politics* vol. 3. Basingstoke: Palgrave Macmillan.

Goggin, M.L., Bowman, A.O'M., Lester, J.P. and O'Toole, L.J., Jr. (1990) *Implementation Theory and Practice: Toward a Third Generation*. Glenview: Scott Foresman/Little, Brown.

Gordon, I., Lewis, J. and Young, K. (1977) 'Perspectives on policy analysis'. *Public Administration Bulletin*, **25**, pp. 26–30.

Gough, I. (1979) *The Political Economy of the Welfare State*. London: Macmillan.

Gouldner, A.W. (1954) *Patterns of Industrial Bureaucracy*. Glencoe, Ill.: Free Press.

Gouldner, A.W. (1957–8) 'Cosmopolitans and locals: Towards an analysis of latent social roles'. *Administrative Science Quarterly*, **2**, pp. 281–306 and 444–80.

Grant, W.P. (1989) *Pressure Groups, Politics and Democracy in Britain*: London: Phillip Allan.

Gray, P.D. and 't Hart, P. (eds) (1998) *Public Policy Disasters in Europe*. London: Routledge.

Greenwood, E. (1957) 'Attributes of a profession'. *Social Work*, **2**, pp. 45–55.

Greenwood, R., Hinings, C.R. and Ranson, S. (1975) 'Contingency theory and the organisation of local authorities: Part One. Differentiation and integration'. *Public Administration*, **53**, pp. 1–24.

Gregory, R. (2003) 'Accountability in modern government', in Peters, B.G. and Pierre, J. (eds) *Handbook of Public Administration*. London: Sage.

Gunn, L. (1978) 'Why is implementation so difficult?' *Management Services in Government*, November.

Gustafssohn, G. (1991) 'Swedish local government: Reconsidering rationality and consensus', in Hesse, J.J. (ed.) *Local Government and Urban Affairs in International Perspective*. Baden-Baden: Nomos Verlagsgesellschaft.

Habermas, J. (1987) *The Theory of Communicative Action*. Cambridge: Polity Press.

Haggard, S. and Moon, C-I. (1990) 'Institutions and economic policy: Theory and a Korean case study'. *World Politics*, **42** (2), pp. 210–37.

Hall, P.A. (1986) *Governing the Economy: The Politics of State Intervention in Britain and France*. Cambridge: Polity Press.

Hall, P.A. (1993) 'Policy paradigms, social learning and the state: The case of economic policy making in Britain'. *Comparative Politics*, **25**, pp. 275–96.

Ham, C. (1992) *Health Policy in Britain*, 3rd edn. London: Macmillan.

Ham, C. and Hill, M.J. (1984) *The Policy Process in the Modern Capitalist State*. Hemel Hempstead: Harvester Wheatsheaf.

Hanf, K. (1993) 'Enforcing environmental laws: The social regulation of co-production', in Hill, M. (ed.) *New Agendas in the Study of the Policy Process*. Hemel Hempstead: Harvester Wheatsheaf.

Hardin, G. (1968) 'The tragedy of the commons'. *Science*, **162**, pp. 1243–8.

Hargrove, E.C. (1975) *The Missing Link*. Washington, DC: The Urban Institute.

Harrison, S. and Pollitt, C. (1994) *Controlling Health Professionals*. Buckingham: Open University Press.

Harrison, S., Hunter, D.J. and Pollitt, C. (1990) *The Dynamics of British Health Policy*. London: Unwin Hyman.

Harrop, M. (ed.) (1992) *Power and Policy in Liberal Democracies*. Cambridge: Cambridge University Press.

Hasenfeld, Y. and Steinmetz, D. (1981) 'Client–official encounters in social service agencies', in Goodsell, C.T. (ed.), *The Public Encounter*. Bloomington: Indiana University Press.

Hawkins, K. (1984) *Environment and Enforcement*. Oxford: Clarendon Press.

Hay, C. (2002) *Political Analysis: A Critical Introduction*. Basingstoke: Palgrave.

Hayek, F.A. (1944) *The Road to Serfdom*. London: Routledge and Kegan Paul.

Hayek, F.A. (1960) *The Constitution of Liberty*. London: Routledge and Kegan Paul.

Hayward, J. and Menon, A. (eds) (2003) *Governing Europe*. Oxford: Oxford University Press.

Heclo, H. (1972) 'Review article: Policy analysis'. *British Journal of Political Science*, **2**, pp. 83–108.

Heclo, H. (1974) *Modern Social Politics in Britain and Sweden*. New Haven, Conn.: Yale University Press.

Heclo, H. and Wildavsky, A. (1981) *The Private Government of Public Money*. London: Macmillan.

Hennessy, P. (1995) *The Hidden Wiring: Unearthing the British Constitution*. London: Gollancz.

Herzberg, F. (1966) *Work and the Nature of Man*. New York: Staples Press.

Higgins, J. (1981) *States of Welfare*. Oxford: Blackwell.

Hill, M. (1969) 'The exercise of discretion in the National Assistance Board'. *Public Administration*, **47**, pp. 75–90.

Hill, M. (1972) *The Sociology of Public Administration*. London: Weidenfeld & Nicolson.

Hill, M. (1983) 'The role of the British Alkali and Clean Air Inspectorate in air pollution control', in Downing, P. and Hanf, K. (eds) *International Comparisons in Implementing Pollution Laws*. Dordrecht: Kluwer-Nijhoff.

Hill, M. (ed.) (1993) *New Agendas in the Study of the Policy Process*. Hemel Hempstead: Harvester Wheatsheaf.

Hill, M. (1996) *Social Policy: A Comparative Analysis*. Hemel Hempstead: Harvester Wheatsheaf.

Hill, M. (2001) 'Social security: Welfare reform or piecemeal adjustment?' in Savage, S.P. and Atkinson, R. (eds) *Public Policy under Blair*. Basingstoke: Palgrave.

Hill, M. and Hupe, P. (2002) *Implementing Public Policy*. London: Sage.

Hill, M. and Hupe, P. (2003) 'The multi-layer problem in implementation research'. *Public Management Review*, **5** (4), pp. 471–90.

Hill, M., Aaronovitch, S. and Baldock, D. (1989) 'Non-decision making in pollution control in Britain: Nitrate pollution, the EEC Drinking Water Directive and agriculture'. *Policy and Politics*, **17** (3), pp. 227–40.

Hirschman, A.O. (1970) *Exit, Voice and Loyalty*. Cambridge, Mass.: Harvard University Press.

Hirst, P. and Thompson, G. (1992) 'The problem of "globalisation": International economic relations, national economic management and the formation of trading blocs'. *Economy and Society*, **21** (4), pp. 355–96.

Hjern, B. and Hull, C. (1982) `implementation research as empirical constitutionalism', in Hjern, B. and Hull, C. (eds) *Implementation Beyond Hierarchy*. Special issue of *European Journal of Political Research*.

Hjern, B. and Porter, D.O. (1981) 'Implementation structures: A new unit of administrative analysis'. *Organisational Studies*, **2**, pp. 211–27.

Hofferbert, R. (1974) *The Study of Public Policy*. Indianapolis, Ind.: Bobbs Merrill.

Hoggett, P. (1991) 'A new management for the public sector?' *Policy and Politics*, **19**, pp. 143–56.

Hoggett, P. (1996) 'New modes of control in the public service'. *Public Administration*, **74** (1), pp. 9–32.

Hogwood, B. (1987) *From Crisis to Complacency? Shaping Public Policy in Britain*. London: Oxford University Press.

Hogwood, B.W. and Gunn, L. (1981) *The Policy Orientation*. University of Strathclyde: Centre for the Study of Public Policy.

Hogwood, B.W. and Gunn, L. (1984) *Policy Analysis for the Real World*. London: Oxford University Press.

Hogwood, B.W. and Peters, B.G. (1983) *Policy Dynamics*. Brighton: Harvester.

Hood, C. (1976) *The Limits of Administration*. Chichester: Wiley.

Hood, C. (1986) *The Tools of Government*. Chatham, NJ: Chatham House.

Hood, C. (1991) 'A public management for all seasons'. *Public Adminstration,* **69** (1), pp. 3–19.

Hood, C. (1995) 'Contemporary public management: A new global paradigm?' *Public Policy and Administration*, **10** (2), pp. 104–17.

Horn, M. (1995) *The Political Economy of Public Administration*. Cambridge: Cambridge University Press.

Howlett, M. (1991) 'Policy instruments, policy styles and policy implementation: National approaches to theories of instrument choice'. *Policy Studies Journal*, **19** (2), pp. 1–21.

Howlett, M. and Ramesh, M. (2003) *Studying Public Policy*, 2nd edn. Don Mills, Ontario: Oxford University Press.

Huber, J.D. and Shipan, C.R. (2002) *Deliberate Discretion? The Institutional Foundations of Bureaucratic Autonomy*. Cambridge: Cambridge University Press.

Hudson, B. (1987) 'Collaboration in social welfare: A framework for analysis'. *Policy and Politics*, **15** (3), pp. 175–82.

Hudson, B. (1989) 'Michael Lipsky and street-level bureaucracy: A neglected perspective', in Barton, L. (ed.) *Disability and Dependency*. Lewes: Falmer Press.

Hudson, B. and Henwood, M. (2002) 'The NHS and social care: The final countdown?' *Policy and Politics*, **30** (2), pp. 153–66.

Hudson, J. and Lowe, S. (2004) *Understanding the Policy Process*. Bristol: The Policy Press.

Hughes, E.C. (1958) *Men and Their Work*. Glencoe, Ill.: Free Press.

Hunter, F. (1953) *Community Power Structure*. Chapel Hill, NC: University of North Carolina Press.

Hupe, P. (1990) 'Implementing a meta-policy: The case of decentralisation in the Netherlands'. *Policy and Politics*, **18** (3), pp. 181–91.

Hurrell, A. and Kingsbury, B. (eds) (1992) *The International Politics of the Environment*. Oxford: Oxford University Press.

Huxham, C. and Macdonald, D. (1992) 'Introducing collaborative advantage'. *Management Decision*, **30** (3), pp. 50–6.

Hwang, Yuan-shie (1995) 'Funding health care in Britain and Taiwan'. PhD diss., University of Newcastle upon Tyne.

Illich, I. (1977) *Limits to Medicine*. Harmondsworth: Penguin.

Immergut, E.M. (1992) 'The rules of the game: The logic of health policy-making in France, Switzerland and Sweden', in Steinmo, S., Thelen, K. and Longstreth, F. (eds), *Structuring Politics: Historical Institutionalism in Comparative Analysis*. Cambridge: Cambridge University Press.

Immergut, E.M. (1993) *Health Policy, Interests and Institutions in Western Europe*. Cambridge: Cambridge University Press.

Jacques, E. (1967) *Equitable Payment*. Harmondsworth: Penguin.

James, O. and Lodge, M. (2003) 'The limitations of "policy transfer" and "lesson drawing" for public policy research'. *Political Studies Review*, **1** (2), pp. 179–93.

Jenkins, W.I. (1978) *Policy Analysis*. London: Martin Robertson.

Jessop, B. (1992) 'Fordism and post-Fordism: A critical reformulation', in Scott, A.J. and Stormper, M. (eds) *Pathways to Industrialisation and Regional Development*. London: Routledge.

John, P. (1998) *Analysing Public Policy*. London: Pinter.

John, P. (2001) *Local Government in Western Europe*. London: Sage.

Johnson, T.J. (1972) *Professions and Power*. London: Macmillan.

Jones, C. (1985) *Patterns of Social Policy: An Introduction to Comparative Analysis*. London: Tavistock.

Jones, P. and Cullis, J. (2003) 'Key parameters in policy design: The case of intrinsic motivation'. *Journal of Social Policy*, **32** (4), pp. 527–48.

Jordan, A. (1997) 'Overcoming the divide between comparative politics and international relations approaches to the EC: What role for "post-decisional politics"?' *West European Politics*, **20** (4), pp. 43–70.

Jordan, A. (2001) 'The European Union: An evolving system of multi-level governance . . . or government?' *Policy and Politics*, **29** (2), pp. 193–208.

Jordan, A.G. (1986) 'Iron triangles, woolly corporatism and elastic nets: Images of the policy process'. *Journal of Public Policy*, **1**, pp. 95–123.

Jordan, A.G. and Richardson, J.J. (1987) *British Politics and the Policy Process*. London: Unwin Hyman.

Jowell, J. (1973) 'The legal control of administrative discretion'. *Public Law*, pp. 178–220.

Kampfner, J. (2003) *Blair's Wars*. London: Free Press.

Katzenstein, P. (1977) 'Conclusion: Domestic structures and strategies of foreign economic policy'. *International Organisation*, **31** (4), pp. 879–920.

Kavanagh, D. and Seldon, A. (2001) *The Power Behind the Prime Minister*. London: HarperCollins.

Kavanagh, G. and Richards, D. (2001) 'Departmentalism and joined-up government: Back to the future'. *Parliamentary Affairs*, **64** (1), pp. 1–18.

Kearns, K.P. (2003) 'Accountability in a seamless economy', in Peters, B.G. and Pierre, J. (eds) *Handbook of Public Administration*. London: Sage.

Keegan, W. (2003) *The Prudence of Mr Gordon Brown*. Chichester: Wiley.

Kelsey, J. (1995) *The New Zealand Experiment*. Auckland: Auckland University Press.

Kennedy, I. (1981) *The Unmasking of Medicine*. London: Allen and Unwin.

Kerr, C. (1973) *Industrialism and Industrial Man*. Harmondsworth: Penguin Books.

Keynes, J.M. (1947) *The General Theory of Employment Interest and Money*. London: Macmillan, rev. edn (original 1936).

Kickert, W.J.M. (1995) 'Steering at a distance: A new paradigm of public governance in Dutch higher education'. *Governance*, **8** (1), pp. 135–57.

Kickert, W.J.M. and van Vucht, F.A. (eds) (1995) *Public Policy and Administration Sciences in the Netherlands*. Hemel Hempstead: Harvester Wheatsheaf.

Kingdon, J.W. (1995) *Agendas, Alternatives and Public Policies*. New York: Addison, Wesley, Longman, 2nd edn (1st edn 1984).

Kingsley, J.D. (1944) *Representative Bureaucracy*. Yellow Springs, Ohio: Antioch Press.

Kinnersley, D. (1994) *Coming Clean: The Politics of Water and the Environment*. Harmondsworth: Penguin Books.

Kiser, L.L. and Ostrom, E. (1982) 'The three worlds of action: A metatheoretical synthesis of institutional approaches', in Ostrom, E. (ed.), *Strategies of Political Inquiry*. Beverly Hills, Cal.: Sage, pp. 179–222.

Knapp, A. and Wright, M. (2001) *The Government and Politics of France*. London: Routledge, 4th edn.

Knill, C. (1998) 'European policies: The impact of national administrative traditions'. *Journal of Public Policy*, **18** (1), pp. 1–28.

Knill, C. and Lenschow, A. (1998) 'Coping with Europe: The impact of British and German administrations on the implementation of EU environmental policy'. *Journal of European Public Policy*, **5** (4), pp. 595–614.

Knoepfel, P. and Weidner, H. (1982) 'Formulation and implementation of air quality control programmes: Patterns of interest consideration'. *Policy and Politics*, **10** (1), pp. 85–109.

Knoke, D. (1990) *Policy Networks: The Structural Perspective*. Cambridge: Cambridge University Press.

Kochan, T.A. (1975) 'Determinants of power boundary units in an interorganizational bargaining relation'. *Administrative Science Quarterly*, **20**, pp. 435–52.

Kormondy, E.J. (ed.) (1989) *International Handbook of Pollution Control*. Westport, Conn.: Greenwood Press.

Krasner, S. (1984) 'Approaches to the state: Alternative conceptions and historical dynamics'. *Comparative Politics*, **16**, pp. 223–46.

Laffin, M. (1986) 'Professional communities and policy communities in central–local relations', in Goldsmith, M. (ed.) *New Research in Central–Local Relations*. Aldershot: Gower.

Lampinen, R. and Uusikylä, P. (1998) 'Implementation deficit – Why member states do not comply with EU directives'. *Scandinavian Political Studies*, **21** (3), pp. 231–51.

Lane, J-E. (1987) 'Implementation, accountability and trust'. *European Journal of Political Research*, **15** (5), pp. 527–46.

Lane, J-E. and Ersson, S.O. (2000) *The New Institutional Politics: Performance and Outcomes*. London: Routledge.

Lansley, S., Goss, S. and Wolmar, C. (1989) *Councils in Conflict: The Rise and Fall of the Municipal Left*. London: Macmillan.

Laski, H.J. (1925) *A Grammar of Politics*. London: Allen & Unwin.

Lasswell, H.D. (1936) *Politics: Who Gets What, When, How*. Cleveland, Ohio: Meridian Books.

Lasswell, H.D. (1951) 'The policy orientation', in Lerner, D. and Lasswell, H.D. (eds) *The Policy Sciences*. Stanford, Cal.: Stanford University Press.

Lasswell, H.D. (1968) 'The policy sciences', in *Encyclopedia of the Social Sciences*, vol. 12. New York: Macmillan.

Lasswell, H.D. (1970) 'The emerging conception of the policy sciences'. *Policy Sciences*, pp. 3–14.

Latham, E. (1952) *The Group Basis of Politics*. Ithaca, NY: Cornell University Press.

Lau, L.J. (1986) *Models of Development: A Comparative Study of Economic Growth in South Korea and Taiwan*. San Fransisco: Institute for Contemporary Studies.

Le Grand, J. (1997) 'Knights, knaves and pawns? Human behaviour and social policy'. *Journal of Social Policy*, **26** (2), pp. 149–70.

Le Grand, J. (2003) *Motivation, Agency and Public Policy*. Oxford: Oxford University Press.

Lenin, V.I. (1917) *State and Revolution*. Moscow: Foreign Languages Publishing House.

Levine, S. and White, P. (1961) 'Exchange as a conceptual framework for the study of interorganisational relationships'. *Administrative Science Quarterly*, **5**, pp. 583–601.

Lewis, J. (1992) 'Gender and the development of welfare regimes'. *Journal of European Social Policy*, **2** (3), pp. 159–73.

Lewis, J. (ed.) (1993) *Women and Social Policies in Europe: Work, Family and the State*. Aldershot: Edward Elgar.

Lewis, J. (1997) 'Gender and welfare regimes: Further thoughts'. *Social Politics*, Summer, pp. 160–77.

Lijphart, A. (1975) *The Politics of Accommodation: Pluralism and Democracy in the Netherlands*, 2nd edn. Berkeley, Cal.: University of California Press.

Lijphart, A. (1999) *Patterns of Democracy*. New Haven, Conn.: Yale University Press.

Lindblom, C.E. (1959) 'The science of "muddling through"'. *Public Administration Review*, **19**, pp. 78–88.

Lindblom, C.E. (1965) *The Intelligence of Democracy*. New York: The Free Press.

Lindblom, C.E. (1977) *Politics and Markets*. New York: Basic Books.

Lindblom, C.E. (1979) 'Still muddling, not yet through'. *Public Administration Review*, **39**, pp. 517–25.

Lindblom, C.E. and Woodhouse, E.J. (1993) *The Policy Making Process*. Englewood Cliffs, NJ: Prentice Hall.

Linder, S.H. and Peters, B.G. (1991) 'The logic of public policy design: Linking policy actors and plausible instruments'. *Knowledge in Society*, **4**, pp. 15–51.

Lipsky, M. (1980) *Street-Level Bureaucracy*. New York: Russell Sage.

Littler, C.R. (1978) 'Understanding Taylorism'. *British Journal of Sociology*, **29** (2), pp. 185–202.

Lowe, P. (1986) *Countryside Conflicts*. Aldershot: Gower.

Lowi, T.A. (1972) 'Four systems of policy, politics and choice'. *Public Administration Review*, **32**, pp. 298–310.

Lowndes, V. and Skelcher, C. (1998) 'The dynamics of multi-organizational partnerships: An analysis of changing modes of governance'. *Public Administration*, 76, Summer, pp. 313–33.

Lukes, S. (1974) *Power: A Radical View*. London: Macmillan.

Macintyre, S. (1985) *Winners and Losers*. Sydney: Unwin Hyman.

MacRae, C.D. (1977) 'A political model of the business cycle'. *Journal of Political Economy*, **85**, pp. 239–64.

Majone, G. and Wildavsky, A. (1978) 'Implementation as evolution', in Freeman, H. (ed.) *Policy Studies Review Annual*. Beverley Hills, Cal.: Sage.

March, J.G. and Olsen, J.P. (1984) 'The new institutionalism: Organisational factors in political life'. *American Political Science Review*, **78**, pp. 734–49.

March, J.G. and Olsen, J.P. (1989) *Rediscovering Institutions*. New York: Free Press.

March, J.G. and Olsen, J.P. (1996) 'Institutional perspectives on political institutions'. *Governance*, **9** (3), pp. 248–64.

Marris, P. and Rein, M. (1967) *Dilemmas of Social Reform*. London: Routledge & Kegan Paul. Marsh, D. and Rhodes, R.A.W. (1992) *Policy Networks in British Government*. Oxford: Oxford University Press.

Marsh, D. and Smith, M. (2000) 'Understanding policy networks: Towards a dialectical approach'. *Political Studies*, **48** (1), pp. 4–21.

Marx, F.M. (1957) *The Administrative State*. Chicago: University of Chicago Press.

Marx, K. (1845) 'Theses on Feuerbach', reprinted in *Marx and Engels: Selected Works*, vol. 2 (1958). Moscow: Foreign Languages Publishing House.

Mashaw, J.L. (1983) *Bureaucratic Justice*. New Haven, Conn.: Yale University Press

Massey, P. (1995) *New Zealand: Market Liberalization in a Developed Economy*. New York: St. Martin's Press.

Matland, R.E. (1995) 'Synthesizing the implementation literature: The ambiguity-conflict model of policy implementation'. *Journal of Public Administration Research and Theory*, **5** (2), pp. 145–74.

May, P.J. (1993) 'Mandate design and implementation: Enhancing implementation efforts and shaping regulatory styles'. *Journal of Policy Analysis and Management*, **12** (4), pp. 634–63.

May, P.J. (1995) 'Can cooperation be mandated? Implementing intergovernmental environmental management in New South Wales and New Zealand'. *Publius*, **25** (1), pp. 89–113.

May, P.J. and Burby, R.J. (1996) 'Coercive versus cooperative policies: Comparing intergovernmental mandate performance'. *Journal of Policy Analysis and Management*, **15** (2), pp. 171–201.

McGregor, D. (1960) *The Human Side of Enterprise*. New York: McGraw Hill.

McLellan, D. (1971) *The Thought of Karl Marx*. London: Macmillan.

Meier, K.J., Stewart, J. Jr and England, R.E. (1991) 'The politics of bureaucratic discretion: Educational access as an urban service'. *American Journal of Political Science*, **35** (1), pp. 155–77.

Merelman, R.M. (1968) 'On the neo-elitist critique of community power'. *American Political Science Review*, **62**, pp. 451–60.

Merton, R.K. (1957) *Social Theory and Social Structure*. Glencoe, Ill.: Free Press.

Meyer, J.W. and Rowan, B. (1977) 'Institutionalized organizations: Formal structure as myth and ceremony'. *American Journal of Sociology*, **83** (1), pp. 340–63.

Meynaud, J. (1965) *Technocracy*. London: Faber.

Middlemas, K. (1979) *Politics in Industrial Society*. London: Andre Deutsch.

Middlemas, K. (1986) *Power, Competition and the State*. Oxford: Blackwell.

Miliband, R. (1969) *The State in Capitalist Society*. London: Weidenfeld & Nicolson.

Millet, K. (1970) *Sexual Politics*. New York: Avon Books.

Mills, C.W. (1956) *The Power Elite*. New York: Oxford University Press.

Milward, H.B. and Francisco, R.A. (1983) 'Subsystem politics and corporatism in the United States'. *Policy and Politics*, **11** (3), pp. 273–93.

Milward, H.B., Provan, G. and Else, B.A. (1993) 'What does the "hollow state" look like?', in Bozeman, B. (ed.) *Public Management: The State of the Art*. San Francisco: Jossey-Bass, pp. 309–22.

Minzberg, H. (1983) *Power in and Around Organizations*. Englewood Cliffs, NJ: Prentice Hall.

Mishra, R. (1984) *The Welfare State in Crisis*. Brighton: Wheatsheaf.

Moe, T.M. (1980) *The Organisation of Interests*. Chicago: University of Chicago Press.

Moran, M. and Prosser, T. (eds) (1994) *Privatisation and Regulatory Change in Europe*. Buckingham: Open University Press.

Moran, M. and Wood, B. (1993) *States, Regulation and the Medical Profession*. Buckingham: Open University Press.

Mosca, C. (1939) *The Ruling Class*, trans. H.D. Kahn. London: McGraw Hill.

Mosley, P. (1984) *The Making of Economic Policy*. Brighton: Wheatsheaf.

Moynihan, D.P. (1969) *Maximum Feasible Misunderstanding*. New York: Free Press.

Musgrave, R.A. (1959) *The Theory of Public Finance*. New York: McGraw Hill.

Newman, J. (2001) *Modernising Governance*. London: Sage.

Niskanen, W.A. (1971) *Bureaucracy and Representative Government*. New York: Aldine-Atherton.

Nordhaus, W. (1975) 'The political business cycle'. *Review of Economic Studies*, **42**, pp. 169–90.

Nordlinger, E.A. (1981) *On the Autonomy of the Democratic State*. Cambridge, Mass.: Harvard University Press.

O'Connor, J. (1973) *The Fiscal Crisis of the State*. New York: St. Martin's Press.

O'Toole, L.J. Jr (1986) 'Policy recommendations for multi-actor implementation: An assessment of the field'. *Journal of Public Policy*, **6** (2), pp. 181–210.

Olson, M. (1965) *The Logic of Collective Action*. Cambridge, Mass.: Harvard University Press.

Olson, M. (1982) *The Rise and Decline of Nations*. New Haven, Conn.: Yale University Press.

Osborne, D. and Gaebler, T. (1992) *Reinventing Government*. Reading, Mass.: Addison Wesley.

Ouchi, W.G. (1980) 'Markets, bureaucracies and clans'. *Administrative Science Quarterly*, **25**, pp. 129–41.

Oye, K. (1985) 'Explaining cooperation under anarchy: Hypotheses and strategies'. *World Politics*, **39** (1), pp. 1–24.

Page, E.C. (2003) 'The civil servant as legislator: Law making in British administration'. *Public Administration*, **81** (4), pp. 651–79.

Page, E.C. and Goldsmith, M. (1987) *Central and Local Government Relations*. Beverley Hills, Cal.: Sage.

Pampel, F.C. and Williamson, J.B. (1989) *Age, Class, Politics and the Welfare State*. Cambridge: Cambridge University Press.

Panitch, L. (1980) 'Recent theorisations of corporatism: Reflections on a growth industry'. *British Journal of Sociology*, **31** (2), pp. 159–87.

Panitch, L. (1994) 'Globalisation and the state', in Miliband, R. and Panitch, L. (eds) *The Socialist Register, 1994*. London: Merlin.

Pareto, V. (1966) *Sociological Writings* (ed. S.E. Finer). London: Pall Mall.

Parry, N. and Parry, J. (1976) *The Rise of the Medical Profession*. London: Croom Helm.

Parsons, W. (1995) *Public Policy*. Aldershot: Edward Elgar.

Peacock, A. (ed.) (1984) *The Regulation Game*. Oxford: Blackwell.

Perri 6: *see* 6, Perri.

Perrow, C. (1972) *Complex Organizations: A Critical Essay*. Cleanview, Ill.: Scott Foresman.

Peters, B.G. and Pierre, J. (eds) (2002) *Handbook of Public Administration*. London: Sage.

Peters, T. and Waterman, R. (1982) *In Search of Excellence*. New York: Harper Collins.

Pierre, J. (ed.) (2000) *Debating Governance*. Oxford: Oxford University Press.

Pierre, J. and Peters, B.G. (2000) *Governance, Politics and the State*. Basingstoke: Macmillan.

Pierson, P. (1994) *Dismantling the Welfare State?* Cambridge: Cambridge University Press.

Pierson, P. (ed.) (2001) *The New Politics of the Welfare State*. Oxford: Oxford University Press.

Piore, M. and Sabel, C.F. (1984) *The Second Industrial Divide*. New York: Basic Books.

Pollitt, C. (1990) *Managerialism and the Public Services*. Oxford: Blackwell.

Pollitt, C. (2003) *The Essential Public Manager*. Maidenhead: Open University Press.

Pollitt, C. and Bouckaert, G. (2000) *Public Management Reform: A Comparative Analysis*. Oxford: Oxford University Press.

Polsby, N.W. (1963) *Community Power and Political Theory*. New Haven, Conn.: Yale University Press.

Popper, K.R. (1966) *The Open Society and Its Enemies*, 5th edn. London: Routledge.

Powell, M., Exworthy, M. and Berney, L. (2001) 'Playing the game of partnership' in Sykes, R., Bochel, C. and Ellison, N. (eds) *Social Policy Review*. Bristol: Policy Press, pp. 39–62.

Power, M. (1997) *The Audit Explosion*. London: Demos.

Pressman, J. and Wildavsky, A. (1973 (1st edn), 1979 (2nd edn), 1984 (3rd edn)) *Implementation*. Berkeley: University of California Press.

Prottas, J.M. (1979) *People Processing: The Street-Level Bureaucrat in Public Service Bureaucracies*. Lexington, Mass.: D.C. Heath.

Pusey, M. (1991) *Economic Rationalism in Canberra*. Cambridge: Cambridge University Press.

Ramesh, M. (2004) *Social Policy in East and Southeast Asia*. London: RoutledgeCurzon.

Ranade, W. (1998) *Making Sense of Multi-Agency Groups*. Newcastle: Sustainable Cities Research Institute.

Ranade, W. and Hudson, B. (2003) 'Conceptual issues in inter-agency collaboration'. *Local Government Studies*, **29** (3), pp. 32–50.

Reissman, L. (1949) 'The study of role conceptions in bureaucracy'. *Social Forces*, **27**, pp. 305–10.

Rex, J. (1986) *Race and Ethnicity*. Milton Keynes: Open University Press.

Rhodes, R.A.W. (1981) *Control and Power in Central–Local Government Relations*. Farnborough: Saxon House.

Rhodes, R.A.W. (1988) *Beyond Westminster and Whitehall*. London: Unwin Hyman.

Rhodes, R.A.W. (1995) 'From prime ministerial power to core executive', in Rhodes, R.A.W. and Dunleavy, P. (eds) *Prime Minister, Cabinet and Core Executive*. Basingstoke: Macmillan.

Rhodes, R.A.W. (1997) *Understanding Governance: Policy Networks, Governance, Reflexivity and Accountability*. Buckingham: Open University Press.

Rhodes, R.A.W. (2003) 'What is new about governance and why does it matter?', in Hayward, J. and Menon, A. (eds) *Governing Europe*. Oxford: Oxford University Press.

Richards, D. and Smith, M.J. (2002) *Governance and Public Policy in the UK*. Oxford: Oxford University Press.

Richardson, J. (ed.) (1982) *Policy Styles in Western Europe*. London: Allen and Unwin.

Richardson, J.J. and Jordan, A.G. (1979) *Governing under Pressure*. Oxford: Martin Robertson.

Rimlinger, G. (1971) *Welfare Policy and Industrialisation in Europe, America and Russia*. New York: Wiley.

Ripley, R.B. and Franklin, G.A. (1982) *Bureaucracy and Policy Implementation*. Homewood: Dorsey Press.

Roethlisberger, F.J. and Dickson, W.J. (1939) *Management and the Worker*. Cambridge, Mass.: Harvard University Press.

Rose, R. (1991) 'What is lesson drawing?' *Journal of Public Policy*, **11** (1), pp. 3–30.

Rose, R. (1993) *Lesson Drawing in Public Policy*. Chatham, NJ: Chatham House.

Rothstein, B. (1992) 'Labor-market institutions and working-class strength', in Steinmo, S., Thelen, K. and Longstreth, F. (eds) *Structuring Politics: Historical Institutionalism in Comparative Analysis*. Cambridge: Cambridge University Press.

Sabatier, P.A. (1986) 'Top-down and bottom-up approaches to implementation research: A critical analysis and suggested synthesis'. *Journal of Public Policy*, **6** (1), pp. 21–48.

Sabatier, P.A. (1999) 'The need for better theories', in Sabatier, P.A. (ed.) *Theories of the Policy Process*. Boulder, Col.: Westview Press, pp. 3–17.

Sabatier, P.A. (ed.) (1999) *Theories of the Policy Process*. Boulder, Col.: Westview Press.

Sabatier, P.A. and Jenkins-Smith, H. (eds) (1993) *Policy Change and Learning: An Advocacy Coalition Approach*. Boulder, Col.: Westview Press.

Sabatier, P.A. and Jenkins-Smith, H. (1999) 'The advocacy coalition framework: An assessment', in Sabatier, P.A. (ed.) *Theories of the Policy Process*. Boulder, Col.: Westview Press, pp. 117–66.

Sabatier, P.A. and Mazmanian, D. (1979) 'The conditions of effective implementation: A guide to accomplishing policy objectives'. *Policy Analysis*, **5** (4), pp. 481–504.

Sabatier, P.A., Loomis, J. and McCarthy, C. (1995) 'Hierarchical controls, professional norms, local constituencies and budget maximisation: An analysis of US Forest Service planning decisions'. *American Journal of Political Science*, **39** (1), pp. 204–42.

Sabel, C.F. (1982) *Work and Politics*. Cambridge: Cambridge University Press.

Sainsbury, D. (ed.) (1994) *Gendering Welfare States*. London: Sage.

Salaman, G. (1979) *Work Organisations*. London: Longman.

Salisbury, R.H. (1979) 'Why no corporatism in the United States?', in Schmitter, P.C. and Lembruch, G. (eds) *Trends Towards Corporatist Intermediation*. London: Sage.

Sandhu, K.S. and Wheatley, P. (1990) *The Management of Success: The Moulding of Modern Singapore*. Boulder, Col.: Westview Press.

Satyamurti, C. (1981) *Occupational Survival*. Oxford: Blackwell.

Scharpf, F.W. (1997) *Games Real Actors Play: Actor-Centered Institutionalism in Policy Research*. Boulder, Col.: Westview Press.

Schattschneider, E.E. (1960) *The Semi-Sovereign People*. New York: Holt, Rinehart and Winston.

Schmitter, P. (1974) 'Still the century of corporatism?' *Review of Politics*, **36**, pp. 85–131.

Schultze, C.L. (1968) *The Politics and Economics of Public Spending*. Washington, DC: Brookings.

Schumpeter, J. (1947) *Capitalism, Socialism and Democracy*, 2nd rev. edn. London: Allen & Unwin.

Schwarzmantel, J. (1994) *The State in Contemporary Society*. Hemel Hempstead: Harvester Wheatsheaf.

Scott, W.R. (1995) *Institutions and Organizations*. Thousand Oaks, Cal.: Sage.

Seebohm Report (1968) *Report of the Committee on Local Authority and Allied Personal Social Services*. London: HMSO, Cmnd. 3703.

Selden, S.C. (1997) 'Representative bureaucracy: Examining the linkage between passive and active representation in the farmers' home administration'. *American Review of Public Administration*, **27** (1), pp. 22–42.

Self, P. (1985) *Political Theories of Modern Government*. London: Allen & Unwin.

Self, P. (1993) *Government by the Market?* Basingstoke: Macmillan.

Selznick, P. (1949) *TVA and the Grass Roots*. Berkeley: University of California Press.

Selznick, P. (1957) *Leadership in Administration*. New York: Harper & Row.

Selznick, P. (1996) 'Institutionalism "old" and "new"'. *Administrative Science Quarterly*, **41**, pp. 270–7.

Shambaugh, D. (1995) *Deng Xiaoping*. Oxford: Clarendon Press.

Shawcross, W. (2003) *Allies: The United States, Britain, Europe and the War with Iraq*. London: Atlantic Books.

Shin, D-M. (2003) *Social and Economic Policies in Korea: Ideas, Networks and Linkages*. London: RoutledgeCurzon.

Sieber, S. (1981) *Fatal Remedies: The Ironies of Social Intervention*. New York: Plenum.

Simon, H.A. (1957) *Administrative Behaviour*, 2nd edn. New York: Macmillan.

Skocpol, T. (1994) *Social Policy in the United States*. Princeton, NJ: Princeton University Press.

Skocpol, T. and Finegold, K. (1982) 'State capacity and economic intervention in the early New Deal'. *Political Science Quarterly*, **97**, pp. 255–78.

Skok, J.E. (1995) 'Policy issue networks and the public policy cycle: A structural-functional framework for public administration'. *Public Administration Review*, **55** (4), pp. 325–32.

Smith, B.C. (1976) *Policy Making in British Government*. London: Martin Robertson.

Smith, B.C. (1988) *Bureaucracy and Political Power*. Brighton: Harvester.

Smith, G. (1981) 'Discretionary decision-making in social work', in Adler, M. and Asquith, S. (eds) *Discretion and Welfare*. London: Heinemann.

Smith, G. and May, D. (1980) 'The artificial debate between rationalist and incrementalist models of decision-making'. *Policy and Politics*, **8** (2), pp. 147–61.

Smith, M.J. (1993) *Pressure, Power and Policy*. Hemel Hempstead: Harvester Wheatsheaf.

Solomos, J., Findlay, B., Jones, S. and Gilroy, P. (1982) 'The organic crisis of British capitalism and race: The experience of the seventies', in Centre for Contemporary Cultural Studies, *The Empire Strikes Back*. London: Hutchinson.

Stephens, P. (1996) *Politics and the Pound*. London: Macmillan.

Stewart, J. and Clarke, M. (1987) 'The public services orientation: Issues and dilemmas'. *Public Administration*, **65**, pp. 161–77.

Stoker, R.P. (1991) *Reluctant Partners: Implementing Federal Policy*. Pittsburgh, Penn.: University of Pittsburg Press.

Stoker, R.P. and Wilson, L.A. (1998) 'Verifying compliance: Social regulation and welfare reform'. *Public Administration Review*, **58** (5), pp. 395–405.

Stone, C. (1989) *Regime Politics: Governing Atlanta, 1946–1988*. Lawrence: University Press of Kansas.

Surel, Y. (2000) 'The role of cognitive and normative frames in policy-making'. *Journal of European Public Policy*, **7** (4), pp. 495–512.

Taylor, F.W. (1911) *The Principles of Scientific Management*. New York: Harper.

Taylor, I. (2003) 'Policy on the hoof: The handling of the foot and mouth disease outbreak in the UK, 2001'. *Policy and Politics*, **31** (4), pp. 535–46.

Taylor, M. (2003) *Public Policy in the Community*. Basingstoke: Palgrave Macmillan.

Taylor-Gooby, P. (2002) 'The silver age of the welfare state: Perspectives on resilience'. *Journal of Social Policy*, **31** (4), pp. 597–622.

Taylor-Gooby, P. (ed.) (2001) *Welfare States under Pressure*. London: Sage.

Thelen, K. and Steinmo, S. (1992) 'Historical institutionalism in comparative politics', in Steinmo, S., Thelen, K. and Longstreth, F. (eds), *Structuring Politics: Historical Institutionalism in Comparative Analysis*. Cambridge: Cambridge University Press.

Thomas, H. (ed.) (1968) *Crisis in the Civil Service*. London: Blond.

Thomas, P.G. (2003) 'Accountability: Introduction', in Peters, B.G. and Pierre, J. (eds) *Handbook of Public Administration*. London: Sage.

Thompson, G., Frances, J., Levacic, R. and Mitchell, J. (eds) (1991) *Markets, Hierarchies and Networks: The Coordination of Social Life*. London: Sage.

Thompson, J.B. (1967) *Organizations in Action: Social Science Bases of Administrative Theory*. New York: McGraw-Hill.

Thompson, J.B. (1989) 'The theory of structuration', in Held, D. and Thompson, J.B. (eds) *Social Theory of Modern Societies: Anthony Giddens and His Critics*. Cambridge: Cambridge University Press.

Thurber, J.A. (1991) 'Dynamics of policy subsystems in American politics', in Cigler, A.J. and Loomis, A. (eds) *Interest Group Politics*, 3rd edn. Washington, DC: Congressional Quarterly.

Toke, D. and Marsh, D. (2003) 'Policy networks and the GM crops issue: assessing the utility of a dialectic model of policy networks'. *Public Administration*, **81** (2), pp. 229–51.

Tomlinson, S. (2001) *Education in a Post-Welfare Society*. Buckingham: Open University Press.

Truman, D. (1958) *The Governmental Process*. New York: Alfred Knopf.

Tuchman, B. (1962) *August 1914*. London: Constable.

Tullock, G. (1967) *The Politics of Bureaucracy*. New York: Public Affairs Press.

Tullock, G. (1976) *The Vote Motive*. London: Institute of Economic Affairs.

Uhr, J. (1993) 'Redesigning accountability: From muddles to maps'. *Australian Quarterly*, Winter, pp. 1–6.

Urwick, L.F. (1943) *The Elements of Administration*. London: Pitman.

Van Meter, D. and Van Horn, C.E. (1975) 'The policy implementation process, a conceptual framework'. *Administration and Society*, **6** (4), pp. 445–88.

Visser, J. and Hemerijck, A. (1997) *A Dutch Miracle: Job Reform and Welfare Growth in the Netherlands*. Amsterdam: Amsterdam University Press.

Wade, H.W.R. (1982) *Administration Law*, 5th edn. Oxford: Oxford University Press.

Wallas, G. (1948) *Human Nature in Politics*. London: Constable.

Wallerstein, I. (1979) *The Capitalist World Economy*. Cambridge: Cambridge University Press.

Wallis, J. (1997) 'Conspiracy and the policy process: A case study of the New Zealand experiment'. *Journal of Public Policy*, **17** (1), pp. 1–29.

Walsh, K. (1995) *Public Services and Market Mechanisms*. Basingstoke: Macmillan.

Walter, A. (1993) *World Power and World Money*. Hemel Hempstead: Harvester Wheatsheaf.

Weale, A. (1992) *The New Politics of Pollution*. Manchester: Manchester University Press.

Weatherley, R. (1979) *Reforming Special Education: Policy Implementation from State Level to Street Level*. Cambridge, Mass.: MIT Press.

Weatherley, R. (1980) 'Implementing social programs: The view from the front line'. Paper delivered at the annual meeting of the American Political Science Association, Washington, DC.

Weatherley, R. and Lipsky, M. (1977) 'Street-level bureaucrats and institutional innovation: Implementing special education reform'. *Harvard Educational Review*, **47** (2), pp. 171–97.

Webb, A. and Wistow, G. (1982) *Whither State Welfare?* London: RIPA.

Weber, M. (1947) *The Theory of Social and Economic Organization*, trans. A.M. Henderson and T. Parsons. Glencoe, Ill.: Free Press.

Weir, M., Orloff, S. and Skocpol, T. (eds) (1988) *The Politics of Social Policy in the United States*. Princeton, NJ: Princeton University Press.

Weissert, C.S. (1994) 'Beyond the organization: The influence of community and personal values on street-level bureaucrats' responsiveness'. *Journal of Public Administration Research and Theory*, **4** (2), pp. 225–54.

Westergaard, J. (1977) 'Class, inequality and "corporatism"', in Hunt, A. (ed.) *Class and Class Structure*. London: Lawrence and Wishart.

Whetstone, G.S. and Rosencranz, A. (1983) *Acid Rain in Europe and North America*. Washington: Environment Law Institute.

Whitmore, R. (1984) 'Modelling the policy/implementation distinction'. *Policy and Politics*, **12** (3), pp. 241–68.

Wildavsky, A.B. (1979) *Speaking the Truth to Power: The Art and Craft of Policy Analysis*. Boston, Mass.: Little, Brown and Co.

Wilding, P. (1982) *Professional Power and Social Welfare*. London: Routledge.

Wilensky, H.L. (1964) 'The professionalisation of everyone'. *American Journal of Sociology*, **70**, pp. 137–58.

Wilensky, H.L. (1975) *The Welfare State and Equality*. Berkeley: University of California Press.

Wilensky, H.L. and Lebaux, C.N. (1965) *Industrial Society and Social Welfare*. Glencoe, Ill.: Free Press.

Wilenski, P. (1986) *Public Power and Public Administration*. Sydney: RAIPA.

Wilks, S. and Wright, M. (1987) 'Conclusion: Comparing government–industry relations: States, sectors and networks', in Wilks, S. and Wright, M. (eds) *Comparative*

Government Industry Relations: Western Europe, the United States and Japan. Oxford: Clarendon Press.

Williamson, O. (1975) *Markets and Hierarchies*. New York: Free Press.

Williamson, O. (1985) *The Economic Institutions of Capitalism*. New York: Free Press.

Wilson, J.Q. (1973) *Political Organizations*. Beverley Hills, Cal.: Sage.

Wilson, W. (1887) 'The study of administration'. *Political Science Quarterly*, **2**, pp. 197–222.

Winkler, J. (1976) 'Corporatism'. *Archives Européennes de Sociologie*, **17** (1), pp. 100–36.

Wittfogel, K.A. (1963) *Oriental Despotism: A Comparative Study of Total Power*. New Haven, Conn.: Yale University Press.

Wolf, A. (2002) *Does Education Matter? Myths about Education and Economic Growth*. London: Penguin Books.

Wolfe, A. (1977) *The Limits of Legitimacy*. New York: The Free Press.

Wolfinger, R.E. (1971) 'Nondecisions and the study of local politics'. *American Political Science Review*, **65**, pp. 1063–80.

Wood, D.B. and Waterman, R. (1994) *Bureaucratic Dynamics*. Boulder, Col.: Westview Press.

Woodward, J. (1965) *Industrial Organisation: Theory and Practice*. London: Oxford University Press.

World Bank (1994) *Averting the Old Age Crisis*. Oxford: Oxford University Press.

Yanow, D. (1993) 'The communication of policy meanings: Implementation as interpretation and text'. *Policy Sciences*, **26** (1), pp. 41–61.

Yanow, D. (1996) *How does a policy mean? Interpreting policy and organizational actions*. Washington, DC: Georgetown University Press.

Yergin, D. (1991) *The Prize: The Epic Quest for Oil, Money and Power*. London: Simon and Schuster.

Young, K. (1977) 'Values in the policy process'. *Policy and Politics*, **5** (2), pp. 1–22.

Zimmerman, D.H. (1971) 'The practicalities of rule use', in Douglas, J.D. (ed.) *Understanding Everyday Life*. London: Routledge & Kegan Paul.

Index